"This book provides an illuminating collection of a wide range of sources, bringing together, perhaps for the first time, epigraphic evidence about associations in the Greco-Roman world. I look forward to using it."

—**Ilias Arnaoutoglou**, *Senior Researcher, Research Centre for the History of Greek Law, Academy of Athens*

"This is a valuable sourcebook that makes available in English a representative and comprehensive collection of texts on the associations in the Greco-Roman world."

—**Everett Ferguson**, *Distinguished Scholar in Residence, Abilene Christian University*

ASSOCIATIONS
IN THE GRECO-ROMAN WORLD

A Sourcebook

Richard S. Ascough
Philip A. Harland
John S. Kloppenborg

BAYLOR UNIVERSITY PRESS

DE GRUYTER

Cover Design by Natalya Balnova
Cover Image: SEG 31 (1981), no. 122 (photo: R.S. Ascough). See inscription #9.

Library of Congress Cataloging-in-Publication Data

Ascough, Richard S.
Associations in the Greco-Roman world : a sourcebook / by Richard S.
   Ascough, Philip A. Harland, John S. Kloppenborg.
   436 p. cm.
   Includes bibliographical references and index.
   ISBN 978-1-60258-374-0 (pbk.: acid-free paper)
   1. Associations, institutions, etc.—Greece—History—To 1500—Sources.
   2. Associations, institutions, etc.—Rome—History—Sources. 3. Social structure—Greece—History—To 1500—Sources. 4. Social structure—Rome—
   History—Sources. 5. Greece—Social life and customs—To 146 B.C—Sources.
   6. Rome—Social life and customs—Sources. 7. Christians—Social life and customs—Sources. 8. Jews—Social life and customs—Sources. 9. Greece—Religious
   life and customs—Sources. 10. Rome—Religious life and customs—Sources.
   I. Harland, Philip A. II. Kloppenborg, John S., 1951– III. Title.
   DE71.A83 2012
   068.37--dc23

                                                    2011051772

ISBN 978-1-60258-374-0 (Baylor University Press)
ISBN 978-3-11-026972-7 (De Gruyter)

Printed in the United States of America on acid-free paper with a minimum of 30% pcw recycled content.

Dedicated to Peter Richardson and Stephen G. Wilson
for their support and encouragement throughout various aspects
of our work on associations.

TABLE OF CONTENTS

INSCRIPTIONS AND PAPYRI

SOUTHERN AND CENTRAL GREECE

ATTICA

EGYPT

Delta Region

Fayûm Region

Upper Egypt

CYRENAICA

BUILDINGS AND MEETING-PLACES

SOUTHERN AND CENTRAL GREECE

MACEDONIA

ASIA MINOR

GREEK ISLANDS OF THE AEGEAN

ITALY

LITERARY REFERENCES

GENERAL REFERENCES

LIST OF ILLUSTRATIONS

EPIGRAPHIC AND PAPYROLOGICAL ABBREVIATIONS

Nb: For author–date citations (e.g., Foucart 1873; Gabrielsen 1994), see the annotated bibliography for full information.

AÉ   *L'Année épigraphique.*

BE   *Bullétin épigraphique* (printed with *Revue des études grecques* and cited by year and entry number).

BGU   *Aegyptische Urkunden aus den Königlichen* (later *Staatlichen*) *Museen zu Berlin, Griechische Urkunden.* Berlin: Weidmann, 1895–.

CCCA   Vermaseren, Maarten Jozef. *Corpus cultus Cybelae Attidisque.* EPRO 50. Leiden: E.J. Brill, 1977–1989.

CIG   Boeckh, A., ed. *Corpus inscriptionum graecarum.* 4 vols. Berlin: Georg Reimer, 1828–1877. I. ed. A. Boeckh (1828); II. ed. A. Boeckh (1843); III. ed. J. Franz (1845–1853); IV. ed. E. Curtius, A. Kirchhoff (1856–1859); Index (1877).

CIJ   Frey, J. B., ed. *Corpus inscriptionum iudaicarum: Recueil des inscriptions juives qui vont du IIIe siècle avant J.-C.* 2 vols. Rome: Pontificio istituto di archeologia cristiana, 1936–1952. I. Europe (1936); II. Asia–Africa (1952).

CIL   *Corpus inscriptionum latinarum,* Consilio et Auctoritate Academiae Litterarum Regiae Borussicae editum. Berlin: Georg Reimer, 1863–1974.

CIRB   Struve, V. V., ed. *Corpus inscriptionum Regni Bosporani: Korpus bosporskikh nadpisei.* Moscow: Nauka, 1965.

CJZC   Lüderitz, G., and J. M. Reynolds. *Corpus jüdischen zeugnisse aus der Cyrenaika.* Beihefte zum Tübinger Atlas des Vorderen Orients. Reihe B. Geisteswissenschaften 53. Wiesbaden: Dr. Ludwig Reichert, 1983.

CMRDM   Lane, Eugene N. *Corpus monumentorum religionis dei Menis.* EPRO 19. 4 vols. Leiden: E.J. Brill, 1971–1978.

DFSJ	Lifshitz, Baruch. *Donateurs et fondateurs dans les synagogues juives: Répertoire des dédicaces grecques relatives à la construction et à la réfection des synagogues.* Cahiers de la Revue biblique 7. Paris: J. Gabalda, 1967.
EpThess	Nigdelis, Pantelis M. Ἐπιγραφικὰ Θεσσαλονίκεια. Συμβολὴ στὴν πολιτικὴ καὶ κοινωνικὴ ἱστορία τῆς ἀρχαίας Θεσσαλονίκης. Thessaloniki: University Studio Press, 2006.
GCRE	Oliver, James H. *Greek Constitutions of Early Roman Emperors from Inscriptions and Papyri.* Memoirs of the American Philosophical Society 178. Philadelphia: American Philosophical Society, 1989.
GRA	Kloppenborg, John S., Philip A. Harland, and Richard S. Ascough. *Greco-Roman Associations: Texts, Translations, and Commentary.* BZNW 181. Berlin: Walter de Gruyter, 2011–. Vol. 1. *Attica, Central Greece, Macedonia, Thrace* (2011).
IAlexandriaK	Kayser, François. *Recueil des inscriptions grecques et latines (non funéraires) d'Alexandrie impériale.* Bibliothèque d'étude 108. Cairo: Institut français d'archéologie orientale du Caire, 1994.
IAnazarbos	Sayar, Mustafa Hamdi, ed. *Die Inschriften von Anazarbos und Umgebung,* 2 vols. IGSK 56. Bonn: Rudolf Habelt, 2000.
IAnkyraBosch	Bosch, E. *Quellen zur Geschichte der Stadt Ankara im Altertum.* Ankara: Türk Tarih Kurumu Basimevi, 1967.
IApamBith	Corsten, Thomas. *Die Inschriften von Apameia (Bithynien) und Pylai.* IGSK 32. Bonn: Rudolf Habelt, 1987.
IBerenike	Reynolds, Joyce. "Inscriptions." In *Excavations at Sidi Khrebish Benghazi (Berenice).* Vol. I: *Buildings, Coins, Inscriptions, Architectural Decoration,* ed. J. A. Lloyd, 233–54. Supplements to Libya Antiqua 5. Libya: Department of Antiquities, Ministry of Teaching and Education, People's Socialist Libyan Arab Jamahiriya, 1977.
IBeroia	Gounaropoulou, L., and M. B. Hatzopoulos. *Inscriptiones Macedoniae Inferioris I: Inscriptiones Beroiae* (in Greek). Athens: Hypourgeio Politismou, 1998.
IByzantion	Lajtar, Adam. *Die Inschriften von Byzantion,* Teil 1, *Die Inschriften.* IGSK 58.1. Bonn: Rudolf Habelt, 2000.
IDelos	Roussel, Pierre, and Marcel Launey. *Inscriptions de Délos: Décrets postérieurs à 166 av. J.-C. (nos. 1497–1524). Dédicaces postérieures à 166 av. J.-C. (nos. 1525–2219).* Académie des Inscriptions et Belles-lettres. Paris: Librairie Ancienne Honoré Champion, 1937.

IDelosChoix	Dürrbach, Felix. *Choix d'inscriptions de Délos: avec traduction et commentaire.* Paris: E. Leroux, 1921.
IDelta	Bernand, A., ed. *Le delta égyptien d'après les texts grecs 1: Les confines libyques.* 3 vols. Mémoires publies par les membres de l'Institut français d'archéologie orientale du Caire 91. Cairo: Institut français d'archéologie orientale, 1970.
IDidyma	Rehm, Albert. 1958. *Didyma. Zweiter Teil: Die Inschriften,* ed. Richard Harder. Deutsches archäologisches Institut. Berlin: Verlag Gebr. Mann.
IEgJud	Horbury, William, and David Noy. *Jewish Inscriptions of Graeco-Roman Egypt.* Cambridge: Cambridge University Press, 1992.
IEph	Engelmann, H., H. Wankel, and R. Merkelbach. *Die Inschriften von Ephesos.* IGSK 11–17. Bonn: Rudolf Habelt, 1979–1984.
IFayum	Bernand, E., ed. *Recueil des inscriptions grecques du Fayoum.* Leiden: E.J. Brill, 1975–1981.
IG II²	Kirchner, Johannes, ed. *Inscriptiones Atticae Euclidis anno anteriores.* 4 vols. Berlin: Walter de Gruyter, 1913–1940.
IG IV	Fränkel, M., ed. *Inscriptiones graecae Aeginae, Pityonesi, Cecryphaliae, Argolidis.* Berlin: Georg Reimer, 1902.
IG IV²	Hiller von Gaertringen, Friedrich F., ed. *Inscriptiones Epidauri.* Berlin: Walter de Gruyter, 1929.
IG V,1	Kolbe, W., ed. *Inscriptiones Laconiae et Messeniae,* part 1. Berlin: Georg Reimer, 1913.
IG VII	Dittenberger, W., ed. *Inscriptiones Megaridis et Boeotiae.* Berlin: Georg Reimer, 1892.
IG IX/1²	Klaffenbach, Gunther, ed. *Inscriptiones graeciae septentrionalis.* 2nd ed. Berlin: Walter de Gruyter, 1932–1968. Fasc. 1, *Inscriptiones Aetoliae* (1932); fasc. 2, *Inscriptiones Acarnaniae* (1957); fasc. 3, *Inscriptiones Locridis occidentalis* (1968).
IG X/2.1	Edson, Charles, ed. *Inscriptiones graecae Epiri, Macedoniae, Thraciae, Scythiae.* II: *Inscriptiones Macedoniae*; fasc. 1: *Inscriptiones Thessalonicae et viciniae.* Berlin: Walter de Gruyter, 1972.
IG XI,4	Roussel, Pierre. *Inscriptiones Deli liberae. Decreta, foedera, catalogi, dedicationes, varia.* Berlin: Georg Reimer, 1914.
IG XII,1	Hiller von Gaertringen, Friedrich F., ed. *Inscriptiones Rhodi, Chalces, Carpathi cum Saro, Casi.* Berlin: Georg Reimer, 1895.

IG XII,2	Paton, W. R., ed. *Inscriptiones Lesbi Nesi Tenedi.* Berlin: Georg Reimer, 1899.
IG XII,3	Hiller von Gaertringen, Friedrich F., ed. *Inscriptiones Symes Teutlussae Teli Nisyri Astypalaeae Anaphes Therae et Therasiae Pholegandri Meli Cimol.* Berlin: Georg Reimer, 1898.
IG XII,5	Hiller von Gaertringen, Friedrich F., ed. *Inscriptiones Cycladum.* 2 vols. Berlin: Georg Reimer, 1903–1909. I: *Inscriptiones Cycladum praeter Tenum* (1903); II: *Inscriptiones Teni insulae* (1909).
IG XII,7	Delamarre, J., ed. *Inscriptiones Amorgi et insularum vicinarum.* Berlin: Georg Reimer, 1908.
IG XII,8	Friedrich, C., ed. *Inscriptiones insularum maris Thracici.* Berlin: Georg Reimer, 1909.
IG XII,Suppl	Hiller von Gaertringen, Friedrich F., ed. *Supplementum.* Berlin: Walter de Gruyter, 1939.
IG XIV	Kaibel, G. *Inscriptiones Graecae, XIV. Inscriptiones Siciliae et Italiae, additis Galliae, Hispaniae, Britanniae, Germaniae inscriptionibus.* Berlin: Georg Reimer, 1890.
IGBulg	Mikhailov, Georgi, ed. *Inscriptiones graecae in Bulgaria repertae.* 5 vols. Sofia: Academia Litterarum Bulgarica, 1956–1997. I: *Inscriptiones orae Ponti Euxini* (1956); II: *Inscriptiones inter Danubium et Haemum repertae* (1958); III/1: *Inscriptiones inter Haemum et Rhodopem reperta: a territorio Philippopolis* (1961); III/2: *Inscriptiones inter Haemum et Rhodopem reperta: a territorio Philippopolitano usque ad oram Ponticam* (1964); IV: *Inscriptiones in territorio Serdicensi et in vallibus Styrmonis Nestique repertae* (1966); V: *Inscriptiones novae, addenda et corrigenda* (1997).
IGBulg I²	Mihailov Georgi, ed. *Inscriptiones graecae in Bulgaria repertae.* Sofia: Academia Litterarum Bulgarica, 1958–1997. Vol. 1, 2nd ed.: *Inscriptiones orae Ponti Euxini* (1970).
IGLSkythia	Pippidi, D. M., and Iorgu Stoian, eds. *Inscriptiones Scythiae Minoris graecae et latinae. Inscripțiile din Scythia Minor grecești și latine.* Bucharest: Editura Academiei Republicii Socialiste Romania, 1983–. I: *Inscriptiones Histriae et vicinia* (1983); II: *Tomis et territorium* (1987); III: *Callatis et territorium* (2000).
IGRR	Cagnat, R. L., J. F. Toutain, V. Henry, and G. L. Lafaye, eds. *Inscriptiones graecae ad res romanas pertinentes.* 4 vols. Paris: E. Leroux, 1911–1927. I: (nos. 1–1518) ed. R. L. Cagnat, J. F. Toutain, and P. Jouguet (1911); II: never

published; III: ed. R. L. Cagnat and G. L. Lafaye (1906); IV: *Asia* (nos. 1–1764), ed. G. L. Lafaye (1927).

IGSK   *Inschriften griechischer Städte aus Kleinasien.* Bonn: Rudolf Habelt, 1972-.

IGUR   Moretti, L., ed. *Inscriptiones graecae urbis Romae.* Istituto italiano per la storia antica, studi nos. 17, 22, 28, 47. Rome: Istituto Italiano per la storia antica, 1968–1990.

IHierapJ   Judeich, Walther. "Inschriften." In *Altertümer von Hierapolis,* ed. Carl Humann, Conrad Cichorius, Walther Judeich, and Franz Winter, 67–181. Jahrbuch des kaiserlich deutschen archäologischen Instituts, Ergänzungsheft 4. Berlin: Georg Reimer, 1898.

IJO   *Inscriptiones Judaicae Orientis.* Tübingen: Mohr Siebeck, 2004. I: David Noy, Alexander Panayotov, and Hanswulf Bloedhorn, *Eastern Europe.* TSAJ 101 (2004); II: Walter Ameling, *Kleinasien.* TSAJ 99 (2004); III: David Noy and Hanswulf Bloedhorn, *Syria and Cyprus.* TSAJ 102 (2004).

IKilikiaBM   Bean, George E., and Terence Bruce Mitford. I: *Journeys in Rough Cilicia 1962 and 1963 [I].* Denkschriften der österreichischen Akademie der Wissenschaften in Wien, philosophisch-historische Klasse 85. Vienna: Hermann Böhlaus, 1965; II: *Journeys in Rough Cilicia 1964–1968 [II].* Denkschriften der österreichischen Akademie der Wissenschaften in Wien, philosophisch-historische Klasse 102.3. Vienna: Hermann Böhlaus, 1970.

IKilikiaHW   Heberdey, Rudolf, and Adolf Wilhelm. *Reisen in Kilikien.* Denkschriften der kaiserlichen Akademie der Wissenschaften in Wien, philosophisch-historische Klasse 44.6. Vienna: Alfred Hölder, 1894.

IKios   Corsten, Thomas. *Die Inschriften von Kios.* IGSK 29. Bonn: Rudolf Habelt, 1985.

IKöln   Galster, Brigitte, and Hartmut Galsterer, eds. *Die römischen Steininschriften aus Köln.* 2 vols. Mainz: Philipp von Zabern, 2010.

IKosPh   Hicks, E. L., and W. R. Paton. *The Inscriptions of Cos.* Oxford: Clarendon, 1891.

IKyme   Engelmann, H., ed. *Die Inschriften von Kyme.* IGSK 5. Bonn: Rudolf Habelt, 1976.

IKyzikos   Schwertheim, Elmar. *Die Inschriften von Kyzikos und Umgebung.* IGSK 18, 26. Bonn: Rudolf Habelt, 1980–.

ILindos   Blinkenberg, C., ed. *Lindos: Fouilles et recherches, 1902–1913. II: Inscriptions.* 2 vols. Berlin: Walter de Gruyter, 1931–1941.

ILS	Dessau, Hermann. *Inscriptiones latinae selectae*. 3 vols. Berlin: Weidmann, 1892–1916. Repr., Dublin: Weidmann, 1974; repr., Chicago: Ares, 1979.
ILydiaKP	Keil, J., and A. von Premerstein, eds. *Bericht über eine Reise in Lydien und der südlichen Aiolis*. Vienna: Alfred Hölder, 1910. II: *Bericht über eine zweite Reise in Lydien*. Vienna: Alfred Hölder, 1911. III: *Bericht über eine dritte Reise in Lydien und den angrenzenden Gebieten Ioniens* Vienna: Alfred Hölder, 1914.
IMagnMai	Kern, Otto. *Die Inschriften von Magnesia am Maeander*. Königliche Museen zu Berlin. Berlin: W. Spemann, 1900.
IMakedD	Demitsas, M. G. Ἡ Μακεδονία ἐν λίθοις φθεγγομένοις καὶ μνημείοις σῳζομένοις. Athens: Perre, 1896. Repr. as *Sylloge inscriptionum graecarum et latinarum Macedoniae*. Chicago: Ares, 1980.
IMilet	Wiegend, Theodor, Georg Kawerau, Albert Rehm, and Peter Herrmann. *Milet: Ergebnisse der Ausgrabungen und Untersuchungen seit dem Jahre 1899*. Berlin: Walter de Gruyter, 1889–1997.
IMT	Barth, Matthias, and Josef Stauber, eds. *Inschriften Mysia und Troas*. Munich: Leopold Wenger-Institut, 1993.
INapoli	Miranda, Elena, ed. *Iscrizioni greche d'Italia, Napoli*. 2 vols. Rome: Quasar, 1990–1995.
IPergamon	Fränkel, M., ed. *Die Inschriften von Pergamon*. 2 vols. Berlin: W. Spemann, 1890–1895. I: *Bis zum Ende der Königzeit* (1890); II: *Römische Zeit* (1895).
IPergamonSupp	Müller, Helmut, ed. *Supplement zum Corpus der Inschriften von Pergamon*. Deutsche archäologische Institut. http://www.dainst.org/de/node/23938?ft=all.
IPerinthos	Sayar, Mustafa Hamdi, ed. *Perinthos-Herakleia (Marmara Ereğlisi) und Umgebung. Geschichte, Testimonien, griechische und lateinische Inschriften*. Österreichische Akademie der Wissenschaften. Philosophisch-historische Klasse. Denkschriften, 269 = Veröffentlichungen der kleinasiatischen Kommission 9. Vienna: Österreichischen Akademie der Wissenschaften, 1998.
IPessinous	Strubbe, Johan. *The Inscriptions of Pessinous*. IGSK 66. Bonn: Rudolf Habelt, 2005.
IPontEux	Latyšev, Basilius, ed. *Inscriptiones antiquae orae septentrionalis Ponti Euxini graecae et latinae*. Saint Petersburg: Petropoli, 1885–1901 I: *Inscriptiones Tyrae, Olbiae, Chersonesi, Tauricae*; II: *Inscriptiones Regi Bosporani*. Repr., Hildesheim: Georg Olms, 1965.

IPrusaOlymp	Corsten, T., ed. *Die Inschriften von Prusa ad Olympum.* IGSK 39–40. Bonn: Rudolf Habelt, 1991–1993.
IRhodM	Maiuri, A., ed. *Nuova silloge epigrafica di Rodi e Cos.* Florence: Le Monnier, 1925.
ISardBR	Buckler, W. H., and D. M. Robinson, eds. *Sardis.* VII, 1: *Greek and Latin Inscriptions.* Leiden: E.J. Brill, 1932.
ISmyrna	Petzl, Georg, ed. *Die Inschriften von Smyrna.* IGSK 23–24/1–2. Bonn: Rudolf Habelt, 1982–1900. Vol. 1: 1982; vol. 2.1: 1987; vol. 2.2: 1990.
ITrall	Poljakov, F. B., ed. *Die Inschriften von Tralleis und Nysa: Teil 1. Die Inschriften von Tralleis.* IGSK 36/1. Bonn: Rudolf Habelt, 1989.
JIWE	Noy, David. *Jewish Inscriptions of Western Europe.* Cambridge: Cambridge University Press, 1993–1995. I: *Italy (excluding the City of Rome)* (1993); II: *The City of Rome* (1995).
LSAM	Sokolowski, Franciszek. *Lois sacrées de l'Asie Mineure. École française d'Athènes.* Travaux et mémoires, fasc. 9. Paris: E. de Boccard, 1955.
LSCG	Sokolowski, Franciszek. *Lois sacrées des cités grecques. École française d'Athènes.* Travaux et mémoires, fasc. 18. Paris: E. de Boccard, 1969.
LSCGSup	Sokolowski, Franciszek. *Lois sacrées des cités grecques: supplément. École française d'Athènes.* Travaux et mémoires, fasc. 11. Paris: E. de Boccard, 1962.
MAMA	Calder, W. M., E. Herzfeld, S. Guyer, and C. W. M. Cox, eds. *Monumenta Asiae Minoris antiqua.* 10 vols. American Society for Archaeological Research in Asia Minor. Publications 1–10. London: Manchester University Press, 1928–1993.
NewDocs I–V	Horsley, G. H. R. *New Documents Illustrating Early Christianity.* North Ryde, Australia: Ancient History Documentary Research Centre, Macquarie University, 1981–1989.
NewDocs VI–IX	Llewelyn, S. R. *New Documents Illustrating Early Christianity.* North Ryde, Australia: Ancient History Documentary Research Centre, Macquarie University, 1992–2002.
NGSL	Lupu, Eran. *Greek Sacred Law: A Collection of New Documents.* Religions in the Graeco-Roman World 152. Leiden: E.J. Brill, 2005.
OGIS	Dittenberger, Wilhelm, ed. *Orientis graeci inscriptiones selectae. Supplementum Sylloge inscriptionum graecarum.* 2 vols. Leipzig: S. Hirzel, 1903–1905. Repr., Hildesheim: G. Olms, 1970.

PCairDem	Spiegelberg, W., ed. *Die demotischen Denkmäler. II. Die Demotischen Papyrus.* Leipzig: Dragulin, 1908.
PEnteuxeis	Guéraud, O., ed. *ΕΝΤΕΥΞΕΙΣ: Requêtes et plaintes addressées au roi d'Egypte au IIIe siècle avant J.-C.* Publications de la Société Royale Égyptienne de Papyrologie. Textes et documents 1. Cairo: Imprimerie de l'Institut Français d'Archéologie Orientale, 1931.
PH	Packard Humanities Institute numbers for Greek inscriptions. The Greek texts are available online at http://epigraphy.packhum.org/inscriptions/.
Philippi II	Pilhofer, Peter. *Philippi.* Band II. *Katalog der Inschriften von Philippi.* WUNT 119. Tübingen: Mohr Siebeck, 2000.
PLond	*Greek Papyri in the British Museum.* London: British Museum, 1893–1974. I: ed. F. G. Kenyon, 1893; II: ed. F. G. Kenyon, 1898; III: ed. F. G. Kenyon and H. I. Bell, 1907; IV: *The Aphrodito Papyri*, ed. H. I. Bell, with appendix of Coptic papyri, ed. W. E. Crum, 1910; V: ed. H. I. Bell, 1917; VI: *Jews and Christians in Egypt; The Jewish Troubles in Alexandria and the Athanasian Controversy*, ed. H. I. Bell, 1924; VII: *The Zenon Archive*, ed. T. C. Skeat, 1974.
PMich	Boak, A. E. R. *Papyri from Tebtunis* (Michigan papyri II and V), 2 vols. Ann Arbor: University of Michigan Press, 1933–1944.
PPetaus	Hagedorn, Ursula, Dieter Hagedorn, Louise C. Youtie, and Herbert C. Youtie. *Das Archiv des Petaus (P.Petaus).* Papyrologica Coloniensia 4. Cologne: Westdeutscher Verlag, 1969.
PRyl	Johnson, J. M., V. Martin, A. S. Hunt, C. H. Roberts, and E. G. Turner. *Catalogue of the Greek Papyri in the John Rylands Library, Manchester.* Manchester: Manchester University Press, 1911–1952.
RIB	Collingwood, R. G., and R. P. Wright. *Roman Inscriptions of Britain.* Oxford: Clarendon, 1965.
RIG	Michel, C., ed. *Recueil d'inscriptions grecques.* Brussels: Lamertin, 1900. Repr., Hildesheim: G. Olms, 1976; *Supplément*, Brussels: Lamertin, 1912; repr., Hildesheim: G. Olm, 1976.
SB	Preisigke, F., F. Bilabel, et al., eds. *Sammelbuch griechischer Urkunden aus Ägypten.* Strasbourg: K. J. Trubner; Wiesbanden: Otto Harrassowitz, 1915–.
SEG	*Supplementum epigraphicum graecum.* Leiden: E.J. Brill, 1923–.

*SIG*²	Dittenberger, Wilhelm, ed. *Sylloge inscriptionum graecarum.* 2nd ed., 3 vols. Leipzig: S. Hirzel, 1898–1901.
*SIG*³	Dittenberger, Wilhelm. *Sylloge inscriptionum graecarum.* 3rd ed., 4 vols. Leizpig: S. Hirzel, 1915–1924.
SIRIS	Vidman, Ladislaus. 1969. *Sylloge inscriptionum religionis Isiacae et Sarapiacae.* RGVV 28. Berlin: Walter de Gruyter.
TAM	Österreichische Akademie der Wissenschaften. *Tituli Asiae Minoris.* Vienna: Hoelder–Pichler–Tempsky, 1901–. I: Ernst Kalinka, *Tituli Lyciae lingua Lycia conscripti* (1901); II/1–3: Ernst Kalinka, *Tituli Lyciae linguis Graeca et Latina conscripti.* 1 vol. in 3 (1920–1944); III: Rudolf Heberdey, ed., *Tituli Pisidiae linguis Graeca et Latina conscripti* (1941); IV: Friedrich Karl Dörner and Maria-Barbara von Stritzky, eds. *Tituli Bithyniae linguis Graeca et Latina conscripti* (1978); V/1–2: Peter Herrmann, *Tituli Lydiae linguis graeca et latina conscripti* (1981).
TitCam	Segre, M., and G. Pugliese Carratelli. "Tituli Camirenses." *Annuario della scuola archeologica di Atene e delle missione Italiane in oriente,* n.s. 11–13 (1949–1951): 141–318.

ACKNOWLEDGMENTS

A scough, Harland, and Kloppenborg have translated into English all of the texts included in this *Sourcebook*. Many of the translations of inscriptions and papyri also appear (or will appear) in the multivolume *Greco-Roman Associations*, published in the BZNW series by Walter de Gruyter GmbH in Germany. We are grateful to the editors at de Gruyter and at Baylor University Press for granting a reciprocal relationship that allows for the dual use of these translations. We would especially like to thank Carey Newman at Baylor for his enthusiastic support for this project. Other than this overlap, the two publication projects differ in many significant ways. The BZNW volumes, of which four are projected, are critical editions with newly edited original texts (Greek and Latin), full publication information, and comprehensive notes and commentary. Their primary audience will be researchers who want a full detailed discussion of the texts. The *Sourcebook*, on the other hand, includes many features not contained in the BZNW volumes—texts from Greco-Roman writers, descriptions of association buildings, and an annotated bibliography of secondary sources. The *Sourcebook* also includes a number of translations of inscriptions and papyri that are not included in the BZNW volumes. Thus, the *Sourcebook* will appeal to researchers who want a broad overview and introduction into the study of ancient associations. Neither the BZNW volumes nor the *Sourcebook* makes any claim to be complete; there are many more texts concerning associations available than was possible to include in either project.

The editors wish to acknowledge the involvement of a number of graduate students and former graduate students who contributed in many ways to the translation of the inscriptions and the composing of the annotated bibliography: William Arnal, Rene Baergen, Alicia Batten, Callie Callon, Agnes Choi, Michelle Christian, Jenn Cianca, Maria Irchenhauser, David Kaden, Richard Last, Jason Pollick, David Reed, Kevin Rodrigues, Sarah

Rollens, Ryan Schellenberg, Svenja Schmidt, Erin Vearncombe, Stéphane Vermette, and Caroline Whelan. Rachel McRae was particularly helpful in contributing to the annotated bibliography and reading drafts of various sections of the manuscript. Ilias Arnaoutoglou made many beneficial suggestions and corrections to the translations from southern Greece, Macedonia, and Thracia.

We are grateful to the Ancient World Mapping Center (http://www.unc.edu/awmc/) for permission to use and adapt the map base.

This project has been supported at various stages by generous funding from the Social Sciences and Humanities Research Council of Canada and by grants from the Premier's Research Excellence Award (Government of Ontario), Queen's University, and York University.

Richard S. Ascough
Philip A. Harland
John S. Kloppenborg

Map of the Ancient Mediterranean

with Regions

INTRODUCTION

A broad cross section of people in the ancient Mediterranean world was affiliated with some type of unofficial association. These associations provided members with a sense of belonging, along with some practical benefits such as opportunities for networking, regular banquets, and a decent burial. The unofficial groups that can be discussed under the rubric of "associations" were in fact diverse, with differences in nomenclature, organization, cult practice, and social makeup. Still, this broad category of "associations" has important heuristic benefit, especially for studying Christian groups and Judean synagogues, which are often treated as groups unto themselves. To place Judean synagogues and early Christian congregations alongside various other types of associations documented in this volume affords us an unusually rich set of comparative materials. Studying these groups together will provide insights into social and religious life within elite and non-elite segments of the population.

Indeed, as scholars work with inscriptions, papyri, and literary texts attesting to the associations, they are recognizing the significant roles played by associations within social and religious life in the Hellenistic and Roman eras. In addition, scholars of early Judaism and Christian origins are increasingly acknowledging that, sociologically, these associations provide a framework for understanding groups of Judeans and of Christians in this period. Unfortunately, many of the epigraphic and papyrological texts for associations are difficult to assess since they are scattered across numerous collections and journals, some of which are not readily available at most libraries. Students face a yet greater challenge because many of these texts are not translated into English when they are published or discussed by scholars. Moreover, scholars of Christian origins tend to rely upon the same few readily accessible inscriptions when discussing associations in relation to Christian groups: *IG* II² 1368 from Athens (**7**), *SIG*³ 985 from Philadelphia in Lydia (**121**), *CIL* XIV 2112

1

from Lanuvium in Italy (**310**), and *CIL* VI 10234 from Rome (**322**).
Although these inscriptions are important, focus on them to the neglect of
other evidence leaves the bulk of the data untapped. This *Sourcebook* aims
to rectify the situation by giving scholars and students easy access to English translations of representative epigraphic, papyrological, and literary
texts; descriptions of the remains of the buildings where some associations
met; and brief annotations on select books and articles in the three primary languages of scholarship (English, German, and French). This work
would also be well suited as a primary text for courses dealing with the
cultural context of Diaspora Judeans (Jews) and Christians or with social
and religious life in the Greco-Roman world generally.

This introduction will be brief, serving more as an orientation to the
Sourcebook itself than as an overview of Greco-Roman associations. There
are indeed other good overviews of associations published elsewhere, and
the editors of this volume have likewise made known their own views on
associations through publication (see works in the annotated bibliography). Yet the purpose of this volume is to invite others into the conversation by offering easy access to some of the extensive evidence. To attempt to
encapsulate the nature of associations here, however, would be to frame the
debate toward our own particular understandings of the associations—the
very thing that we hope to invite others to form for themselves. Indeed,
there are some key areas in which the three of us would disagree, so any
attempt at a synthesis would be artificial. For example, each of us has his
own view of how best to categorize or form a taxonomy of associations:
cultic and occupational (Ascough 2003, 20–24); household connections,
ethnic/geographic connections, neighborhood connections, occupational
connections, cultic or temple connections (Harland 2003a, 28–52); or family-based groups, cultic groups, and ethnic, neighborhood, and occupational groups (Kloppenborg 2006, 323–25). Still, there are also places where
we are in fundamental agreement, as in the rejection of the common yet
problematic category of "funerary association" (*collegia funeraticia*)—that
is, an association devoted exclusively to burial of the dead (see Ascough
2003, 21; Harland 2003a, 28–29; Kloppenborg 1996a, 20–23). There remain
many areas that are in need of continued exploration through careful analysis of the association inscriptions and papyri, and this *Sourcebook* hopes
to inspire such analysis by others, including the continuation of comparisons with Judean gatherings and Christian congregations.

Using This Sourcebook

Selection of Materials

Currently, there are no English-language sourcebooks or annotated bibli-
ographies for the study of Greco-Roman associations. There are only three
comparable comprehensive sourcebooks on associations, all of which are

more than a century old, two in French and one in German: Foucart (1873), Waltzing (1895–1900), Poland (1909). Our own work builds on these resources and numerous other more recent publications to present translations of 337 inscriptions and papyri (chap. 1), descriptions of twenty-eight association meeting places (chap. 2), and translations of fifty-four literary passages involving associations (chap. 3), particularly materials in Greek but also some representative Latin materials. It becomes clear that this is a very small selection of inscriptions when one realizes that there are more than three thousand Latin inscriptions in Waltzing's collection alone, and the evidence for associations from Greek materials is similarly vast, if not greater. In making our choices we have selected texts that are representative of a broad range of texts (e.g., decrees, dedications, regulations, graves), groups (e.g., occupational, ethnic, cultic), group memberships (e.g., citizen, noncitizen, male, female, mixed), and purposes (e.g., cultic, social, burial). Our own research interest in the study of Christian origins has led us to focus primarily, although not predominantly, on areas where Christianity was present in the first and second centuries CE: Attica, Macedonia, Asia Minor, Egypt, and Rome (but few relevant inscriptions have survived from Corinth, for instance). We have included a scattering of other texts from various regions to demonstrate the range and diversity of available evidence. It remains the case that for each region many more texts could have been added to our list. Alongside other immigrant or ethnic associations, we have included inscriptions (about thirty) and literary passages involving Judean (Jewish) *groups*. As the literary materials for early Christian associations are readily available, we have not attempted to include them here, but hope that the *Sourcebook* might serve well within a course aimed at placing Christian groups within the cultural context of group life in the Roman Empire. We have also excluded texts from official boards of temples or official age-based organizations linked to education (i.e., *paides, ephebes, neoi, neoteroi, gerontes*), although reference to them sometimes occurs alongside other types of associations in the inscriptions we have collected. Nevertheless, since these more official groups occasionally provide a context for understanding unofficial associations, we have included some books and articles in the annotated bibliography regarding the age-based organizations.

Arrangement of Materials

For section 1, Inscriptions and Papyri, we have arranged the entries according to geographic region, beginning with southern and central Greece, moving north to Macedonia and Thracia, then north and northeast through the lower Danube region and the Bosporan Kingdom. We then make our way through Asia Minor and south through Greater Syria before turning westward through Egypt and Cyrenaica and then north again into Italy and the western provinces.

Inscriptions and papyri are presented in the following manner:

MAJOR REGION (e.g., Macedonia, Asia Minor, Egypt)
Sub-region (if applicable; e.g., Ionia, Fayûm)
   121. Type of Monument and Our Title

   City or locale (subregion). Some sources where the original text
   can be found.

   Date or approximate date (arranged chronologically by locale)

   Description of the monument and current location, if available.
   Explanation of foreign concepts or items.

   Translation of the inscription or papyrus.

As seen above, entries are grouped first by major geographical region (e.g.,
Asia Minor, Egypt), then, if applicable, by subregion (e.g., Ionia, Fayûm),
and finally by city, town, or locale. There are subheadings for major
regions and sub-regions, but not for locales, which are specified immediately below the number and our title for the inscription. For each locale,
the inscriptions are then presented chronologically, based on known or
approximate dates (with undated inscriptions coming last for each locale).
    The majority of inscriptions in the *Sourcebook* are Greek; inscriptions
in Latin or Demotic are clearly identified as such in the description. Our
list of where each entry is published is meant to provide only a few examples of where the Greek or Latin inscription can be found in the primary
collections, and the abbreviations used for these inscriptional collections
(e.g., *IG, IEph, IJO*) can be found listed in the pages before the introduction
to this *Sourcebook*. When an entry includes a reference in the name–date
format (e.g., Jaccottet 2003, vol. 2, no. 13), the user should consult information in the annotated bibliography, which can be found in the final
section of the book.
    An important online resource for the original Greek inscriptions is the
Packard Humanities Institute (PHI) website at http://epigraphy.packhum
.org/inscriptions/. That website is both browsable by region and subregion
and searchable by keyword or by corpora. Although not yet implemented,
plans exist to add the ability to search that database of inscriptions by
PHI's own internal numbering system (e.g., PH232990), so we do include
these numbers wherever possible so that students and scholars can more
directly look up the Greek text of a given inscription in the future (without
having to browse that website by region and subregion). The Epigraphik-
Datenbank Clauss/Slaby (http://oracle-vm.ku-eichstaett.de:8888/epigr/
epigraphik_en), which makes available the text of Latin inscriptions
and some photos, can also be searched by corpus, location, or key-
words. The *Corpus inscriptionum latinarum* (http://cil.bbaw.de/cil_en/

index_en.html) includes photos (when available) and secondary bibliography, but not the texts themselves.

With the English translations of inscriptions, we have attempted to be consistent in translating the names for associations and associates, along with titles of officials, but we often include in brackets the transliterated Greek or Latin term for clarification. Some recurring association self-designations or names for association members (with our equivalent translated term) include *collegium* ("association"), *koinon* ("association"), *eranos* ("club"), *orgeōnes* ("sacrificing associates"), *synodos* ("synod"), *synergasia* ("guild"), *thiasos* ("society"), *synagōgē* ("synagogue" or "gathering"), *eranistai* ("club members"), *mystai* ("initiates"), and *thiasōtai* ("society members"). There are, of course, many other terms used for associations and associates, all of which are indexed for ease of reference, as are terms for officials such as *archeranistēs* ("head of the club"), *epimelētēs* ("supervisor"), *grammateus* ("secretary"), and *prostates* ("president"). We have made sporadic use of other parenthetical material in order to provide clarification of terms or concepts. For example, the general meaning of epithets or descriptors used to name a particular deity are clarified in English in parentheses and quotation marks: for example, Zeus Dionysos Gongylos ("Round"), Men Tyrannos ("Absolute Ruler"), Theos Hypsistos ("Highest God"). For convenience and ease of access, we have included a list of inscriptions and papyri cited. This is far from a complete list of all the publications that might have been cited for any given entry, but it will allow the reader to find texts from a particular inscriptional collection in this *Sourcebook*.

Although associations are widely attested in inscriptions and papyri, there are other types of archaeological evidence, and archaeologists have excavated more than fifty buildings used by associations. In order to provide a sampling of these remains, we have included in section 2, Buildings and Meeting Places, twenty-eight brief descriptions of association meeting places (numbered **B1**, **B2**, etc.). These descriptions are meant to be representative rather than comprehensive. These are the main building remains extant, and much of the material remains that we did not include comes from Ostia and from smaller locations in Italy where the name of the association affiliated with a building is unknown. Many other associations are known to have had buildings from references in inscriptions (descriptions of which can be found in Bollmann 1998), but the material remains have not survived or been found by archaeologists. Although we include inscriptions that involve groups of Judeans, we have not included descriptions of Judean synagogues, which are well covered in other publications (see Richardson 2003; Runesson 2001). We also do not include many temples and buildings discussed in other publications regarding specific deities, such as Mithras (see

L. Michael White, *The Social Origins of Christian Architecture*, vol. 2 [Valley Forge, Pa.: Trinity Press International, 1997], 259–429), Dionysos (see Jaccottet 2003, 1:147–96), or Egyptian deities (see Robert A. Wild, "The Known Isis-Sarapis Sanctuaries of the Roman Period," *Aufstieg und Niedergang der römischen Welt* II.17.4 [1984]: 1740–1851). The descriptions of the buildings are arranged by major geographical regions in the same general order as the inscriptions and papyri. The bibliography cited by name–date (e.g., Arnaoutoglou 2002) in each building entry refers to the annotated bibliography; otherwise full details are provided.

Section 3, Literary References, gathers together about fifty-four significant references to associations in literary sources by Greek and Latin literary sources (numbered **L1**, **L2**, etc.), again without claiming to be exhaustive. We have classified these entries according to three broad areas: general references, dealings with civic or imperial authorities, and legal documents in the *Digest* of Justinian (which dates to the sixth century CE but contains evidence from earlier). Under each section, literary passages are arranged chronologically (either by the author or by the incidents described). Each item is prefaced by a brief introduction that provides context for understanding the passage quoted and an identification of the original language, whether Greek or Latin. The writers are given in alphabetical order in the index of literary references at the end of the *Sourcebook*.

Section 4, the Annotated Bibliography containing more than 350 secondary sources, is also comprehensive without claiming to be exhaustive. We have attempted to include most significant works in English, German, and French, each one of them with a brief annotation. Space limitations prevented us from including all that we would have liked, and many entries were omitted in order to make room for more inscriptions in the volume. We have not generally included dictionary and encyclopedia entries, except where these are fairly substantial contributions. Specialized studies on a particular text and articles that collect inscriptions are usually excluded, unless the book or article places an inscription or inscriptions within a broader descriptive or argumentative context. Finally, we have not sought to include every book and article that touches on associations, but only those works that significantly engage material regarding associations.

The index of subjects and locales aims to facilitate researchers in tracing a particular locale, word, or topic across a number of entries and in making connections among the primary and secondary works in the *Sourcebook*. Using this index, researchers can easily navigate the material to focus on texts and scholarship that are directly pertinent to their own scholarly interests.

As we noted for each section of the *Sourcebook*, we have tried to be representative without making any claim to be exhaustive in our selection of texts and bibliography. However, we invite the reader to visit the companion website for this volume at http://www.philipharland.com/greco-roman -associations/, which will continue to supplement and illustrate the materials gathered in this *Sourcebook*.

INSCRIPTIONS AND PAPYRI

Southern and Central Greece

Attica

1. Decree of the Sacrificing Associates of Echelos and the Heroines

Athens (Attica). Arthur Geoffrey Woodhead, *Inscriptions: The Decrees* (The Athenian Agora, 16; Princeton, N.J.: American School of Classical Studies at Athens, 1997), no. 161 = *LSCGSup* 20 = *GRA* I 14 = PH232990.

Early third century BCE

> Slab of Hymettian marble found on the Areopagos (inv. no. Agora I 1906). Since the hero Echelos is associated with the district of Echelidai, near Neon Phaleron (southwest of Athens), this inscription must come from the precinct "of the heroines," apparently near the Areopagos.

. . . the motion that Lysias son of Periander of Plotheia made: For good fortune, the sacrificing associates (*orgeōnes*) approved. In order that the partnership (*koinōnia*) in the sacrifices be maintained for all time for the association (*koinon*) that is near Kalliphanes' property and that of the hero Echelos, it was resolved: to inscribe the names of those who owe anything to the partnership—both the principal and the interest, as much as each owes—on a monument (stele) and set it up by the altar in the temple, and to inscribe the ancient decrees on the monument. And further that . . . supervise the inscribing and its erection in the temple and render an account to the association of whatever has been spent for these purposes. This was approved by the sacrificing associates.

Furthermore, the host (*hestiator*) should offer the sacrifice on the seventeenth and eighteenth of the month of Hekatombaion. On the first day he should sacrifice a young pig to the Heroines, sacrifice an adult animal to the Hero, and prepare an offering table. On the last day he should sacrifice an adult animal to the Hero. He must render an account of whatever he has expended and must not spend more than the income. Let him distribute shares of the meat to the sacrificing associates who are present—as well as up to a half share to their sons—and to the women of sacrificing associates, giving to free women the same share and up to a half share to their daughters and up to a half share for one female attendant. Let him hand over the woman's share to the man. It was approved by the sacrificing associates.

Let the host . . . of the interest. . . .

2. Decree of Society Members Honoring a Treasurer

Athens (Attica). *IG* II² 1323 = *RIG* 971 = *SIG*³ 1103 = *GRA* I 31 = PH3539.

194/193 BCE

Plaque of Pentelic marble, broken at the bottom.

Gods! In the year that Dionysios was civic leader (*archōn*), in the month of Elaphebolion, during the regular assembly, the society members (*thiasōtai*) approved the motion that Zeno son of Zenodotos of Erikeia proposed: Whereas Theon, having been appointed as the treasurer for the year that Nikophon was civic leader (*archōn*), has rendered this service for many years; further, he has allocated funds for the sacrifices at the appropriate times with honesty; and, further, he has paid immediately the burial expenses for those who have died. Likewise also the secretary (*grammateus*) has rendered service for many years. Whereas these two continue to show goodwill toward the association of society members and to put themselves at its disposal, and . . . the same. . . .

3. List of New Members in a Synod of Herakles

Attica (uncertain location). *SEG* 36 (1986), no. 228 = *GRA* I 38 = PH294182.

159/158 BCE

Slab of white marble with a triangular top (pediment), now in the Liebieghaus Museum, Frankfurt (inv. no. 1570). The inscription records the entrance of fourteen new members into the association, which is composed of members of the subdivisions (*demes*), resident foreigners (*metics*), and slaves.

In the year that Aristaichmos was civic leader (*archōn*) and Sosander son of Philinos of Kydathenaion was priest, the following entered the synod (*synodos*) of Herakles, Sosander son of Philinos of Kydathenaion having paid for the monument (stele): Demetrios of Paiania, Timagoras of Rhamnous, Sothrichos of Antioch, Petron the house-bred slave, Sodas of Potamos, Glaukias of Antioch, Zopyros of Aphidna, Spercheios, Meleagros, Sindes, Sosibios, Hippodromos, and Attas.

4. Dedication to the Egyptian Gods

Athens (Attica). *SEG* 42 (1992), no. 157 = Sterling Dow, "The Egyptian Cults in Athens," *Harvard Theological Review* 30 (1937): 183–232 (no. VIII) = *SIRIS* 5 = *GRA* I 41 = PH229685.

ca. 116/115–95/94 BCE

> Base of Hymettian marble, now in the Epigraphical Museum, Athens (EM 649). This was found in Athens in the same neighborhood as the ancient Sarapis sanctuary, about forty-five meters away from where the Metropolitan Church now stands. The leaders in this association include both Athenian citizens (priest, temple guardian) and resident aliens (attendant, interpreter of visions).

To Isis, Sarapis, Anubis, and Harpokrates.

Megallis daughter of Magas of Marathon set this up on behalf of her daughter Demarion and her sons, in accordance with a command, during the priesthood of Menandros son of Artemon of Alopeke, when Asopokleus of Phlya was temple guardian, Sosikratos of Laodikea was the attendant, and Dionysios of Antioch was judge of the spectacles (or: interpreter of visions).

5. Honorary Decree of a Society of Ship Owners and Merchants

Athens (Attica). *IG* II² 1012 = *CIG* 124 = *RIG* 1502 = *GRA* I 42 = PH3232.

112/111 BCE

> Now in Naniano (in Venice). The association requests permission of the Athenian Council to erect a statue of its "host," the person who welcomed visitors to the city, suggesting a close relationship between the city officials and this association composed largely of foreigners.

In the year that Dionysios, who followed Paramonos, was civic leader (*archōn*), during the seventh civic presidency of Aiantides, when Lamios son of Timouchos of Rhamnous was the secretary, eighth day of Gamelion, eighth day of the civic presidency, with the Council in the Council chamber: Stratophon son of Stratokles of Sounion, one of the presidents with his fellow presidents put to a vote—and the Council approved—the motion that Rhesos son of Artemon of Halai proposed: Whereas Diognetos of Oe, the treasurer of the ship owners and merchants who pay dues to support the shrine of Zeus Xenios ("of foreigners"), has made an overture to the Council, and explained to the Council that the synod (*synodos*) wishes to set up in his (Dionysios') record office a shield with an image of their host (*proxenos*), Dionysios son of Theophilos of Halai, who has also been appointed the supervisor over the harbor. Therefore they petitioned the Council to ratify the motion for itself. For good fortune, the Council has resolved to permit Diognetos and the synod to erect a shield with an image of Dionysios son of Theophilos of Halai in his record office, as they have petitioned the Council.

6. Regulations of the Heroists

Athens (Attica). *IG* II² 1339 = Foucart 1873, no. 21 = *RIG* 1562 = *GRA* I 46 = PH3555.

57/56 BCE

> Slab of Hymettian marble found near the temple of the Dioskouroi on the slope of the Acropolis, now in the Epigraphical Museum, Athens.

To good fortune! In the year that Diokles son of Diokles was civic leader (*archōn*), when Aropos son of Seleukos was treasurer . . . of the Heroists of Diotimos, Zenon, and Pammenes, whose head of the club (*archeranistēs*) was Zenion son of Diotimos of Marathon, the association (*koinon*) of the Heroists resolved to make provision for the income of the association, so that those of the Heroists who are away from home for whatever reason shall pay three drachmas for the sacrifices, and those living at home but not in attendance shall be required to pay six drachmas as the contribution, and they shall not receive the portion of the sacrifice. And if they do not make a contribution, it was resolved that they should not participate in the club (*eranos*), except if one should be absent because of mourning or because of sickness. Likewise it was resolved to allow those who have contributed thirty drachmas to introduce new members to the club and . . . of six drachmas and not . . . let them cast their ballot regarding the things. . . .

7. Regulations of a Bacchic Association—The Iobacchoi

Athens (Attica). *IG* II² 1368 = *LSCG* 51 = Jaccottet 2003, vol. 2, no. 4 = *GRA* I 51 = PH3584.

164/165 CE

> Column found in the apse of a Roman building (see **B2**) between the Pynx and the Areopagus in Athens, on the western slopes of the Acropolis, now in the Epigraphical Museum, Athens. The top of the column depicts the head of a bull above two panthers on either side of a large drinking vessel (see sketch in figure 1). The members of this group are called Iobacchoi, a variant on *bakchoi* or bacchants (devotees of Bacchos).

To good fortune! In the year that Arrius (or: Aurelius) Epaphroditos was civic leader (*archōn*), on the eighth of Elaphebolion, an assembly (*agora*) was first convened by the priest who was nominated by Aurelius Nikomachos, who had served as vice priest for seventeen years and as priest for twenty-three years and had, for the order and glory of the Baccheion, resigned while still living in favor of his excellency Claudius Herodes, by whom he was nominated as vice priest.

He (the vice priest) read the statutes drawn up by the former priests, Chrysippos and Dionysios, and after the priest and head of the bacchic devotees (*archibakchos*) and the president had approved, they all shouted: "We will use these forever!" "Bravo for the priest!" "Revive the statutes!" "It is fitting for you to do so!" "Health and good order to the Baccheion!" "Inscribe the statutes on the monument (stele)!" "Put the question!"

The priest said: "Since it is pleasing to me and to my fellow priests and to all of you, as you ask, we shall put the question." And the president (*proedros*), Rufus son of Aphrodisios, put the question: "To whomever it seems good that the statutes that have been read out should be ratified and inscribed on a monument (stele), raise your hand." Everyone raised his hand. They shouted: "Long life to his excellency, the priest Herodes!" "Now you have good fortune!" "Now we are the best of all Bacchic societies!" "Bravo to the vice priest!" "Let the monument be made!" The vice priest said: "The monument will be set on the column and inscribed. For the presiding officers shall be empowered to prevent any of those decrees from being violated."

It is not allowed for anyone to become an Iobacchos (i.e., a member of the Bacchic association) unless he has first registered with the priest the customary notice and is approved by a vote of the Iobacchoi, if he appears to be worthy and suitable for the Baccheion. The entrance fee shall be fifty denarii and a libation for one whose father was not a member.

Figure 1
Sketch of the inscribed column of the Iobacchoi (7; from Jane Ellen Harrison, Primitive Athens as Described by Thucydides *[Cambridge: Cambridge University Press, 1906], 90, figure 25.*

Similarly, those whose fathers were members should be enlisted, giving an additional twenty-five denarii—that is, half the usual rate—until puberty.

The Iobacchoi shall meet together on the ninth of each month, on the annual festival, and on the Bacchic days (*Bakcheia*), and if there is any occasional feast of the god. Each member shall speak and act and be zealous for the association, contributing to the fixed monthly dues for wine. If he does not fulfill these obligations, he shall be shut out of the gathering (*stibas*). Those named in the decree shall be empowered to enforce this, except in the cases of persons who are out of town, in mourning, ill, or if someone to be admitted to the gathering is completely indispensable. The priests shall judge these cases.

If a brother of an Iobacchos should enter, having been approved by a vote, he shall pay fifty denarii. If an uninitiated boy active in sacred services has paid the fee to the gods and the Baccheion, he shall be an Iobacchos with his father, on the basis of one libation by his father. The priest shall give a letter to everyone who has been submitted a notice and has been approved by vote indicating that he is an Iobacchos—after the member pays the entrance fee to the priest. The priest shall indicate the payments made, and for which purpose, in the letter.

In the gathering no one is allowed to sing, cause a disturbance, or applaud. Rather, with all order and decorum members shall speak and do their parts, as the priest or the head of the bacchic devotees directs. None of the Iobacchoi who has not paid the contributions for either the meetings on the ninth of the month or the annual festival is permitted to enter into the gathering, until it has been decided by the priests whether he should pay the fee or be allowed to enter anyway. Now if anyone begins a fight or is disorderly or sits in someone else's seat or insults or abuses someone else, the person abused or insulted shall produce two of the Iobacchoi as sworn witnesses, testifying that they heard the insult or abuse. The one who committed the insult or the abuse shall pay to the common treasury (koinon) twenty-five light drachmas, or the one who was the cause of the fight shall either pay the same twenty-five drachmas or not come to any more meetings of the Iobacchoi until he pays. If someone comes to blows, the one who was struck shall file a report with the priest or the vice priest, who shall without fail convene a meeting and the Iobacchoi shall judge by a vote with the priest presiding. The offender shall be penalized by not being permitted to enter for a time—as long as it seems appropriate—and by paying a fine up to twenty-five silver denarii. The same penalty shall also be applied to the one who is beaten and does not go to the priest or the head of the bacchic devotees but instead brings a charge with the public courts. The penalty shall be the same for the officer in charge of order (eukosmos) if he does not expel those who fight.

If one of the Iobacchoi, knowing that a meeting ought to be convened for this purpose, does not attend, he shall pay a fine of fifty light drachmas to the common treasury (koinon). If he fails to pay, the treasurer shall be permitted to prevent him from entering the meetings of the Baccheion until he pays. If one of those who enters does not pay the entrance fee to the priest or the vice priest, he shall be expelled from the banquet until he pays and he shall pay in whatever way the priest orders.

No one is permitted to recite a speech (or: perform a hymn [?]) unless the priest or the vice priest gives permission. Otherwise he is liable to pay a fine of thirty light drachmas to the treasury. The priest shall perform the customary services (*litourgia*) of the gathering and of the yearly festival in a fitting manner: He shall set before the gathering one libation of the Festival of Return (*Katagogia*), and shall give the discourse about the god (*theologia*), which the former priest Nikomachos inaugurated out of his zeal. The head of the bacchic devotees shall sacrifice to the god and make a libation on the tenth day of the month of Elaphebolion. When the parts of the sacrificial victims are distributed, let them go to the priest, the vice priest, the head of the bacchic devotees, the treasurer, the cowherd (*boukolos*), "Dionysos," "Kore," "Palaimon," "Aphrodite," "Proteurythmos." Let these roles be apportioned among all by lot.

If any of the Iobacchoi receives a legacy, honor, or appointment, he shall make a libation for the Iobacchoi commensurate with the occasion—a marriage, birth, pitcher festival, coming of age, grant of citizenship; being honored as a rod bearer, Council member, president of the games, Panhellene, member of the elders' council (*gerousia*), member of the lawgivers (*thesmothesia*), or any magistracy whatsoever; an appointment as a fellow sacrificer, police chief, or sacred victor, and if any who is an Iobacchos should obtain any promotion.

The officer in charge of order shall be chosen by lot or be appointed by the priest, bearing the wand (*thyrsos*) of the god for anyone who is disorderly or creates a disturbance. Now if the wand is laid on anyone—and the priest or the head of the bacchic devotees approves—the one who made the disturbance shall leave the banquet hall. If he refuses, those who have been appointed by the priests as "horses" (i.e., bouncers) shall take him outside of the door. And he shall be liable to the punishment that applies to those who fight.

The Iobacchoi shall choose a treasurer by vote every two years. He shall receive for registration all of the property of the Baccheion. He shall likewise hand over everything to his successor. He shall provide at his own expense the lamp oil for the meetings on the ninth of the month, the annual festival, and the gathering, as well as all the usual days of the god and the days on which legacies, honors, and appointments are celebrated. If he so wishes, he shall choose a secretary at his own risk, and the treasurer's libation shall be given to him and he shall be exempt from membership fees for two years.

If an Iobacchos dies, a wreath worth up to five denarii, and a single jar of wine shall be provided for those who attend the funeral. But no one who is absent from the funeral itself shall have any wine.

8. Regulations of a Club on Admission and Discipline

Liopesi (Attica). *IG* II² 1369 = Foucart 1873, no. 20 = *LSCG* 53 = *GRA* I 49 = PH3585.

Second century CE

> This is the foundational document of an association, one of the
> duties of which is the care of the tomb of a hero.

(*17 lines missing due to damage*) . . . set up this in memory of the dead and the others. . . (*5 lines too damaged to translate*) . . . In the year that Tauriskos was civic leader (*archōn*), in the month of Mounichion on the eighteenth day, the male friends convened a club (*eranos*) and by common council subscribed to an ordinance of friendship.

The law of the club members (*eranistai*): It is not lawful for anyone to enter this most holy synod (*synodos*) of club members without being first examined as to whether he is pure, pious, and good. Let the president (*prostatēs*), the head of the club (*archeranistēs*), the secretary, the treasurers, and the advocates (*syndikoi*) examine the candidate. Except for the president, let these positions be chosen by lot each year. The one who has been entrusted with the tomb of the hero shall be in charge of the service for his lifetime. May the club increase because of the zealousness of its members! But if anyone of those should be seen where fighting or disturbances occur, he shall be expelled from the club, being fined twenty-five Attic drachmas or being punished with double the blows in addition to judgment (?).

9. Regulations of a Club on Sacrifice and Discipline

Liopesi (Attica). *SEG* 31 (1981), no. 122 = *NGSL* 5 = *GRA* I 50 = PH293233.

Early second century CE

> Two fragments of Pentelic marble, now in the Getty Museum, Malibu, California (inv. no. 78.AA.377). The plaque has a decorated triangular top (pediment with a shield and three acroteria). The base has a roughly cut tenon that could be inserted into a socket base. A photograph of this monument appears on the cover of this book.

To good fortune! In the year that Titus Flavius Konon was civic leader (*archōn*) and the priest of the consul Drusus, on the eighteenth of the month of Mounichion, it seemed good to Marcus Aemilius Eucharistos of Paiania, the head of the club (*archeranistēs*) of the synod (*synodos*) of Heraklists in the Marshes, to approve the following regulations:

If someone in the synod should cause a fight, on the following day let him pay a fine. The one who initiated the fight should pay ten drachmas and whoever joined in should pay five drachmas. After his fellow club members (*eranistai*) have taken a vote to expel him, let him pay the fine without fail.

Concerning the endowment that has been deposited by the head of the club and whatever other endowment has been collected, let no one in any way whatsoever touch it, beyond the interest that accrues. The treasurer shall not expend more than three hundred drachmas from the interest. If he should lay hold of more or take from the endowment, or more of the interest, he shall pay a fine of three times what was taken. Likewise, if a former treasurer has been proved to have put money away for himself, let him be fined three times the amount taken.

Concerning the priesthoods: If someone should agree to purchase one, let him make the payment immediately to the head of the club in the following year and let him receive a receipt from the head of the club. In accordance with custom, let him receive a double portion, except for the wine. Those who contract for the pork and the wine who do not hand them over during the year that they are providing the dinners shall be fined a double portion.

Those who contract to supply provisions must present acceptable sureties to the treasurer and the head of the club. They shall appoint three able-bodied night watchmen. If any of them should refuse, then let them be selected by lot and whoever is chosen shall accept. If he should not accept or if he does not want to be a night watchman after having been chosen, he shall pay a fine of one hundred drachmas. It is necessary to appoint from the synod ten collectors (*praktores*). If they do not wish to be collectors, let ten be chosen by lot from the general membership. Likewise, when the treasurer provides an accounting, after a meeting has been called, they shall appoint three auditors and the auditors shall swear by Herakles, Demeter, and Kore.

They shall choose by lot two men every day to be in charge of the meat. Likewise, two men in charge of the rolls. If anyone who is entrusted with this task is found to have done something sordid, he shall be fined twenty drachmas. Let the head of the club choose three people—whomever he wants—from the synod to assist him in paying out the endowment. But let all of them give ... *x* measures (*choinixes*) of fine wheat flour, by the public measure. Each year the treasurer shall take care that a sacrifice to the god is performed consisting of a boar weighing twenty minas.

If a member of the club (*eranos*) wishes to initiate his child ..., let him provide 16.5 minas of pork. If someone wants to enter himself, let him provide 33 minas of pork. Let the account be closed when the auditors, having taken an oath, return the accounts to the head of the club, and indicate whether the treasurer owes anything. Firewood should be supplied by the treasurer each year. The dues must be brought to the treasurer so that loans can be made. Whoever does not pay shall be fined a double amount. Whoever does not pay at all shall be expelled from the club (*exeranos*). It shall not be lawful to touch the firewood in the grove. Everyone is to wear a wreath in honor of the god.

10. Decrees Regarding a Kitian Temple for the Syrian Aphrodite

Piraeus (Attica). *IG* II² 337 = *LSCG* 34 = *GRA* I 3 = PH2554.

333/332 BCE

> Slab of Pentelic marble, now in the Epigraphical Museum, Athens (EM 7173). Athenian decrees typically begin with the expression "Gods!" to indicate that appropriate rites and invocations have been performed.

Gods! In the year that Nikokrates was civic leader (*archōn*), in the first presidency of the tribe of Aigeis, Theophilos of Phegaia, chair of the presiders, put the following to a vote and the Council made the resolution:

Antidotos son of Apollodoros of Sypalettos made the following motion: In regard to what the Kitians (i.e., immigrants from Kition on Cyprus) propose concerning the establishment of the temple to Aphrodite, it is resolved by the Council that the presiders, who are chosen by lot to preside in the first session (*ekklēsia*), shall bring them forward and deal with the business and put to the People the proposal of the Council: that it seems good to the Council that the People, having listened to the Kitians regarding the foundation of the temple and to any other Athenian who wishes to speak, should decide whatever seems best.

In the year that Nikokrates was civic leader (*archōn*), during the second presidency of the tribe of Pandionis, the question was put by Phanostratos of Philaidai, chair of the presiders. The Council made the resolution:

The motion of Lykourgos son of Lykophron of Butadai: Since the Kitian merchants are making a legitimate request in asking the People for the right to lease the land on which they propose to establish a temple of Aphrodite, let it be it resolved by the assembly to grant to the Kitian merchants the right to acquire land to establish the temple of Aphrodite, in the same way that the Egyptians also established the temple of Isis.

11. Decree of the Sacrificing Associates of Bendis

Piraeus (Attica). *IG* II² 1361 = *LSCG* 45 = *GRA* I 4 = PH3577.

330–324/323 BCE

> Plaque of Pentelic marble damaged at the top and bottom, now in
> the Epigraphical Museum, Athens. The occurrence of sacrifices
> after the sixteenth of the month of Thargelian suggests a connec-
> tion with Bendis, a goddess associated with Thrace.

. . . as many persons as are inscribed on the monument (stele) and their
descendants. If any of the sacrificing associates (*orgeōnes*) who have a
claim in the sanctuary should sacrifice to the goddess, they shall do so
without any cost. However, if a private individual should sacrifice to the
goddess, he shall pay the priestess for a suckling pig: one (?) obol, along
with the skin and the entire right thigh; for a mature animal: three obols,
along with the skin and the thigh on the same conditions; and, for an ox:
one (?) obol and the skin. They shall give the priestly portion of females
to the priestess and of males to the priest. No one is permitted to sacrifice
anything in the sanctuary beside the altar. If they do, they will owe a fine
of fifty drachmas.

In order that the house and the sanctuary be maintained in good
repair, the income from the house and the sale of water—however much it
costs for the maintenance of the sanctuary and the house—is to be spent
on it and not for any other reason, until the sanctuary and the house are
repaired, unless the sacrificing associates agree by a vote to do something
different . . . for the sanctuary. They should leave water for the occupant
of the house so that he may use it. If someone should move or introduce
a motion in violation of this law, they will owe fifty drachmas to the goddess—both the one who formulated the motion and the one who moved
it—and let them not participate in the common activities. The supervisors
(*epimelētai*) are also to inscribe on a monument (stele) the names of these
persons who owe this money to the goddess.

The supervisors and performers of the sacrifices (*hieropoioi*) shall
arrange an assembly and convocation in the sanctuary to discuss the association's affairs on the second day of each month. Each of the sacrificing
associates who have a claim in the sanctuary shall give to the performers
of the sacrifices two drachmas during the month of Thargelian for the sacrifice, before the sixteenth day. Whoever is at home in Athens and in good
health but does not contribute, owes two drachmas, sacred to the goddess.

So that there may be as many sacrificing associates of the sanctuary as
possible, it is permitted for anyone who wishes to contribute . . . *x* drachmas to become a member of the sanctuary and to be inscribed on the

monument (stele). Let the members approve those who are to be inscribed on the monument, and hand over the names of those approved to the secretary in the month of Thargelion . . .

12. Decree of the Sacrificing Associates of Bendis Honoring Supervisors

Piraeus (Attica). *IG* II² 1256 = Cynthia J. Schwenk, *Athens in the Age of Alexander: The Dated Laws and Decrees of "the Lykouran Era" 338–322 B.C.* (Chicago: Ares, 1985), no. 52 = *GRA* I 5 = PH3471.

329/328 BCE

Slab of Pentelic marble with a rectangular plaque (*pinax*) at the top of a shaft containing the inscription, now in the Ny Carlsberg Glyptothek, Copenhagen (inv. no. 1043a). The relief (figure 2) depicts the goddess Bendis on the right, wearing a Phrygian cap and dressed

Figure 2
Relief of the goddess Bendis and her consort Deloptes, with two bearded supplicants on the left and members of the association in low relief, now in the Ny Carlsberg Glypote (**12**; *photo by Kloppenborg*).

in an animal skin with a spear in her left hand and a bowl or plate
extended in the right hand. The other figure is likely Deloptes, her
consort. Two bearded male worshipers appear at the left, probably
representing the two honorees. In the upper-left corner there are
five smaller figures carved in low relief. There are two olive wreaths
on the shaft below the inscription. It is not clear whether the membership of this association consists of Athenian citizens or Thracians (possibly slaves).

Gods! Philokrates proposed the following motion: Whereas Euphyes
and Dexios, who were supervisors (*epimelētai*) of the sanctuary during
the year that Kephisophon was civic leader (*archōn*), performed their service honorably and with ambition and in a manner worthy of the goddess and of the sacrificing associates (*orgeōnes*), the sacrificing associates
have resolved to crown Euphyes and Dexios on account of their honesty
and care, each with a gold crown worth one hundred drachmas, and to
inscribe this decree on a monument (stele) and to set it up in the sanctuary
of the goddess.

13. Regulations Outlining Obligations of Society Members

Piraeus (Attica). *IG* II² 1275 = *LSCGSup* 126 = *GRA* I 8 = PH3489.
325–275 BCE

> Slab of gray marble with damage at the top, now in the British
> Museum. This law (*nomos*) of the society obliges members to pro-
> vide burial for members and to assist living members financially.

... and if a member ... of the society members (*thiasōtai*) ... and if any of
them should die ... or a son or a ... or a father or whoever is his closest relative in the society (*thiasos*), and they shall attend the carrying out of the
deceased—both the members and all the friends (*philoi*). And if a member
should be wronged, they and all the friends shall come to his assistance,
so that everyone might know that we show piety to the gods and to our
friends. To those who do these things, may many blessings come upon
them, their descendants, and their ancestors. Whenever the society members have ratified this law, let there be nothing to take precedence over it.
And if someone should either speak or act in contravention of the law, an
accusation against him may be lodged by any of the society members who
so wishes. If he convicts him, let them assess the penalty, whatever seems
appropriate to the association (*koinon*).

14. Honorary Decrees by a Society Devoted to Aphrodite

Piraeus (Attica). *IG* II² 1261 = *SIG³* 1098 = *GRA* I 9 = PH3476.

302/301 BCE (A); 301/300 BCE (B); 300/299 BCE (C)

Plaque of marble containing three decrees set up by the society
members in successive years.

(A) When Nikokles was civic leader (*archōn*), the society members
(*thiasōtai*) approved the following motion: Whereas Stephanos the breast-
plate maker, when he became the supervisor (*epimelētēs*) of all the association's affairs, administered them with the appropriate care and continued
to be ambitious in other matters concerning the association (*koinon*). And
whereas he conducted the procession in honor of Adonis in accordance
with ancestral customs. To good fortune! The society members resolved:
to commend Stephanos the supervisor on account of the ambition and the
nobility of character that he has exhibited toward the association of the
society members; to crown him with an olive wreath; and, to give to him
ten drachmas. Having been crowned by the association, he dedicated the
statue of Demeter Homonoia ("Concord") of the association.

The society members of Aphrodite honored Stephanos son of
Mylothros.

(B) When Klearchos was civic leader (*archōn*), the society members
approved the following motion: Whereas Stephanos, formerly having
been a supervisor and now having been chosen as a performer of the sacrifices (*hieropoios*) with his fellow performers of the sacrifices, has been a
generous person and has offered to the gods the sacrifices which by ancestral custom are offered to them, and whereas he has exercised care over
the other matters that are his to care for. To good fortune! The society
members resolved to commend Stephanos the performer of sacrifices on
account of the ambition and the nobility of character that he has exhibited
toward the association of the society members; to crown him with an olive
wreath; and, to give to him ten drachmas.

The society members of Aphrodite honored Stephanos son of
Mylothros   .

(C) When Hegemachos was civic leader (*archōn*)—to good fortune—Sokles made the following motion: Whereas Stephanos, having
become a performer of sacrifices, has conducted faithfully the sacrifices
to Aphrodite, the society members resolved to commend Stephanos son
of Mylothros; to crown him with an olive wreath; and, to give him twenty
drachmas from the treasury. Having received this money, he shall dedicate a statue in the temple, inscribing it with this decree, so that as many

as are ambitious will see that the society members know how to return appropriate thanks.

15. Honorary Decree of the Society Members of Tynaros

Piraeus (Attica). *IG* II² 1262 = *GRA* I 10 = PH3477.

300/299 BCE

> Slab of Hymettian marble, now in the National Museum, Athens.

When Klearchos was civic leader (*archōn*), month of Skirophorion. Kantharion made the following motion:

The society members (*thiasōtai*) resolved: Whereas the supervisors (*epimelētai*) have faithfully and ambitiously executed their responsibilities, both in regard to the sacrifices and all the other affairs of the association (*koinon*), it is resolved to commend them and to crown them with olive wreaths and to provide for them at the association's expense a votive plaque in the amount of twenty drachmas. Both the crowns and the decree are to be inscribed on the plaque, so that all the others might know that the association renders appropriate thanks to those who are ambitious toward the members in acts of benefaction.

(*left column*)
The society members of Tynaros honor Drakon and Kittos.

(*right column*)
The society members of Tynaros honor Drakon and Kittos.

16. Decree of a Society Honoring Their Secretary

Piraeus (Attica). *IG* II² 1263 = Foucart 1873, no. 30 = *GRA* I 11 = PH3478.

300/299 BCE

> Plaque of Pentelic marble, now in the Museum in Piraeus.

When Hegemachos was civic leader (*archōn*) in the month of Pyanopsion on the fifth day of the present month in the regular assembly of the society members (*thiasōtai*), the society members approved the motion that Kleon son of Leokrates from Salamis proposed: Whereas Demetrios, who was chosen secretary (*grammateus*) by the society members when Klearchos was civic leader (*archōn*), took care of all of the affairs of the association (*koinon*) honorably and justly; rendered the accounts in good order and justly; and, gave a public accounting both of what he had controlled himself and what he had delegated to the others—whatever he administered belonging to the society members. Whereas he now continues to do what is helpful and speaks on behalf of the society members, both as a group and individually, and after the society members approved a motion to give him a reward from the treasury, he even returned this to the society members.

To good fortune! As a result of these things, it seemed good to the society members to commend Demetrios son of Sosandros of Olynthos on account of the excellence and honesty which he continues to have with respect to the association of society members; to crown him with a votive plaque worth fifty drachmas; and, to set up the plaque in the temple, wherever he should wish it, after asking the society members. This is so that others will also be ambitious toward the society members, knowing that they will receive thanks from the society members commensurate with the benefactions.

The treasurer, who was elected during the civic leadership (archonship) of Hegemachos, shall provide the money for the monument and he shall be responsible for the monument so that it will be completed quickly. It was also resolved to crown him immediately with an olive wreath. The performers of sacrifices (*hieropoioi*) who have been chosen at that time to serve as performers of sacrifices shall announce this crowning publicly after the libations: "The association crowns Demetrios with this wreath on account of the excellence and good will that he continues to show toward the society members." And if they do not publicly announce this, let them pay a fine of fifty drachmas. It was also resolved to inscribe this decree upon the monument.

(*In an engraved crown*) The society members honored Demetrios of Olynthos.

17. Decree of the Sacrificing Associates of Bendis Honoring Two Members

Piraeus (Attica). *IG* II² 1284 = *GRA* I 22 = PH3498.

241 BCE

Marble slab, now in the Museum in Piraeus.

. . . sacrificing associates (*orgeōnes*) . . . so that . . . and in other matters he proved to be of service and displayed the good will which he held toward all of the sacrificing associates. So that all who wish to be ambitious toward the sacrificing associates might know that they shall receive thanks worthy of whoever should act as a benefactor. To good fortune! The sacrificing associates resolved to commend Olympos son of Olympiodoros and to crown him with an oak wreath, on account of the ambition and good will that he continually exhibits toward both the temple and the sacrificing associates. The secretary shall inscribe this decree on a monument (stele) and set it up in the temple, and the treasurer shall pay . . . drachmas. . . .

In the year that Lykeas was civic leader (*archōn*), on the eighth day of the month of Skirophorion, in the regular assembly, Sosias son of Hippokrates made the following motion: Whereas Eukleides, who was chosen as secretary (*grammateus*) has for many years managed in a proper and upright manner those matters that were made his responsibility by the laws, showing himself to be blameless, and whereas he gave an accurate account in regard to the things he managed. For good fortune, it was resolved by the sacrificing associates to commend Eukleides son of Antimachos and to crown him with an oak wreath on account of the ambition and honesty that he has exhibited with respect to the sacrificing associates. The secretary shall inscribe the decree on a monument (stele) and set it up in the temple, and the treasurer shall pay . . . drachmas. . . .

18. Decree of the Thracian Sacrificing Associates of Bendis

Piraeus (Attica). *IG* II² 1283 = *LSCG* 46 = Brigitte Le Guen-Pollet, *La vie religieuses dans le monde grec du Vᵉ au IIIᵉ siècle avant notre ère. Choix de documents épigraphiques traduits et commentés* (Toulouse: Presses universitaires du Mirail, 1991), no. 7 = *GRA* I 23 = PH3497.

240/239 BCE

> Slab of white marble with a relief, now in the Piraeus Museum. This inscription records the forming of a new Thracian group in the Asty in Athens and their construction of a temple. The new group desires to accompany the Piraean group in procession from the Prytaneion (civic presidency building) in Athens to the Bendis shrine in the Piraeus, perhaps as part of the festival of the *Bendideia*. For another monument from the Piraeus that depicts devotees (probably athletes) approaching the Thracian goddess Bendis, see figure 3.

Gods! In the year that Polystratos was civic leader (*archōn*), on the eighth of the month of Hekatombaion, at the regular assembly, Sosias son of Hippokrates made the motion: Whereas, the People of Athens granted to the Thracians, alone of all of the immigrant groups (*ethnē*), the right to own property (*enktēsis*) and to build a sanctuary in accordance with the oracle of Dodona and to have a procession from the hearth of the building of the civic presidency (*prytaneion*). Now those who have been chosen to build a sanctuary in the Asty think that both groups should be favorably disposed to each other, so that the sacrificing associates (*orgeōnes*) may also be seen

Figure 3
Relief of athletic youths approaching the goddess Bendis from Attica (ca. 400–375 BCE),
now in the British Museum (photo by Kloppenborg).

to be obedient to the law of the city, which orders the Thracians to have
their procession continue to the Piraeus, and being favorably disposed
toward the sacrificing associates who are in the Asty. For good fortune,
the sacrificing associates resolve that, when those in the Asty choose to
arrange the procession, the procession shall therefore proceed from the
building of the civic presidency to the Piraeus in the same procession with
those members from the Piraeus. Further, they resolve that the supervisors in the Piraeus shall promise to supply sponges in the sanctuary (or:
during the festival) of the Nymphs and to supply cups, water, wreaths, and
a meal in the sanctuary, just as they prepare for themselves.

When the sacrifices occur, the priest and the priestess shall pray—in
addition to the prayers that they normally pray and in the same way—for
the sacrificing associates who are in the Asty, so that when these things
take place and the entire immigrant group (*ethnos*) lives in concord, the
sacrifices and other rites shall be made to the gods, in accordance with
both the ancestral customs of the Thracians and the laws of the city. So
that it will turn out well and in a manner reflecting piety for the entire
immigrant group (*ethnos*) in matters concerning the gods.

Furthermore, if one of the sacrificing associates (of the Asty) should
wish to have access to the sacrificing associates (of the Piraeus) concerning

some other matter, they shall always have priority following the sacred rites. Also, if one of the sacrificing associates of the Asty should wish to join the sacrificing associates, they may do so, and receive portions of the sacrifice without paying the fee, for life, the portion. . . .

19. Regulations of the Sacrificing Associates of the Mother of the Gods

Piraeus (Attica). *IG* II² 1328 = *LSCG* 48 = *CCCA* 263 = *GRA* I 34 = PH3544.

183/182 BCE (A); 175/174 BCE (B)

> Plaque of Pentelic marble, now in the Epigraphical Museum of Athens (EM 10550). The second of these two decrees conflicts with the regulation of the first by granting a permanent role to Metrodora.

The sacrificing associates (*orgeōnes*) honor those who have contributed.

(A) In the year that Hermogenes was civic leader (*archōn*), in the month of Mounichion, at a regular assembly, Simon son of Simon of Poros made the following motion: Whereas there have been many expenses, and because of these expenses any woman who obtains the priesthood is expecting that there be a certain appropriate distribution of funds for them, so that they can perform their service with no additional expense being imposed on them.

For good fortune, it has been agreed by the members that the one who happens to be chosen as priestess for the year following Hermogenes' civic leadership (archonship) shall, in accord with these and the other things, furnish two thrones of the finest quality, and give an ornament of silver to the cupbearers and those who attend the goddess for the collection of the contributions. If someone acts in violation of these rules, the sacrificing associates are empowered to fine the priestess who offends against any of these rules, up to fifty drachmas. They will exact it in whatever manner seems best to them and it is unlawful for anyone to confer upon them the customary honors. They (the sacrificing associates) shall also be empowered to . . . the leaf concerning the disobedient priestess. Whichever priestess has obtained the priesthood shall appoint an attendant from among those who have already been priestesses. But it is not permitted to appoint the same person twice until all have had their turn. Otherwise, the priestess will be liable to the same fines. The secretary (*grammateus*) shall inscribe the decree on a stone monument (stele) and set it up in the temple.

(B) In the year that Sonikos was civic leader (*archōn*), in the month of Mounichion, at the regular assembly, the sacrificing associates approved the motion that Kleippos of Aixone proposed: Whereas Metrodora, having been deemed worthy by the priestess Archedike—who became priestess during the civic leadership (archonship) of Hippakos—to serve as an attendant and to coadminister with her for a year, devoted herself to this role and coadministered the matters pertaining to the goddess in an honorable, appropriate, and pious manner, and she fulfilled her obligations both to the priestesses and to the sacrificing associates without reproach. And whereas, accordingly, when Simale became priestess in the year that Sonikos was civic leader (*archōn*), and when she requested that the sacrificing associates agree to appoint for her Metrodora as an attendant. After the sacrificing associates agreed with her, she coadministered the priesthood—namely what pertained to the goddess, the priestesses, and the sacrificing associates—in an honorable, appropriate, and pious manner. For this reason, the priestesses also are eager to appoint her as attendant to the goddess for life. Therefore in order that they might be seen to be taking the best care of the goddess and that they might act in an honorable and pious manner in relation to the matters of the goddess—for good fortune—it has been resolved by the sacrificing associates to act in all matters that pertain to the decree that was proposed by Simon of Poros and to appoint Metrodora as an attendant to the goddess for life, that she serve indefinitely those who happen to be priestesses and that she meets their needs in an honorable and appropriate manner. It was also resolved that they take care that all things pertaining to the goddess take place in a pious manner, just as her mother, Euaxis, continued to do these things. And let the secretary inscribe this decree on the monument (stele) of the sacrificing associates.

20. Decree of the Sacrificing Associates of the Mother of the Gods

Piraeus (Attica). *IG* II² 1327 = *CCCA* 264 = *GRA* I 35 = PH3543.

178/177 BCE

> Plaque of Pentelic marble, with a decorated triangular top (pediment with acroteria), now in the Epigraphical Museum, Athens (EM 7854). This association includes both citizens and resident foreigners, the latter of whom stand to benefit the most from the benefaction of the honoree in covering their funeral expenses.

Gods! In the year that Philon was civic leader (*archōn*), in the month of Mounichion, at regular assembly—for good fortune, Euktemon son of Eumarides of Steiria, proposed the motion: Whereas Hermaios son of Hermogenes of Paionidai, having been treasurer (*tamias*) for many years, has continually acted piously toward the gods; he has proved himself generous to the sacrificing associates (*orgeōnes*) both collectively and individually, putting himself at the disposal of each; he has been zealous that the customary sacrifices to the gods be made, often generously paying for these from his own resources; he has paid for the tomb for some who had died when the treasury had no money, so that the deceased might be treated decently even in death; he made expenditures for repairs and he was the one who organized the original collection of the common fund; he continually talks about and advises what is best; and, he shows himself to be well-intentioned in all things. For good fortune! The sacrificing associates resolved to commend Hermaios son of Hermogenes of Paionidai and to crown him on account of the excellence that he has shown to the gods and, collectively, to the sacrificing associates, so that there might be a rivalry among the rest who aspire to honor, knowing that they will receive thanks benefitting those who are benefactors of the association of sacrificing associates. And let there be set up an image of him with a plaque in the temple and let it be crowned at every sacrifice. And let the supervisors (*epimelētai*) inscribe this decree on a stone monument (stele) and set it up in the Metroon (the sanctuary of the Mother). And the cost of both the plaque and the monument are to be paid from the treasury.

This was done when Neon of Cholargos, Simon of Poros, and Ergasion were supervisors.

21. Decree of the Dionysiasts Recognizing a Hero

Piraeus (Attica). *IG* II² 1326 = *LSCG* 49 = Jaccottet 2003, vol. 2, no. 2 = *GRA* I 36 = PH3542.

176/175 BCE

> Plaque of Pentelic marble found near the ruins of a sanctuary to Dionysos, now in the Epigraphical Museum, Athens.

Gods! To good fortune! In the year that Hippakos was civic leader (*archōn*), in the month of Poseideon at the regular assembly, Solon son of Hermogenes of Cholargos proposed the following motion: Whereas it has happened that Dionysios has left this life, and he had displayed in many things the goodwill that he had and continued to have toward all who brought the synod (*synodos*) together for the god. Also, when he was asked he was always the cause of some good thing, both for individuals and for the common good, being a benefactor (*philanthrōpos*) at all times. Whereas he has already been honored by the Dionysiasts, he has received the priesthood of the god, and he has been appointed treasurer, further increasing the common revenues by contributing one thousand silver drachmas from his own resources. And after all of the other expenditures he contributed a place in which they could come and sacrifice each month to the god in accordance with their ancestral customs.

He contributed in addition another five hundred silver drachmas, from which funds the statue of Dionysos was prepared for the sacrificing associates (orgeōnes), and it was installed in accordance with the oracle of the god. With respect to these matters, the plain demonstrations that exist concerning this man are registered in the archives for all time. On account of these things, the Dionysiasts, recognizing them, have honored him as being worthy and have crowned him in accordance with the law, so that the members who bring the synod together for the god might be seen to remember him, both while he was alive and after he died, remembering his beneficence and his goodwill toward them. Because of these things, they have publicly honored his children, since it happened that he has left behind successors to the things he possessed with glory and honor.

Concerning these successors, the law of the sacrificing associates also invites, first in this case, the eldest of the sons, just as also he had been introduced into the group in the place of his brother Kallikrates while his father was still alive. The sacrificing associates resolve that the priesthood of Dionysios be given to Agathokles son of Dionysios of Marathon, and that he hold it for life on account of all the honors with which his father has been honored. This was done because he has continued to maintain the treasury for the period after Dionysios' death and has enhanced the revenue, devoting himself to these things without hesitation, wishing to demonstrate his own goodwill and beneficence to all of the Dionysiasts. He also introduced his brother Dionysios son of Dionysios of Marathon into the synod in virtue of the possessions of his father, possessions which he shares, in accordance with the law. Furthermore, the sacrificing associates resolved to recognize that Dionysios has been canonized as a hero and to set up a statue of him in the temple beside the statue of the god, where there is also a statue of his father, so that he may have the most beautiful memory for all time. Let this decree be inscribed on a stone monument (stele) and erected beside the sanctuary of the god. The cost of the monument and its erection shall be borne by the treasurer (tamias). These things were moved by Solon.

22. Regulations for a Sanctuary and Association of the God Men Tyrannos

Laurion (north of Cape Sounion, Attica). *IG* II² 1365 + *IG* II² 1366 = *CMRDM* I 12 + *CMRDM* I 13 = *GRA* I 53 = PH3581 + PH3582.

Late second or early third century CE

Two monuments with similar inscriptions, now in the Epigraphical Museum, Athens. *IG* II² 1365 has an inscribed crescent at the top, which may have been painted. *IG* II² 1366 (a later expanded version) has a large, deeply incised, U-shaped crescent at the top, which resembles a horseshoe. At the base is a large lug used to secure the stone in place. Men is a moon god particularly attested in the region of Phrygia in Asia Minor. The founder of this cult, Xanthos, is an immigrant from the region of Lycia, south of Phrygia.

(*IG* II² 1365—*Version 1*)

Xanthos the Lycian consecrated the sanctuary of Men—the god having chosen him.

To good fortune! No one shall enter while impure, but let him be purified after eating garlic and pork.

And no one shall offer sacrifice without the permission of the founder. If anyone does this by force, the sacrifice will be unacceptable to the god. The sacrifice shall include what is prescribed for the god: a right leg, the skin, olive oil for the altar, a lamp, and a libation.

Let him be purified from contact with a corpse on the tenth day; from menstruation on the seventh day; but do not let a murderer around the place; from miscarriage (or: abortion) on the fortieth day; from intercourse with a woman on the same day, having washed themselves from head to foot. May the god be merciful to those who serve the god with a simple soul.

If the founder dies or is sick or out of town, let people serve the god with the approval of the one to whom the founder hands over authority.

Anyone who is a busybody or meddles will incur sin against Men Tyrannos ("Men the Absolute Ruler") that cannot be expiated. Let him give to the priest a head and feet and a breast.

(*IG* II² 1366—*Version 2*)

Xanthos the Lycian slave of Gaius Orbius, consecrated the sanctuary of Men Tyrannos ("Men the Absolute Ruler")—the god having chosen him.

To good fortune! No one shall enter while impure, but let them be purified after eating garlic or pork and after intercourse with women.

When members have washed from head to foot on the same day, they may enter. And a woman, having washed from head to foot for seven days after menstruation, may enter on the same (i.e., seventh) day. And likewise for ten days after contact with a corpse, and forty days after a miscarriage (or: abortion).

Nor shall anyone offer sacrifice without the permission of the founder of the sanctuary. If anyone does this by force, the sacrifice will be unacceptable to the god. The sacrificer shall provide what is prescribed for the god: a right leg, the skin, head, feet, breast, olive oil for the altar, a lamp, kindling, and a libation. May the god be merciful to those who serve with a simple soul.

If the founder dies or is sick or out of town, let no one have authority except the one to whom he hands it over.

Anyone who is a busybody or interferes with the property of the god will incur sin against Men Tyrannos which he certainly cannot expiate.

And the one who offers sacrifices on the seventh day of the month should perform all that is appropriate for the god. Let him receive a leg and shoulder from the sacrifice which is brought; let the remainder be cut up at the temple. And if anyone offers a sacrifice to the god from new moon till the fifteenth and if someone fills a table for the god, let him receive a half portion of its contents.

Those who wish may convene a club (*eranos*) for Men Tyrannos for good fortune. Likewise, the club members (*eranistai*) shall provide what is appropriate for the god: a right leg, hide, a liquid measure (*kotylē*) of oil, a liquid measure (*chous*) of wine (about 3.25 liters), a dry measure (*choinix*) worth of cake, three sacred cakes, two measures (*choinikes*) of small cakes, and fruit. If the club members banquet, they shall provide a wreath and a woolen fillet. May the god be very merciful to those who approach with simplicity.

23. Exemptions by a Dionysiac Society for a Priest of Dionysos

Megara (Attica). Jaccottet 2003, vol. 2, no. 7 = *GRA* I 60.

141 CE

> This text was found in a notebook of A. Boeckh, an epigrapher working in the area in the 1830s.

To good fortune! Year 172, in the month of . . . the meeting (*synodos*) of the society members (*thiasōtai*) of Dionysos resolved that Antipatros, who built the temple of Dionysos for the society (*thiasos*) and was the priest for life, should be exempt from all service, from dues and from providing services (*leitourgiai*).

Peloponnesos

24. Monument for a Founder and Hero

Argos (Peloponnesos). *IG* IV 581 = *CIG* 1134 = PH28100.

Roman period

The leather dressers (*spatoléastai*) set this up for Marcus Antonius Aristokrates son of Anaxion, founder and hero.

25. Grave Mentioning a Female Cowherd

Cenchreae (Peloponnesos). *IG* IV 207 = PH27703.

Roman period

> The term "cowherd" is sometimes used for a member of an association devoted to the god Dionysos. The male name Apphys seems to be a Lydian name (e.g., *TAM* V.1 276, 351, 470a); Apphydis would be the female equivalent. Both likely derive from a term of endearment (*apphys* or *appha*) used among family members.

For Flavius Troilos Phokas, brother, and for Apphydis, (female) cowherd (*boukola*), as a memorial for the worthy deceased. Farewell.

26. Fragmentary Inscription Involving a Society

Corinth (Peloponnesos). John H. Kent, *Corinth: Results of Excavations.* Vol. 8/3: *The Inscriptions 1926–1950* (Cambridge, Mass.: American School of Classical Studies at Athens, Harvard University Press, 1966), no. 308 = PH179295.

44 BCE–267 CE

> Fragmentary inscription legible only on the left side, included here because it is among the few surviving inscriptions concerning associations at Corinth.

(*line or lines missing*) . . . to come . . . two days . . . (*two lines largely missing*) . . . of the market overseer . . . of the society (*thiasos*) . . . honor of the . . . it shall not be permitted . . . (*at least one missing line*)

27. Honors by the City for a Society

Epidauros (Peloponnesos). *IG* IV²,1 688 = PH29129.

Second to third century CE

The city of the Epidaurians honored the Epidaurian society (*thiasos*) of Aristodamos on account of the virtue and goodwill which it (the society) has shown to it (the city).

28. Honors by an Association for a Woman

Gytheion (Peloponnesos). *IG* V,1 1175 = PH31591.

Roman period

> Fragmentary inscription preserved only on the left side. The full name of this "association/meeting" (*koinon*) or "society" (*thiasos*)

likely makes reference to the deity honored (as suggested by the *-iastai* ending on line 3).

To good fortune!

The association (or: meeting; *koinon*) of the . . . (name of a deity)-iasts honored Julia . . . , the most worthy, daughter of . . . , and wife of . . . most worthy . . . because of the piety she has shown toward the god and good-will toward the society (*thiasos*) . . . giving a most worthy favor . . . This was done (?) when . . . *Name* was supervisor (*epimelētēs*). . . .

29. Membership List of an Association of Banqueters

Sparta (Peloponnesos). *IG* V,1 209 = PH30559.

First century BCE

> Slab of marble (broken into two parts) with a relief of the Diosk-ouroi (Dioscuri) gods above. This association consisted of men and women, slaves and free persons, some from the same house-hold. Such diverse membership was mandated by the Spartan state, which established compulsory dining associations that served as loci for reinforcing the state's ideology.

The banqueters (*hoi sitēthentes*) at the time that Nikokles was guardian of the laws (*patronomos*): Eurybanassa daughter of Sidektas, priestess; Tyndares son of Sidektas, priest; Deximachos son of Pratolas; Sidektas son of Pratolas; Damokratidas son of Eudamidas, officer of the youth; Timodamos son of Damostratos, elder; Aristomenes son of Aristomenes, overseer (*ephor*); Philostratos son of Sokrates, guardian of the laws; Dinokrates son of Dinokles, supervisor of women; Pratolaos son of Deximachos; Damokrates son of Aristokratidas, herald; Eukrates son of Eurykrates, seer; Kallikrates son of Nikon, flute player; Nikandridas son of Nikomachos, lyre player; Eudaimokles son of Eudaimokles, teacher according to the law; Damokrates son of Damokrates, master builder; Mantikles son of Sosikrates, carver; Damokrates son of Damokrates, guilder; Philonidas Karneoneikos son of Philonidas; Aristopolis daughter of Damocharis recognized as legitimate; Pratonikos freedman of Perphila, spinner; Hippomedon son of Nikandros, paean singer; Nikokles freedman of Tyndares, maker of palm branch crowns; Andronikos son of Nikokles, purifier; Zelotos freedman of Panteimia, secretary; Damippos son of Agathokles, dyer; Stephanos son of Phoibides, reader; Nikephoros freedman of Damostratos, attendant; Damokrates son of Lysippos, supplier; Eunous freedman of Aristokrates, baker; Clodia, slave of Akamantia, dealer in crowns; Philodamos freedman of Euthykles, butcher; Diokles slave of Kallisthenia.

Central Greece

30. Regulations of a Dionysiac Society

Physkos (Lokris). *IG* IX/1² 670 = *LSCG* 181 = Jaccottet 2003, vol. 2, no. 153 = *GRA* I 61 = PH43568.

Mid-second century CE

> Slab of limestone, broken at the bottom. In this mixed group devoted to Dionysos, the male members are designated "cowherds" and the female "maenads."

For good fortune! The law of the society (*thiasos*) of Amandos that has been ratified by two meetings (*synodoi*). The members of the society (*thiasōtai*) shall contribute fourteen obols, not fewer, to the association. The association (*koinon*) contributes three lamps. No maenad may attack or abuse another maenad. Likewise, no cowherd (*boukolos*) may attack or abuse another cowherd. If someone should do so, they shall pay to the association a fine of four drachmas for each utterance. One who is in town and does not attend the meeting shall pay the same fine. Whoever does not gather on the mountain owes five drachmas to the association. If on the holy night the maenad does not bring . . . fifteen, she will owe a fine of five drachmas to the association. Likewise if a cowherd does not bring. . . .

31. Graves for Members of Associations Devoted to Athena and to Dionysos

Tanagra (Boeotia). *IG* VII 685–88 and *SEG* 32 (1982), no. 488 = *GRA* I 57 and 58.

Third to first century BCE, as specified below.

(A) Over (the body of) Lykaon. The Athenaists buried him (*IG* VII 685, second century BCE).

(B) Galatas: The Dionysiasts buried him (*IG* VII 686, late third century BCE).

(C) Hail, Hippomachos! The Athenaists buried him (*IG* VII 687, late third century BCE)

(D) Elpis. The synod of Athenaists buried her (*IG* VII 688, undated).

(E) Over (the body of) Eutychos. The Dionysiasts and the vine-dressers buried him (*SEG* 32 [1982], no. 488, second to first century BCE).

MACEDONIA

32. Dedication to Augustus by an Association of Roman Merchants

Acanthos (Macedonia). *SEG* 1 (1923), no. 282 = *GRA* I 62 = PH152541.

27 BCE–14 CE

> Drum of white marble, probably the base of a statue of Augustus.

The city, the association of Roman merchants, and the inhabitants dedicated this to emperor Caesar Augustus, god, son of god.

33. Honors by the Craftsmen for Priests of Athena

Amphipolis (Macedonia). *SEG* 48 (1998), no. 716ter = PH312526.

90/89 BCE

> Slab with a triangular top (pediment), now in the Museum of Kavala.

Years 9 and 50. The association (*koinon*) of craftsmen crowned the priests of Athena, Philoxenos son of Perigenes, Euphrosynos son of Nikanor, Marcus Ampius Alexandros, Mainius . . . *Name*. The fellow priests (*syniereis*) crown Euphrosynos son of Nikanor and Philoxenos son of Perigenes.

34. Dedication to the Great Gods of Samothrace by a Coppersmith

Amphipolis (Macedonia). *SIG³* 1140 = *SIG²* 773; *BCH* 55 (1931) 179,8 = PH150499.

Roman period

Marcus Caecilius Sotas, the coppersmith (*chalkeus*) from the guild (*technē*), dedicated this to the great gods in Samothrace.

35. Honors by a Society for Two Men

Beroea (Macedonia). *IBeroia* 22 = *SEG* 48 (1998), no. 751 = Jaccottet 2003, vol. 2, no. 18 = PH149497.

7 BCE

> Slab of marble, now in the Beroea Museum (inv. no. L 585). There is a framed relief under text A depicting two men on either side of an altar. One man offers a libation while the other holds a scepter

in his left hand and a libation cup in his right hand. Beneath the frame there is a crown with the three inscribed lines of text B on either side. Like many associations, this society adopted a civic title (market overseer) for one of its internal functionaries.

(A) In the year 141 in the month Artemisios, Paramonos son of Theogenes, having served as market overseer (*agoranomos*) of the society (*thiasos*), set this up for Dionysos from his own resources.

(B) The association (*koinon*) of society members (*thiasōtai*) honor with a crown Paramonos son of Theogenes.

36. Dedication to Zeus Hypsistos by a Group of Attendants under Rufus

Beroea (Macedonia). *IBeroia* 26 = *SEG* 35 (1985), no. 714 = PH149501.

ca. 100–150 CE

Slab of marble with a relief of an eagle encircled by a wreath and another relief above depicting the bust of a man, now in the Beroea Museum (L 670).

Dedicated to Zeus Hypsistos ("Highest"). Publius Cornelius Rufus and the attendants (or: servants; *diakonoi*) under him set this up when Sextus Publius Philotas was serving as judge.

37. Grave Erected by an Association of Donkey Drivers

Beroea (Macedonia). *IBeroia* 372 = *GRA* I 64 = PH149851.

Second century CE

Slab with a triangular top (pediment) found in a private house, now lost.

For Aelius Orestes. The society (*synētheia*) of donkey drivers set this up as a memorial.

38. Dedication to Zeus Hypsistos by a Group of Attendants under Erotas

Beroea (Macedonia). *IBeroia* 28 = PH149503.

Second to third century CE

Slab of white marble with a relief of a wreath encircling an eagle.

Dedicated to Zeus Hypsistos ("Highest"). The attendants (or: servants; *diakonoi*) associated with Erotas son of Eubiotos set this up.

(*wreath*)

Titus Fabricius . . . (*two lines are illegible*) . . . *Name* son of Apollodoros, Alexandros son of Nikolaos, Menandros Pamphilas (*vacant space*) Titus Mallius Eisieros . . . (*twenty-six remaining lines of names are largely illegible*).

39. Dedication of an Altar for an Association of the Hero God

Kassandreia/Hagios Mamas (Macedonia). *CIG* II 2007f = *IMakedD* 747 = *GRA* I 66 = PH151763.

Second century CE

> Altar of marble found reused in the construction of a shrine to Saint Demetrius (east of the main street in Hagios Mamas).

Aelianus Neikon, the head of the synagogue (*archisynagōgos*) of the hero god, and the association (*kollēgion*) erected the altar for Vibius Antonius. His son-in-law, Axidares, set up this panel.

40. Grave of a Treasurer of the Silversmiths

Kalambaki (Macedonia). *Philippi* II 410/G258 = *SEG* 2 (1924), no. 421 = *GRA* I 67 = PH152562.

Undated

> Slab of white marble found reused in a Turkish cemetery.

Julius Eutyches, treasurer of the silversmiths, lies here.

41. Contributions to the Temple of Silvanus by Members of an Association

Philippi (Macedonia). *CIL* III 633 = *Philippi* II 164/L001, 163/L002, 165/L003, 166/L004 = *GRA* I 68.

Second century CE

> Latin inscriptions carved on the rock face of the acropolis, which had been quarried to serve as the rear wall of a sanctuary of Silvanus. The earliest inscription (I) provides the names of those who have donated to the building and ornamentation of the temple of Silvanus while the second (II) records a full list of association members, with space for more names to be added (figure 4). Inscription III provides the names of new members, added at a later date. The

Figure 4
*Membership list engraved on the rear wall of the sanctuary of Silvanus at Philippi
(41, part II; photo by Ascough).*

latest inscription added (IV) again lists members from a different time, but is somewhat difficult to read. The membership lists show that the members are men who are Roman citizens of western and eastern origin, mostly freedmen, but there are also four slaves.

(I)   Publius Hostilius Philadelphus, on account of the honor of the office of the magistrate of public works (*aedile*), at his own expense, had inscribed the names of the association members who gave funds for the construction of the temple. Domitus Primigenius gave a bronze statue of Silvanus with a house. Gaius Horatius Sabinus gave four hundred roof tiles toward roofing the temple. Nutrius Valens gave two marble statues of Herakles and Mercury. Paccius Mercuriales gave 250 denarii for concrete in front of the temple and 15 denarii for a painted board of Olympus. Publicius Laetus donated 50 denarii for building the temple. Likewise Paccius Mercuriales with his sons and freedman donated

50 denarii for building the temple as well as 25 denarii for a marble statue of Liber. Alfenus Aspasius, priest, gave a bronze image of Silvanus with a base and, while he was still living, deposited 50 denarii for his funeral. Hostilius Philadelphus had the rock ascending into the temple quarried at his own expense.

(II)   Publius Hostilius Philadelphus, freedman of Publius, at his own expense, cut out the frame and set the inscription on the rock below, where he wrote and engraved the names of the worshippers during the time of the priest Urbanus. (*seventy-one names in four columns follow*)

(III)   (*twenty-five names in three columns*)

(IV)   The members of the association (*collegium*) of Silvanus during the time of the priest Magius Victor: (*list of names, one of whom is called "father" [pater], here used as a leadership term*)

42. Grave and Bequest for an Association of Grave-diggers

Philippi (Macedonia). *Philippi* II 029/G215 = PH150480.

Second century CE

> Slab of marble, now in the Museum in Kavala (inv. no. L 68). The inscription appears below a relief of the Thracian Horseman inside a square frame.

Manta set this up for her own child, Soudios son of Paibilas, twenty-six years old, as a memorial. I bequeath to the Kalpapoureitian grave-diggers 150 denarii. Once a year they shall celebrate the Rose festival (*rosalia*).

43. Dedication by a Female Association Devoted to the God Liber (Dionysos)

Philippi (Macedonia). *Philippi* II 340/L589 = Jaccottet 2003, vol. 2, no 25 = *GRA* I 71.

First to second century CE (?)

> Monument with a Latin inscription found in a small building, probably a house, underneath the public baths south of Basilika B.

This is dedicated to Liber, Libera, and Hercules. The society (*thiasus*) of distinguished maenads (i.e., female attendants of the god) brought in water at their own cost.

44. Honors by the City for a Purple Dyer

Philippi (Macedonia). *Philippi* II 697/M580.

Undated

> Slab of white marble first observed in 1872 in a military post that
> was subsequently destroyed. The similarities to a well-known bibli-
> cal character, Lydia the Thyatiran purple dealer at Philippi (Acts
> 16:14), and the circumstances in which it was seen by only one
> individual and subsequently lost have caused some to question its
> authenticity.

The city honored from among the purple dyers an outstanding citizen,
Antiochus the son of Lycus, a native of Thyatira, as a benefactor (*euergetes*).

45. Membership of an Association Devoted to Zeus Hypsistos

Pydna (Macedonia). *SEG* 46 (1986), no. 800 = *NewDocs* I, pp.
26–27 = *GRA* I 72 = PH151223.

250 CE

> Slab of marble inscribed on the face and down the narrow left side,
> now in the Dion museum (inv. no. 5931; figure 5). This association
> consists of citizens, noncitizens, and slaves, as well as both men and
> women.

For good fortune! In the Augustan year 282, which is also year 398, on the
eighteenth day of the month of Daisios, in Pydna. The convened worshippers (*thrēskeutai*) of the god Zeus Hypsistos ("Highest") decided to set up
this monument (stele), when Urbanianus Vilistus was auditor (*logistes*);
Aurelius Nigerion was leader (*archōn*) under the head of the synagogue
(*archisynagōgos*), Aurelius Kepion, formerly of Pieria; Aurelius Severus
was president (*prostatēs*); and Aurelius Theophilus, formerly of Pieria, was
secretary (*grammateus*). The rest of the worshippers are inscribed below.
Prosper!

Aurelius Erotianos, Aurelius Boethos, Titus Octavius Zosimos, Ata-
nius Tatianus, Aurelius Trophimos, Claudius Philoumenos, Aurelia
Sabina, Aurelius Artemidoros, Aurelia Parthenope, Aurelius Elpinikos,
Titus Flavius Julianus, Titus Aelius Julianus, Cornelius Ophelion, Phi-
locuris the household manager, Eleusinis the house slave, Claudius
Ambrosis, Aurelius Epagathos, Aurelius Alexandros, Aurelius Kopryl-
los, Cornificius Kallimorphos, Antonius Paramonos, Aurelius Poluxenos,
Aurelia Atheno, Aurelius Herakleides, Aelius Philo, Aurelius Maximus,
Aurelius Theodoulos, Aelius Kalophronios, Aurelius Leontiscos.

Figure 5
Membership list of an association devoted to Zeus Hypsistos at Pydna
(45; photo by Ascough).

Figure 6
*Anubis in relief on an honorific inscription set up by an association of banqueters
at Thessalonica (47; photo by Ascough)*

(*On the left side of the stele*) Through the agency of Theophilus and Aurelius Kepion, formerly of Pieria.

46. Donation of a Judean Synagogue

Stobi (Macedonia). *IJO* I Mac1 = *CIJ* 694 = *DFSJ* 10 = *GRA* I 73 = PH150506.

Second to third century CE

> Column of marble, now in the Belgrade National Museum (inv. no. 18/IV). The inscription was found inside a fifth-century Christian basilica, which is built upon a synagogue, itself built upon a smaller synagogue, which was, in turn, a renovation of a private villa. This earliest stratum is likely the house of Claudius Tiberius Polycharmos.

Claudius Tiberius Polycharmos, also called Achyrios, the father of the synagogue in Stobi, who has conducted his whole life according to Judean custom, in fulfillment of a vow has donated the rooms (*oikoi*) to the holy place and the dining room with three benches (*triclinium*), along with a portico with four rows of columns (*tetrastoon*), from his own resources without touching the holy revenues at all. All authority over all the upper rooms and the ownership is retained by me, Claudius Tiberius Polycharmos, and by my heirs as long as they are alive. Whoever wants to introduce a novelty against my decision shall pay 250,000 denarii to the patriarch. For this seemed good to me. The repair of the roof tiles of the upper rooms will be done by me and my heirs.

47. Honors by Sacred Object Bearers for a Benefactor (with a Relief of Anubis)

Thessalonica (Macedonia). *IG* X/2.1 58 = *SIRIS* 109 = Nigdelis 2010, no. 2 = PH137240.

First century BCE to first century CE

> Narrow slab of gray marble with a decorated triangular top (pediment with acroteria), now in the Thessaloniki Archaeological Museum (inv. no. MΘ 1254). In the center there is a relief of the Egyptian deity Anubis draped and standing on a small base, encircled by a wreath (figure 6).

For Aulus Papius Chilon who established the meeting place (*oikos*). The sacred object bearers (*hieraphoroi*) and fellow banqueters (*synklitai*): Scanius Felix, Salarius Nikephoros, Lucilius Bassus, Priamos son of Apollonios, Primos son of Archepolis, Dosenius Bacchios, Julius Secundus,

Annius Secundus, Viesius Felix, Secundus son of Euphantos, Menandros son of Nikandros, Apoleus Lucilus, Kalistratos, who is also called Archon (or: who is also the leader [*archōn*]).

48. Donation for an Association of Banqueters

Thessalonica (Macedonia). *IG* X/2.1 70 = Nigdelis 2010, no. 6 = *GRA* I 74 = PH137252.

66–67 CE

Column of marble found near the sanctuary of Sarapis in Thessalonica, now in the Thessaloniki Archaeological Museum (inv. no. MΘ 987).

Year 214. Herennia Procula, fulfilling the promise of her father Marcus Herennius Proculus, has set up for the fellow banqueters (*synklitai*) four columns with capitals and bases as well as the lintel, during the priesthood of Leonidas son of Lysanias.

49. Grave of a Shipper

Thessalonica (Macedonia). *SEG* 42 (1992), no. 625 = Nigdelis 2010, no. 28 = *GRA* I 75 = PH153298.

90–91 CE

Slab of marble with a low relief of a ship with a man sitting at the stern and holding the rudder (figure 7), now in the Thessaloniki Archaeological Museum (inv. no. MΘ 6086). The term *doumos* for an association is well attested in Asia Minor. The native home of the deceased, Amastris, is in the region of Paphlagonia in Asia Minor.

When Gaius Autronius Liberus, also called Glykon, was head of the synagogue (*archisynagōgos*), Quintus Papius Castor was secretary (*grammateus*), and Hermogenes son of Diogenes was accountant (*exetastēs*), the association (*doumos*) of Aphrodite Epiteuxidia ("Successful") set this up as a memorial for Athenion son of Praxiteles of Amastis, who has died while abroad. This was set up through their supervisors (*epimelētai*). Farewell! So also will you be sometime! Year 122.

50. Bequest to an Association of Initiates of Zeus Dionysos Gongylos

Thessalonica (Macedonia). *IG* X/2.1 259 = Nigdelis 2010, no. 12 = Jaccottet 2003, vol. 2, no. 19 = *GRA* I 76 = PH137441.

First century CE

Figure 7
Gravestone of a shipper with a man steering a boat from Thessalonica
*(**49**; photo by Ascough).*

Slab of marble, found in the sanctuary of Sarapis, now in the Thessaloniki Archaeological Museum (inv. no. MΘ 983).

For the good fortune of Zeus Dionysos Gongylos ("Round"). Gaius Julius, cult official, consecrated to the god and gave by bequest to the current and future initiates (*mystai*), as long as they are banded together, one third of five *plethra* (about 4.4 km²) of vineyards located in the village (*asty*) of Perdylia, on the following condition: As long as they maintain the legal

right, they will use the income to hold a banquet of bread for the support-
ers (*threpsantes*), according to the tradition and the donation, on the nineteenth of the month of Dystros, on the thirteenth of the month of Daisios,
and on the twenty-third of the month of Gorpiaios. The current and future
initiates also swear by the god, by the rites (*orgia*), and by the midnight
bread to maintain the above ritual according to the bequest.

The initiates recorded below also consecrated two thirds of the five
plethra. They will share in the income during their lifetime in the presence
of the god and subsequently enrolled initiates will receive the same. The
whole vineyard must remain unsold. The initiates have sworn accordingly
to help to maintain the things agreed together.

(*column 1*)

Lucius Fulvius Felix, priest, Marcus Ombrius Eros, Nikandros son
of Nikandros, Herakeides son of Korragos, Gaius Julius Felix, Marcus
Ombrius Makedon, Titus Sextius, Nonus Terraeus Hyacinthos, Antigonos
son of Nikephoros, Marcus Lollius Attikus,

(*column 2*)

Gaius Julius Agathopous, Avidius . . . Nonus Terraeus Firmanus, Marcus Lollius Sabinus, Gaius Raius Zosimos, Marcus Marius Cerealis, Marcus Antonius Primus.

This was set up with the consent of Straton son of Epikrates, by birth
son of Dionysios, priest for a second time.

51. Dedication to Theos Hypsistos by an Association of Banqueters

Thessalonica (Macedonia). *IG* X/2.1 68 = Nigdelis 2010, no. 4 =
PH137250.

Late first century CE

> Column of gray marble broken in two, now in the Thessaloniki
> Archaeological Museum (inv. no. MΘ 990).

This is dedicated to Theos Hypsistos ("Highest God") on behalf of Titus
Flavius Euktimenos son of Amuntas, head of the banquet (*trikliniarchos*),
by the fellow banqueters (*synklitai*) recorded below: (*a list of thirty-eight
male names follows*).

52. Story of the Foundation of an Association of Sarapis

Thessalonica (Macedonia). *IG* X/2.1 255 = *NewDocs* I 6 = *GRA* I
77 = PH137437.

First to second century CE

Slab of marble found among the ruins of the temple of the Egyptian gods in Thessalonica, now in the Thessalonike Archaeological Museum (inv. no. MΘ 825). This inscription, which is a copy of an inscription from two centuries earlier, records the founding of a household cult of Sarapis in another city, Opus.

. . . during the embassy . . . to enter into the shrine (*oikos*), it seemed in his sleep that Sarapis stood beside him and told him that after having arrived in Opus, he should carry a message to Eurynomos son of Timasitheos to receive Sarapis and his sister Isis, and that he should deliver to him (Eurynomos) the letter under the pillow. And waking up, he (Xenainetos) marveled at the dream and yet he was at a loss about what he should do because he was a political rival to Eurynomos. But, falling asleep again, and seeing the same things, when he awoke he found the letter under the pillow, just as it had been indicated to him. Now when he had returned (to Opus), he gave the letter to Eurynomos and reported the things that were decreed by the god. Now when Eurynomos received the letter and heard the things that Xenainetos said, he was at a loss because they were political rivals toward one other, as was made clear above. After having read the letter and having seen that the things that were written were in agreement with the things first having been said by him (Xenainetos), he (Eurynomos) received Sarapis and Isis. After he provided hospitality in the household (*oikos*) of Sosinike, she received Sarapis and Isis among the household gods. Sosinike offered the sacrifices for a certain time. And after her death Eunosta, the granddaughter of Sosibas, when she received the office, administered the mysteries of the gods among those not initiated into the sacred rites. When Eunosta finally fell ill . . . sacrificed on her behalf. . . .

53. Honors by an Association of "Sport Lovers" for a Man

Thessalonica (Macedonia). *EpThess* II.12 = Nigdelis 2010, no. 41 = *GRA* I 78.

ca. 100–150 CE

Slab found in five pieces in the western cemetery, now in the Thessaloniki Archaeological Museum (inv. no. MΘ 6167). The nature of the association, rendered here rather literally as "lovers of play" (*philopaiktoroi*), is ambiguous but may have to do with athletic or dramatic shows.

The members of the association around Lucius Rusticilius Agathopous from among the sport lovers set this up for Titus Julius Prophetes, also called Secundus.

Figure 8
Relief of a donkey driver on a grave monument from Thessalonica
(54; photo by Ascough).

54. Grave of a Society Member with a Relief of a Donkey and Cart

Thessalonica (Macedonia). *BE* (1972) 263 = *NewDocs* IV, p. 215 no. 17 = Nigdelis 2010, no. 27 = PH150313.

159/160 CE

Slab of marble with a decorated triangular top (pediment with acroteria and acanthus leaves in the center), now in the Thessaloniki Archaeological Museum (inv. no. MΘ 10771). The relief above the inscription depicts a man on a donkey-driven cart (figure 8). The inscription seems to involve an association of transport professionals devoted to Heron Aulonites, who protected those who crossed narrow passages.

Crescens. Year 191. The society (*synētheia*) of Heron Aulonites set this up for Gaius Julius Crescens. The associates of the head of the synagogue (*archisynagōgos*), Artemon the yoke maker and the priest Tryphon paid (for this) from the income from the money chest as a memorial for him.

55. Honors by an Association of Purple Dyers

Thessalonica (Macedonia). *IG* X/2.1 291 = *IMakedD* 439 = Nigdelis 2010, no. 17 = *GRA* I 79 = PH137473.

Late second century CE

Slab of white marble, now in the Istanbul Museum (sculpture cat. no. 271). There is a relief of the Thracian Horseman above the inscription.

The association of purple dyers of the eighteenth street honored Menippos, son of Amios, also called Severus, from Thyatira as a memorial.

56. Grave of a Mule Driver

Thessalonica (Macedonia). *EpThess* II.10 = Nigdelis 2010, no. 39.

ca. 150–200 CE

Column of marble, now in the Thessaloniki Archaeological Museum (inv. no. MΘ 10850). The inscription is in Greek but uses Latin terms for "mule driver" and "colleagues."

Set up for Chryssipos Menecrates the mule driver (*mouliōn*) with his colleagues (*kollēgioi*), as a memorial.

57. Funerary Altar of a Priest of Dionysos

Thessalonica (Macedonia). *IG* X/2.1 506 and p. 288 = *IMakedD* 387 = Jaccottet 2003, vol. 2, no. 21 = *GRA* I 80 = PH137690.

209–210 CE

Square funerary altar of marble with a decorated triangular top (pediment with acroteria and a rose) and circular incision, probably for the insertion of a receptacle for bones, now in the Thessaloniki Archaeological Museum (inv. no. MΘ 1815). This inscription indicates that more than one Dionysiac association existed in Thessalonica in the early third century CE.

Artemin daughter of Markos, the wife of Isidoros son of Isidoros, and Junia daughter of Isidoros set this up for their father Isidoros son of Sabinus, who lived well and was a city councilor and priest of societies (*thiasoi*) of Dionysos, from his own resources, for his memory and on account of his benevolence. In memory.

In the 357th year.

(*On the right side*)
Farewell noble soul!

58. Bequest of a Priestess of Dionysos

Thessalonica (Macedonia). *IG* X/2.1 260 = *IMakedD* 396 and 729 = Jaccottet 2003, vol. 2, no. 22 = Nigdelis 2010, no. 13 = *GRA* I 81 = PH137442.

Third century CE

Altar of marble inscribed on three sides, with the top hollowed out to act as a receptacle, now in the Thessaloniki Archaeological Museum (inv. no. Mθ 1767).

(*C: left side panel*)
The initiates (*mystai*), small and large, are each to bear a crown of roses (i.e., during the Rose festival). The one who does not shall not share in my gift. But if the holm oak bearers (*prinophoroi*) do not do this, then the bequest belongs to the society (*thiasos*) of the oak branch bearers (*dryophoroi*), subject to the same conditions. But if the other society does not do this, then the bequest is to be for the city.

(*A: front panel*)
Euphronsyne, niece of Dioskous, Eueian priestess.

(*B: right side panel*)
. . . being Eueian priestess of Prinophoros, I bequeath for my eternal memory two *plethra* of vineyards [1.76 km^2] with the ditches, in order that from the income sacrifices worth not less than five denarii may be burned for me.

59. Grave of a Judean Mentioning Synagogues

Thessalonica (Macedonia). *IJO* I Mac15 = *SEG* 44 (1994), no. 556 = *GRA* I 82 = PH153445.

Late third century CE

Stone casket of marble found in the eastern necropolis, where other Judeans were interred, now in the Thessaloniki Archaeological Museum (inv. no. Mθ 5674).

Marcus Aurelius Jakob, also called Eutychios, while he was still alive, prepared this for his wife Anna who is also called Asynkrition and for himself as a memorial. If anyone buries another here, he shall pay the synagogues 75,000 shiny denarii.

THRACIA

60. Dedication to the God Dionysos and the Initiates

Abdera (Thrace). Jaccottet 2003, vol. 2, no. 35 = GRA I 83 = PH295285.

Third century CE (?)

> Limestone with a triangular top and a base, most likely originally placed over a doorway of a small building or large room.

For good fortune! Gaius Cassius Sextus, head cowherd (archiboukolos), built this shrine (megaron) for the god Dionysos and for his fellow initiates (mystai) at his own expense.

61. Dedication of an Altar to a Company

Augusta Traiana (Thrace). SEG 39 (1989), no. 649 = Jaccottet 2003, vol. 2, no. 49 = GRA I 84 = PH171860.

Second to third century CE

> Altar inscribed on all four sides.

For good fortune! The initiates of the subterranean sanctuary (magareis) set up this altar for the company (speira) before the city (i.e., outside the city walls). Karteris son of Nannas, member of the elders' council (gerousiastēs); Flavius the manufacturer of hats, initiate of the subterranean sanctuary (magareus); Trophimos son of Apollodoros, also called Asbolis, initiate of the subterranean sanctuary; and, Herakleianos, baker of white bread, initiate of the subterranean sanctuary.

62. Membership List of the Banqueters of Asklepios

Augusta Traiana (Thrace). IGBulg III,2 1626 = GRA I 85 = PH169720.

Second to third century CE

> Plaque of limestone. There is one Roman name, but the majority are Thracian names that seem partially abbreviated (the second name may be an abbreviation of the name of the father).

For good fortune! The symposiasts (banqueters) of the god Asklepios: Germanus son of Germanus, Eptetralis Mouka(?), Kotys Doleos, Mouka-tralis Epte(?), Tarsas Skelenos, Pistous son of Skelos, Doles Deizezene(?), Moukaboris Aulou(?), Moukaboris Bri(?), Moukaporis Mouka(?), Mouka-tralis Dia(?), Doles Beithyos.

63. Dedication of an Altar for a Synagogue of Barbers

Perinthos (later Herakleia, Thrace). *IPerinthos* 49 = *IGRR* I 782 = *GRA* I 86 = PH167259.

First century CE (A); second century CE (B)

> Altar of marble. After the altar was first set up and inscribed (A), it was reused and inscribed on the backside (B) with reference to another association.

(A) *Name* . . . the administrator (*dioikētēs*) and Marcus Pompeius Comicus, son of Comicus, restored the altar to the synagogue (*synagōgē*) of barbers—namely those gathered around the head of the synagogue (*archisynagōgos*) Gaius Julius Valens—and provided the location.

(B) For Zeus Lopheites, the priest Eudion son of Phillys set this up as a gift for the new (*neoi*) goldsmiths.

64. Honors for the Emperor by a Baccheion of Asians

Perinthos (later Herakleia, Thrace). *IPerinthos* 56 = Jaccottet 2003, vol. 2, no. 37 = *IGRR* I 787 = *GRA* I 87 = PH167267.

196–198 CE

> Seen by Cyriacus in the city wall in 1444 CE.

For good fortune! For the health, victory, and eternal duration of our lord emperor Lucius Septimius Severus Pertinax Arabicus Adiabenicus, of Marcus Aurelius Antonius Caesar, of his entire household, of the sacred Senate, and of the People of Perinthos, which oversees the temple. Marcus son of Horos has dedicated the pillar to the Baccheion of Asians (*Asianoi*) from his own resources, for eternal honor and goodwill toward him. This was done when Statilius Barbaros was governor, Pomponius Justinianus was in charge of the sacred things (*hieromnemon*), Maximus son of Claudius was chief initiate, and Eutychos son of Epiktetos was priest. Prosper.

65. Sibylline Oracle Concerning a Dionysiac Company

Perinthos (later Herakleia, Thrace). *IPerinthos* 57 = Jaccottet 2003, vol. 2, no. 36 = *GRA* I 88 = PH167268.

Second century CE (?)

> Seen by Cyriacus in 1444 CE on the right side of the altar in the church of the Virgin Mary. The Greek text of the Sibyl's utterance is partially corrupted and the translation here is just one option. Devotees of the god Dionysos used the cry "euoi!" or "euai!" in rituals.

Greetings! Oracle of the Sibyl: "Whenever the bacchant who cries '*euoi*' is struck with fear (?), then blood and fire and dust will be mixed."

This was set up by Spellios Euethis, the head cowherd (*archiboukolos*); Herakleides son of Alexandros, the head of the initiates (*archimystēs*); Alexandros, the leader of the company (*speirarchos*); Arrianos son of Agathias; Heroxenos son of Magnus; Soterichos son of Dadas; and, Menophilos son of Menophilos.

66. Dedication of an Altar by an Association

Perinthos (later Herakleia, Thrace). *IPerinthos* 55 = *SEG* 26 (1976), no. 826 = PH167266.

Second to third century CE

> Marble altar. Here an association at Perinthos in Thracia (perhaps a group of immigrants from Apamea) expresses connections with the people of Apamea in Bithynia.

For good fortune! The sanhedrin (*synedrion*) of friends of Apamea dedicated this altar to Homonoia (i.e., Concord personified). Prosper!

67. Dedication to a Cult Association of Homonoia

Philippopolis (Thrace). *IGBulg* V 5434 = *SEG* 47 (1997), no. 1089 = *GRA* I 89 = PH170564.

Second to third century CE

> Altar of marble found in the marketplace.

For good fortune! This was dedicated to the household of the Augusti, to the sacred Senate and the People of Rome, to the Council and People of Philippopolis, to the goddess Demeter and Kore, and to the associates (*synētheis*) of Homonoia (i.e., Concord personified). Tiberius Claudius Claudianus Quintillianus and his son Tiberius Claudius Varius Quintillianus set up the altar from their own resources.

68. Dedication by an Association of Initiates

Rhegion (Thrace). *IByzantion* 31 = *SEG* 18 (1962), no. 280 = Jaccottet 2003, vol. 2, no. 38/2 = *GRA* I 90 = PH170872.

85–96 CE

> Slab of white marble with a gable, acroteria, and two reliefs of large
> wreaths, now in the Istanbul Archaeological Museum (inv. no.
> 4797). This association, which is attested in six other inscriptions,
> held athletic games as part of their festivals, which Semnos, along
> with another man, organized and supervised, and for which they
> were honored in other inscriptions.

For good fortune! During the fifth year of the official of the sacred things
(*hieromnemon*; i.e., the eponymous civic official of Byzantion), Domitian
Caesar Augustus Germanicus, in the month of Bosporios, the initiates
(*mystai*) of Dionysos Kallon honored Semnos, the slave (or: freedperson)
of Lollia Katylle, for acting as priest for two years in an exceedingly brilliant and good manner.

LOWER DANUBE AND BOSPORAN KINGDOM

Moesia, Dacia, and Scythia

69. Decree Dissolving an Association

Albernus Major (Dacia). *ILS* 7216 = *CIL* IX 924–927, no. 1 = Liu
2009, 360–61 (no. 117).

167 CE (February 9)

> A triptych (16 × 13 cm) with inscriptions in Latin. The tablets con-
> tain two slightly differing copies of the decree, the first copy (A) on
> the first two interior pages, and the second (B, including the names
> of the witnesses) on the third and fourth pages.

Authenticated copy made from a notice which was posted at Alburnus
Maior near the office of Resculum and in which was written the following: Artemidorus son of Apollonius, president of the association (*collegium*) of Jupiter Cernenus, and Valerius son of Nico and Offas son of
Menofilus, treasurers of the same association, by posting this notice do
publicly attest: that of the fifty-four members that used to constitute the
above-named association, there now remain in Alburnus no more than
seventeen; that even Julius son of Julius, the copresident, has not come to
Alburnus or to the association since the day of his election as copresident;
that (Artemidorus) has rendered an account to those who were present of

what he had of theirs and was returning what he had spent on funerals; that he (Artemidorus) had recovered the security he had posted for these sums; that now there were not sufficient funds for any more funerals, nor did he have a single coffin; that no one had been willing to attend meetings on the days required by the regulations of the society, or to contribute funeral services or fees; and that they (i.e., the remaining officers) accordingly publicly attest by this notice that no member should suppose that, should he die, he belongs to an association or that he shall be able make any request of them for a funeral.

Posted at Alburnus Maior, February 9, during the year that emperor Lucius Aurelius Verus was consul for the third time and Quadratus was co-consul.

Issued at Alburnus Maior.

Seals of Lucius Vasidius Victor, Gaius Secundinus Legitimus, Stertinus Rusticus, Aelius Plator, . . . *Name* Geldon, Ulpius Felix, September Plator

70. Dedication of a Meeting Hall of a Textile Guild

Apulum (Dacia). *CIL* III 1174 = *ILS* 7255a = Waltzing 1895–1900, vol. 3, no. 235.

202/203–205 CE

Plaque of marble with a Latin inscription.

For the welfare of our two emperors, Lucius Septimius Severus Pius Pertinax and Marcus Aurelius Antoninus Publius Septimius Geta, Caesar, the association of textile workers (*collegium centonariorum*) built a meeting hall (*schola*) with pediment (i.e., triangular top) with their own money. Lucius Pomponius Liberalis, consularius of the three Dacian provinces, dedicated this.

71. Dedication for a Company of Asians

Dionysopolis (Moesia Inferior). *IGBulg* I² 23 = Jaccottet 2003, vol. 2, no. 53 = PH167880.

222–235 CE

Slab of limestone. This is one among numerous extant inscriptions involving associations of "Asians" (*Asianoi*), namely groups formed by immigrants from Asia Minor.

For good fortune! On behalf of the fortune and victory of the lord, emperor Marcus Aurelius Severus Alexander Pius Eutyches, Marcus Aurelius

Koures, official in charge of the sacred, dedicated this to the ancient company (*speira*) of Asians (*Asianoi*).
(*Nonsensical letters in another hand follow.*)

72. Dedication of a Dining Room for the Hymn Singers

Histria (Moesia Inferior). *IGLSkythia* I 167 = Jaccottet 2003, vol. 2, no. 63 = PH172833.

ca. 150–200 CE

Slab of marble with a triangular top (pediment).

For good fortune! On behalf of the victory and salvation of the Augusti and on behalf of the Council and People of the Histrians, Zipas son of Diokles made this dining room (*stibas*) from his own resources—rather than the resources of the priesthood—for the victorious elder hymn singers (*hymnōdoi*) who are gathered around Dionysos. This was done when Kokkeios son of Domitian was choirmaster, Aelianus son of Eli was chief of the Muses, Marcus Dionittas son of Artemidoros was secretary for life and zealous friend, and Diogenes and Zoilos were examiners.

73. Decree Concerning Contributions for the Construction of a Temple

Kallatis (Scythia Minor). *IGLSkythia* III 35 = Jaccottet 2003, vol. 2, no. 54 = PH173603.

Late third century BCE

Slab of bluish marble with a decorated triangular top (pediment with acroteria), broken into eight pieces.

For good fortune! When Simos son of Asklapiades was king, during the month of Dionysios, when Hagemon son of Pythion was president, the society members (*thiasitai*) resolved that a temple should be constructed for the god. Let those of the society members who want to contribute toward the construction promise whatever amount each chooses. Those who have promised a gold coin (stater) are granted a crown of honor for life and their name inscribed on the monument. Those promising less than a gold coin up to thirty silver pieces (drachmas) are granted their name inscribed and a crown of glory during the triennial festival for life. The rest who have promised less are granted their name inscribed on the monument.

Let three men be appointed from among all the society members to ensure that the temple is constructed magnificently and quickly. Once they have been chosen, these men will receive the sums from those who have promised and they will administer the expenses, and the written account of the management will be handed over. Upon the completion of the work, those chosen for overseeing construction will be granted a crown for the meetings that the society members will hold during the triennial festival.

For good fortune! Those who promised to contribute to the building of the temple:

(column a)

Apollonymos son of Satyros: a gold coin (stater); Apollonios son of Apollonios; Philippos son of Apollonios; Dionysios son of Kalchadon. To build the temple: Meniskos son of Herakleides (?) . . . a gold coin (stater); Damatrios son of Damatrios: a gold coin (stater); Simos son of Promathion: a gold coin (stater); Kratinos son of Mikos: a gold coin (stater); Nautimos son of Pasiadas: a gold coin (stater); Zopyros son of Protopolis: a gold coin (stater); Harmagenes son of Damophon: a gold coin (stater); Kritoboulos son of Pyrsos: a gold coin (stater); Asklapiodoros son of Apollodotos: a gold coin (stater); Nossion son of Hierokles: a gold coin (stater); Zopyros son of Hestios: a gold coin (stater); Damosthenes son of Dionysios: sheltered, vaulted passageway leading to the doorway.

(column b)

Menis son of Hikesios: thirty silver drachmas; Sosibios son of Protomachos: thirty silver drachmas; Hereas son of Damophon: thirty silver drachmas; Euphraios son of Satyros: thirty silver drachmas; . . . *Name*: thirty silver drachmas; . . . *Name*: thirty silver drachmas; . . . *(two missing lines)* . . . Apollodotos . . . : thirty workers; Promathion son of Promathion: fifteen workers. Hagemon son of Pythion: a work horse and fifteen workers; Olympos son of Soterichos: fifteen workers; Dion son of Aristokles: fifteen workers; Hapheistion son of Skythas: fifteen workers; Dionysios wreath dealer: ten workers; Apollonios Simos: ten workers.

74. Honorary Decree of a Society

Kallatis (Scythia Minor). *IGLSkythia* III 44 = Jaccottet 2003, vol. 2, no. 58 = PH173612.

12–15 CE

Slab of marble with a triangular top (pediment), broken into five pieces.

During the kingship of Kotys son of Rhoimetalkas, in the month of Dionysios at the time of the triennial festival, the society members (*thiasitai*) approved the motion made by Diodoros son of Damatrios: Whereas

Ariston son of Ariston, whose father was the benefactor and founder of the city and was zealous toward the society (*thiasos*), is continually increasing the virtue of his family; and whereas he likewise shows his own commitment to the People, saving them on every occasion and in every danger, being a benefactor to the citizens, promising always to be the cause of something good, presenting himself as well-intentioned toward our society, and increasing the honors for Dionysos; and whereas, although young, he displayed more ambition toward the citizens than those who were chosen earlier as benefactors. Therefore, in order that the society members might be seen maintaining their goodwill toward him and remembering the sincerity he has toward them, having previously granted to his father the greatest honors of any of those granted to any other benefactor, and having recently proclaimed a crown for him because the People honored him with the same honors as his father, the society members resolved to crown Ariston son of Ariston at every meeting (*synodos*) and on every day on which they gather, as "benefactor of the People and as zealous toward the society." Further, they resolved that the crown be given in perpetuity both on account of the benefactions and virtues that he has displayed to the People and on account of the goodwill and zealousness that he has had for the society members. Further, it was resolved that the society members should inscribe this decree on the base of white stone in the month of Lykeos during the festival of the Xenia Dionysia and should set it up in the most prominent place inside the shrine.

75. Association of Banqueters

Kallatis (Scythia Minor). *IGLSkythia* III 68,A = PH173637.

50–100 CE

Sacred table of marble.

The banqueters (*thoinētai*) who are gathered around the priest Herakleon son of Pyrsos dedicated this to Herakles Alexikakos ("Averter of Evil") as a thanksgiving (*eucharistērion*).

76. Dedication by Family Members and Society Members

Marcianopolis (Moesia Inferior). *IGBulg* V 5364 = *SEG* 28 (1978), no. 603 = PH170537.

First half of the third century CE

Block of limestone.

Martiales the priest, the rest of the kin (*syngeneis*), and the rest of the society members (*thiasitai*) set this up for god Aularkenos.

77. Dedication to a Company of Asians

Municipium Montanensium (Moesia Inferior). *IGBulg* II 480 = Jaccottet 2003, vol. 2, no. 70 = PH68530.

Second century CE (?)

Plaque of marble.

The sweet offspring of Zeus and Semele, Lenaios, bestower of lavish gifts. The priest Saturninus with his dear wife Magna set up this most excellent gift of his own production for the company (*speira*) of Asians (*Asianoi*) during the time of his priesthood.

78. Dedication of a Column by a Priest of a Baccheion of Asians

Nikopolis ad Istrum (Moesia Inferior). *SEG* 53 (2003) no. 726 = *AÉ* (2003), no. 1563 = PH32659.

Early third century CE

Column of limestone set up by a priest on behalf of the association.

Pautalos son of Cornutus, priest of the Baccheion (*Bakcheion*) of Asians, set up this column from his own resources.

79. Dedication by an Association of Fishermen

Odessos (Moesia Inferior). *IGBulg* I² 77(2) = *AÉ* (1928), no. 146 = PH167955.

Imperial period

The inscription appears below a relief.

The tuna fishermen of Hermas who are gathered around the priest Eptaikenthos from Asia dedicated this to the Hero Manimazos when Theodotos son of Herakon and Zeno son of Posidonios were supervisors.

80. Dedication of a Statue by a Dionysiac Society

Tomis (Scythia Minor). *IGLSkythia* II 120 = Jaccottet 2003, vol. 2, no. 62 = PH173220.

First half of the first century BCE

Plaque of marble that accompanied a statue.

This pure statue is dedicated on behalf of the society (*thiasos*) to you, blazing one, as a gift from the workshop of Parmis, crowned initiate (*mystikos*) among the bacchants (i.e., devotees of Bacchos), who reveals the ancient rite. But you, bull-horned one, receive the handwork of Hermagenes and save the sacred society (*thiasos*) of Parmis.

81. Statue Erected by a Guild of Shippers for the Emperor's Son

Tomis (Scythia Minor). *IGLSkythia* II 60 = *IGRR* I 610 = PH173159.

139–161 CE

Round statue base.

For good fortune! The association (*oikos*) of shippers in Tomis honored the son of emperor Marcus Aurelius Verus Caesar out of their own resources and Titus son of Titus the Younger dedicated this statue out of his own resources.

82. Dedication of an Altar for the "House" of Alexandrians

Tomis (Scythia Minor). *IGLSkythia* II 153 = *IGRR* I 604 = PH173253.

160 CE

Altar of marble.

Dedicated to the great Sarapis, to the gods who share his temple, to the emperor Titus Aelius Hadrianus Antoninus Augustus Pius, and to Marcus Aurelius Verus Caesar. Karpion son of Anubion set up the altar for the house (*oikos*) of the Alexandrians from his own resources. This was done in the 23rd year on the first of the month of Pharmouthi, when Cornutus, also called Sarapion, and Polymnos, also called Longinus, and . . . were priests.

Bosporan Kingdom

83. Dedication of a Manumitted Slave to Theos Hypsistos in a Prayer House

Gorgippia (Bosporan region). *IJO* I BS20 = *CIRB* 1123 = *IPontEux* II 400 = PH183859.

41 CE (October/November)

Plaque of white marble, now in the Hermitage Museum (inv. no. Гп20), Saint Petersburg. Possibly Judean, based on the use of "blessed" (*eulogētos*) in connection with the god's attributes together with the reference to a prayer house. The inscription ends with an oath involving three other deities (Zeus, Earth, and Sun).

To Theos Hypsistos ("Highest God"), all-powerful, blessed. During the reign of king Mithridates, friend of . . . and friend of the homeland, in the 338th year in the month of Deios, Pothos son of Strabon dedicated a house-bred slave, who is named Chrysa, to the prayer house (*proseuchē*) in accordance with a vow, on the condition that she will not be hindered or bothered by any heir, under Zeus, Ge ("Earth"), and Helios ("Sun").

84. Dedication to Poseidon by a Society of Shippers

Gorgippia (Bosporan region). *CIRB* 1134 = PH183870.

173–211 CE

For good fortune! Time of the reign of king Tiberius Julius Sauromates (?), friend of Caesar and friend of the Romans, pious one . . . in the *x*th year in the month . . . of Daisios.

The society (*thiasos*) of shippers (*nauklēroi*) dedicated this to the god Poseidon during the time of king Sauromates son of the great king Rhoimetalkas. They also made the images and built the temple, raising it up from the foundations for which purpose also the king honored the god and the society with funds in the amount of one thousand artabas. The society members are gathered around the priest: Athenodoros son of Seleukos, foremost in the kingdom; the synagogue leader (*synagōgos*), Moirodoros son of Neokles, who is who is also the governor of Gorgippia; the procurators (*phrontistēs*), Kossos son of Attas Kossos; and, Pharnakes son of Noumenios, administrator of sacred affairs.

The society members are: Pantaleon son of Pharnake, commander (*stratēgos*); Moirodoros son of Atamazos, commander; Chrestion son of Papas, Makarios son of Athenodoros . . . ; *Name* . . . administrator of the taxes (*oikonomos enkykliōn*); Gaganos . . . , administrator of the taxes; Aspourgos . . . administrator of the taxes; . . . (*at least thirty-three other members without any clear designation of roles are listed in the fragmentary lines that follow*).

85. Honors by a Society for the Royal Family of the Bosporan Kingdom

Pantikapaion (Bosporan region). *CIRB* 75 = *IPontEux* II 19 = PH182790

ca. 150–125 BCE

Plaque of Tauric limestone, with a relief at the top depicting Aphrodite Ourania ("Heavenly") riding a swan and holding a scepter with Eros to the right and two female figures of Victory (Nikai) above.

Of Pairisades. Of Camasarye. Of Argotas. (*with a crown under each name*)

On behalf of the leader and king Pairisades (IV, reigned 150–125 BCE), son of the mother-adoring king Pairisades (III, reigned 180–150 BCE) and queen Camasarye, the daughter of the child-adoring Spartokos and Argotas son of Isanthos, husband of queen Camasarye, the synagogue leader (*synagōgos*), Theokritos son of Demetrios, and the society members (*thiasitai*) dedicated the monument to Aphrodite Ourania ("Heavenly") Apatouros, guardian goddess.

Theokritos son of Demetrios son of Theokritos, Papias son of Papias . . . , Straton son of . . . Papias son of . . . , Papias son of . . . , Kallistratos . . . Poseidonios. . . .

86. Manumission in a Judean Prayer House

Pantikapaion (Bosporan region). *CIRB* 70 = *IJO* II BS5 = *PontEux* II 52 = PH182785.

81 CE (January/February)

Plaque of white marble, broken in two.

During the reign of king Tiberius Julius Rheskouporis, friend of Caesar and friend of the Romans, pious one, in the year 377 on the twelfth of the month Pereitios, I, Chreste former wife of Drusus, permanently set free my house-bred slave, Heraklas, in the prayer house in accordance with my vow. Not subject to control and undisturbed by any heir, he can go wherever he wants unhindered, just as I have vowed, apart from reverence and devotion toward the prayer house (*proseuchē*). My heirs, Herakleides and Helikonias, have agreed to this and the synagogue (*synagōgē*) of the Judeans has been designated joint guardian.

87. Grave for a Member of a Synod

Pantikapaion (Bosporan region). *CIRB* 79a = *IPontEux* II 63a = PH182794.

Late first to early second century CE

Plaque of limestone.

In memory of Logon son of Rhodon. The synod (*synodos*) is gathered around the synagogue leader (*synagōgos*), Tryphon II; the goodness-loving official (*philagathos*), Kesstios son of Bacchios; the official in charge of affairs (*pragmatas*), Araton; and the rest of the society members (*thiasitai*) set up as a memorial.

88. Grave for a "Brother" of the Synod

Pantikapaion (Bosporan region). *CIRB* 104 = PH 182821.

ca. 200–250 CE

> Gravestone on which members of an association, including the "father" of the group, set up a memorial for a fellow member who is referred to as a "brother."

For good fortune! Those gathered around the priest, Valeris son of Nei-kostratos, and the father (*patēr*) of the synod (*synodos*), Kallistos the younger, and the rest of the members of the synod (*synodeitai*) honored their own brother (*adelphos*), Symphoros son of Philippos.

89. Manumission in a Judean Prayer House

Phanagoria (Bosporan region). *SEG* 43 (1993), no. 510 = *IJO* I BS18 = PH339520.

52 CE (March / April)

> Block of light yellow marble, reused several times.

During the reign of king Kotys in the 348th year on the first of the month of Xandikos, Psycharion and his sons, Sogos and Anos, set free Karsan-danos, Karagos, and Metroteimos in the prayer house (*proseuchē*), uncontrolled and unhindered apart from devotion and reverence toward the prayer house, and to establish their freedoms (?). The synagogue (*synagōgē*) of the Judeans has been designated joint guardian.

90. Dedication of a Relief of a Figure Mounted on a Horse

Tanais (Bosporan region). *CIRB* 1259 = PH184000.

104 CE

> Slab decorated with a relief of a mounted horseman (dressed in the Sarmatian/Iranian manner) as an altar blazes before him. Yulia Ustinova (1999, 192–95) argues that this is likely a depiction of the Sarmatian (Iranian) deity Theos Hypsistos, but it may also be a royal figure (Sauromates). Although the patron deity of the group is unnamed, this too is most likely Theos Hypsistos, since that is the only god attested in connection with other associations at Tanais, associations that also share the same leadership structure (e.g., father, synagogue leader, and goodness-loving official).

During the reign of king Tiberius Sauromates, friend of Caesar and friend of the Romans, pious one, in the year 401 (Bosporan era), celebrating the . . . day of Tanais in the month of Apellaios, this was set up by those gathered around the priest, Xenon son of Eros; the synagogue leader (*synagōgos*), Gaius son of Chariton; the goodness-loving official (*phila-gathos*), Neikostratos II; and, the assistant to the goodness-loving official (*paraphilagathos*), Euporos son of Makaros. Of the rest of the society members (*thiasitai*): Metrophanes son of Alexandros, Herakleides son of Pabas, Kalligenes son of Theneikos, Dadas son of Theneikos, Thorax son of Gastes, Eros son of Zenobios, Boidas son of Apollonios, Sousas son of Pabas, Attas son of Diophantes, Ariston son of Deios, Mastous son of Papias, Theagenes son of Metrophanes, and Eukrates (?) son of Psycharion.

91. Dedication to Theos Hypsistos by a Synod

Tanais (Bosporan region). *CIRB* 1277 = *IPontEux* II 445 = *IGRR* I 917 = PH184019.

ca. 173–211 CE

> Plaque of marble broken in several pieces. The identity of the unnamed Theos Hypsistos ("Highest God") is uncertain, but this may be a Sarmatian (Iranian) deity, as argued by Ustinova (1999). There are no indications of a Judean presence at Tanais.

To Theos Hypsistos ("Highest God"). For good fortune! During the reign of king Tiberius Julius Sauromates, friend of Caesar and friend of the Romans, pious one, the synod (*synodos*) which is gathered around the priest, Julius son of Rhalchados; the father (*patēr*) of the synod, Chorouathos . . . ; the synagogue leader (*synagōgos*), Ardarakos son of Synegdemos; the goodness-loving official (*philagathos*), Diaos son of Kerdonakos; the assistant to the goodness-loving official (*paraphilagathon*) . . . *Name* son of Phorgabakos; the head of the youths (*neaniskarchēs*), Demetrios son of Apollonios; the head of the gymnasium, Basileides son of Theoneikos; the friend (?) of the synod, Attas son of Herakleides; and the rest of the society members (*thiasitai*): (*a fragmentary list of at least twenty-nine names follows*) . . . in the . . . year and the month of Loon. . . .

92. Dedication to Theos Hypsistos by an Association of Adopted "Brothers"

Tanais (Bosporan region). *CIRB* 1283 = *IPontEux* II 452 = *IGRR* I 920 = PH184025.

228 CE

> Plaque of marble. The use of fictive sibling terminology ("brothers") among members has been integrated within the title of the group.

There is no evidence pointing to the presence of Judeans at Tanais, so any suggestion of a Judean connection would be speculation.

For good fortune! Vow for Theos Hypsistos ("Highest God").

During the reign of king Tiberius Julius Kotys, friend of Caesar and friend of the Romans, pious one, the adopted brothers who revere (*eispoiētoi adelphoi sebomenoi*) Theos Hypsistos inscribed their names alongside the elder *Name* . . . II, Nigosa son of Herakleides, Ariston son of Menestrates, Kalligenes son of Myron, Alexiona son of Patroklos, Eutychianos son of *Name* . . . , Eutyches son of Theagenes, Sozomenos son of Styranos, Maes son of Sala, Phadious son of Philemon, Dionysios son of Sogos, Eutychianos son of Gorgias, Dalosakos son of Symphoros, Kardious son of Dadas, Phosakos II, Diophantos son of Dionysios, Eutyches son of Antimachos, Dadas son of Chodiakios, Sambion son of Elpidion, Myreinos son of Mastos, and Asklas son of Herakleides. Sambion son of Elpidion gave this monument as a gift to the brothers. Phourtas son of Agathos and Agathemeros son of Publius made this (?).

In the 525th year on first day of the month Gorpiaios.

Asia Minor

Bithynia and Pontus

93. Grave of a Dionysiac Initiate and Performer

Amastris (Pontus). *SEG* 35 (1985), no. 1327 = PH265443.

August 31, 155 CE

> Large base of marble with upper moulding. Satyrs are mythical attendants of the god Dionysos. Here Dionysos is designated with an epithet that derives from the ritual cry "euoi!"

It was now my thirtieth year. My father named me Aemilianus. Geminos, a man of the nobility, brought me up. In the presence of burning incense (or: burnt offerings), I led the band of revelers (*kōmos*) mystically in the rite for the triennial god Euios (i.e., Dionysos). I was also revered in the gymnasia and experienced in wrestling, javelin throwing, kickboxing (*pankration*), discus throwing, circular racing (or: using a hoop), jumping, and all rhythmic ball playing, each of which my foster father taught me. I won with a satyr play (or: satyr dance) at Kyzikos and Pergamon. At Kyzikos I myself won the crown, but at Pergamon cruel fate carried off the crown. Misfortune withered my body on Dorian soil, but Geminos my foster father, carrying my bones to my homeland, placed them into a stone chest which was adorned with eternal crowns. Year 225, 31 August, Loos 17.

94. Honors by a "House" of Shippers for a Leader

Amastris (Pontus). Gustave Mendel, "Inscriptions de Bithynie [II]," *Bulletin de correspondance hellénique* 25 (1901): 5–92, (no. 184) = PH265198.

imperial

> Fragment damaged on all sides.

The "house" (*oikos*) of the shippers honored M. Ulpius Rufonianus the president (or: patron; *prostatēs*) for life on account of his virtue. The shippers set this up.

95. Honors by a Society for a Priestess (with a Relief of Cybele and Apollo)

Apamea Myrleia area, town of Triglia (Bithynia). *IApamBith* 35 = PH277592.

119 or 104 BCE

> Slab with a relief divided into three panels and an inscription beneath. The upper panel depicts a sacrifice in honor of Cybele (seated on a throne) and Apollo. The priestess Stratonike approaches the altar with upraised hands in adoration and is accompanied by a girl playing a double flute and a boy bringing forward the sheep. The middle panel depicts the association eating and drinking. The lower panel depicts musicians and a dancer.

For her benevolence, the male and female members of the society (*hoi thiasitai kai thiasitides*) crowned Stratonike daughter of Menekrates, who was priestess of Cybele and Apollo in the 178th year, with a crown with a band engraved on a plaque that was announced and another crown with a band that was announced in the synagogue of Zeus.

96. Grave of a Boy Mentioning Fellow Initiates

Apamea Myrleia area, Pylai (Bithynia). *IApamBith* 103 = PH277623.

ca. 250–300 CE

> Slab with a relief of a funerary meal with a seated woman to the left and two men reclining to the right. Discovered built into a house in Yalova.

The young boy Dion, friend of the town of Abarsakos, was snatched by the goddess Fate, having lived fifteen years. Also for his father Dion, having lived forty-five years. The fellow initiates of Abarsakos set this up for the sake of remembrance.

97. Honors by a Society of Isis Devotees for Anubion

Kios (Bithynia). *IKios* 22 = PH277701.

Late Hellenistic or early imperial period

> Discovered under a fountain on the road behind the modern market.

The society members (*thiasitai*) honored Anubion son of Nikostratos, who as a benefactor equipped the sacred ship with two full-sized painted images and another painting. They honored the same Anubion, as a benefactor, with a painted portrait image. They honored the same Anubion, who also served as monthly officer, with a painted image. They honored the same Anubion for piously and generously taking on the Charmosyna (i.e., joyful festival) of Isis with two life-sized painted images, with another painted image on a shield, with a stone monument, and with a proclamation of these honors each month through the year during the Isis celebrations, during the other festivals of the members of the society, and during the regular common assemblies (*synodoi*).

98. Grave with an Epitaph in Verse for an Initiate of Isis

Prusa near Olympos (Bursa) Museum, provenance unknown (Bithynia). *IPrusaOlymp* 1054 + 1028 = *SEG* 42 (1992), no. 1112 + *SEG* 28 (1978), no. 1585 = Richard W. V. Catling and Nikoletta Kanavou, "The Gravestone of Meniketes Son of Menestheus: 'IPrusa' 1028 and 1054," *ZPE* 163 (2007) 103–17 = PH278747.

Late Hellenistic or early imperial period

> Slab of marble, broken in two with a relief of a family (two adults and three children) on each panel and an epigram in the Doric dialect.

Menekites son of Menetheus.

I did not travel the murky way of Acheron where the dead travel by ferry, but I, Meniketes, sped into the harbors of those who are blessed. For I furnished for her house the linen-covered beds of the goddess of Egypt, which are unutterable for those who are impure. Honored by dead men, oh stranger, I gained a remarkable reputation among the Isis-devotees (*Isiakoi*) as a testimony. For I have brought about glory for my father Menesthes, leaving behind three children. You, however, walk this way without causing harm!

99. Honors by an Association of Companions and Friends for a High Priest

Prusa near Olympus (Bithynia). *IPrusaOlymp* 24 = PH278515.

First century CE

> Slab of marble with a partially preserved relief depicting a man with a flaming altar to the left over which he is holding a libation bowl and another large bowl to the right with a palm branch on either side.

The companions (*hetairoi*) of the elder Ophelion and close friends (*synētheis philoi*) honored Sakerdos son of Menandros the high priest and head of the gymnasium, their own benefactor for life, who took care of setting up the statue freely on behalf of the association (*koinon*). Themistokles son of Lysikles, who is also called Phoibos, made this.

100. Honors by Initiates of Sarapis and Isis for a Benefactor

Prusa near Olympus (Bithynia). *IPrusaOlymp* 48 = PH278539.

ca. 150 CE

> Slab of marble in two parts. The upper part contains a relief of the busts of Isis and Sarapis decorated in the temple (*naiskos*) style with part A of the inscription between the two busts. The lower part contains part B of the inscription.

(A) The initiates (*mystai*) dedicated this to Hermes (?).

(B) The initiates thanked Lucius Julius Frugi on behalf of Potamon son of Sostratos because of his (Frugi's) benefactions toward him (Potamon). This is a thanksgiving for Sarapis and Isis. The initiates and tenth-day-celebrators (*dekatistai*) around Leonides son of Hermesilaos, the priest, erected this as a thanksgiving for Sarapis and Isis.

> Hagias son of Hermesilaos, Diodoros son of Hermesilaos, T. Flavius Perseus, Meidias son of Alexandros, Diogenes son of Apollonios, Potamon son of Demosthenes.

> I Potamon son of Sostratos thank L. Julius Frugi, benefactor and nurturer. . . Diogenes son of. . . .

101. Grave of a Sack Weaver

Prusa near Olympos (Bursa) Museum, provenance unknown (Bithynia). *IPrusaOlymp* 1036 = *SEG* 43 (1993), no. 898 = PH278755.

Second century CE

> Slab of marble with a relief depicting a bust of a man.

The sack weavers set this up for Ariston, their fellow society member (*synthiasitēs*), for the sake of remembrance.

102. Grave Prepared by Fellow Initiates

Prusa near Olympos area, Kestel (Bithynia). *IPrusaOlymp* 159 = *SEG* 36 (1986), no. 1114 = PH278647.

Late second or early third century CE

> Slab of white-gray marble with a relief depicting a man in a short tunic who holds a staff in his right hand and a snake in his left hand.

The fellow initiates (*synmystai*) set this up for Rufus son of Gaius for the sake of remembrance. He lived in an appropriate way for sixty years.

Mysia, Troad, and Aeolis

103. Imperial Decree and Proconsular Letter Involving a Society Devoted to Dionysos (Liber Pater)

Kyme (Aeolis). *IKyme* 17 = *SEG* 18 (1962), no. 555 = Robert K. Sherk, *Roman Documents from the Greek East:* Senatus Consulta *and* Epistulae *to the Age of Augustus* (Baltimore: Johns Hopkins University Press, 1969), 313–20 (no. 61) = Jaccottet 2003, vol. 2, no. 104.

ca. 28/27 BCE

> Slab of marble, now in the Rijksmuseum van Oudheden in Leiden. Here an association devoted to Dionysos (Liber Pater) engages in diplomatic contacts with the Roman governor of Asia in order to have an imperial decree applied to their situation concerning a temple and meeting place. References to "the Noracean" and "the Tycallean" pertain to sub-divisions of Kyme.

(*I. Decree of Augustus and Agrippa in Greek*)

Emperor Caesar Augustus, son of god, and Marcus Agrippa son of Lucius, consuls: If there are securities on places owned by the People or temples in the cities or in front of the city of each province, and if there are or will be any dedications in these places, let no one take these things, or buy them, or sell them, or receive them as a gift. Whatever has been taken, bought, or given as a gift, let whoever is in charge of the province consider it to be restored as a place owned by the People or a temple of the city. And whatever object . . . may be given, let him not administer justice concerning this.

(*II. Letter from Vinicius in Latin*)

L. (?) Vinicius, proconsul, sends greetings to the magistrates of Cyme. Apollonides son of Lucius, the Noracean, your citizen, has come to me and shown that the temple of Liber Pater is, through sale, a possession of Lysias son of Diogenes, the Tycallean, your citizen. Since the members of the society (*thiaseitae*) want to restore the sacred objects to the god as Augustus Caesar has ordered, after having paid the price written on the temple of Liber Pater by Lysias, I want you to see to it that, if this is true, Lysias receives the price written on the temple and restores the temple to the god, and that the following be inscribed on it: "Restored by emperor Caesar Augustus, son of the deified Julius." But if Lysias disputes Apollonides' claim, let Lysias give a security to ensure his appearance in court wherever I am. I think it is proper for Lysias to offer the temple as security.

(*III. Partially preserved letter from Vinicius in Greek*)

L. (?) Vinicius sends greetings to the leaders of the Kymaians: Apollonides son of Lucius, Noracean, a citizen of yours, came and indicated to me that the temple of Dionysos, through sale, is possessed by Lysias son of Diogenes, a citizen of yours, and since. . . .

104. Dedication to Zeus Soter by a Brotherhood

Kyme area, Ali-aga (Aeolis). *IKyme* 39 = PH268310.

Second to third century CE

> Part of a column. *Phratra* is a Greek term used in Lydia for an association (rather than a civic division, usually spelled *phratria*).

The brotherhood (*phratra*) which is around Dionysodotos dedicated this column to Zeus Soter ("Savior") and Ktistes ("Founder").

105. Honors by a Synagogue of Judeans for a Female Benefactor

Kyme or Phokaia (Aeolis). *IJO* II 36 = *CIJ* 738 = *IKyme* 45 = PH252856.

Third century CE

> Found in Yeni Foça/Nea Foca.

Tation daughter of Straton, son of Empedon, having built the building (or: house; *oikos*) and the open-air enclosure from her own resources, granted them to the Judeans. The synagogue of the Judeans honored Tation daughter of Straton, son of Enpedon, with a gold crown and with the front seats.

106. Grave Prepared by the Fellow Initiates

Kyzikos area, Aisepos (Mysia). *IMT* 1181 = *IKyzikos* I 312 = PH288557.

Third to second century BCE

> Found and copied by Metropolitan Nikodemos of Kyzikos on a stone in the vicinity of Gönen.

Memorial of Menekrates son of Androneikos which the fellow initiates (*symmystai*) of Poimanenians (i.e., inhabitants of Poimanenos) prepared for him.

107. Honors by Roman Businessmen for a Deceased Woman (Apollonis)

Kyzikos (Mysia). *IMT* 1435 = *SEG* 28 (1978), no. 953 = *NewDocs* IV 2 = PH288713.

ca. 25–50 CE

> Large block of white marble. Lines 7–36 of column 1 are very damaged and largely unintelligible. The inscription mentions a cult of Artemis Pythia, which is a goddess well attested at Miletos (see *IDidyma* 312, 326, 329, 333, 352, 360, 373, 381, 382). Kyzikos was originally a colony of Miletos.

(*column 1*)
The People and the Romans engaged in business in the city honored Apollonis daughter of Prokles because of her parents' virtue, her husband's virtue, and her own moderation. . . .

(*lines 7–35 are too fragmentary to translate*)
. . . Because of these things . . . in a large gathering of the city, the gathering instructed all the civic leaders (*archontes*) to introduce appropriate honors for her. Because of this, the People has indeed resolved as follows:

She is to be mourned by the entire people, all those living in the city, both men and women, and the sacred buildings, sanctuaries, and all the temples are to be closed . . . until the burial. During the burial ceremony the presidents (*prytaneis*) and civic leaders, as well as the boys, youths (*ephebes*), the citizens, and all the free men of the city, are to follow. Likewise the unmarried girls, the female citizens, and the remainder of the free women living in the city are to follow.

(column 2, beginning at line 48)

Furthermore, since she has been granted a funeral adorned in beautiful clothing, it was also resolved for her to be interred within the ancestral tombs of her husband which are in the area of the great harbor. Now the presidents who are serving as presidents in the month of Anthesterion are to crown her statue each year with a gold crown during the Anthesteria festival (i.e., a festival in honor of Dionysos) on the twelfth and thirteenth days, as the sacred herald proclaims with those having been honored beforehand: "The People crowns Apollonis daughter of Prokles because of her parents' virtue, her husband's virtue, and her own moderation with this perpetual crown." And a place for her statue is to be prepared in the sanctuary of the Graces (*Charitesion*) on the right side for those entering from the sacred market, in which her statue is to be set up.

Now, since she held the priesthood of Artemis of the Pythaistridists (i.e., devotees of Artemis Pythia) and as a witness of her piety concerning sacred things, the priestesses, the Pythaistridists, and the temple overseers are to crown her statue when they annually enter together into the sanctuary of the Graces on the seventh day of the month of Artemision. In order that a memorial of her moderation may be visible to the entire city, a statue of her is to be set up in one of the rooms of the square marketplace in the roofed colonnade at the east end, between the office of the property assessors and the office of the market overseer. After it is decorated, it will be used forever as the office of the marriage registrar and those who serve in the office of the marriage registrar. Those registering the finalization of their marriages with the marriage registrar are required to crown the statue of *(column 3, beginning at line 71)* Apollonis which is dedicated in the office. Now statues of her are to be set up . . . *(lines 71–79, which make reference to Aphrodite and possibly a temple of Artemis, are too fragmentary to translate)* . . . golden statues are to be set up in whatever place her relatives choose. Beneath the statues an inscription is to be written as follows: "The People and the Romans engaged in business in the city honored Apollonis daughter of Prokles because of her parents' virtue, her husband's virtue, and her own moderation." The decree is also to be inscribed on the tomb by the treasurer. The decree is to be for the preservation of the city.

108. Decree of the Traders from Asia Granting Honors to Antonia Tryphaena

Kyzikos (Mysia). *IMT* 1431 = *IGRR* IV 144 = PH288709.

41–54 CE

Marble block discovered in 1872.

When Pausanias son of Eumenes was commander of the cavalry (*hipparchos*; i.e., eponymous official of Kyzikos), in the month of Kalamaion, the Council and the People resolved: When Demetrios was presiding, Pausanias son of Eumenes of the Aigikoreis tribe put the motion: Since Antonia Tryphaena, daughter of King Polemon (i.e., king of Pontus in 37/36 BCE) and Queen Pythodoris, being pious with respect to everything toward the eternal household of the greatest of the gods, Tiberius Augustus Caesar, and his eternal rule, joined in dedicating a statue of his mother Augusta Nikephora ("Bringer of Victory") to Athena Polias ("of the City"). And since Antonia Tryphaena has received her priesthood from the city during the Panathenaian celebrations last year, she accomplished everything for the Augusti (*Sebastoi*) with respect to piety toward the gods and in keeping with her character, performing many sacrifices in a distinguished manner, and she treated local inhabitants and foreigners with a natural love of humanity so that the foreigners were amazed with favor at her piety, holiness, and love of glory. And since, even though she was away the year after, everything was being fully accomplished in keeping with her piety, the traders and foreigners from the world who had come to the festival wanted to set up a golden shield with an image of her, and for this reason approached the Council and the People for permission to make the dedication.

The Council and the People resolved to join with them in dedicating the shield in the temple of Polias, and to write on it: "The traders from Asia who have come to the tax-free festival, which was held in Kyzikos for the Augusti (*Sebastoi*) and for Athena Polias, honored Antonia Tryphaena daughter of King Polemon and Queen Pythodoris Philometor, priestess of Augusta Nikephora, because of her piety regarding the household of the greatest of the gods, Tiberius Augustus Caesar, and because of her dignity in every respect and her beneficence toward them."

109. Dedication to Sarapis and Isis by the Therapeutists

Kyzikos (Mysia). *IMT* 1542 = *SIRIS* 318 = PH288822.

First century BCE or first century CE

Plaque of margle, now in the Kestner Museum, Hannover, Germany.

The therapeutists (*therapeutai*; i.e., servants of the gods) who are with Andreas son of Menestrates—namely, Promachos son of Aristonikos, Teimon son of Menophilos, Zenon son of Meniketes, Menophilos son of Theodotos, Theodotos son of Theodotos, Dionysios son of Eisarchos, Ktesibios son of Hermonax, Zmaragdos son of Parthenios, Athenos son of Theodoros, Promachos son of Promachos, Menodoros son of Menandros,

Figure 9
*Monument dedicated to Zeus Hypsistos from Panormos (**110**; photo by Harland).*

Athenagoras son of Menekrates, Philoxenos son of Apollodoros, Diagoras son of Lysagoras—dedicated this to Sarapis and Isis.

110. Dedication to Zeus Hypsistos with a Relief of the Gods and a Banquet Scene

Kyzikos area, Panormos (Mysia). Gustav Hirschfeld, *The Collection of Ancient Greek Inscriptions in the British Museum: Part IV* (Oxford: Clarendon, 1893–1916), 153 (no. 1007) = PH289198.

First century BCE to second century CE

> Slab of white marble with a triangular top (pediment) and with a three-paneled relief. The top panel depicts Zeus, Artemis, and Apollo; the second panel shows a banqueting scene with six male figures; and the bottom panel portrays four figures, namely a seated figure playing the double flute, a nude female dancing, a nude dancing figure with a Phrygian cap and percussion instruments, and a man at the wine bowl (figure 9).

Thallos, eponymous official of the association (or: of the festival, or of the village [?]), dedicated the monument to Zeus Hypsistos ("Highest") and the place (or: village).

111. Grave with Fines Payable to the Porters

Kyzikos area, Panormos (Mysia). *IMT* 1937 = *IKyzikos* I 291 = PH289217.

Undated

Memorial of . . . *Name* who prepared it for himself, for his most sweet wife, Matrona, and for our common children. I forbid anyone else from being buried in it. Now if anyone dares to deposit another here, he will pay one thousand denarii to the most sacred sanhedrin of sack bearers (i.e., porters) of the harbor.

112. Grave with Fines Payable to the Clothing Cleaners

Kyzikos area, Tatlisu (Mysia). *IMT* 1801 = *IKyzikos* I 211 = PH289084.

Undated

Grave of Eutychia which she prepared for herself, for her parents, and for her children. I forbid anyone else from using this grave. Now whoever dares to deposit another dead body will pay 1,500 denarii to the most sacred sanhedrin (*synedrion*) of clothing cleaners.

113. Dedication to King Eumenes II by a Bacchic Group

Pergamon (Mysia). *IPergamonSupp*, AM 27, 1902, no. 86 = Jaccottet 2003, vol. 2, no. 91 = PH316398.

after 158 BCE

> Altar of white marble, now in the Bergama (Pergamon) Museum. King Eumenes II reigned from about 197–159 BCE over the Attalid kingdom centered on Pergamon.

The bacchants (*bacchoi*) of the god of the ritual cry "euoi" (i.e., Dionysos) dedicated this to King Eumenes, god, savior, and benefactor.

114. Honors by the People of Amisos and the Corporate Body of Romans for Augustus

Pergamon (Mysia). *IPergamonSupp*, AM 24, 1899, no. 16 = *IGRR* IV 314 = PH316328.

27 BCE–14 CE (time of Augustus)

> Slab of white marble, now in the Bergama Museum.

Emperor Caesar, god Augustus, son of god. The People of Amisos and the fellow members of the corporate body (*sympoliteuomenoi*) of Romans honored their own savior and founder.

115. Honors by Dionysiac Cowherds for a Leader

Pergamon (Mysia). *IPergamon* II 485 = *SIG*³ 1115 = Jaccottet 2003, vol. 2, no. 94 = PH302149.

First century CE

> Slab of white marble (broken in two) with a large engraved crown at the top. Herders appear in mythology associated with the god Dionysos and the term "cowherds" is sometimes used within associations as a title for members, as here. Silenos was a mythical figure known as the nurturer or foster father of Dionysos, often portrayed as an old man. In this group at Pergamon, several people played this role as Silenoi (plural). For the building in which a group of Dionysiac cowherds met, see **B6** and figure 21.

The cowherds (*boukoloi*) honored Soter son of Artemidoros, the chief cowherd (*archiboukolos*), because of his pious and worthy leadership at the divine mysteries of Dionysos Kathegemon ("Dionysos the Leader").

These are the cowherds: L. Aninius Gallus; Perigenes son of Perigenes; Menodoros son of Asklepiades; Hermaiskos son of Hermaiskos; L. Julius Diokles; Tryphon son of Tryphon also called Koralles; Diomedes son of Diomedes; Hermaiskos son of Posidonios; Monogenes son of Asklepiades also called Minnas; Nikomachos son of Nikomachos; Hermogenes son of Agathoboulos; L. Aninius Joulianos; G. Iulius Rufus, also called Aphrodeisios; Asklepiades son of Zotaios also called Epineikos; Agathoboulos son of Hermogenes; Apollonios Publius son of Apollonios; Iustus; Apollonios.

Hymn instructors: Menophilos Felix son of Herakleides; Asklepiades son of Moschos also called Paris.

The Silenoi are: Menophantos son of Menophantos also called Polybios; Thalamos son of Asklepiades; P. Vedius Nason, the chorus leader.

116. Honors by Dancing Cowherds for a Proconsul of Asia

Pergamon (Mysia). *IPergamonSupp*, AM 24, 1899, no. 31 = Jaccottet 2003, vol. 2, no. 98 = PH316343.

Post-109/110 CE (the year of Quadratus' proconsulship)

> Slab of white marble, broken on the right side and the bottom. For
> the building in which a group of cowherds met, see **B6** and figure 21.

For good fortune! On the occasion of the triennial festival, the dancing cowherds (*boukoloi*) honored Gaius Antius Aulus Julius Quadratus,
twice consul, proconsul of Asia, and priest of noble ancestry of Dionysos
Kathegemon ("Dionysos the Leader"). Auphidia Polla daughter of Publius; Claudius Quadratus, the assigner of offices; Gaius Silius Maximinus
(?) . . . the head cowherd (*archiboukolos*); Lucius Aninius Flaccus (?). . . . The
cowherds: Claudius Epaphos who is also called Diad . . . , Flavius (?) Julius
Diokles, Menandros son of Menandros As . . . , Kapiton son of Menophantos, Titus Flavius Athen . . . Gaius Julius Bassos Claudianus (?), Bion son of
Bion, Hermaiskos Apoll . . . , Charmides son of Eikadios, Titus Claudius
Lindos, Tiberius Flavius Secundus, Philetairos son of Philetairos, Epineikos son of Epineikos.

117. Dedication of an Altar to Hadrian with a Calendar of the Hymn Singers' Celebrations

Pergamon (Mysia). *IPergamon* II 374 = PH302029.

129–138 CE

> Altar of blue-white marble with an inscription on each of the four
> sides (A–D).

(A) For good fortune! The hymn singers (*hymnōdoi*) of god
Augustus and goddess Roma dedicated this to emperor Cae-
sar Trajan Hadrian Olympios, savior and founder. T. Flavius
Philoxenos, P. Quintilius Meidon, T. Claudius Scribonius,
T. Claudius Marcianus, Dionysios son of Hermogenes, T.
Claudius Asklepiades, C. Silius Otacilianus, A. Jul. Hip-
pokrates Ulpianus son of Hippokrates, Gn. Otacilius Pollion
son of Pollion, L. Aninius Flaccus, L. Statilius Moschianos, P.
Aelius Dionysios descendant of Ae. Dionysios, T. Flavius Her-
mogenes grandson of Flavius Quint. Hermogenes, T. Ulpius
Diogenes, Moschos son of Moschos the olympic champion,
M. Ju. Ulpianus Asklepiadoros, A. Castricius Paulus . . . , T.
Claudius Paulinus . . . , T. Flavius Alexandros . . . , A. Julius
Dionysios, A. Gessius Alexandros, C. Julius Hermaiskos
Bassianos, M. Albinius Bassos Sempronianus, Menippos
son of Menippos, P. Silius Pollianus, T. Flavius Pollianus, T.
Flavius Julianus, Caecus son of Caecus, A. Julius Noetos, L.
Annius, Claudius Philetos son of Julianus, T. Flavius Caecilia-
nus, Aelius Tatianos, and T. Claudius Procillianus have set up

the altar from their own foundation established by the Castricius family . . . Capiton, the theologian (i.e., expounder of the stories of the gods). . . .

(B) For good fortune! During his year in office, the keeper of order (*eukosmos*) supplies:

Month of Caesar, Augustan day, birthday of Augustus (i.e., September 23, the first of the new year in the province of Asia): one mina (i.e., one hundred drachmas);

Month of Peritios (= December 24–January 23), first kalends of January: one mina, one bread;

Month of Panemos (= May 24–June 22), Augustan day, Rose festival (i.e., May 24–26): 1 mina, 1 bread;

Month of Loös, third day (= June 25) for the mysteries: wine, one mina and one bread; and

Month of Hyperberetaios, twenty-ninth day (= September 21): one mina, one bread.

The keeper of order (*eukosmos*) will also supply wreaths for the hymn singers on the monthly celebration of Augustus' birthday and on the remaining birthdays of the emperors. He will supply wreaths in the hymn singers' meeting place and wreaths for the hymn singers and their sons each day during the mysteries, as well as cakes, incense, and lamps for Augustus.

The leader (*archōn*) will furnish fifteen denarii toward the incense for the deceased, which will be received near the entrance into the place. The children connected by marriage will receive twelve denarii from the common treasury toward incense.

(C) For good fortune! During his year in office, the priest (*hiereus*) supplies:

Month of Peritios, Kalends of January: wine, a table setting, one mina, three breads;

Month of Panemos, second day, Rose festival: wine, a table setting, one mina, three breads;

Month of Loös, second day for the mysteries: wine, one mina, three breads;

Month of Hyperberetaios, twenty-ninth day: wine, a table setting, one mina, three breads;

Same month, thirtieth day: wine for the altar, a table setting, one denarius.

Also, the outsiders (*exōtikoi*) newly appointed as hymn singers shall give fifty denarii toward the images of the Augusti (*Sebastoi*; i.e., members of the imperial family as revered gods).

(D) For good fortune! During his year in office the secretary (*grammateus*) supplies:

Month of Hyperberetaios, twenty-ninth day, birthday of Augusta (i.e., Livia, the wife of the emperor): wine, a table setting worth two denarii, one mina;

Month of Peritios, Kalends of January: one mina, one drachma, and nine assaria coins;

Month of Panemos, third day, Rose festival: a table setting worth one denarius, one mina, and one bread;

Month of Loös, Augustan day, mysteries: wine, a table setting, one bread. . . .

The appointed hymn singer will supply one hundred denarii toward the sacrifices of Augustus and Roma; fifteen denarii to each hymn singer; double, that is thirty denarii, as well as wine and three breads to the gods; and, one bread and half of a mina to the sons of members.

Now the one who succeeds his father shall give fifteen denarii to the gods, seven denarii to each hymn singer, wine, and a table setting. But the leaders will also give back to the sons who have paid the choral fee half of all their fees.

118. Honors by Settlers for a Consul

Pergamon (Mysia). *IPergamonSupp*, AM 27, 1902, no. 102 = *OGIS* 491 = PH316413.

Post-142 CE

Base of white marble.

The settlers (*hoi katoikountes*) on Paspareitai street honored L. Cuspius Pactumeius Rufinus, consul, benefactor, and founder of the homeland, when Menandros II the dyer and C. Julius Eutaktos were supervisors. They gave one hundred denarii and the base from their own resources.

119. Dedication Involving an Association Devoted to the Dioskouroi Gods

Pergamon (Mysia). *IPergamon* II 321 (notes) = *CIG* 3540 = PH317090.

Roman imperial period

> The Dioskouroi (or Dioscuri) gods were the twin sons of Zeus: Castor and Pollux.

... *Name* dedicated this to the Dioskouroi and to the association (*symbiōsis*) of male Dioskourites (i.e., devotees of the Dioskouroi) when Telesphorion was the leader and Asklepiades was secretary.

120. Dedication of an Altar for an Association of Friends of the Augusti

Pergamon (Mysia). C. Habicht, ed., *Die Inschriften des Asklepieions. Die Inschriften von Pergamon* (Berlin: Walter de Gruyter, 1969), no. 85 = PH303090.

Roman imperial period

> Small altar of marble found near the Asklepieion.

For good fortune! Epiktesis daughter of Heraklas, who has served as priestess, has set up this altar for Asklepios Soter ("Savior") and for the association (*symbiōsis*) of friends of the Augusti (*philosebastoi*) from her own resources.

Lydia

121. Divine Instructions for the Household Association of Dionysios

Philadelphia (Lydia). *LSAM* 20 = *SIG*³ 985 = Barton and Horsley 1981.

Late second century to early first century BCE

> Slab of white marble with damage along the right side. Zeus Eumenes in this inscription may be a reference to Zeus identified with king Eumenes II, former ruler of the Attalid kingdom centered on Pergamon. Philadelphia itself was founded after 189 BCE by Eumenes II or by his successor, Attalus II Philadelphus. Eumenes may also be simply an epithet of the god Zeus, meaning "kindly."

For good fortune! For health, common salvation, and the best reputation, the instructions that were given to Dionysios in his sleep were written down, giving access into his house (*oikos*) to men and women, free people and household slaves. For in this house altars have been set up for Zeus Eumenes and Hestia his consort, for the other Savior gods, and for Eudaimonia ("Prosperity"), Ploutos ("Wealth"), Arete ("Virtue"), Hygeia ("Health"), Agathe Tyche ("Good Fortune"), Agathos Daimon ("Good Spirit"), Mneme ("Memory"), the Charitae ("the Graces"), and Nike ("Victory"). Zeus has given instructions to this man for the performance of the purifications, the cleansings, and the mysteries in accordance with ancestral custom and in accordance with what has now been written here.

When entering this house let men and women, free people and household slaves, swear by all the gods that they do not know about any deceptive action against a man or a woman or about any drug harmful to people, and that they neither know nor use harmful spells, a love charm, an abortive drug, or a contraceptive. Nor should they use any other thing fatal to children, or give advice or connive with another person about such things. Now no one should withdraw their goodwill toward this house, and if anyone should do any of these things or plan them, the others are neither to look the other way nor remain silent, but shall expose and avenge the violations.

Beyond his own wife, a man is not to seduce someone else's wife, whether free or slave, nor a boy, nor a virgin girl. Nor shall he advise someone else to do so. Should he connive at it with someone, they shall expose such a person, both the man and the woman, and not conceal it or keep silent about it. Let the woman and the man, whoever does any of the things written above, not enter this house. For the gods set up in it are great, and they watch over these things and will not tolerate those who transgress the instructions.

A free woman is to be pure and not know the bed of another man, nor have intercourse with anyone except her own husband. But if she does know the bed of another man, such a woman is not pure, but defiled, full of endemic pollution, and unworthy to revere this god whose sacred things have been established here. She is not to be present at the sacrifices, nor cause offence at the purifications and cleansings, nor see the mysteries being performed. If she does any of these things after the instructions have been inscribed, she will have evil curses from the gods for disregarding these instructions. For the god does not want these things to happen at all, nor does he wish it. Rather, he wants obedience.

The gods will be merciful to those who obey and will always give them all good things, whatever things gods give to people whom they love. But if any transgress, the gods will hate such people and inflict upon them great punishments. These instructions were stored with the goddess Agdistis, the holiest guardian and mistress of this house. May she create good thoughts in men and women, free people and household slaves, so that they may obey the things written here. During the monthly and annual sacrifices, may those men and women who have confidence in themselves touch this stone on which the instructions of the god have been written, so that those who obey these instructions and those who do not obey these instructions may become evident.

Zeus Soter ("Savior"), accept the touch of Dionysios mercifully and kindly, and be gentle with him and his family. Provide good rewards, health, salvation, peace, safety on land and sea . . . likewise. . . .

122. Honors by the Therapeutists of Zeus for a Civic Leader

Sardis (Lydia). *ISardBR* 22 = PH263133.

ca. 100 BCE

Slab of blue marble found near the temple of Artemis.

The therapeutists (i.e., servants) of Zeus who enter the shrine have consecrated and crowned Sokrates Pardalas son of Polemaios, the foremost man of the city, for following in his ancestors' footsteps in his piety toward the deity.

123. Petitions by a Priest of Apollo on the Shores to a High Priest

Sardis area, village of Yeniköy, north of Koloe/Gygaia lake (Lydia). *SEG* 46 (1996), no. 1519.

ca. 150 BCE

Slab of marble with a moulding and an olive branch at the top. The bottom of the monument is missing. This inscription documents several stages of successful diplomacy between the priest of Apollo and Hellenistic authorities.

When Euthydemos was high priest and Kadoas son of Pleri was priest. Petition by Kadoas the priest of Apollo on the Shores (*Pleura*), who held the priesthood for many years, to the high priest Euthydemos: Previously, when Antiochos was king, I made a request before Nikanor the high priest "that a monument would be set up in the temple recording his name, mine, and those of the initiates (*mystai*). Now if it seems agreeable, I request for you to write Asklepiades the manager in order that he may assign me a place in which to set up the monument on which I will record your name, my name, and those of the initiates."

"Diophantos to Attinas: I have appended for you a copy of the letter written to me by Euthydemos the high priest."

"Euthydemos to Asklepiades: Concerning the petition which was sent to me by Kadoas, the priest of Apollo on the Shores (*Pleura*), let it be just as he requested."

Menekrates son of Hermogenes, Metrodoros son of Mithres. . . .

124. Honors by Workers of the Slave Market for T. Julius Lepidus

Sardis (Lydia). *SEG* 46 (1996), no. 1524 = *AÉ* (1996), no. 1452.

Late first century to early second century CE

> Slab of white marble built into an Islamic funerary wall near the Roman baths.

According to a decree by the entire assembly of the People, the People of the Sardians honored T. Julius Lepidus . . . of Asia and of the city, Caesar loving high priest, foremost man of the city, because of his love of glory and incomparable goodwill toward the homeland. Those engaged in business in the slave market set up the honor from their own resources.

125. Monument Erected by the Initiates of Apollo

Sardis (Lydia). Herrmann 1996, 318–19 (no. 2) = *SEG* 46 (1996), no. 1528.

First century CE (?)

> Fluted column found in the area of the building known as the "Monumental Mudbrick Structure."

The initiates of Apollo set up this monument.

126. Edict Concerning Zeus and the Mysteries of Sabazios, Agdistis, and Ma

Sardis (Lydia). Herrmann 1996, 329–35 (no. 4) = Louis Robert, "Une nouvelle inscription grecque de Sardes: Règlement de l'autorité perse relatif à un culte de Zeus," *Comptes-rendus des séances de l'Académie des Inscriptions et Belles-Lettres* (1975): 306–30 = *SEG* 29 (1979), no. 1205 = *CCCA* 456 = *NewDocs* I 3 = PH277091.

Second century CE (claiming to be a copy of a document from ca. 365 BCE)

> This document is presented as though it is a copy of an earlier edict from about 365 BCE, during the time of Artaxerxes III, king of

Persia. Baradatian Zeus may be identified with the Persian deity Ahura Mazda with the epithet meaning "the Legislator," as suggested by Louis Robert. However, this may also be a reference to the founder of a Lydian cult of Zeus (with no specific Persian connection), a man named Baradates (see *SEG* 46 [1996], no. 1720). The god Sabazios and the goddesses Agdistis and Ma were native to Anatolia for some time.

In the thirty-ninth year of Artaxerxes' reign, Droaphernes Barakis, the governor of Lydia, dedicated the statue to Baradatian Zeus. He instructs his temple warden therapeutists (i.e., servants) who enter into the shrine and who crown the god not to participate in the mysteries of Sabazios with those who carry the burning incense (or: burnt offerings) and not to participate in those of Agdistis and Ma. They instruct Dorates, the temple warden, to abstain from these mysteries.

127. List of Fountains Used by Mystery Associations, a Synagogue, and Others

Sardis (Lydia). *ISardBR* 17 = PH263128.

ca. 200 CE

Slab seen and documented in 1874 in the vicinity of the marketplace.

. . . and to whomever the water is being apportioned. The fountain opposite the gymnasium of the elders' council (*gerousia*); the fountain opposite the two mystery halls (*mysterioi*); the fountain of Domitia, five hundred liquid measures (500–*chous*; i.e., about 1,640 liters); the fountain of *Name* . . . ; the fountain of Lenaeitis near the . . . ; the fountain of the mystery hall of Attis opposite and flowing into Zeus' sanctuary; the fountain of the synagogue . . . ; the fountain near the Odeion, three hundred liquid measures (i.e., about 984 liters); the fountain of . . . near the two story-building of the . . . which also has towers, two four-amphorae measures (i.e., about 208 liters); the fountain of the guard house which is on the descending road of the marketplace near . . . sends water; the fountain from the reservoir . . . ; the fountain of Lysimachos (?), three hundred liquid measures; the fountain of . . . *Name* near the Menogeneion, three hundred liquid measures; the fountain of Arsinoe (?); the fountain flowing from the Arsinoean fountain near the god Men's sanctuary; the fountain in . . . which is near the gate; the fountains which Rufus and Lepidus built . . . Aurelia Julia Meno . . . the fountain of . . . *Name*, two four-amphorae measures; the fountain built by (?) Asinnius M . . . one four-amphorae measure (about 104 liters) . . . Flavius Secundus (?). . . .

128. Honors by the People and the Roman Businessmen for a Resident Foreigner

Thyatira (Lydia). *TAM* V.2 924 = PH264354.

50–1 BCE

Slab of gray marble.

The People and the Romans engaged in business honored Quintus Baebius Fiscus, sojourning as a foreigner in a fair and humane manner.

129. Honors by Dyers for a Priestess of the Augusti

Thyatira (Lydia). *TAM* V.2 972 = *IGRR* IV 1242.

ca. 50 CE

Base of marble.

The dyers (*bapheis*) set this up from their own resources to honor Claudia Ammion—daughter of Metrodoros Lepidus and wife of Tiberius Claudius Antyllos who was head of the gymnasium three times—priestess of the Augusti (*Sebastoi*) and high priestess of the city for life, having served as director of contests in a magnificent and extravagant manner, and having conducted her life in purity and with self-control.

130. Dedication of a Hero Cult and an Association Devoted to Gaius Julius Xenon

Thyatira area (Lydia). *TAM* V.2 1098 = *ILydiaKP* II 74 = *IGRR* IV 1276.

First century CE

Slab of marble.

The People dedicated the Xenon shrine and the hewn stone to Gaius Julius Xenon son of Apollonides, hero and benefactor, who had become high priest of Caesar Augustus and goddess Roma and who had made the greatest benefactions for all of Asia. He was a savior, benefactor, and founder in relation to all and became father of the fatherland, foremost among the Hellenes. The Juliasts prepared this monument.

131. Honors by Leather Cutters for the Leader of an Association of Romans

Thyatira (Lydia). *TAM* V.2 1002 = *IGRR* IV 1169.

Late first century CE

Base of marble.

The leather cutters (*skytotomoi*) honored T. Flavius Alexandros son of Metrophanes of the tribe of Quirina, who was market overseer in a vigorous and extravagant manner for six months, curator of the association (*conventus*) of Romans, ambassador to the emperor in Rome three times, legal representative in the laborious cases concerning the Attaleians (?) at his own expense, and priest of Artemis in a manner displaying piety and love of honor. This was set up on behalf of Flavia Alexandra and Flavia Glykinne, his daughters.

132. Honors by Dyers for a High Priest of Asia

Thyatira (Lydia). *TAM* V.2 978 = *IGRR* IV 1239 = PH264408.

ca. 106–114 CE

Base of gray marble, likely a statue base.

The dyers (*bapheis*) set this up to honor Tiberius Claudius Sokrates of the Quirina tribe, son of Sokrates, high priest of Asia of the temple in Pergamon, director of contests for the city, head of the gymnasium, who supplied numerous and great things every time including the erection of buildings and generously arranging immunity for the homeland. This was done when Tiberius Claudius Anthus, Menodotos son of Menodotos, Menandros Olympikos son of Menogenes, and Lucius Kranion son of Apollonios were supervisors (*epimelētai*).

133. Honors by Dyers for a Civic Leader

Thyatira (Lydia). *TAM* V.2 989 = *CIG* 3496 = PH264420.

ca. 120–130 CE

Base of marble.

For good fortune! The Council and the People honored . . . *Name* son of Makedon, a noble, good and patriotic man, who has served as chief of police in a remarkable manner, market overseer in a brilliant and glory-loving manner for six months, commander in a pure and careful manner, and member of the Board of Ten. He has also supplied all the other needs of the city zealously. The dyers (*bapheis*) set up this honor from their own resources when Apollonios son of Apollonios was supervisor (*epimelētēs*).

134. Grave Near a Sambatheion in the Chaldean Quarter

Thyatira (Lydia). *IJO* II 146 = *CIJ* 752 = *TAM* V.2 1142 = PH264573.

Second century to early third century CE

> Coffin (sarcophagus) of marble. The building here designated a "Sambatheion" may or may not have some connection to the Judean "Sabbath" and, therefore, with a Judean association. Josephus uses the term "Sabbateion" in a decree attributed to Augustus; there it is used in reference to a place where sacred books and the collection for the temple taxes were stored by Judeans in Roman Asia (Josephus, *Antiquities* 16.164). The fact that this building is in the Chaldean quarter also suggests the possibility of some connection with Babylonian immigrants.

Flavius Zosimos, having prepared the grave, placed it in a pure place outside the city by the Sambatheion in the quarter (or: precinct) of the Chaldean, alongside the public road, for himself and for his most sweet wife Aurelia Pontiane. No one else has the authority to put anyone into this grave. Now whoever dares or does these things will give 1,500 silver denarii to the city of the Thyatirans and 2,500 denarii to the most sacred treasury, also becoming liable under the law of grave robbing. This inscription was written twice, with the other copy being placed into the archives. This was done by Menophilos son of Julianus, public official, in the most brilliant city of the Thyatirans under the proconsul Catillius Severus, on the thirteenth day of the month Audnaios.

135. Honors by Devotees of the God Herakles for a Man

Thyatira (Lydia). *TAM* V.2 959 = *ILydiaKP* II 51 = PH264389.

Second century CE

> Round base of blue and red marble decorated with an engraved crown. Attalus II Philadelphus was coruler of the Attalid kingdom with Eumenes II around 160–158 BCE, when the mentioned settlement was established.

For good fortune! The Herakleists from the settlements established by Attalus and Eumenes at Mernouphyta honored Glykon Neikandros, a man who loves honor, with a gold crown.

136. Honors by Dyers for a Roman Military Official

Thyatira (Lydia). *TAM* V.2 935 = *CIG* 3497 = *IGRR* IV 1213.

Post-199/200 CE (under Caracalla)

Base of marble.

For good fortune! T. Antonius Claudius Alfenus Arignotus, the most excellent procurator of Augustus responsible for the treasury of Liviana; prefect of the second wing of Flavia Agrippiana; commander of the exclusive wing; military tribune of the first Cilician cohort; commander of the first Gaetulian cohort; procurator of the second Flaviana cohort of Numidians; commander of the second Flaviana cohort of Bessorians; quartermaster of god Antoninus and of the harbors of Seleucia Pieria; Roman equestrian of the Quirina tribe; relative of consuls; son and grandson of high priests of Asia; cousin of Alfenus son of Apollinarios who is responsible for the census of Augustus; temple warden of the most brilliant metropolis of Kyzikos; curator of Seleucia Pieria, of Alexandria near Issos, of Rhossos, of Trajanopolis, and of the Tropesians; performer of every kind of military service in the colonies; and, priest of the ancestral god Tyrimnos (i.e., patron deity of Thyatira). The dyers (*bapheis*) set this up.

137. Honors by a High Priest of the "Whole Athletic Meeting" for a Friend

Thyatira (Lydia). *TAM* V.2 984 = Millar 1999, 92 (no. 1).

ca. 220 CE

Base (?) found in private home in Akhisar.

For good fortune! Aurelius Alexandros, high priest of the whole athletic meeting for life, leader of athletics as well as the baths of Augustus, priest of the ancestral god Helios Pythios Apollo Tyrimnaios honored his own benefactor and the benefactor of everyone in the city, M. Gnaius Licinius Rufinus, most brilliant man of consular rank, founder and benefactor of the homeland, friend of Augustus.

138. Honors by Bakers for an Asiarch and High Priest

Thyatira (Lydia). *TAM* V.2 966 = *IGRR* IV 1244 = PH264396.

Second to third century CE

Base of marble found in a private home in Akhisar. The position of "Asiarch" was taken on by wealthy inhabitants with Roman citizenship in the province of Asia. The precise functions of this position remain unclear, although it is unlikely to be identified with the high priesthood in the provincial imperial cult, as previously believed.

For good fortune! The bakers (*artokopoi*) set this up from their own resources to honor Gaius Julius Julianus Tatianus, who was director of contests, Asiarch, high priest for life, distributor (*triteutēs*) and director of the market in the same year, and ambassador to the emperors at his own expense with success for the greatest homeland. He was son of C. Julius Hippianos and Cornelia Secunda the high priests of Asia, grandson of Flavius Moschios the high priest, descendant of Flavius Hippianos and Flavia Tatia who, like their ancestors, acted as high priests with their kin, contributed to public buildings, and acted with zeal all the time, and were founders of the homeland. Lesbios Philotas the supervisor set up the statue and the altar with his son Asklepiades from their own resources.

139. Funerary Altar and Coffin of a Priestess Prepared by Initiates

Thyatira (Lydia). *TAM* V.2 1055.

Second to third century CE

Funerary altar.

For Ammias. Her children and the initiates (*mystai*) of the deities set up the funerary altar together with the coffin (sarcophagus) . . . for the priestess of the gods for the sake of remembrance. Now if anyone wants to learn the truth from me, let him come to the funerary altar and one will attain whatever one wants through a vision during the night or day.

140. Honors by Civic Institutions for a Priestess in Connection with Mysteries of Artemis

Thyatira (Lydia). *TAM* V.2 995 = *CIG* 3507 = PH264426.

Second to third century CE

Base (?)

For good fortune! The Council and the People honored Ulpia Marcella, the priestess of Artemis, daughter of the admirable Marcus Ulpius Damas and of Kanidia Bassa, who performed the mysteries of the goddess and the sacrifices in a brilliant and extravagant manner. Androneikos son of Androneikos and Stratoneike daughter of Menogenes, her household slaves, set this up from their own resources.

141. Honors by Wool Workers for the Athlete Alexandros

Thyatira (Lydia). *TAM* V.2 1019 = *IGRR* IV 1252 = PH264450.

ca. 218–222 CE

Base of marble found in a private home in Akhisar.

C. Perelius Aurelius Alexandros, the outstanding and foremost member of the eternal and immortal athletes of the worldwide competitions of the Pythian Augusteian games and the anointed ambassador. The wool workers (*lanarioi*) set this up in his honor when Aurelius Moschianos son of Ammianos was supervisor.

142. Honors by Hymn Singers of the Mother Goddess for a Benefactor

Thyatira (Lydia). *TAM* V.2 955 = *ILydiaKP* II 49.

Third century CE

> Base of marble found between Thyatira and Hierocaesareia.

For good fortune! The hymn singers (*hymnōdoi*) of the Mother of the Gods honored with the erection of a statue Aurelius Polythallos, son of Aurelius Menophilianos Fronton Polythallos, a man proven in every position of leadership and service.

143. Honors by Slave Traders for a Slave Merchant

Thyatira (Lydia). *TAM* V.2 932 = *IGRR* IV 1257 = *OGIS* 524.

Undated

> Base of marble.

The workers (*ergastai*) of the slave market and the slave brokers (*proxenētai*) set this up in honor of Alexandros son of Alexandros, slave merchant (*sōmatemporos*), who has served as director of the market for a four-month period in an upright manner and who has given extravagantly from his own resources to the city during the days of the festivals of the Augusti (*Sebastoi*; i.e., members of the imperial family as revered gods).

144. Grave Prepared by Children and Members of a Brotherhood

Thyatira (Lydia). *TAM* V.2 1148.

Undated

> Slab found in a private home in the vicinity of Kennez. The term *phratores* (cf. *phratra*) was a native Lydian term for an association, here translated "brotherhood."

The children and the members of the brotherhood (*phratores*) set up this monument. If anyone knocks down or vandalizes this monument, the gods will not be gracious to them or to their children, nor will the earth bear fruit for the offender.

Phrygia

145. Honors by a Judean Synagogue for Julia Severa and Others

Akmoneia area, Ercis (Phrygia). *IJO* II 168 = *CIJ* 766 = PH270132.

Late first century or early second century CE

> Slab of white marble with a panel, now in the museum at Afyon Karahisar.

The building (or: house; *oikos*), which was built by Julia Severa, was renovated by P. Tyrronius Klados, head of the synagogue for life, Lucius son of Lucius, also head of the synagogue, and Publius Zotikos, leader (*archōn*), from their own resources and from the common deposit. They decorated the walls and ceiling, made the windows secure, and took care of all the rest of the decoration. The synagogue honored them with a gold shield because of their virtuous disposition, goodwill, and diligence in relation to the synagogue.

146. Honors by Clothing Cleaners for a Prefect and Sebastophant

Akmoneia (Phrygia). *MAMA* VI, p. 149 (no. 164) = *IGRR* IV 643 = PH272554.

98–117 CE

> T. Flavius Montanus was also a benefactor at Ephesos, where he contributed structures in the theater, dedicating them to Artemis, Trajan, and the People of Ephesians (*IEph* 2037, 2061, 2063). A sebastophant, or revealer of the Augusti, played an important role in mysteries for the emperors and imperial family members as gods (comparable to the hierophant in other mysteries).

For good fortune! T. Flavius Montanus son of Hiero of the tribe of Quirina, prefect of the artisans (*eparchon techneitōn* = *praefectus fabrum*) for the second time, high priest of Asia in the temple of the Assembly of Asia in Ephesos, revealer of the Augusti (*sebastophantēs*), and director of contests for life. The guild (*synergasia*) of clothing cleaners (*gnapheis*) honored their own benefactor.

147. Dedication of a Statue of Council Personified by Dyers

Hierapolis (Phrygia). *SEG* 41 (1991), no. 1201 = PH273100.

ca. 100–150 CE

Large base of marble found in the theater.

The guild (*technē*) of dyers (*bapheis*) dedicated this to the Council, and Glykonianos Menandros son of Glykon, Gaius Julius Lucius Crescens of the Fabian tribe, Gaius Baevius Glykon II, and Antiochos son of Zosimos were responsible to setting it up.

148. Dedication to Dionysos Kathegemon by a Hierophant

Hierapolis (Phrygia). *SEG* 41 (1991), no. 1202 = PH273101.

Second century CE

Base of marble found near the theater.

C. Ambibius Phrygianos, the revealer of sacred things (*hierophantēs*), dedicated this to Dionysos Kathegemon ("Dionysos the Leader").

149. Grave of a Judean Family Mentioning a Synagogue

Hierapolis (Phrygia). *IJO* II 191 = Miranda 1999, 124 (no. 14) = *SEG* 49 (1999), no. 1827 = *AÉ* (1999), no. 1585a–b.

ca. 200 CE (A); post-250 CE (B)

Reused limestone coffin (sarcophagus) in the northern necropolis.

(A) The grave, the burial ground beneath it, and the area around it belong to Nikotimos Lykidas son of Artemisios. In it he has buried Apphia, his wife. A copy of this inscription was stored in the archives. Judean.

(B) The grave and the place around it belong to Aurelius Heortasios Julianus, from Tripolis, Judean, now living in Hierapolis. In it he and his wife Glykonis will be buried, and let their children be buried here as well. It is not lawful for anyone else to be buried in it. If someone does such things, he will pay two silver coins to the most holy synagogue (*synagōgē*).

150. Grave of a Judean Family Mentioning the Settlement of the Judeans

Hierapolis (Phrygia). *IJO* II 205 = *IHierapJ* 212 = *CIJ* 775 = Miranda 1999, 44 (no. 16) = PH271826.

ca. 150–200 CE

Limestone coffin (sarcophagus) located in the northern necropolis.

This grave and the surrounding place belong to Aurelia Augusta daughter of Zotikos. In it she, her husband, who is called Glykonianos, also known as Hagnos, and their children will be buried. But if anyone else is buried here, the violator will pay a fine of three hundred denarii to the settlement (*katoikia*) of the Judeans who are settled in Hierapolis and one hundred denarii to the one who found out about the violation. A copy of this inscription was stored in the archives of the Judeans.

151. Grave of a Judean Family Mentioning the People of the Judeans

Hierapolis (Phrygia). *IJO* II 206 = *IHierapJ* 69 = Miranda 1999, 118–19 (no. 5).

ca. 150–200 CE

Limestone coffin (sarcophagus) in the northern necropolis (figure 10).

The grave and the burial ground beneath it together with the base and the place belong to Aurelia Glykonis daughter of Ammianos, and her husband Marcus Aurelius Alexandros Theophilos, also known as Aphelias, both Judeans. They will be buried in it, but it is not lawful for anyone else to be buried in it. If this is violated, the guilty one will pay a fine of one thousand denarii to the people (*laos*) of the Judeans. A copy of this inscription was stored in the archives.

152. Grave of Publius Aelius Glykon Mentioning Purple Dyers and Carpet Weavers

Hierapolis (Phrygia). *IJO* II 196 = *SEG* 46 (1996), no. 1656 = Miranda 1999, 131–32 (no. 23).

150–250 CE

Limestone coffin (sarcophagus) located in the southeastern necropolis near the remains of the Martyrium of St. Philip (figure 11).

This grave and the burial ground beneath it together with the surrounding area belong to Publius Aelius Glykon Zeuxianos Aelianus and to Aurelia Amia daughter of Amianos Seleukos. In it he will bury himself, his wife, and his children, but no one else is permitted to be buried here. He left behind 200 denarii for the grave-crowning ceremony to the most holy

Figure 10
*Grave mentioning the "people of the Judeans" at Hierapolis (*151*; photo by Harland).*

Figure 11
*Grave of P. Aelius Glykon from Hierapolis (*152*; photo by Harland).*

presidency of the purple dyers (*porphyrobapheis*), so that it would produce from the interest enough for each to take a share in the seventh month during the festival of Unleavened Bread. Likewise he also left behind 150 denarii for the grave-crowning ceremony to the sanhedrin (*synedrion*) of carpet weavers (*akairodapistai*), so that the revenues from the interest should be distributed, half during the festival of Kalends on the eighth day of the fourth month and half during the festival of Pentecost. A copy of this inscription was stored in the archives.

153. Honors by Institutions and Associations for a Civic Leader

Hierapolis (Phrygia). *IHierapJ* 32 = *IGRR* IV 818 = PH271647.

pre-212 CE

Column of white marble found in "the halls" near the theater.

The most distinguished Council (?), the most distinguished People of Hierapolis, the elders' council (*gerousia*), the sanhedrin (*synedrion*) of Romans, the young men (*neoi*), and the many synods honored Gaius Ageleius Apollonides of the Aniensis tribe, member of the virtuous councilors, commander of the city, market overseer, member of the Board of Ten, leader of the association (*conventus*) of the Romans, provider of the oil, auditor of public accounts, director of public works, and useful in meeting imperial needs.

154. Grave of P. Aelius Hermogenes Mentioning Dyers

Hierapolis (Phrygia). *IHierapJ* 195 = PH271809.

ca. 138–212 CE

Coffin (sarcophagus) from the northern necropolis.

This grave and area belongs to Publius Aelius Hermogenes son of Charopeinos (?). His son (?) will be buried in it, his wife has been buried in it, and Hermogenes will be buried in it as well, but no one else. But if someone violates this by burying someone else here, that person will pay 2,500 denarii to the most holy treasury (?), 1,600 denarii to Apollo, and 800 denarii to the one prosecuting the case. The guild (*ergasia*) of dyers (*bapheis*) will supervise the grave. He has provided the grave-crowning funds, as contained in the inscription about the grave-crowning funds, in order that the grave-crowning funds be given each year in the amount of 1,000 denarii . . . a copy of this inscription has been stored in the archives.

155. Grave of M. Aurelius Diodoros Mentioning Purple Dyers

Hierapolis (Phrygia). *IHierapJ* 227 = PH271841.

ca. 190–250 CE

> From the northern necropolis. The "foundling guild" (*tēs ergasias tēs thrematikēs*) mentioned near the end of this bequest may be a reference to a group of cattle breeders or some other occupation dealing with foundlings.

(A) This grave and the area around it, together with the underlying base, belong to Marcus Aurelius Diodoros Koriaskos, also known as Asbolos. In it, he, his wife, and his children will be buried. I will bury whomever I want around it. It is not lawful for anyone else to be buried here. But if someone does so, that one must pay a fine of five hundred denarii to the most holy treasury and five hundred denarii to the most sacred elders' council (*gerousia*). However much you give life, oh friend passing by, know that this is the fulfillment of your life!

(B) He has also left behind three thousand denarii for the sanhedrin (*synedrion*) of the presidency of the purple dyers (*porphyrobapheis*) for burning the incense on the customary day using the interest from the funds. But if anyone is neglectful of his role in burning the incense, the funds that are left behind are to be used by the foundling guild (*ergasia*). And my wife will also be buried here.

156. Honors by Wool Cleaners for Tiberius Claudius Zotikos Boa

Hierapolis (Phrygia). *IHierapJ* 40 = *IGRR* IV 821 = PH271655.

Third century CE

> Slab of white marble found in "the halls" near the theater.

The most sacred guild (*ergasia*) of wool cleaners (*erioplytai*) honored Tiberius Claudius Zotikos Boa, the foremost civic commander, honor-loving director of contests, and secretary of the temples which are in Asia, esteemed ambassador, high priest, and benefactor of the homeland. The erection of this monument was planned by the associates of Marcus Aurelius Apollonios Pylon son of Marcus Aurelius Apollonios, Marcus Aurelius Ammianos son of Ammianos and grandson of Ammianos Glykon, and Aurelian Arruntianus son of Hermippos.

157. Honors by Purple Dyers for Tiberius Claudius Zotikos Boa

Hierapolis (Phrygia). *IHierapJ* 41 = *IGRR* IV 822 = PH271656.

Third century CE

> Block of white marble.

The most sacred guild of purple dyers (*porphyrobapheis*) honored Tiberius Claudius Zotikos Boa, foremost civic commander, honor-loving director of contests, secretary of the temples which are in Asia, esteemed ambassador, high priest, and benefactor of the homeland.

158. Grave of Aurelius Zotikos Epikrates Mentioning Guilds

Hierapolis (Phrygia). *IHierapJ* 133 = PH271749.

Post-212 CE

> Coffin (sarcophagus) in the northern necropolis.

(a.1) Grave of Aurelius Zotikos Epikrates

(b.1) . . . Zotikos (?) and him. Now I leave behind a hundred and fifty denarii to the guild (*syntechnia*) of nail workers (*hēlokopoi*) for the yearly grave-crowning ceremony. But if they fail to provide the service, then the guild (*syntechnia*) of coppersmiths (*kalkeis*) will do so. But if they fail to provide the service, the funds are to be given to the purple dyers (*porphyrobapheis*) for supervision of the grave. It is not lawful for anyone else to be buried here, and if this is violated the offender will pay five hundred denarii to the most sacred elders' council (*gerousia*), five hundred denarii to the most holy treasury, and the same to the one prosecuting the case. A copy of this inscription was stored in the archives. And nothing will be given. . . .

Ionia

159. Honors by Demetriasts and the People of Ephesos for Benefactors

Ephesos (Ionia). *IEph* 4337 = *SEG* 4 (1930), no. 515 = PH247714.

ca. 19–23 CE

> Slab of blue marble discovered in two separate pieces. The beginning of the decree is missing but some key honors referring to cults of imperial figures (Augusta and sons of Drusus Caesar) identified

with gods (Demeter Karpophoros and the "new" Dioskouroi) are
preserved. The Dioskouroi (or Dioscuri) gods were the twin sons of
Zeus: Castor and Pollux.

. . . deemed worthy of every testimonial by us and by the People. Now
gladly contributing with the same generosity just as he does yearly with
the children, in a singular and exemplary fashion he continued to meet
the yearly expenses of the positions of director, head of the gymnasium,
night watcher, and supplier of water. Because of this, the Demetriasts who
marveled at his goodwill toward them decided to respond with a reward of
appropriate honors. Therefore, the following priests will exist for life with
a double share and freedom from liturgy: Bassos priest of Artemis, Servilia
Secunda priestess of Augusta Demeter Karpophoros ("Fruit Bringer"),
and Proklos priest of the new Dioskouroi, the sons of Drusus Caesar. The
Demetriasts also decided to have images of them made. These images
will be set up in an ideal location in a public place, having an appropriate
inscription. They will also set up the resulting decree by the Council and
the People. The Demetriasts before the city resolved how what is written
above should be done.

160. Honors by the Provincial Assembly of Asia for Hymn Singers

Ephesos area, Hypaipa village (Ionia). *IEph* 3801 = *SEG* 4 (1930),
no. 641.

41–54 CE

> Slab of marble found in the village of Hypaipa, east of Ephesos.
> Column 1 contains the hymn singers' honors for the imperial
> household and the beginning of a letter from emperor Claudius to
> the group. Column 2 is a resolution by the provincial Assembly of
> Asia honoring the hymn singers for their participation in provin-
> cial imperial cult celebrations at Pergamon in honor of the goddess
> Roma (Rome personified) and god Augustus Caesar (who is identi-
> fied with Ancestral Zeus).

(*column 1*)
. . . on behalf of the eternal, enduring Tiberius Claudius Caesar Augustus Germanicus and his whole household. During the crown bearing
of Tiberius Claudius Asklepiodoros son of the Quirinian Tryphon, and
while Alexandros son of Apollonides was secretary of the People and both
temple warden and distributer of the properties of the temple of Augustus,
the hymn singers (*hymnōdoi*) set this up according to the existing decree
which was engraved by the sacred synod (*synodos*) in Pergamon, inasmuch

as this offering is just and kind toward them (i.e., toward members of the imperial household). Hosios son of Apollonios Herm . . . took care of it. . . .

Tiberius Claudius Caesar Augustus Germanicus, twice proclaimed emperor (*imperator*), high priest, with tribunician power, twice appointed consul, proconsul, father of the fatherland, to the sacred synod of the hymn singers, greetings. Acknowledging the decree which. . . .

(*column 2*)

. . . resolved by the Hellenes of Asia (i.e., the provincial Assembly of Asia) on the motion of G. I. Anaxagoras son of . . . Caesar-loving high priest of Asia and life-long director of contests for goddess Roma and god Augustus Caesar, Zeus Patroos ("Ancestral"), emperor and greatest high priest, father of the fatherland and of the whole race of humankind: Since it is proper to offer a visible exhibition of piety and of every intention befitting the sacred to the Augustan household each year, the hymn singers from all Asia, coming together in Pergamon for the most sacred birthday of Augustus Tiberius Caesar, god, accomplish a magnificent work for the glory of the synod, singing hymns to the Augustan household, accomplishing sacrifices to the Augustan gods, leading festivals and banquets.
. . .

161. Grave with Fines Payable to the Silversmiths

Ephesos (Ionia). *IEph* 2212 = *NewDocs* IV 1 = PH249888.

41–54 CE (time of emperor Claudius), or later

Grave inscription.

The grave, the area around it, and the underground tomb belong to M. Antonius Hermeias, silversmith (*argyrokopos*) and temple keeper (*neopoios*), and to his wife Claudia daughter of Erotion. No one may be buried in this grave except those written above. But if anyone dares to bury a body or to erase the inscription, that one will pay one thousand denarii to the silversmiths in Ephesos. The sanhedrin (*synedrion*) of silversmiths takes care of this grave and Erotion dedicated five hundred denarii, and the inheritance was given in the sixth month on the established eighth day.

162. Donations to the Fishery Toll Office by Fishermen and Fish Dealers

Ephesos (Ionia). *IEph* 20 = *NewDocs* V 5 = PH247975.

54–59 CE

A large slab found in the harbor area and inscribed on two sides (figure 12). If the list of donors to the construction of the toll office are themselves members of the fishermen and fish dealers, then there were both Roman and non-Roman citizens among the members of this occupation at Ephesos (cf. *NewDocs* V 5); however, it is possible that the donors were joining with the fishermen in contributing to the building and were not themselves members of the occupational group. The cubit was a measurement equivalent to the space from the elbow to the fingertips.

(A) This is dedicated . . . to the emperor Nero Claudius Caesar Augustus Germanicus; to Julia Agrippina Augusta, his mother; to Octavia, the emperor's wife; to the People of the Romans; and, to the People of the Ephesians. The fishermen and fish dealers set this up from their own resources, having received the place by decree from the city and having built the toll booth for the fish market. The following contributed to the work according to the amount indicated:

(*column 1*)

Publius Hordeonus Lollianus with his wife and children: four columns; Publius Cornelius Alexandros: paving of one hundred cubits of the open area with Phokaian stone; Tib. Claudius Metrodoros with his wife and children: three columns and paving of the colonnade beside the monument with Phokaian stone; P. Gerellanus Melleitos, two columns; Euporos son of Artemidoros: one column and twelve denarii; Philokrates son of Apellas with his children: one column and twelve denarii; L. Octavius Macer with his brothers: one column; P. Anthestius son of Publius: one column; Onesimos son of Apollonios and Dionysios son of Charisios: a painted column; P. Cornelius Felix with Cornelia Ision: one column; Septimius Trophimos with his children: a column; Herakleides son of Herakleides and grandson of Herakleides: . . . *x* denarii; Epaphras son of Tryphon with his son: three hundred tiles; P. Naevius Niger with his children: fifty denarii; P. Vedius Verus with his son: fifty denarii; L. Fabricius Tosides with his son: fifty denarii; P. Cornelius Philistion with his son: fifty denarii; L. Octavius Rufus with his sons: fifty denarii; Tryphon son of Artemidoros: thirty-seven denarii; Isas son of Artemidoros: thirty-seven denarii; Attalos Hamaxas son of Charixenos with his son: thirty denarii; Epikrates Kroukras son of Antiochos with his sons: thirty denarii; Isas son of Isidoros: thirty denarii.

(*column 2, to the right of column 1*)

Hesperos son of Demetrios with his sons: twenty-five denarii; Q. Laberius Niger with his son: twenty-five denarii; Isas son of Hermochares with his sons: twenty-five denarii; C. Furius with his son: twenty-five

Figure 12
*Monument of the fishermen and fish dealers at Ephesos (**162**; photo by Harland).*

denarii; M. Valerius Fronto with his daughter: twenty-five denarii; Artemisios son of Lesbios: twenty-five denarii; P. Savidius Amethystos with
his sons: twenty-five denarii; Hierax son of Hermokrates with his wife:
twenty-five denarii; Didymos son of Theudas: twenty-five denarii; Demetrios Kenartas son of Demetrios: twenty-five denarii; Xanthos son of
Pythion: two thousand bricks; Phorbos, the watchman: one thousand
bricks; Secundus, the watchman: one thousand bricks; M. Antonius Bassus with his daughter: all the mats used for binding bricks in the stoa;
Syeros son of Kleanax with his son: twenty denarii; Vetulenus Primus with
his son: twenty denarii; Cn. Cornelius Eunous with his child: fifteen denarii; Attalos son of Attalos and grandson of Kassiades: fifteen denarii; Diogenes son of Diogenes with his son: fifteen denarii; Vettidius Nikandros
with his sons: fifteen denarii; Gaius Roscilius: fifteen denarii; Zosimos son
of Gaius Furius: fifteen denarii; Bacchios son of Euphrosynos with his

mother: fifteen denarii; L. Vitellius with his son: fifteen denarii; L. Consius Epaphroditos: fifteen denarii; Aristeas son of Aristoboulos with his son: fifteen denarii; Ruficius Faustus: fifteen denarii; P. Livius: fifteen denarii; Antiochus Psychas with his son: fifteen denarii; Chares son of Chares with his sons: fifteen denarii.

Along with his wife, L. Fabricius Vitalis, who superintended the works and procured the construction of the work, also dedicated at his own expense two columns together with the adjacent altars beside the temple of the Samothracian gods.

(*Side B, which is heavily damaged, has approximately thirty names, and all legible amounts are five denarii.*)

163. Letter of the Demetriasts Concerning Mysteries

Ephesos (Ionia). *IEph* 213 = *NewDocs* IV 22 = PH247918.

88/89 CE

> Statue base of marble. Members of the imperial family, or Augusti (*Sebastoi*), are here placed alongside the patron deity of the association.

To Lucius Mestrius Florus, proconsul, from Lucius Pompeius Apollonios of Ephesos. Mysteries and sacrifices are performed each year in Ephesos, lord, to Demeter Karpophoros ("Fruit Bringer") and Thesmophoros ("Law Bringer") and to the Augustan (*Sebastoi*) gods by initiates (*mystai*) with great purity and lawful customs, together with the priestesses. In most years these rites were protected by kings and emperors, as well as the proconsul of the period, as contained in their enclosed letters. Accordingly, as the mysteries are pressing upon us during your time of office, through my agency the ones obligated to accomplish the mysteries necessarily petition you, lord, in order that, acknowledging their rights. . . .

164. Honors by Silversmiths for a High Priest

Ephesos (Ionia). *IEph* 425 (+ *IEph* 636 notes for a correction to line 10) = PH248044.

ca. 81–117 CE

> Base built into the Baths of Varius.

T. Claudius Aristion, high priest of Asia for the third time . . . (*three untranslatable lines*), president, and temple warden, who arranged many great works in our city from his own resources. The silversmiths (*argyrokopoi*) set up this monument when Furius Secundus was superintendent of works.

165. Honors by Physicians for the Chief Physician of Emperor Trajan

Ephesos (Ionia). *IEph* 719 = PH249247.

ca. 102–114 CE

> Base found in the "apsidal building."

The physicians (*iatroi*) who sacrifice to ancestor Asklepios and to the Augusti (*Sebastoi*) honored T. Statilius Crito, chief physician (*archiatros*), procurator of emperor Nerva Trajan Caesar Augustus Germanicus Dacicus, and priest of the shrine of King Alexander and of Gaius and Lucius, descendants of Augustus. When Tiberius Claudius Demostratos Caelianus was priest and L. Atilius Varus was leader (*archōn*) of the physicians, C. Arrius Hermerotos and his sons, Arrius Celsianus and Arrius Celsus, set up the honor from their own resources as he (Hermerotos) had promised the physicians.

166. Dedication by a Dionysiac Society with Honorary Membership for Emperor Trajan

Ephesos area, Tire village (Ionia). *IEph* 3329 = Jaccottet 2003, vol. 2, no. 142.

Early second century CE

> Found in the Church of the Taxiarchoi in Tire.

For Dionysos and emperor Nerva Trajan Caesar Augustus Germanicus, who is also a member of the society of Dionysos. Euboulos Kassandros son of Apollonios, "the old man," Menestratos son of Menestratos, Attalos son of Metrodoros. . . .

167. A "Family" of Gladiators

Ephesos (Ionia). *IEph* 1182 = PH249615.

Early second century CE

> Slab of white marble. The position of "Asiarch" was taken on by wealthy inhabitants with Roman citizenship in the province of Asia, but the functions of this position remain unclear.

(*column 1*)
Family (*phamilia*) of gladiators of

(*column 2*)
   T. Claudius Tatianus Julianus, Asiarch.

168. Honors by Initiates of the God Dionysos for Emperor Hadrian

Ephesos (Ionia). *IEph* 275 = *SEG* 26 (1976), no. 1272 = Jaccottet 2003, vol. 2, no. 136 = PH248718.

117–138 CE

> Altar of white marble found in the eastern portion of the sanctuary of Artemis.

Emperor Caesar Trajan Hadrian Augustus, son of god Trajan Parthicus and grandson of god Nero, greatest high priest, with tribunician power, three times consul. The initiates (*mystai*) before the city (*pro poleōs*), enthroned with Dionysos, honored him when Claudius Romulus was priest, Claudius Eubios was the revealer of sacred things (*hierophantēs*), and Antonius Drosus was supervisor. Theodotos son of Theodotos Proclion, initiation leader, with his children, Proklos, hymn singer, and Athenodoros set up this honor from their own resources.

169. Dedication of a Statue of Isis for Workers in the Fishery Toll Office

Ephesos (Ionia). *IEph* 1503 = *SIRIS* 301 = PH248503.

138–161 CE (time of Antoninus Pius)

> Rounded statue base found near the Ephesian harbor.

This is dedicated to the Ephesian Artemis, to the emperor Titus Aelius Hadrian Antoninus Caesar Augustus Pius, to the first and greatest metropolis of Asia, twice temple warden of the Augusti (*Sebastoi*), the city of the Ephesians, and to those who are engaged in the toll booth for the fish market. Cominia Junia dedicated this statue of Isis and an altar at her own expense when Tiberius Claudius Demostratos was civic president.

170. Honors by Civic Institutions and Wine Tasters for P. Vedius Antoninus (II)

Ephesos (Ionia). *IEph* 728 = PH249108.

162/163 CE (time of Vedius II)

> Base of marble situated in the Scholastikia baths.

The Council and the People of the first and greatest metropolis of Asia, twice temple warden of the Augusti (*Sebastoi*), the city of the Ephesians, honored P. Vedius Antoninus son of P. Vedius Antoninus. The elder Antoninus was civic president, head of the gymnasium, twice secretary of the People, Asiarch, festival leader of the great Ephesian and Pasithean festivals, and legate to the senate and the emperors. The honoree, Antoninus the younger, himself was civic president, secretary, Asiarch, festival leader of the great Ephesian games and chief officer of the Olympian games. He served as ambassador to the senate and the emperors concerning the greatest matters, and he was himself a victor. He served as head of the gymnasium unfailingly during the visit of the greatest emperor Lucius Aurelius Verus all the days he visited. He has also adorned the city with many and great works, and he has shown love of honor readily and voluntarily each time. Those who are engaged in the taste (i.e., likely wine tasters) set up this statue.

171. Honors by Wool Workers for P. Vedius Antoninus (II or III)

Ephesos (Ionia). *IEph* 727 = PH249109.

Mid-second century CE (time of Vedius II or III)

Statue base found near the civic Council building.

The guild (*synergasia*) of wool workers (*lanarioi*) honored P. Vedius Antoninus, the founder of the city of the Ephesians.

172. Reservations in the Latrines of the Vedius Gymnasium

Ephesos (Ionia). *IEph* 454a, b (+ addenda p. 12), c, d, e, f = *SEG* 4 (1930), no. 541a–f.

Post-160 CE

Reservations on columns in the area of the latrines in the Vedius bath-gymnasium.

(A) Of the bankers, three spaces.

(B) Of the hemp workers from the Servilius stoa.

(C) Of the astiopolist (*meaning unknown*) wool dealers.

(D) Of those from Branchiane street.

(E) Of the linen weavers.

(F) Of the guild of basket makers (?).

173. Honors by Initiates for Commodus as the "New Dionysos"

Ephesos (Ionia). *IEph* 293 = PH248767.

ca. 180–192 CE (time of Commodus)

> Found near the old harbor in the apsidal building near the so-called baptismal font of John. Here the emperor is identified with a god as a "new Dionysos."

The emperor-loving, hair-cloth-wearing (or: sack-bearing) initiates (*sakēphoroi mystai*) of the primal god Dionysos Koreseitos set this up in honor of emperor Caesar M. Aurelius Commodos Antoninus Augustus, new Dionysos, during the priesthood of M. Aurelius Menemachos, the high priest and president.

174. Grave of a Chief Physician Cared for by the Judeans

Ephesos (Ionia). *IJO* II 32 = *CIJ* 745 = *IEph* 1677 = PH250100.

150–250 CE

> Slab of white marble.

This is the memorial of Julius (?) . . . chief physician (*archiatros*), and his wife, Julia . . . and their children, living. The Judeans in Ephesos take care of this grave.

175. Grave of a Physician Cared for by the Physicians

Ephesos (Ionia). *IEph* 2304 = PH250309.

Undated

> Coffin (sarcophagus) between the Koressian Gate and the temple of Artemis. The term "Mouseion" was used for buildings dedicated to the Muses (mythical figures of intellectual and artistic inspiration), in this case a place of learning.

This grave and the altar beneath it belong to Marcus Pompeius Boron, emperor-loving physician (*iatros*)—living—and to his wife Ulpia Neike—living. It is not lawful for anyone else to be buried in it. Now if anyone places a body in it, erases the inscription, or tries to sell it, may that person not be satisfied in life, children, body, selling, or buying. The sanhedrin (*synedrion*) of physicians (*iatroi*) from the Mouseion in Ephesos take care of the grave. He left to them a legacy worth 4,600 denarii.

176. Grave of Alkmeionis Involving Devotees of the God Bacchos (Dionysos)

Miletos (Ionia). *SEG* 17 (1977), 503 = Jaccottet 2003, vol. 2, no. 149 = PH252546.

Late third to second century BCE

Poetic grave inscription.

"Farewell holy priestess," say the female bacchants (*bakchai*) of the city. This is appropriate for a good woman. She led you to the mountain, and carried all ritual implements and sacred objects, proceeding before the city. Now if some stranger inquires about her name, she is Alkmeionis daughter of Rhodios, who knew her share of blessings.

177. Membership of the Temenizontes of Apollo, Zeus, and Aphrodite

Miletos (Ionia). *IMilet* 797 = *SEG* 30 (1980), no. 1339 = PH252320.

First century BCE

Two fragments of a block of gray marble.

When Metrodoros (?) son of Hermias was treasurer of the gold and Andronikos son of Myonides was secretary, the members of the sanctuary association (*temenizontes*) gathered for Apollo, Zeus, and Aphrodite: Zenon son of Asklepiades, Ision son of Apollodoros, Zenon son of Demetrios, Theon son of Zenon, Artemidoros son of Her . . . , Damas son of Dionysios (?), Oiax son of Hekatomnos, Hekataios son of Hekatomnos, Hekatodoros son of Apoll. . . .

178. Letter of Emperor Claudius to the Sacred Victors and Performers of Dionysos

Miletos (Ionia). *IMilet* 156 = *GCRE* 29 = PH252173.

48 CE

Base of gray marble found in the temple of Apollo (the Delphinion).

Tiberius Claudius Caesar Augustus Germanicus, with tribunician power for the eighth time, consul for the fourth time, proclaimed emperor (*imperator*) for the fifteenth time, father of the fatherland, and censor, to the sacred victors (*hieroneikai*) and performers (*technitai*) gathered around Dionysos, greetings.

I acknowledge your memory regarding the things I supplied when I maintained the rights which were granted by the Augusti before me and by the Senate, and I will try to increase these rights in light of your pious disposition toward my household. Now Marcus Valerius Junianus of my household drew my attention to this, and I also praised him for his positive disposition toward you. Farewell.

179. Oracle from Didyma Involving Builders at Miletos

Miletos (Ionia). *IMilet* 935 = Joseph Fontenrose, *Didyma: Apollo's Oracle, Cult and Companions* (Berkeley: University of California Press, 1988), 193–94 (no. 19) = PH252569.

ca. 120 CE

Block of limestone with an oracle in hexameter verse.

Should the builders (*oikodomoi*) associated with . . . Epigonos—that is, the contractors for the section of the theater in which the prophet of the god, the late Ulpianus, was superintendent of works and the architect, Menophilos, assigns the work—fashion and construct the arches and the vaults over the columns or should they consider other work?

The god answered: For good uses of wise building techniques, it is expedient to consult a skillful man for the best suggestions, performing sacrifices to thrice-born Pallas (i.e., the goddess Athena) and strong Herakles.

180. Honors by Performers from Asia for a Benefactor

Miletos area, Didyma (Ionia). *IDidyma* 107 = *OGIS* 472 = PH247174.

First to second century CE

The goddess Artemis Pythia also appears in an inscription from Kyzikos, a Milesian colony (*IMT* 1435).

The performers (*technitai*) from Asia working at the temple in Didyma honored Meniskos Melanos son of Zopyros, sacred victor, who was thrice victor at the Didymeia games; he was their foremost head of the gymnasium who accomplished the remaining things with extreme love of glory; and, he was ambassador to Augustus with respect to the inviolability of Didymean Apollo and the privileges of the city. He has also been honored by Asia, by the People of the Milesians, and by the elders' council (*gerousia*) with golden images and statues and with other great honors, being a descendant of king Lykomedes. They dedicated this to the Didymean god (i.e., Apollo) and to Pythian Artemis (i.e., sister of Apollo) on account of his virtuous behavior and good will toward them.

181. Honors by "Worldwide" Linen Workers for a Prominent Athlete

Miletos (Ionia). *SEG* 36 (1986), 1051 = PH252448.

Late second century CE

> Base of white marble found in excavations of the theater, now in the Louvre (MA 2806).

For good fortune! M. Aurelius Thelymitres, victor in the Pythian games, victor in the Capitoline games, incredible victor in all the great games, son of the incredible M. Aurelius Thelymitres, voluntary benefactor of the homeland in many ways. Because he has granted freedom from disturbance during the athletic contest, both communally and individually, the world-wide and most sacred sanhedrin (*synedrion*) of linen-weavers (*linourgoi*) honored him in the section of the stage which he had built. Farewell!

182. Honors by Gardeners for Ulpius Karpos

Miletos (Ionia). *OGIS* 755 and 756 = PH252479 and PH252480.

ca. 130 CE

> Although the descriptor or epithet Hypsistos ("Highest," or "Most high") could be used of the Judean God, it was also used of other deities, as is most likely here.

(A) The priest of the most holy god Hypsistos ("Highest"), Savior, Ulpius Karpos, member of the Council. The station (*station*) of gardeners (*kēpouroi*) opposite the city honored their benefactor on behalf of their own salvation (*OGIS* 755).

(B) Ulpius Karpos, a prophet of the most holy god Hypsistos ("Highest"). The fleet of shellfish (or: razor fish) fishermen honored their own benefactor because of everything (*OGIS* 756).

183. Reserved Seating in the Theater for Goldsmiths, Judeans, and Others

Miletos (Ionia). *IMilet* 940.

Various dates second to fifth century CE

> Reservations inscribed on the seats in the theater in the first, second, and fourth sections on the first level. The designation "blue" here most likely refers to supporters of a particular team of competitors

that wore the color blue. For a photo of one of the Judean inscriptions (f), see figure 13.

(A) Place of the blue goldsmiths (*aurarioi*).
(B) Place of the goldsmiths.
(C) Place of the victorious goldsmiths.
(D) Place of the emperor-loving goldsmiths.
(E) Place of the younger ones.
(F) Place of the Judeans who are also god fearers (or: Place of the Judeans and god fearers).
(G) God fearer.
(H) Place of the blue Judeans.
(I) Place of Diodotes.
(J) Thelymitres.

184. Honors by Dionysiac Worldwide Performers for T. Aelius Alcibiades

Nysa (Ionia/Caria). *IEph* 22 (side A only) = M. Clerc, "Inscription de Nysa," *BCH* 9 (1885): 124–31 = PH261503.

ca. 142 CE

> Column of white marble. Only the inscription pertaining to the Ephesian branch of performers on side A is translated here. Side B of the inscription (not translated here, but available in Clerc) refers to an association (*kollegion* = *collegium*) of Nysaians at Rome, who likewise benefited from Alcibiades' benefactions.

Figure 13
Theater seating for the Judeans and god fearers at Miletos
(**183f**; *photo by Harland*).

On the proposal of Publius Aelius Pompeianus Paion of Side, Tarsus and Rhodes, winner of many poetic contests, composer of songs and rhapsodist of god Hadrian, theologian of the temples which are in Pergamon, appointed director of contests of the Augustan Pythian games, and by the vote of P. Aelius . . . of Kyzikos, harpist, unexpected winner of the Capitolinian games and Olympian games: Since Aelius Alcibiades is an educated and generous man, excelling in other virtues, providing for a long time continuously, even twelve years, doing good for the musicians, receiving honor and magnificence together with the synod (*synodos*), and displaying love of honor in many matters both for us and for the common good. Furthermore, since he honored the sacred precinct of the worldwide performers (*technitai*) at the temple of Rome by donating excellent books, and since he granted magnificent gifts of properties, including stabling facilities, from which we reap the continuous, everlasting rent, distributing the rents among ourselves annually on the birthday of god Hadrian. In response, the performers at Rome reciprocated with favor, voted on other honors for him, appointed him high priest through all eternity, and thought him worthy to be honored along with the company of the other high priests by having his name inscribed first on the plaques. For, on the one hand, he adorned the imperishable memory of Hadrian and, on the other, he has made known the highly regarded synod through his gifts. As a result, the synod participates in magnificent parades and carries out costly religious services during holidays.

Because of these things and for good fortune, the game-conquering and crown-winning worldwide performers associated with Dionysos and emperor Caesar T. Aelius Hadrian Antoninus Augustus Pius and the fellow contestants whom they met during the quinquennial contests of the great Ephesian games in the greatest and first metropolis of Asia—the city of the Ephesians, twice temple warden of the Augusti (*Sebastoi*)—have passed a resolution that, in addition to the honors decreed to the man, they will vote for a well-balanced favor of exchange by doing the following: They will set up golden images and statues in the holy temples of the emperors in Asia and in Nysa, the emperor-loving homeland of Alcibiades. They will inscribe the voted decrees on a monument (stele) in the temple of Apollo, as well as in the rest of his public works and throughout all the cities, in order that it may be a good memorial of both Alcibiades' generosity and his well-received favors. They will publicly honor him with a gold crown in services and libations during the contest. And they will make a public announcement and honor him during each meeting (*synlogos*). A copy of the decrees will be sent out to his brilliant fatherland, the city of Nysa—by way of the elders P. Aelius Pompenianus Paion of Side,

Tarsus and Rhodes, winner of many poetic contests, composer of songs and rhapsodist of god Hadrian, theologian of the temples which are in Pergamon, appointed director of contests of the Pythian Augustan games, and Aristides son of Aristides Pergaion of Pergamon, incredible poet.

Copies of the inscription will be sent by an embassy of elders to the greatest emperors and to the synod in Rome for the sake of acknowledging together what the benefactor Alcibiades has done.

185. Dedication to the God Anubis for Queen Stratonike by the Fellow Anubiasts

Smryna (Ionia). *ISmyrna* 765 = *SIRIS* 305 = PH255005.

Third to second century BCE (time of Queen Stratonike wife of Seleukos I Nikator or of Eumenes II, kings of the Attalid kingdom centered on Pergamon)

> Two column pieces (a and b) of blue marble, one found on mount Pagus and the other in the agora. Anubis was an Egyptian deity.

(A) The fellow Anubiasts dedicated this to Anubis on behalf of Queen Stratonike and on behalf their own Herakleitos son of Archigenes: Philodemos son of Apollonios, Artemidoros son of Horos, Eudoros son of Apollonios, Dakon son of Lakon, Aristophanes son of Artemidoros, Kaphisias son of Menekrates, Mnesimachos son of Theodoros, Hermias son of Horos, Apollonios son of Menon, Dionysios son of Loulanabos, Philostratos son of Demokrates, Demokrates son of Philostratos, Zenon son of Loulabelos, Trochilos son of Pyrgion, Epikouros son of Stratippos, Artemidoros son of Dionytas, Dionysios son of Pythion, . . . *Name* son of Dionysios . . . (*lines missing between A and B*)

(B) . . . Parmen . . . son of . . . *Name*, Zoilos son of Horaios, Philoxenos son of Poseidonios, Apelles son of Dionysios, Telemachos son of Nikanor, Zopyrion son of Kratinos, Xouthos son of Nikanor, Eumedes son of Protarchos, Euandros son of Sphodrios.

186. Restoration of a Statue of Athena by Silversmiths and Goldsmiths

Smyrna (Ionia). *ISmyrna* 721 = *SIG*³ 1263 = PH254932.

ca. 14–37 CE

> Type of monument unknown.

For good fortune! The guild (*synergasia*) of silversmiths (*argyrokopoi*) and goldsmiths (*chrysochooi*), having repaired the statue of Athena, restored her for the homeland when L. Vinicius was commander of the military.

187. Grave of a Cilician Prepared by the Friends-of-Agrippa Companions

Smyrna (Ionia). *ISmyrna* 331 = *SEG* 18 (1978), no. 518 = PH255489.

First century to early second century CE (after the time of Marcus Agrippa)

> Slab of blue marble. This association was evidently devoted to Marcus Agrippa, son-in-law of Augustus. Adana was located in the province of Cilicia.

The friends-of-Agrippa companions (*philagrippai symbiōtai*) prepared the memorial for their own companion, Marion from Adana, who is also known as Mareis, for the sake of remembrance.

188. Honors by Civic Institutions and Initiates for Two Female "Theologians"

Smyrna (Ionia). *ISmyrna* 653 = PH255060.

First to second century CE

> Base of white marble, now in the Ashmolean Museum at Oxford. As their title indicates, "theologians" (*theologoi*) expounded the stories (*logoi*) or accomplishments of gods or goddesses. The goddess remains unnamed in this inscription, but Demeter or Kore is probably in mind, as initiates for each of these goddesses are attested at Smyrna in this period (*ISmyrna* 655 and 726).

The Council, the People, and the synod (*synodos*) of initiates (*mystai*) of the goddess honored the sisters Claudia Antonia Sabina Prokliane and Claudia Antonia Juliane, the theologians (*theologoi*), for everything which they zealously offered with respect to piety toward the goddess and the festival of the initiates. Claudius Antonius Lamos, their father, set up the honors when T. Claudius Zenon and M. Vibius Theodoros were treasurers.

189. Honors by Devotees of the God Dionysos Breiseus for a Benefactor

Smyrna (Ionia). *ISmyrna* 652 = Jaccottet 2003, vol. 2, no. 115 = PH255058.

ca. first century CE

Piece of a column base of gray marble.

For good fortune! The sacred synod (*synodos*) of Breiseans honored C. Julius Cheirisophos, son of the literary expert (or: teacher of grammar; *grammatikos*) C. Julius Mousonios, who has displayed love of honor in serving as director of contests.

190. Subscriptions of the Initiates of Dionysos with Imperial Dedications

Smyrna (Ionia). *ISmyrna* 731 = Jaccottet 2003, vol. 2, no. 116 = PH254991.

80 CE (no. 731, lines 1–20), 83 CE (no. 731, lines 21–27)

> Fragmentary slab of marble that also contains *ISmyrna* 600, an imperial letter to the synod of Dionysos Breiseus. Members described with the term "ancestral initiate" (*patromystēs*) are likely descendants of initiates from previous generations.

This was dedicated to emperor Titus Caesar Vespasian Augustus, great high priest, with tribunician power for the ninth time, proclaimed emperor (*imperator*) for the fifteenth time, father of the fatherland, consul for the eighth time, and to Caesar Domitian son of god Vespasian Augustus, consul for the seventh time. This was done when C. Julius Fabias Mithres, the emperor-loving son of the People, was serving as priest by family descent, T. Claudius Bion Nonianos was crown bearer, L. Licinius Proklos was director of contests, . . . *Name* was president of athletics, and L. Sulpicius Firmus was administrator.

Those who have fully paid the entrance fee are: Sulpicius Firmus, Artemidoros Artemas, ancestral initiate (*patromystēs*), Apollonios Eudemos, ancestral initiate, Trophimos Asklepiades, Tyrannos Papios son of Menandros.

This was dedicated to emperor Caesar Domitian Augustus, proclaimed for the ninth time, and to Quintus Petillius Rufus, consul for the second time. This was done when Koskonias Myrton was crown bearer, L. Caecilius Fronto the younger was director of contests, and Dionysios Cicinius the younger was president of athletics.

191. Honors by Initiates of Dionysos Breiseus for Emperor Hadrian

Smyrna (Ionia). *ISmyrna* 622 = Jaccottet 2003, vol. 2, no. 119 = PH255039.

ca. 129–132 CE

Base of stone found in the agora.

The initiates (*mystai*) of the great Breiseus Dionysos before the city honored emperor Trajan Hadrian Caesar Augustus Olympios, savior and founder. This was done when Dikaios Heliodoros son of Alexandros, their own treasurer, was supervisor.

192. Letter of Emperor Marcus Aurelius to the Synod of Dionysos Breiseus

Smyrna (Ionia). *ISmyrna* 600, lines 1–18 only = *SEG* 34 (1984), no. 1191 = Jaccottet 2003, vol. 2, no. 122 = PH254910.

March 3, 158 CE or earlier

> Fragmentary slab of marble with two imperial letters (on the same stone as *ISmyrna* 731). Only the first, complete letter (lines 1–18) is presented here. Only the opening of another letter (*ISmyrna* 600, lines 19–26) from Antoninus Pius to the "synod of initiates in Smyrna" is preserved. (For a photo of a bust of emperor Marcus Aurelius, see figure 14.)

Marcus Aurelius Caesar son of emperor Caesar Titus Aelius Hadrian Antoninus Augustus, father of the fatherland, with tribunician power, consul for the second time, to the synod (*synodos*) which is gathered around Breiseus Dionysos, greetings.

Your goodwill which you displayed in sharing with me the birth of a son—even though this turned out badly (i.e., the child had died)—became no less evident. Statilius Maximus, the greatest proconsul and our friend, sent the decree. I wish you good health. March 28th, from Lorium.

M. Antonius Artemas had this inscription engraved as a gift when Sulpicius Rufinus was treasurer.

193. Honors by Performers and Initiates of the God Dionysos Breiseus for a Benefactor

Smyrna (Ionia). *ISmyrna* 639 = *CIG* 3190 = *IGRR* IV 1433 = Jaccottet 2003, vol. 2, no. 121 = PH255050.

ca. 150–200 CE

> Marble stone.

The sacred synod (*synodos*) of performers (*technitai*) and initiates (*mystai*) gathered around Dionysos Breiseus honored Marcus Aurelius Julianus son of Charidemos, twice Asiarch, crown bearer, temple warden of the Augusti (*Sebastoi*), and bacchant (*bacchos*) of the god. They did this

Figure 14
Bust of emperor Marcus Aurelius, now in the Ephesos Museum in Vienna
(photo by Harland).

because of his piety toward the god and goodwill toward the homeland in
everything, the greatness of the works which he prepared for it, and his
disposition. This took place when Menophilos Amerimnos son of Metrophanes was treasurer and Aphrodisios Paulus son of Phoibion was supervisor of works.

194. List of Donors (Including Judeans) for Building Projects

Smyrna find location, from Smyrna or perhaps from the vicinity
of Erythrai (Ionia). *ISmyrna* 697 = *IGRR* IV 1431 = *SEG* 32 (1982),
no.1203 = PH254946.

ca. 124 CE

Slab of white marble, in the Ashmolean Museum at Oxford. There
has been some scholarly debate regarding the phrase *hoi pote Ioudaioi* (here translated "those formerly from Judea"), with some
suggesting that these were apostate Jews and others suggesting a
geographical understanding of the term (in reference to immigrants). For a discussion of the debate and an argument for the geographical understanding, see Harland (2009, 150–52).

. . . during Euarestos' sixth time in overseeing the temple, when he was
serving as commander, the following were supplied: Claudius Bassos,

director of contests of the festival of Nemesis, paved the basilica; Fuscus did work worth seventy thousand denarii; Chersiphron the Asiarch contributed toward the gardens in the palm grove; Lucius Pompeius contributed fifty thousand toward the palm grove; Lucius Vestinus paved the basilica which is near the Council's meeting place and had the bronze door made; Smaragdos the civic president had the temple of Tyche built in the palm grove; Claudianus the civic president gilded the roof of the place of anointing in the elders' gymnasium and provided the columns along with the bases and capitals for the thank offering in the temple; Nymphidia the priestess, Claudia Artemulla, Claudia Polla, Claudia daughter of Neiketes, Theudianos the crown bearer for the second time, Flavia Asklepiake, Isidoros the sophist, Antonia Magna, Claudius Aristion, and Albidia Magna contributed ten thousand; Claudia Hedeia contributed ten thousand; Claudia Charis contributed ten thousand; Claudius Leontion contributed ten thousand; Claudia Aurelia contributed fifty-two toward the kymbellitic marble columns along with the bases and capitals in the palm grove; those formerly from Judaea (*hoi pote Ioudaioi*) contributed ten thousand; Metrodoros son of Neikanor contributed seven thousand five hundred toward the palm grove; and, Murdius Caecilianus contributed twenty thousand.

Also, because of Antonius Polemon, we were successful in gaining from lord Caesar Hadrian a second senatorial decree in which we have become twice temple warden, as well as sacred contests, immunity, theologians (*theologoi*), hymn singers (*hymnōdoi*), 1,500,000 denarii, and columns for the place of anointing, including seventy-two made from Synnadian marble, twenty from Numidian stone, and six from purple stone. And the sun room in the gymnasium was supplied by Sextos the high priest.

195. Regulations of a Sanctuary of the God Dionysos Bromios

Smyrna (Ionia). *ISmyrna* 728 = Reinhold Merkelbach and Josef Stauber, *Steinepigramme aus dem griechischen Osten, Band 1: Die Westküste Kleinasiens von Knidos bis Ilion* (Stuttgart: Teubner, 1998), 502 = Jaccottet 2003, vol. 2, no. 126 = PH255128.

Second century CE

Slab of white marble with the beginning and ending of the inscription missing, in the Reichsmuseum in Leiden. The inscription is in verse.

. . . son of Menandros, the revealer of the god (*theophantēs*), set this up. All who pass through the sanctuary and shrines of Bromios ("Thunderer") should refrain from the exposure of newborn infants for forty days, so that wrath does not ensue. Likewise a woman is to refrain from abortion (or: miscarriage) for as many days. Now if death and fate descends on someone in the household, perform the rites outside the gateway of the household after one third of the month (i.e., ten days), and if some defilement comes from other households, stay away three days after encountering a decaying corpse. Nor should those wearing black clothing approach the altars of the lord, nor should anyone lay hands on un-offered sacrifices (or: nor should anyone lay hands on sacrifices that are unfit for offering) pertaining to sacred things, nor bring an egg into the Bacchic festivities, especially during the banquets, nor offer a heart on the sacred altars . . . also abstain from mint, which Demeter (?) scattered (?) . . . make a proclamation about the Titans to the initiates (*mystai*) . . . and it is not lawful to rattle the reeds . . . thrown, by whom the initiates . . . sacrifices . . . nor carry. . . .

196. Family Grave of Rufina the Head of the Synagogue

Smyrna (Ionia). *IJO* II 43 = *CIJ* 741 = *ISmyrna* 295 = PH255755.

Second to third century CE

Slab of marble.

Rufina, Judean head of the synagogue, prepared the burial niche for her freedmen and house slaves. No one else has the authority to bury anyone else here. Now if anyone dares to do so, he will pay fifteen hundred denarii to the most holy treasury and one thousand denarii to the people (*ethnē*) of the Judeans. A copy of this inscription was stored in the archives.

197. Family Grave with Fines for Violation Payable to the Porters

Smyrna (Ionia). *ISmyrna* 204 = *IGRR* IV 1459 = PH255205.

ca. 150–200 CE

Slab of marble found on the slope of mount Pagus, now in the Epigraphical Museum in Athens.

Publius Aelius Nikostratos prepared the grave for himself, his wife, his children, their descendants, and house slaves. It is not lawful for anyone to sell or to transfer ownership of the grave. But if anyone does these things, he will pay two hundred fifty denarii to the porters around "the jug" (likely a topographical nickname). A copy of this inscription is stored in the archive in Smyrna.

198. Dedication of an Altar for the Fellow Hymn Singers of Hadrian

Smyrna (Ionia). *ISmyrna* 595 = *IGRR* IV 1436 = *SEG* 26 (1986), no. 1299 = PH255002.

ca. 200 CE

Column of white marble.

. . . *Name*, hymn singer (*hymnnōdos*) . . . by the ancestors, son of Gaius Claudius Pompeius, member of the Council and civic president, descendant of Gaius Claudius Valerius Licinnianus, priest of Asklepios and chief of police of the Olympic games at Pisa, has set up the altar for the genuine fellow hymn singers (*synymnōdoi*) of god Hadrian.

199. Reserved Seating for an Association of Porters Devoted to Asklepios

Smyrna (Ionia). *ISmyrna* 713 = *IGRR* IV 1414 = PH254989.

225 CE

Block of gray marble.

For good fortune! According to the decree of the most excellent Council and by the confirmation of the illustrious proconsul Lollianus Avitus, four seats in a row have been given to the porters (*phortēgoi*) devoted to Asklepios from the trading station. This was done when Aurelius Aphrodisios was treasurer.

200. Honors by Initiates of Demeter for a Benefactor

Smyrna (Ionia) perhaps. *ISmyrna* 655 = *CIG* 3194 = PH255068.

Undated

Base of a statue depicting a crowned man wearing a toga.

The synod of initiates (*mystai*) of the great goddess before the city, Demeter Thesmophoros ("Law Bringer"), honored Metrodoros Matreas son of Hermogenes, son of Metrodoros, fellow witness of *Name* . . . the crown bearer.

201. Common Grave of a Guild of Flax Workers

Smyrna (Ionia). *ISmyrna* 218 = PH255722.

Undated

Slab of coarse marble, now in the Ashmolean Museum at Oxford.

Epaphroditos son of Hapalos, son of Perigenes, prepared for the association (*symbiōsis*) of flax workers (*syppinadoi*) this vault, located on the right-hand side for those who approach the tomb. If anyone has been approved for membership, he will be placed in this vault by the guild (*synergasia*).

Caria

202. Oracle from Delphi on the Introduction of Dionysiac Societies to Magnesia

Magnesia on the Maeander (Caria). *IMagnMai* 215 = *SEG* 17 (1977), no. 495 = Jaccottet 2003, vol. 2, no. 146 = PH260765 (A) + PH260613 (B).

ca. 150 CE (dealing with supposed incidents in the fourth or third century BCE)

> Slab of marble. In the mid-second century CE, an initiate has a supposedly ancient oracular response (which likely places itself in the fourth or first half of the third century BCE) reengraved. This consultation of Apollo at the oracle at Delphi results in the establishment of associations at Magnesia headed by maenads (lit. "mad women" or "raving women," attendants of Dionysos). In some versions of mythology, the archetypal maenad Ino (a daughter of Kadmos, founder of Thebes) was considered the foster mother of Dionysos. A monument from the Villa Quintiliana in Rome depicts a maenad leading two satyrs in a procession for the god Dionysos (figure 15).

(A) For good fortune! When Akrodemos son of Dioteimos was civic president (*prytanis*), the Magnesian People consulted the god concerning the sign which occurred: An image of Dionysos was discovered in a plane tree, located opposite the city, which made a loud piercing sound caused by the wind. What does this mean? Why does it continue? For this reason, the oracular messengers Hermonax son of Epikrates and Aristarchos son of Diodoros were sent to the Delphians.

The god answered: Magnesians, who obtained the holy city on the Maeander, defenders of our possessions: You came to hear from my mouth what the appearance of Bacchus in the bush means for you. He appeared as a youth, when the clear-aired city was founded but well-cut temples were not yet built for Dionysos.

Do the following, oh exceedingly strong people: Dedicate temples which delight in the wand (*thyrsos*) and appoint

Figure 15
*Relief of a maenad and two satyrs in a procession for Dionysos, from the Villa Quintiliana in Rome (ca. 100 CE), now in the British Museum (**202**; photo by Harland).*

a perfect and sacred priest. And come onto Thebes' holy ground, so that you may receive maenads from the race of Ino daughter of Kadmos. They will also give to you good rites (*orgia*) and customs (*nomima*) and will consecrate Bacchic societies (*thiasoi*) in the city.

According to the oracle, by way of the oracular messengers, the three maenads, Kosko, Baubo, and Thettale, were brought from Thebes: Kosko gathered together the society (*thiasos*) of the plane tree, Baubo the society before the city, and Thettale the society of Kataibatai. They died and were buried by the Magnesians: Kosko lies at the Hill of Kosko, Baubo in Tabarnis, and Thettale near the theater.

(B) This is dedicated to the god Dionysos. Apollonios Mokolles, ancient initiate, had this ancient oracle inscribed upon a slab together with the altar.

203. Donations by Initiates of the God Dionysos in the Village of Klidon

Magnesia on the Maeander (Caria). *IMagnMai* 117 = *SEG* 17 (1977), no. 496 = Jaccottet 2003, vol. 2, no. 147 = PH260567.

Second century CE

> Block of marble found west of the gymnasium. This inscription documents donors who left funds to the Dionysiac association upon their deaths. Several mention the title or position that the person had held within the group, and these seem to be closely associated with the mythology of Dionysos, including a "nurse" and two "papas" or foster fathers of Dionysos. The foster father Silenos (who is not expressly mentioned) was often pictured as an old man who adopted and cared for the baby Dionysos.

When Claudia Appia Tatiane was crown-bearer, . . . *Name* son of Philetos, the head initiate (*archimystēs*) along with Hermeros son of Euporos (?) arranged to record the following so as not to forget the initiates (*mystai*) who left behind funds for them as a remembrance, so that the customary offerings will be offered in the month of Leneon for them by the initiates of Klidon who meet in the sacred house (*oikos*).

Here is an indication of how much each of them left behind: Philemon the "pappa" of Dionysos: eighteen denarii; Posidonia the priestess and crown bearer: twenty-five denarii; Antiochos (?) the revealer of sacred things (*hierophantēs*): eighteen denarii; Elpis the "nurse": fifteen denarii; Agathia . . . : *x* denarii; . . . Anaxagoras (?) the "pappa": eighteen denarii. Whatever is lent out at interest by the initiates . . .

204. Honors by Civic Institutions and the Settlement of Romans for a Benefactor

Tralles (Caria). *ITrall* 80 = *CIG* 2927 = PH262950.

Post-127 CE

> No description of stone available (based on Böckh's sketch in *CIG*).

The Council, the People, and the settlement (*katoikountes*) of Romans in Tralles honored Aulus Fabricius Priscianus Charmosynus. He has been commander of the city voluntarily; he has been manager of the grain including the sixty thousand measures (*modii*) of grain from Egypt which came into his homeland by agreement with lord Caesar Trajan Hadrian Augustus; he has paid in advance from his own resources the honor of grain as well as the expenses incurred until now; and, he is a good and patriotic man adorned with every kind of virtue and trustworthiness. Even as the homeland gave witness for him many times through the honor that was granted to him in the registers and decrees of the Council and the People. This took place when Claudius was crown bearer. . . .

205. Honors by Initiates for a Priest of Isis and Sarapis

Tralles (Caria). *ITrall* 86 = *SIRIS* 295 = PH262929.

Post-132 CE

> Slab found in Aydin. The man honored in this inscription was likely a member of the Panhellenion institution at Athens, which was founded by emperor Hadrian in about 130 CE. The Panhellenion drew members from the upper echelons of Greek cities, and its focus was on preserving the cultural heritage of the Hellenes.

The initiates (*mystai*) honored the Panhellene, Julius Amyntianus, priest of Isis and Sarapis.

206. Honors by a Synod for C. Julius Philippus

Tralles (Caria). *ITrall* 50 = *OGIS* 501 = PH262933.

ca. 150–200 CE

> Base. The C. Julius Philippus in this inscription has sometimes been identified with the Asiarch Philippus (at Smyrna) mentioned in the *Martyrdom of Polycarp* (12.2).

C. Julius Philippus, procurator of the Augusti, father of Julius Philippus the senator, and praetor of the Romans. The synod (*synodos*) of those from Ionia and the Hellespont honored their own director of contests, financial auditor, and benefactor when the supervisors were Serapion II of Magnesia on Sipylos, the olympic victor, and Tib. Claudius Spercheios.

207. Honors by Linen Weavers for a Market Overseer

Tralles (Caria). *ITrall* 79 = PH262924.

Second to third century CE

> A well-preserved monument found at Utch Geuz.

The guild (*syntechnia*) of linen weavers (*linyphoi*) honored Eutyches, the most remarkable and sole market overseer through the whole year.

Lycia, Pamphylia, and Pisidia

208. Honors by Milyadians, Roman Businessmen, and Thracian Settlers for Augustus

Milyas area, Kozluca (Pisidia). *SEG* 36 (1986), no. 1207 = *AÉ* (1986), no. 688 = PH282515.

5–4 BCE

Three blocks of white limestone.

The Milyadians, the Romans engaged in business alongside them, and the Thracians who are settled alongside them dedicated this to Roma and emperor Caesar Augustus, son of god, high priest, with tribunician power for the nineteenth time, consul for the twelfth time, and proclaimed emperor (*imperator*) for the fourteenth time, their own savior.

209. Honors by Dyers for a Benefactor of the Gladiatorial Contests

Sagalassos (Pisidia/Lycia). Louis Robert, *Les gladiateurs dans l'orient grec* (Bibliothèque de l'école des hautes études IVe section, sciences historique et philologiques; 1940; repr., Amsterdam: Adolf M. Hakkert, 1971), 142 (no. 97) = *IGRR* III 360 = PH281875.

Undated

Statue base found northwest of the temple of Antoninus.

P. Aelius Quintus Claudius Philippianus Varus, director of contests for life of the Klareian and Varian contests, high priest of Augustus, glory loving during the entire four days of the gladiatorial contests to the finish with iron weapons and each of the five days with barbed iron spears. The guild (*syntechnia*) of dyers (*bapheis*) honored their own benefactor, according to the decree of the Council and the People, when Claudius Menis was superintendent.

Cilicia and Galatia

210. Honors by Linen Workers for Emperor Hadrian

Anazarbos (Cilicia). *IAnazarbos* 3 = *IGRR* III 896 = PH311573.

136 CE

Statue base of limestone.

Emperor Caesar Trajan Hadrian Augustus, son of god Trajan Parthicus and grandson of god Nero, greatest high priest, with tribunician power for the twentieth time, proclaimed emperor (*imperator*) for the second time, consul for the third time, father of the fatherland, and benefactor of the world. The guild (*syntechnia*) of linen workers (*linourgoi*) set this up.

211. Honors by Sacred Object Bearers for Emperor Caracalla

> Anazarbos (Cilicia). *IAnazarbos* 4 = PH311574.
>
> 207 CE
>
>> Statue base of limestone.

The sacred object bearers (*hieraphoroi*) gathered around Marcellus son of Elis, Hermogenes son of Deios, Sokrates son of Germanus, and Hermogenes son of Tiberius, the sacred object bearers of the wool-carding guild and, through them, the rest of the sacred object bearers and the porters (or: door keepers; Latin: *ostiarii*) of the industrious marketplace in the metropolis of Anazarbos—chief seat of the three provinces of Cilicia, Isauria, and Lykaonia and twice temple warden—honored emperor Caesar Marcus Aurelius Antoninus Pius Augustus, greatest high priest, with tribunician power for the tenth time, proclaimed emperor (*imperator*) for the second time, consul for the second time, son of the most divine emperor Severus, and lord and benefactor of the world.

212. Honorary Decree of the Worldwide Performers for Ulpius Aelius Pompeianus

> Ankyra (Galatia). *IAnkyraBosch* 128 = *IGRR* III 209 + 211 = PH267069.
>
> 128 CE
>
>> Pedestal of marble from the temple of Augustus at Ankyra.

For good fortune! Decree of the worldwide performers (*technitai*) gathered around Dionysos and emperor Trajan Hadrian Augustus Caesar, new Dionysos, namely, those who are crowned sacred victors, fellow contestants, and registered members of the sacred theatrical synod (or: as well as the members of the sacred theatrical synod). Since the most sacred Council established Ulpius Aelius Pompeianus as director of contests for the mystical (*mystikon*) contest, which was granted to the city by the emperor in a speedy manner. Since he accepted the appointment quickly, and he accomplished the contest in an conspicuous manner from his own resources, leaving no brilliant and generous thing undone. He confirmed the piety of the homeland toward both gods, and all the benefactions were given freely, sparing no expense. Acting very quickly, the contests were already called again, and he assisted in every part of the mystery. The prizes were being established for the synod, and the contest involving mysteries was being held because he alone preferred to do good for the city.

Therefore, for the sake of preserving honors for both the emperor and Dionysos and maintaining the contest for the city, it was resolved by us to honor the man with a statue which will be set up in the most noticeable place in the metropolis, and a separate one for the competitors will be set up in the theater as a most beautiful model of virtue for the spectators. The competitor who enters into the contest involving mysteries should adorn it (i.e., the second statue) with the crowns that are brought in. But if a competitor does not do this, he is to be excluded from the contest because of his lack of gratitude toward a virtuous man and the competitor's failure to obey the things that have been decreed by the synod. Furthermore, a statue of the man is to be set up in Neapolis. The decree will display the greatness of the man and the proper thanksgiving of the synod to the greatest emperor Caesar Trajan Hadrian Augustus and the greatest governor Trebius Sergianus.

This was brought forward by Gaius Antonius Pol . . . , comic actor and olympian victor, and has been carried to vote by Gaius Julius Collega son of Neocaesarus, incredible comic actor. The performance of the contest involving mysteries took place in the metropolis of Ankyra in Galatia when Ulpius Aelius Pompeianus was leader of the Assembly of Hellenes (helladarch), Memmius . . . was high priest, . . . Name son of Dionysios was leader of the Assembly of Hellenes (helladarch); when Titus Flavius Julianus was foremost leader, Alexandros Sopatros was secretary, . . . Name the Laodicean, cithara player and incredible victor in the Augustan games, was high priest for the third time, . . . Name son of Epoptos from the Troad, greatest victor, was legal expert; and, when Nonius Torquatus Asprenas and Marcus Annius Libo were consuls.

213. Regulations of the Sabbatists

Elaeussa Sebaste area (Cilicia). *OGIS* 573 = *LSAM* 80 = PH285719.

Late first century BCE to early first century CE (time of Augustus)

> Inscription engraved on a rock. This association of Sabbatists may or may not have some connection to the Judean Sabbath and the Judean God. In other words, they may be a group of gentile devotees of the Judean God. Sabbatistes may also be the name of a non-Judean deity. The name Aithibelios likely has an Aramaic origin or Phoenician origin.

It was resolved by the companions (*hetairoi*) and the Sabbatists (*sabbatistai*) who gathered together by the providence of the god Sabbatistes: No one is to nullify the authority of the engraved inscription. Rather, let it be strictly observed. If anyone wants to make a dedication, the one who wants to make a dedication is allowed to do so.

Protos put the motion to crown Aithibelios, the synagogue leader (*synagōgeus*). No one is allowed to leave undone, damage, or change the dedications which are in the temples and the things written on the plaques and on the dedications. If anyone does what is forbidden or fails to do what is prescribed, he will pay one hundred drachmas to the god Sabbatistes, one hundred drachmas to the Sabbastists, one hundred drachmas to the city, and one hundred drachmas to the chief ruler (*dynastēs*). Now let the monument (stele) be a record of oath. No one is to entertain during the day (perhaps the Sabbath day, if a Judean connection is involved). The priest should allocate contributions to the god for the preparation of the place.

214. Grave of an Association

Lamos/Adanda (Cilicia). *KilikiaBM* I 34 + *IKilikiaBM* II 172n38 for lines 1–6 + *IKilikiaBM* II 175n41 for line 17 = PH285154.

First century CE (before the time of Vespasian)

Built tomb on the eastern hill of Adanda.

The artisan brothers made this, Attalos son of Attalos and Meneas son of Attalos, Selgians.

The ones who have joined together, Mobrenis son of Rhondos and those with him—namely Motas son of Oxalibes, Komdi son of Oxalibes, Rhondas son of Konnis Merdoutos, Mos son of Rhondos, Mos son of Eneknes, Rhondas son of Knes—made this in agreement. May it bring good health to us. Now if we should suffer anything which is in accordance with being human (i.e., death), only our children and our wives will be buried in the above memorial monument. Now if in the course of these things time should take our relatives, the male relatives among us should be placed in the above memorial monument, and the female relatives should be placed beneath. Now if any of our female relatives is given away in marriage, do not let her be placed in this memorial. Now if anyone should do any of these forbidden things, let that one pay to the People one thousand drachmas, ten white and ten black bulls, ten rams, and ten goats. Let that one not (?) open the memorial. Let him not remove the conditions written above, nor remove the conditions by going to court, nor. . . . Now if anyone should remove another person buried here, he should pay the above stated fines. This is not a common memorial (i.e., not for use by anyone outside of this group). Now if anyone . . . (*something to do with a daughter*) . . . placed into this memorial . . . giving . . . Leonidon . . . this memorial . . . the part the ones who have joined together . . . into the base of the monument . . . our male relatives, elders, the things written above. If anyone reaches up by force . . . the things written above.

215. Grave of an Association of Selgians and Other Immigrants ("Brothers")

Lamos (Cilicia). *IKilikiaBM* II 201 = PH285220.

First century CE (before the time of Vespasian)

> Rock-cut tomb with separate coffin (sarcophagus) lid and busts of a man and a woman (?). Column b is below the left-hand bust, and column c is below the right-hand bust. This is among the clearest cases of the use of fictive sibling language ("brothers") within associations.

(*a = lines 1–20*)

Rhodon son of Kydimasas, Selgian, and those with him: Pyramos son of Pyramos, Selgian; Mindyberas son of Arestes, Selgian; Aetomeros Manis; Lylous son of Menos, Selgian; Ketomaneis son of Kibrios; Zezis son of Oubramis; Kendeis son of Zenonis; Aigylis son of Oubramis; and Dinneon son of Pigemis, Selgian. This is our common memorial and it is not lawful for anyone to bury another body here. But if anyone buries another here let him pay a pair of oxen and three mina (= one hundred drachmas) to Zeus, three mina and a pair of oxen to Apollo, and three mina to the People. But if anyone should go up and wish to sell his common ownership, it is not lawful . . .

(*b = lines 21–35*)

For it is not lawful to sell from abroad (or, possibly: sell outside the group), but let him take from the common treasury thirty coins (staters) and let him depart. But if some brother (*adelphos*) wants to sell, let the other brothers (*adelphoi*) purchase it. But if the brothers so wish, then let them receive the coins mentioned above and let them depart from the association (*koinon*). But whenever someone dies, and has no one to carry out the funeral. . . . (*fragmentary column c follows*).

216. Honors by Attabokaist Initiates for a Priest of the Great Mother

Pessinous area, near village of Sivrihisar (Galatia). *IPessinous* 17 = *OGIS* 540 = PH267445.

Second century CE

Slab of marble.

Tiberius Claudius Heras son of . . . *Name*, of the Quirina tribe, tenth after the high priest, fifth priest of the Galatians for life of the great Mother of the gods who is in Pessinous and Meidaion, six times high priest of the Augusti (*Sebastoi*) for the Assembly of the Augustan Galatians, director of contests, revealer of the Augusti (*sebastophantēs*) in the temple which is in Pessinous, having been the first priest to do so, head of the gymnasium, giving gifts freely, prefect of the Iturean cohort, twice tribune of two legions, namely the twelfth Fulminata and the third Cyrenaica. He has been honored by the Augusti (*Sebastoi*) with a pure spear and a crown for being first on the defensive wall of the enemy camp (*corona vallaris*). The Attabokaists who are initiates (*mystai*) in the mysteries of the goddess honored him. . . .

217. Dedication for Demeter Karpophoros by a Guild of Gardeners

Pessinous area, near village of Ballihisar (Galatia). *IPessinous* 22 = PH267454.

Roman imperial period

Votive slab.

For good fortune! Klaros son of Eudaimon and Akylas son of . . . *Name*, superintendents of the association (*systēma*) of gardeners (*kēpouroi*) dedicated this to goddess Demeter Karpophoros ("Fruit Bringer") using funds from the treasury.

218. Funerary Dedication to Dionysos and the Initiates

Seleucia area, between Kelendera and Seleucia (Cilicia). *IKilikiaHW* 183 = PH285461.

First to second century CE

Metrical epitaph in a wall near the graves by the theater.

Athenaios son of Chareinos dedicated this to Dionysos, head of the bacchants (*archebacchos*), and to the initiates (*mystai*) when Sopatros son of Apollonios was priest.

219. Grave of a High Priest Erected by an Association of Friends

Seleucia (Cilicia). L. Duchesne, "Les nécropoles chrétiennes de l'Isaurie," *Bulletin de correspondance hellénique* 4 (1880): 195–97 = PH285125.

Undated

The friends (*philoi*) set this up for Apollonios son of Python, the high priest, for the sake of remembrance.

GREEK ISLANDS OF THE AEGEAN

Southwestern Islands (off the coast of Attica)

220. Decree of the Milesian Settlers at Aegiale

Aegiale on Amorgos (Cyclades). *IG* XII,7 396 = *SIG*³ 866 = PH79047.

153–154 CE

> This is one of numerous inscriptions that attest to a well-organized group of Milesian immigrants on Amorgos. The association structures itself in imitation of a typical city (*polis*) and here passes a decree in honor of a well-respected deceased man.

The leaders (*archontes*), Council, and People of the Milesians who are settled (*katoikountes*) at Aegiale on Amorgos made a resolution on the proposal of the commanders and Board of Ten who have the presidential power. Serapion son of Serapion introduced the decree and Iason son of Straton put it to the vote. Aristeas son of Preimos has been a good man with respect to all the leadership positions and services which he accomplished alongside us in the homeland. He has lived a reverent and quiet life throughout his whole life, just as all the citizens have witnessed through his lovable character. Certainly that which is fixed by fate for all people has happened, as Aristeas has died while still in the prime of life, leaving behind orphaned children and grief for Aristeas' son and another infant forever. Therefore, it was resolved through the decree to comfort his children, his female relatives, and his friends in proportion to their grief, knowing that the fate which is determined for all people is inevitable.

Two decrees were inscribed concerning this, one of which was stored in the archives. This happened at Aigiale on Amorgos on the twelfth day before the first day (kalends) of the month of Dekenbrion, when Bruttius Lateranus and Junius Rufinus were consuls. Serapion son of Serapion introduced it and Iason son of Straton put it to the vote. Epikrates son of Agatheinos, leader (*archōn*) for the second time, declared and approved it.

221. Story Concerning a Temple for the Egyptian God Sarapis

Delos (Cyclades). *IG* XI,4 1299 = *SIG*² 663 = *SEG* 24 (1974), no. 1158 = PH63784.

ca. 200 BCE

> Free-standing column found in the courtyard of the building iden-
> tified as "Sarapieion A," now in the Archaeological Musem at Delos
> (inv. no. E 767). Other inscriptions from Delos refer to a group that
> met in this small temple as "the ones who serve" (*hoi therapeuontes*)
> the god (*IG* XI,4 1217 and 1290), a variant on the "therapeutists"
> attested elsewhere in this volume. There were at least two other
> structures dedicated to Sarapis on Delos: Sarapieion B, where sev-
> eral associations met, and Sarapieion C, a larger civic temple. Only
> the first, prose part of this inscription (lines 1–28) is translated here;
> lines 29–94 present a poetic retelling of the same events in hexa-
> meter verse.

The priest Apollonios [II] inscribed this according to the command of the god. For our grandfather, Apollonios, an Egyptian from the priestly class, having brought his god with him from Egypt, continued serving (*therapeuōn*) his god according to ancestral custom and, it seems, lived for ninety-seven years. My father, Demetrios, followed him in serving the gods and, because of his piety, he was honored by the god with a bronze image which was set up in the temple (*naos*) of the god. He lived for sixty-one years.

After receiving the sacred things and being appointed to perform the services (*therapeiai*) in a diligent manner, the god instructed me through a dream that I should dedicate his own temple of Sarapis (*Sarapieion*), and that he was not to be in rented rooms anymore. Furthermore, he would find the place where the temple should be located, indicating this by a sign. And this is what happened. For there was this place full of manure which was advertised for sale on a small notice on a passage to the marketplace. Now since the god willed it, a contract of purchase was completed and the temple was quickly built in six months.

Now certain people conspired against us and the god. They sought a judgment against the temple and myself in a public trial, seeking either punishment or a fine. But the god promised me in a dream that we would win the case. Now that the proceedings have ended and we have won as is worthy of the god, we praise the gods by demonstrating appropriate gratitude.

*The remainder of the inscription (lines 29–94) is a poetic
retelling and expansion of the incidents above in the form
of a hymn. In its description of the temple, the hymn mentions "seats and dining couches" which were installed
"for the feast to which the god invites us." The hymn also
expands on a description of the victory at the trial which,
the hymn claims, was a result of Sarapis himself paralyz-
ing the opponents as if they were statues that could not
utter the charges. The hymn also mentions that there was
a mixed crowd of foreigners (xenoi) attending the trial,
which took place within the temple itself.*

222. Honors by Israelites for Benefactors

Delos (Cyclades). *IJO* I Ach 66 and 67 = *SEG* 32 (1982), 810 and
809 = *NewDocs* VIII 12b and *NewDocs* VIII 12a = PH215712 and
PH215711.

ca. 250–175 BCE (A); ca. 150–50 BCE (B)

Slabs of white marble with large wreaths.

(A) The Israelites on Delos who contribute toward the holy temple
on (or: contribute toward sacred and holy) Gerizim honored
Menippos son of Artemidoros from Herakleia, himself and
his descendants, who furnished and dedicated from his own
resources on account of a prayer (*proseuchē*) of God (or: in
fulfillment of a vow to God; or: for the prayer house of God)
. . . (*about two lines missing*) and they crowned him with a
gold crown and . . . (*the rest of inscription missing*).

(B) The Israelites on Delos who contribute to the temple on (or:
to sacred) Gerizim crown with a gold crown Sarapion son of
Jason from Knossos because of his beneficence toward them.

223. Honorary Decree of Tyrian Immigrants for a Member and Priest

Delos (Cyclades). *IDelos* 1519 = *IDelosChoix* 85 = PH63955.

153/152 BCE

Delian marble, now in the Louvre. This honorary decree was passed
by an association of immigrants from Tyre in Phoenicia for a fellow member of the association. Several different terms for an "association," "gathering," or "meeting" are used in this decree (e.g.,

ekklēsia, thiasos, synodos, koinon), and it is not always clear how to sort out the relations or distinctions between these different designations. Some terms likely designate subgroups within the broader association.

When Phaidrias was civic leader (*archōn* in Athens) on the eighth of the month of Elaphebolion, during an assembly (*ekklēsia*) in the temple of Apollo:

Dionysios son of Dionysios the head of the society (*archithiasitēs*) said: Since Patron son of Dorotheos, who is a member of the synod (*synodos*), approached the assembly and reaffirmed his existing goodwill toward the synod, and because he has fulfilled numerous needs without hesitation and continues to speak and do what is advantageous both for the association (*koinon*) and for the synod all the time in accordance with his own existing goodwill toward everyone of the merchants and shippers who sail on the sea. Now adding even more goodwill with the goodwill of the gods, he invited the association to dispatch an embassy to the People of the Athenians in order that it might grant to them a place in which to build a sanctuary of Herakles, the cause of the greatest good things that happen to people and the founder of our original homeland. Being chosen ambassador to the Council and the People of Athens, he sailed, readily taking upon himself the expenses from his own resources and demonstrating the goodwill of the synod toward the People. In this way he accomplished the will of the society members (*thiasitai*) and increased honor for the gods, just as it suited him. He spoke often and in a manner demonstrating love of humanity at suitable times and he also spoke appropriate things on the synod's behalf at the most pressing moment with every kindness and with love of honor, and he received the society (*thiasos*) for two days on behalf of his son.

Therefore, in order that he may provide in the future without being asked and the synod may display its consideration for people who show goodwill toward it by returning appropriate favors to benefactors, and in order that still other people may become zealous admirers of the synod because of the thanks shown toward that person and in order that those who show love of honor may compete for the favor of the synod: For good fortune! It was resolved by the association of the Tyrian Herakleists of merchants and shippers to praise Patron son of Dorotheos and to crown him with a gold crown each year during the performance of the sacrifices to Poseidon on account of the virtue and goodness which he continues to have toward the association of the Tyrian merchants and shippers. It was also resolved to set up a painted image of him in the sanctuary of Herakles and in another place where he decides. Let him be free of paying his share and free from service with regard to everything that happens in the synods. Let the appointed leaders of the society, the treasurers, and the secretary take care of proclaiming the following proclamation during the sacrifices as they are taking place and in the synods: "The synod of the Tyrian merchants and shippers crown Patron son of Dorotheos, the benefactor." Let them write this decree on a stone plaque and let them set it up in the sanctuary of Herakles, and let the treasurer and the head of the society share the cost of this.

This was done when Dionysios son of Dionysios was leader of the society and Patron son of Dorotheos was priest.

The People of Athens. The synod of Tyrian merchants and shippers.

224. Honors by Berytian Immigrants for a Roman Banker

Delos (Cyclades). *IDelos* 1520 = Tod 1934 = PH63956.

Post-153/152 BCE

> This decree by immigrants from Berytos (Beirut) in Phoenicia honors a Roman banker. As with the Tyrian decree (above), numerous terms are used for the group or its meetings. See **B8** for information on the meeting place of the Berytians, which had several shrines dedicated to Poseidon, Roma, and likely Melqart and Astarte.

(*Lines 1–5*)

For good fortune! When . . . *Name* was civic leader (*archōn*) . . . decision of the association (*koinon*) of Berytian, Poseidoniast merchants, shippers, and warehouse workers. Since the synod (*synodos*) was in need of one who would contribute toward the completion of the building (*oikos*) and toward the payment of the common funds for the synod. In order that not only the things which were decreed would be completed properly, but also that others, observing how easy it is to deal with the synod, may themselves contribute toward what is advantageous for the common fund.

(*Lines 6–20*)

Marcus Minatius son of Sextus, Roman, is a noble and good man, acting piously toward the gods and glory loving in relation to the synod, displaying love of glory both to individuals and to the association (*koinon*) in such a way that the plan of the association may be fulfilled and the building may be completed according to what was previously decreed. He contributed the interest, which was considerable, and contributed what was gathered together, from which he made an advance of money for the ones who were chosen to carry out the construction of the sanctuary. Following this, he also made a voluntary contribution of seven thousand drachmas to the association on his own. Furthermore, he also invited all of us to the sacrifice, which he prepared for the gods to be accomplished for the synod, and he invited us to the banquet. He also promised that for the future he would always have the same inclination to be a contributing cause of something good for the association (*koinon*), in order that the synod may appear to be honoring good men, never neglecting any opportunity to return favor.

(*Lines 20–34*)

For good fortune! It was resolved by the association to praise Marcus Minatius son of Sextus, Roman, and to accept the promise he made in a friendly way, since he is a glory-seeking person. The association will also grant him a place chosen by him in the courtyard for setting up his statue, or in whatever other place he may decide, except a place in the temples, the porticos, and the sacred place—whatever he may want for the setting up of the portrait. The following will be inscribed on the statue: "The association of Berytian, Poseidoniast merchants, shippers and warehouse workers set this up for Marcus Minatius son of Sextus, Roman banker, their own benefactor on account of the virtue and goodwill which he continues to have toward the association." And the same inscription will accompany the portrait. Let him also be assigned a dining couch with that of the sacrificer during the festivities in honor of Poseidon and the foremost dining couch in all the other synods.

(*Lines 34–53*)

Also, let one day each year be celebrated for him on the day following the procession of the festivities in honor of Apollo, and let him invite two people of his choice. Now a gold crown will be placed upon him, upon him who "crowned" the synod. Let the following be proclaimed during the festivities in honor of Poseidon: "The association crowns Marcus Minatius son of Sextus with a gold crown on account of the virtue and goodwill which he continues to have toward the association. For good fortune!" Furthermore, proclaim the following on the same day: "The association crowns Marcus Minatius son of Sextus and celebrates a day in his honor, both now and forever, on account of the virtue and goodwill which he continues to have toward the association. For good fortune!" And in the monthly synods proclaim: "The association crowns Marcus Minatius son of Sextus with a gold crown, being a benefactor of the synod. For good fortune!" Let the proclamations of the crowns always be done in front of the people. Also let him bring one guest to each procession. Let him be free from service in every office and every expenditure. Let a bull be brought on his behalf for the procession during the festivities in honor of Apollo each year for all time. The inscription on the bull (?) should be as follows: "The association of Berytian Poseidoniasts on behalf of Marcus Minatius son of Sextus."

(*Lines 53–69*)

Now, in order that the honors being given by the synod to Marcus may remain for all time in accordance with the rule, let there be many emulators to display love of glory toward the synod, who know that the synod is useful and that it not only decrees appropriate honors for benefactors but eagerly promotes them. This is essential in order that the honors given to benefactors may continue forever. It is not permitted for anyone, whether a common man or a ruler, to say or to write something as though it is necessary to change the honors which have been given, or to take away or invalidate anything arranged to be done in the decree, neither the one who has written such things, nor the one who has said such things, nor the one who has read such things, nor the one who has proposed such things, nor the one who has voted such things. May anyone who has written or proposed something contrary to this be completely destroyed, both him and his children. Now let the ones who watch for violations have enjoyment of life, children, and possessions, and may they be kept safe by land and by sea. Also let the one who does these things that are forbidden pay six thousand drachmas with crowns pressed on them that are sacred to Poseidon and let that one be liable for the wrong that was done. Likewise let the head of the society (*archithiasitēs*) who does not follow the commands pay the same penalty and be liable for the wrong that was done.

(*Lines 69–81*)

Let the treasurers in leadership at the time pay the herdsmen, who were chosen according to the law, one hundred and fifty drachmas for the processional bull on behalf of Marcus, and let them pay another hundred and fifty drachmas for the reception which the association holds each year on behalf of Marcus. Now let the herdsmen who receive the money written above lead the bull in procession and let them do the same for the banquet according to the decree. Let them (i.e., the treasurers) provide a written account of what funds they managed in the first meeting after the reception. But if any of the chosen herdsmen does not do any of the things ordered for them to do, let that one pay one thousand sacred drachmas of Poseidon and let him be liable for the wrong that was done.

(*Lines 81–96*)

Now let those who do not do what is recorded in the decree also be subject to a curse, and let any member of the society who wants to accuse them do so, for this is permitted for them. Let the one in leadership as head of the society at the time bring in the prosecutor and the defendant, and let him distribute a pebble for voting to the members of the society . . . (*one or two words missing*) let the culprit be accused (?) by the one bringing the accusation, who will be given one third of the fine which has been paid. But if the head of the society does not do something as stipulated here, let him be prosecuted concerning these things when he is no longer an official

of the association. Let the head of the society have the decree inscribed on
a white plaque and let it be placed in the courtyard . . . this was done when
Phaidrios was civic leader (*archōn*). . . . Let those in leadership as treasurers at the time pay the expense for these things.

225. Dedication of a Statue Group by a Berytian Immigrant

Delos (Cyclades). *IDelos* 1783 = PH64223.

After 153 BCE

> Base for a statue group of Aphrodite, Eros, and Pan.

Dionysios son of Zenon and grandson of Theodoros, Berytian, benefactor,
dedicated this to the ancestral gods on behalf of himself and his children.

226. Dedication of a Statue to the Goddess Roma by the Berytians

Delos (Cyclades). *IDelos* 1778 = *OGIS* 591 = PH64218.

130–69 BCE

> Statue base of marble found in a northern room of the Berytians'
> building.

The association of Berytian Poseidoniast merchants, shippers, and warehouse workers dedicated this to the goddess Roma, benefactor, on account
of the goodwill which she has in relation to the association and the homeland. This was done when Mnaseas son of Dionysios, benefactor, was head
of the society (*archithiasitēs*) for the second time. Menandros son of Melas,
Athenian, made this.

227. Dedication of an Altar to Roma by the Berytians

Delos (Cyclades). *IDelos* 1779.

130–69 BCE

> Plaque on the back of an altar from the meeting place of the
> Berytians.

The association of Berytian Poseidoniast merchants, shippers, and warehouse workers. Altar of Roma. This was done when Dionysios son of Sosi-
pater was head of the society (*archithiasitēs*).

228. Honors by Berytians for the Praetor Gnaeus Octavius

Delos (Cyclades). *IDelos* 1782 = PH64222.

Pre-128 BCE, or pre-87 BCE

> Slab of blue marble discovered in a building southwest of the meeting place of the Berytians.

The association of the Berytian Poseidoniast merchants, shippers and warehouse workers in Delos set this up for Gnaeus Octavius son of Gnaeus, praetor of the Romans, benefactor.

This was done when Gorgias son of Apollodoros was head of the society (*archithiasitēs*).

229. Renovation of a Temple for the Pure Goddess by an Association of Syrians

Delos (Cyclades). Gérard Siebert, "Sur l'histoire du sanctuaire des dieux syriens a Délos," *Bulletin de correspondance hellénique* 92 (1968): 359–74.

166–88 BCE

> Slab of blue marble found southwest of the sanctuary of the Syrian gods. Numerous other inscriptions from the final decades of the second century BCE attest to a cult of Syrian deities on Delos centered around the worship of a goddess called variously "Pure Goddess," "Pure Aphrodite," "Pure Aphrodite, the Syrian Goddess," or "Atargatis, Pure Goddess" (see *IDelos* 2220–2304).

The priest, Nikon son of Apollonios, and the priestess, his wife Onesako daughter of Xenon, arranged for the reconstruction of the previously existing building (*oikos*), by which it was separated from the area of the temple of Sarapis (or: which was extended as far as the temple of Sarapis), on behalf of themselves and their children as a thanksgiving to Hagne Thea ("Pure Goddess"). The association (*koinon*) of society members (*thiasitai*) of Syrians which the goddess gathers together on the twentieth day of the month have also made a collection toward the renovation of the building in the amount of fifty Delian drachmas.

230. Honors by Alexandrian Warehouse Workers for a Ptolemaic Governor of Cyprus

Delos (Cyclades). *IDelos* 1528 = PH63964.

Post-127 BCE

Krokos, the kinsman of King Ptolemy (VIII [?]), his sister Queen Cleopatra, and his wife Cleopatra, naval leader, absolute highest commander, and high priest of the temples at Cyprus. The synod (*synodos*) of the elder warehouse workers (*egdocheis*) from Alexandria honored him on account of his goodwill and justice toward their synod and toward the other foreigners, dedicating this to Apollo, Artemis, and Leto.

231. Dedication to Apollo by the Italian Apolloniasts

Delos (Cyclades). *IDelos* 1730 = *IDelosChoix* 97 = PH64170.

ca. 125 BCE

> Round base of gray-blue marble found in the marketplace of the Competaliasts in the south end by the portico of Philip.

Quintus Tullius son of Quintus, Marcus Paconius son of Lucius, Lucius Mamilius son of Lucius, Decimus Fulvius son of Quintus, Marcus Granius son of Marcus, Lucius Maecius son of Lucius, who are the Apolloniasts, dedicated this to Apollo.
Ammonios son of Zopyros made this.

232. Dedication to the Gods Hermes (Mercury) and Maia (Maiae) by the Italian Hermaists

Delos (Cyclades). *IDelos* 1733 = *IDelosChoix* 96 = PH64173.

ca. 125 BCE

> Slab of marble found in the south end of the marketplace of the Competaliasts by the portico of Philip. Bilingual inscription with Latin and Greek. Two of those named in the inscription are freedmen of two former owners, who are brothers. The translation is from the Greek, with clarifications from the Latin in parentheses.

Marcus Pactomeius son of Marcus (Pactomeius), Marcus Toscenius Nobilior son of Lucius, Decimus Fulvius son of Decimus, Decimus Gessius son of Decimus, Publius Granius, (freedman) of Aulus (Granius) and Publius (Granius), Lucius Arellius (freedman) of Lucius and Aulus. The Hermaists dedicated this to Hermes and Maia (Mercury and Maiae).

233. Dedication to the God Poseidon (Neptune) by the Italian Poseidoniasts

Delos (Cyclades). *IDelos* 1751 = *IDelosChoix* 98 = PH64191.

ca. 125 BCE

> Block of white marble found north of the marketplace of Theophrastos. Bilingual Latin and Greek inscription. The Latin portion of the inscription clarifies the fact that one of the honorees is a freedman.

Maraeus Gerillanus son of Statius, Gaius Laronius son of Gaius, Gaius Licinius freedman of Gaius, Publius Tutorius Antiochus. The Poseidoniasts (Latin: Neptunales) dedicated this to Poseidon (Neptune, in the Latin).

234. Dedication of a Temple of Herakles by the Oil Merchants

Delos (Cyclades). *IDelos* 1713 = PH64153.

ca. 100 BCE

The oil-merchants (*elaiopōlai*) dedicated the temple and the statue of Herakles, when the appointed supervisors were Zenon and Theon, sons of Hermon, both of Elea, and Publius Plotius Patron, and Posidippos son of Titus of Herakleia, and Eirenaios son of Zoilos of Azetium, and Sporius Arius son of Decimus, Roman, . . . Menekles son of Pankratos . . . Dedicated to Herakles and Hermes.

235. Membership List of the Competaliasts

Delos (Cyclades). *IDelos* 1760 = PH64200.

ca. 100–98 BCE

> Base of white marble found in the round building in the marketplace of the Competaliasts.

Damas Clavius son of Manius, Thraseas Samiarius freedman of Quintus Samiarius, Agathokles Placonius, (slave) of Lucius Paconius, Alexander Babullios (slave) of Lucius Babullius, Aulus Atanius (slave) of Decimus Atanius, Apollodoros, Xenon Mundicius freedman of Lucius Mundicius and Marcus Mundicius, Stephanos . . . freedman of Quintus Name, Damonicus Maecius freedman of Quintus Maecius, Antiochos Creperius slave of Titus Creperius, Tryphon Audius slave of Lucius Audius. These are the Competaliasts who set this up in the year that Theodosios was the civic leader (*archōn*).

236. Dedication to the Gods Hermes, Dionysos, and Apollo by the Wine Merchants

Delos island (Cyclades). *IDelos* 1711 = PH64151.

98/97 BCE

The wine merchants (*oinōpolai*) dedicated this to Hermes, Dionysos, and Apollo when Medeios son of Medeios from the Piraeus was superintendent of the island and Dionysios Eupirides son of Athenobios was in charge of the trading station.

237. Dedication to the God Apollo and the Italians by an Association

Delos (Cyclades). *IDelos* 1758 = PH64198.

74 BCE

> Base of white marble found in the marketplace of the Italians, now in the British Museum (figure 16). This association is devoted to the gods Hermes, Apollo, and Poseidon.

(*left column*)

Marcus Calvius son of Aulus, Aulus Claudius son of Bacchius, Aulus Rotilius son of Lucius, Lucius Sulpicius son of Lysimachos, Marcus Plaetorius Flaccus son of Marcus, Aulus Castricius Achaios son of Decimus, Aulus Sulpicius Onesas son of Servius, Decimus Claudius Demetrios, son of Decimus.

(*right column*)

Diogenes Herakleios son of Protogenes, Sextus Oppius Zeuxis son of Nemerius, Publius Servelius Epagathos son of Aulus, Titus Clodius Tryphon son of Gaius, who are Hermaists, Apolloniasts, and Poseidoniasts,dedicated this to Apollo and to the Italians, when Lucius Licinius Lucullus and Marcus Aurelius Cotta were consuls.

Figure 16
Monument dedicated "to Apollo and the Italians" from Delos
(**237**; *photo by Harland*).

238. Honors by Athenians and a Synod of Pompeiasts for Pompey

Delos (Cyclades). *IDelos* 1641 = PH64080.

Post-65 BCE

The People of the Athenians and the synod of the Pompeiasts who are in Delos honored Gnaeus Pompeius son of Gnaeus, great absolute ruler, dedicating this to Apollo, Artemis, and Leto (?). This was done when Zenon son of Zenon was leader (*archōn*) of the synod and Aulus Calvius was leader of the gathering (*synagōgeus*) for life, and L. Dionysios son of Lenaeus, public servant (or: public official), was secretary of the synod for the third time.

239. Honors by Shippers for a Nikaian from Bithynia

Delos (Cyclades). *IDelos* 1705 = PH64145.

Undated

The merchants (*emporoi*) and shippers (*nauklēroi*) who sail into Bithynia honored Meleagros son of Zmertomaros from Nicaea, on account of the goodness he has shown toward them, dedicating this to Apollo, Artemis, and Leto.

240. Grave Set Up by an Association

Euboea, town of Eretria (Cyclades). *SEG* 50 (2000), no. 876.

ca. 150 BCE

> Slab of marble with a triangular top set up by a group that cele-
> brated its rituals on the eighth day of each month, perhaps on a day
> sacred to Poseidon.

. . . of the living. The association (*koinon*) of eighth-day worshippers set this up for Zoilos son of Theophilos.

241. Statue Base of the Association of Followers of Amphias

Euboea, town of Eretria (Cyclades). *SEG* 31 (1981), no. 807 = PH323310.

ca. 150 BCE

> Statue base of marble.

The association (*koinon*) of Amphiasts set this up for Amphias son of Aristodemos and dedicated it to Asklepios and Hygieia ("Health" as a goddess).

242. Herm Set Up by Members of a Friendship Association

Tenos (Cyclades). *IG* XII,5 912 = *CIG* 2339b = PH78269.

Undated

> A marble herm (now missing its head) with the inscription engraved on the torso and around and below the genitalia. A herm, which derives its name from the god Hermes, is a plain rectangular monument with sculpted head and genitalia.

For good fortune! When Apollonides was chief sailor, Protion was messenger, Damon was secretary, and Pythion was sacred physician, this was set up by the friends (*philoi*): Tauros, Hierax, Moschos the younger, Neiketes son of Perigenes, Tryphon son of Neiketes, Flavius son of Zoilos—a friendship association (*symbiōsis philia*).

243. Regulation of the Association of Epikteta's Relatives

Thera (Cyclades). *IG* XII,3 330 = *LSCG* 135 = Laum 1914, II 43–52 (no. 43) = PH75847.

210–195 BCE

> Four plaques of marble that were attached to a base that supported four statues, with an inscription engraved in eight columns. Engraved crowns decorate the top and bottom of each plaque. The "Mouseion" mentioned here is a sanctuary dedicated to the Muses, which also seems to have housed memorial buildings for deceased family members.

(*Part A: Identification of Statues*)

Phoenix son of *Name* (?) . . . Andragoras son of Phoenix. Epikteta daughter of Grinnos. Kratesilochos son of Phoenix.

(*Part B: Testament of Epikteta*)

During the presidency of those associated with Phoiboteles, Epikteta daughter of Grinnos, acting with her guardian, Hypereides son of Thrasyleon, and with the consent of her daughter Epiteleia, being in sound mind and knowingly, has made the following will: While I am in good health and alive, I shall administer what belongs to me. But if I should die, I leave behind what is outlined here. This is done in accordance with the instructions given to me by my husband Phoenix, who also built the Mouseion for our deceased son, Kratesilochos; who brought the statues and images of himself and of Kratesilochos and the heroic monuments; and, who asked that I complete the construction of the Mouseion and place the statues of the Muses, the images, and the heroic monuments there.

Two years later, after my only remaining son Andragoras died, Andragoras ordered that I complete the instructions of his father Phoenix and that I set up an image and a heroic monument for him (Andragoras), as for his father and his brother; establish a men's association (*koinon*) consisting of relatives; and give to this men's association three thousand drachmas as income, from the time that they are established. Therefore, since everything has been completed and established in accordance with those instructions, and the association of relatives has been established, whose names are subscribed, so that the association may assemble in the Mouseion, I am giving three thousand drachmas to the previously indicated men's association of relatives. These funds are owed on the lands that I own and acquired on my own in Melainai . . . when they inherit . . . I leave the Mouseion and the sacred enclosure of the Heroon to my daughter Epiteleia, so that, when she has received the income of all of my possessions, she shall pay each year in the month of Eleusinios the sum of two hundred ten drachmas to the men's association of relatives.

No one shall have the authority to sell the Mouseion, the sacred enclosure of heroic monuments, the statues that are in the Mouseion or in the sacred enclosure of heroic monuments, or to mortgage, change, or remove them in any way at all, or to fabricate some pretext, or to build anything other than a stoa in the sacred enclosure. Nor can anyone use the Mouseion except if one of Epiteleia's relatives has a wedding. Otherwise, they shall be prevented by the association and the association shall have authority in whatever it does. No one shall have the authority to remove anything that is in the Mouseion. If they do, they shall be prevented by the association of relatives, and the association shall have the right to prevent it.

Andragoras, the son of my daughter, shall hold the priesthood of the Muses and the heroic monuments. If he should suffer death, then the eldest of the family of Epiteleia shall be priest.

The men's association of relatives shall assemble in the Mouseion yearly in the month of Delphinios, receiving from my successors the two hundred ten drachmas. For three days they shall designate one of them as the monthly priest, and shall sacrifice on the nineteenth of the month to the Muses; on the twentieth to the Heroes, Phoenix and Epikteta; and on the twenty-first to Kratesilochos and Andragoras. If Epiteleia or her successors do not pay the two hundred ten drachmas in the month of Eleusinios to the men's association of relatives, the produce of the previously indicated lands in Melainai shall belong to the men's association of relatives, up to the value of two hundred ten drachmas. If the successors prefer to give a security to the men's association for the three thousand drachmas also on other lands, they shall have the authority to do this when they give secure mortgages.

Subscribed are the names of the relatives that have been assembled: Hypereides son of Thrasyleon; Antisthenes son of Isokles and, by adoption, son of Grinnos; Aristodamos son of Isokles; Timesios son of Praxiteles; Euagoras son of Prokleidas; Prokleidas son of Euagoras; Kartidamas son of Prokleidas; Hagnosthenes son of Kartidamas; Prokleidas son of Alcimedon; Bolakrates son of Aglosthenes; Archinikos son of Gorgopas; Startophos son of Bolakrates; Gorgopas son of Archinikos; Gorgopas son of Echestrates; Gorgopas son of Kartidamas; Agathostratos son of Kratesilochos; Mollis son of Polymedes; Kartidamas, Kratesilochos, Dion, and Dorokleidas, sons of Agathostratos; Himertos son of Himerophon; Kritos son of Teisanor; and, Polynikos and Evagoras, sons of Soteles.

Also, the wives who live with them and their children shall be admitted, the female children as long as they are under parental authority, the males when they have reached the appropriate age, and their children under the same conditions. Also to be admitted are the women who have inherited from me, their husbands, and their children, under the same conditions as those noted above. Also to be admitted are my namesake Epikteta; my daughter Epiteleia; Mnaso and Ainesippa, the daughters of Gorgopas; Basilodika and Telisippa, the daughters of Thrasyleon; and Kallidika, the daughter of Isokles; and, their husbands. Also to be admitted are Epiteleia, daughter of Aristarchos, and her children.

Witnesses: Charon . . . , Euagoras son of Prokleidas, Antisthenes son of Isokles, who is also by adoption son of Grinnos.

(Part C: Regulation)

During the leadership of those associated with Himertos in the month of Diosthyos, Epikteta daughter of Grinnos, along with her guardian and husband of her daughter, Hypereides son of Thrasyleon, with the consent also of her daughter Epiteleia, has provided in her will three thousand drachmas for the purpose of sacrifice to the Muses and the heroes, and for a meeting (*synagōgē*) of the men's association of relatives, for which also it shall receive yearly from her descendants two hundred ten drachmas, so that there shall be a meeting for three days in the Mouseion. At the meeting, they shall prepare sacrifices for her husband Phoenix and herself, and her sons Kratesilochos and Andragoras. The one who becomes the monthly official (*epimēnios*) shall sacrifice on the first day to the Muses; on the second day to the heroes, Phoenix and Epikteta; and, on the third day to the heroes Kratesilochos and Andragoras.

For good fortune! It has been resolved to accept her (Epikteta's) proposal and to hold the meeting after the first payment and, after the meal, to pour out all of the first cup as a libation for the Muses, Phoenix, Epikteta, Kratesilochos, and Andragoras. The meeting of the men's association of relatives shall take place for three days yearly in the Mouseion in the month of Delphinios. And all persons will freely provide service once, according to descending age. Likewise, their children, who enter the association after their departure from youth (*ephebes*), will first officiate freely. Those who officiate freely shall provide imported wine, enough for three cups per person, one each for the crowning, the music, and the perfume. If someone should not officiate according to what has been written, he will pay to the association one hundred drachmas. This payment will be arranged by the administrator (*artutēr*) according to the law. Now the one who violates what has been arranged in this regard will be excluded from the association until it has been paid.

During these years of free service, the administrator will collect the revenue due to the association during the meeting, and let it be applied to the loans secured for mortgaged properties, separating a deduction sufficient for the sacrifices to the Muses and to the heroes, according to the testament. He will also set aside no more than fifteen drachmas for entertainment during the meeting. If there is no longer a person that must provide the service without charge, all members will each take his turn, by rank of age, just as it is prescribed for those that undertake it freely. Ten days before the meeting is to take place, they shall receive from the administrator fifty drachmas. But if he does not serve after having received the money, let him pay one hundred fifty drachmas, which the administrator will arrange, and let his property be seized as security, according to the law. Until it has been paid he shall not participate in the association. In this case, let the administrator provide the service and recover the cost first from the revenue. Let the banquet take place as the association decides and for the amount that it decides. If the administrator does not provide funds to the officiants according to the regulations, let the officiant complete everything and offer the sacrifice for which he is responsible. But the administrator shall owe one hundred fifty drachmas to the monthly officer he did not pay, and the right of execution on the debt shall lie with the one who did not receive the money and will be against the administrator, in accordance with a surety, in accordance with the law. And he shall not participate in the association until he pays.

Let the one officiating on the first day offer to the Muses a victim and offerings consisting of cakes made with five measures (*choinika*) of wheat and a dry cheese costing one coin (*stater*). And also let him provide crowns for the gods and all the other things necessary for the entire sacrifice. And from these things he will set aside for the gods the customary parts from the victim that are sacred, and a cake. Let the one officiating on the second day offer to the heroes Phoenix and Epikteta a victim and offerings, consisting of cakes made with five measures of wheat and a dry cheese costing one coin (*stater*). And also let him provide crowns for the heroes and all the other things necessary for the entire sacrifice. He will also set aside the customary parts of the victim that are sacred, a cake, a loaf of bread, a parax-cake, and three fish. Let the one officiating on the third day sacrifice in honor of the heroes, Kratesilochos and Andragoras, in the same manner as has been prescribed for Phoenix and Epikteta. When the officiants offer these sacrifices, they will hand over to the association all the cake and half of the entrails, and will keep the rest for themselves. The administrator will distribute the offerings to those present. If the monthly offering should be made freely, the supervisor (*epissophos*) who offers these sacrifice shall sell the remainder, in accordance with what is written; whatever it paid, the administrator shall disburse.

Let the association choose a supervisor. Let the one chosen convene a meeting annually on the second day of the festival and let him plan everything to do with the association, so that it shall be administered as it written in the testament and the law. Let him also record the official (*epimēnios*) and the administrator (*artutēr*) by age and the supervisor and the amount loaned, and if anyone does not serve as a monthly officer, the penalty he owes according to the law, or anything else that falls to him as prescribed in the law or the testament or the decisions of the association. Let him also record the income and expenditures made under his supervision and whether anything else is owed to the association. If he should not do the things set out, let him owe to the association three hundred drachmas, and he shall not participate in the association until he pays it. And the right of execution shall be with men chosen by the association by way of seizure, according to the law.

Let the chosen administrator collect what is owing to the association according to the testament and all the other things assigned to him by the supervisor. Let him hand over to the monthly official the amount prescribed in the law and also the amount collected for the sacrifices that was not spent, and anything else the association decides. Let him hand over the remainder at the meeting (*syllogos*). Now if he should not pay any of that which is prescribed or the excess funds should be handed over to the meeting, let him owe to the association twice the amount he did not give. Also, let the supervisor record in the association's record books the amount not paid as being owed double. And he shall be excluded from the association until he pays, and the right of execution shall be with men chosen for seizure, according to the law. And if he does not pay the monthy officials, the ruling shall be against him in accordance with what is written in the law.

In order that everything will be administered thoroughly according to the testament and the law and the decisions of the association for all time, and in case anyone should not act according to the law or the testament or the decisions, let the association strike a committee of elected men, however many they decide, which will ensure all things are done as decided by the association. Also let the supervisor write these things down. Now if the supervisor should choose not to write it, let the association immediately appoint a man to write it down. Let the man chosen write all the things decided by the association.

That which is decided by the majority of the association, let these things be authoritative except concerning dissolution. But concerning this let it not have authority either by oral or written request to dissolve the association or the prescribed sacrifices, or to do any harm to the association or create division or to malign anything traditional. Now if any such request is made orally or in writing, let the word or writing be invalid, and the one who spoke or wrote be expelled from the association and owe to it five hundred drachmas, and let it be done by seizure, according to the law, for all relatives who desire the same thing.

To ensure that the supervisor is approved and the one chosen writes down all things according to the law, let the meeting be convened by the leadership (ephorate) of Himertos on the tenth of the month of Diosthyos and the supervisor shall be elected. Let this supervisor write down all the things according to the law, and also take care that the law and the testament be engraved and set up on the base of the statues in the Mouseion, and be written on a writing tablet. The supervisor shall also provide a box in which the writings of the association are to be placed. Likewise the meeting will elect a male archivist (*grammatophylax*), who will receive an account from the supervisor, the writing tablet with the transcription of the law and testament, and he shall guard the box with the papyri in it, for as long as the association decides. He will also bring them to the meeting. Now if the association should choose another archivist, he shall hand over these items to the one chosen after him in the meeting for reason of accountability.

Southeastern Islands (off the coast of Caria)

244. Decree of the Syrian Immigrants Devoted to Atargatis

Astypalaia (Dodecanese). *IG* XII,3 178 = PH75690.

Late third to second century BCE

Slab of marble with an inscription in the Doric dialect.

When Ophelion son of Enation was priest and Syros son of Biettos was presiding, it was resolved by the goddess Atargatis and the meeting (*koinon*) of the society (*thiasos*) of the ancestral gods: Since Ophelion son of Enation, who has been approved by the goddess through the casting of lots, has been a priest of the ancestral gods and a good man, and since he demonstrated great zeal and love of glory both concerning the priesthood of the gods and concerning the meeting (*koinon*) of the ... (*remainder lost*).

245. Collective Graves of Associations on Kos

Kos (Dodecanese). *IKosPh* 155–58 and *SEG* 55 (2005), no. 937bis.

Individual dates given below

> The following inscriptions were found in the outer wall of a house in the village of Kermeti, which is built on part of the site of the necropolis of the ancient city of Kos.

(A) Boundary marker of the cemetery of the society (*thiasos*) of the Aphrodisiasts associated with Eutychos (*IKosPh* 155; first century BCE to first century CE).

(B) Boundary marker of the cemetery of the society (*thiasos*) of the Hermaists associated with Nikophoros son of Hermaios, the Laodicean (*IKosPh* 156; first century BCE to first century CE).

(C) Boundary marker of the cemetery of the Athenaists associated with Drakon (*IKosPh* 157; first century BCE to first century CE).

(D) Boundary marker of the cemetery of the society (*thiasos*) of the Athenaists associated with Asklepiades (*IKosPh* 158; Roman imperial period).

(E) Boundary marker of the cemetery of the society (*thiasos*) of the Homonoists (i.e., devotees of Concord personified) associated with Dositheos son of Nikanor from Damaskos (*SEG* 55 (2005), no. 937bis; third century CE).

246. Honors by Associations for a Civic Priest of the Augusti

Nisyros (Dodecanese). *IG* XII,3 104 = *IGRR* IV 1110 = PH75614.

Roman imperial period

> This partially preserved honorary monument makes reference to previous honors for Gnomagoras by various associations, including devotees of the god Hermes, Syrian immigrants devoted to

Aphrodite, devotees of Zeus Meilichios ("Gentle One"), and devotees of Dionysos.

Gnomagoras son of Dorotheos, Nisyrian, who has been a soldier on the warship which was called Euandria Sebasta; who has frequently been crowned with gold crowns by the Council; who has served as priest of the Augusti (*Sebastoi*) in Nisyros; who has served as magistrate of the People; who has been head of the gymnasium in Nisyros, supplying the oil for all the free persons and the settlers in Nisyros, as well as the resident foreigners on the thirteenth of the month; who is pleasant toward all of the associations (*koineia*) in Nisyros; who has been crowned with gold crowns numerous times by the Hermaists, by the Syrian Aphrodisiasts, and by the Milichiasts of Zeus, as well as being honored by them; and who has been crowned by the Eurythemidian Dionysiasts . . . (*the remaining lines do not survive*).

247. Dedication of a Statue of Aristombrotidas by Family Members

Rhodes, town of Kamiros (Dodecanese). *TitCam* 84 = PH193388.

Post-167 BCE

> Statue base. This dedication of a statue makes reference to previous honors granted by several associations, including those devoted to the gods Asklepios, Hermes, and Sarapis.

Aristombrotidas son of Aristombrotidas. This statue was set up by Kritoboulos son of Aristombrotidas on behalf of his brother Aristombrotidas, Nausippos son of Kritoboulos on behalf of the deity, Damaineta daughter of Kritoboulos on behalf of her husband, who has served as priest of Athena Polis ("of the City") and Zeus Polieus ("of the City") and as director of public works. Aristombrotidas has been honored and crowned with a gold crown by the Kamirians, crowned with gold crowns by the Asklepiasts who are in Kamiros, crowned with a gold crown by the Hermaists in Kamiros, crowned with gold crowns by the Sarapiasts who are in Kamiros, crowned with a gold crown by the Kouraists who are in Kytelos; and, crowned with a gold crown by those of the third district who are in Lelos.

This is dedicated to the gods.

Pythokritos and Asklepiodoros son of Zenon, Rhodians, made this.

248. Honorary Statue by Family Members

Rhodes, town of Kamiros (Dodecanese). *TitCam* 87 = PH193391.

ca. 27 BCE–14 CE

> This statue is dedicated to a family member whose name is lost. The inscription includes a list of previous honors including those by various associations. The association of Eretheibiazonts appears to be connected with Apollo Erethimios/Erythibios ("Averter of Mildew"; viz., protector of crops; see Strabo, *Geogr.* 13.1.64). The Pasiphonteian association devoted to the god Asklepios was evidently founded by a man named Pasiphontos, a common name on Rhodes.

. . . This was set up by Theuphanes III of Plarios deme and Auxesis of Plarios daughter of Athanodoros on behalf of their son; by Euphranax of Plarios, Mentor of Plarios and Theuphanes IV of Plarios on behalf of their brother; by Iason son of Euphranax, on behalf of the deity; and, by Theuphanes V of Plarios on behalf of the deity. He has been crowned by the Kamirians . . . and by the Homonoian (i.e., devoted to Concord personified) association of Eretheibiazonts and by the Pasiphonteian association of Asklepiasts on account of his goodwill toward the association.

This is dedicated to the gods.

Anthos from Knidos, resident foreigner, made this.

249. Honors by Devotees of the God Hermes for a Priest

Rhodes, town of Lindos (Dodecanese). *ILindos* 251 = PH190969.

ca. 115 BCE

> Round statue base of Lartian marble with traces of the statue's feet. The Alkimedontian Hermaists were a group devoted to the god Hermes and, most likely, founded by a man named Alkimedon.

Mikythos son of Mikythos and adopted son of Eubolos, who served as priest of Athena Lindia ("of Lindos"), Zeus Polieus ("of the City"), Artemis in the village of Kekoia, and Pythian Apollo, and who served as sacrificing priest.

The Alkimedontian Hermaists honored their own benefactor.

This is dedicated to the gods.

250. Associations in a List of Donors to Athena Lindia and Zeus Polieus

Rhodes, town of Lindos (Dodecanese). *ILindos* 252, lines 222–27, 250–59 = PH190970.

ca. 115 BCE

> Fragments of a large slab of gray-blue Lartian marble. This inscrip-
> tion, which lists multiple donors to the temple of Athena Lindia
> (Athena of Lindos), includes both private individuals and several
> associations, illustrating the way in which diverse associations were
> connected to the life of the town. The man Timapolis also provides
> a clear case of one person's multiple affiliations with various asso-
> ciations (also see the dossier of Dionysodoros in the town of Rhodes
> [255]).

(lines 222–27)

. . . Agathostratos son of Agathokles of Lindos, Nikostratos son of
Archokrates of Ladarmios deme, as well as the head sacrificing-priest,
priests, sacrificing-priests, and the association (*koinon*) of Timopoleian
Athenaists: donation of twenty. . . .

(lines 250–59)

. . . Timapolis and the Timapoleian association; Timapolis and the
association of Agathodaimoniasts; Timapolis and the association of Ages-
tratians and Leukarians; Timapolis and the association of . . . (*name lost*)
and Apolloniasts; Timapolis and the association of Arsinoeians (?), Aphrodisiasts and . . . (*name lost*): donation of ten; Timapolis and the Soteriasts . . . (*following seven lines do not survive*)

251. Honors by Numerous Associations for a Priest

Rhodes, town of Lindos (Dodecanese). *ILindos* 264 = PH190982.

ca. 125–100 BCE

> Block of white marble. This honorary inscription makes reference
> to previous honors by various associations, including two differ-
> ent groups of Dionysiac performers, a group devoted to the god-
> dess Athena, immigrant groups, and the "Letodorian Pausistratian
> association," most likely a group founded by men named Letodoros
> and Pausistratos.

. . . *Name*, who served as priest of Athena Lindia and Zeus Polieus, has
been praised and crowned with a gold crown by the association (*koinon*)
of sacrificial priests and head sacrificial priests; he has been praised and
crowned with a gold crown by the civic leaders (*archontes*) and commanders (?) of the association of Athenaists, by the performers gathered around
Dionysos . . . and by the performers gathered around Dionysos Kathegemon ("Dionysos the Leader") who meet in the temple of Dionysos; he has
been praised and crowned by the Letodorian, Pausistratian (?) association with a gold crown and it will publicly proclaim the honor on account

of his virtue, goodwill, and benefaction toward the Letodoreian, Pausis-trateian association; and, he has been praised and crowned with a gold crown by the settlements of foreigners in the city of Lindos. He has also served as priest of Artemis in the village of Kekoia and of Pythian Apollo and . . . head sacrificial priest.

This took place on the occasion of his having presided over and led the chorus to a win (?).

252. Honors by Devotees of the Dioskouroi Gods for a Priest

Rhodes, town of Lindos (Dodecanese). *ILindos* 285 = PH191003.

93 BCE

> Round base of Lartian marble. These honors are granted by an asso-ciation devoted to the Dioskouri (Diocuri) gods, Castor and Pollux, with the group being founded by a man named Philokrates.

Nikagoras son of Nikagoras and adopted son of Peisias, priest of Athena Lindia, Zeus Polieus, and Artemis who is in the village of Kekoia. The association (*koinon*) of the Philokrateian Dioskouriasts honored him on account of his piety, goodwill, and benefaction toward them, dedicating this to the gods.

Charmolas son of Artemidoros, Rhodian, made this.

253. Honors by Associations Devoted to the God Helios and the Panathenaia for a Soldier

Rhodes, town of Lindos. *ILindos* 292 = PH191010.

ca. 88–85 BCE

> Two fragments of a round base of Lartian marble.

Timachidas son of Hagesitimos, who served in the navy on both unforti-fied and fortified ships and was a noble man in the battles, has been hon-ored by the association (*koinon*) of Hesteian Haliast Haliads with a gold crown and by the association (*koinon*) of Panathenaists who are fellow soldiers and tent mates with a gold crown. The feasting mates (*syssitoi*), namely Dionysios son of Hierokles, Aristokrates son of Hagesandros, Dionysios son of Leon, Hagesandros son of Hagesandros and grandson of Athenodoros, Aristeidas son of Pythodoros and adopted son of Aris-teidas, Aischinas son of Aischinas, Alexidamos son of Aristophilos, set this up on account of his goodwill toward them, dedicating the monu-ment to the gods.

Agathokles of Antioch made this.

254. Grave Prepared by Devotees of the Savior God

Rhodes, town of Lindos (Dodecanese). *ILindos* 630 = PH191359.

ca. 51–50 BCE

> Gravestone of Lartian marble decorated with wreaths. This monument records the honors granted by an association devoted to a savior god (likely Zeus) which was founded by a man named Lysistratos.

Athanodoros, native, was honored by the Lysistrateian Soteriasts (i.e., Saviorists) with a gold crown and with a laurel crown. Farewell good man!

255. Dossier of Dionysodoros the Alexandrian

Rhodes, town of Rhodes (Dodecanese). *IG* XII,1 155 = Gabrielsen 1994 = Jaccottet 2003, vol. 2, no. 156 = PH138693.

Second century BCE

> Slab, now in the Museo del Seminario Patriarcale of Venice. The text of the inscription is here arranged chronologically as outlined in *IG* (rather than in the order presented by Dionysodoros). This is among the most extensive inscriptions that documents one person's multiple affiliations with associations of various kinds (see also the case of Timapolis in the town of Lindos on Rhodes [250]). Dionysodoros was a member and leader of the association devoted to the god Helios and the god's offspring (the Haliads), of the association devoted to Pan, and of the association devoted to the god Dionysos. At least two of these affiliations lasted for decades. Toward the end of his life, he had several inscriptions (gathered here) reengraved together.

(A) The head of the club (*archeranistes*) of the Haliasts and Haliads, Dionysodoros the Alexandrian, benefactor, having been praised and crowned for virtue with a gold crown by the association of Dionysiasts and having been honored for his benefaction and with freedom from service of all kinds; and, having been crowned with two gold crowns in the reception of the Baccheia (*Bakcheia*) during the triennial festival by his fellow club members (*syneranistai*), who have received benefactions from him, he made a dedication to triennial festival personified and to the association (*koinon*).

(B) He was praised and crowned by the association of Paniasts with a laurel crown, crowned for virtue with a gold crown made from ten gold pieces, crowned with a crown of white poplar, and honored for benefaction and with freedom from duties of all kinds on two occasions. These honors will be proclaimed perpetually in these burial places. Since he has served as head of the club for eighteen years, he has made the club (*eranos*) increase.

(C) Since the head of the club, Dionysodoros the Alexandrian, benefactor, has served as head of the club of the Haliasts and the Haliads for twenty-three years in a row and has increased the club, he was praised and crowned with a laurel crown by the association of Haliasts and Haliads. Also, having been crowned with a gold crown for virtue and honored for benefaction and with freedom from duties of all kinds, he dedicated this to Baccheian Dionysos and the association.

(D) When Damainetos was priest on the twelfth of Diosthyos, Boulagoras the Rhodian made the motion: Since Dionysodoros the Alexandrian, benefactor of the festal association (*koinon*) for thirty-five years, continues to be a good man in relation to the group (*plēthos*) of Haliads and Haliasts, and he supplied for numerous, substantial needs of the association. Therefore, in order that the Halids and Haliasts may display that they honor good men, whether living or dead, and that they return worthy favors to the ones who choose to be benefactors of the club and who make a good display in everything that is done.

For good fortune! It was resolved by the association of the Haliads and the Haliasts, after the ratification of the proposed honor, to praise and to crown perpetually with the largest possible gold crown—in accordance with our rule regarding the size of crowns—Dionysodoros the Alexandrian, benefactor of the association. Let the secretary have the resolutions engraved, and let the head of the club, the appointed leaders (*archontes*), and, as always with these things, the ones who are chosen give attention to taking care that three obols (i.e., half a drachma) be taken out to pay for the crown at each meeting (*synodos*). Let the honors begin now and continue after his death. Also, in order that everything takes place according to the decree and according to the laws, let his crowning be proclaimed in the meetings on the second day after the sacred rites. The head of the club and those who are currently leaders should take care of this. Let the overseer of the association or the sacred herald proclaim the following announcement:

"The association of the Haliads and the Haliasts honored with a perpetual gold crown Dionysodoros the Alexandrian, benefactor of the association with a commendation. It gives to him the honors both while he is living and after his death on account of the virtue and goodwill which he continues to have both toward the common good and toward his club members!"

When he dies, let the head of the club, the financial officers, and the overseers—those who are currently in leadership—receive the funds set aside for obtaining the perpetual crown. After buying a crown and a double ribbon and after making the proclamations on the second day of the meetings, let the overseer deposit the income in the assembly (*syllogos*) in the month following the meetings (*synodoi*). Also, let the secretary write into the accounts the following: "Concerning Dionysodoros the benefactor, who was crowned with a perpetual gold crown, from the sale of the crown." The proclamations and crownings are to begin for him during the funerary rites (or: at the tombs) for the dead in the month of Hyakinthios. Likewise, the head of the club and the leaders, who are always chosen after (or: always taking care of) these things, should give attention to this. The leaders shall use up the amount set aside for the perpetual crown in the month of Hyakinthios each year for the crown proclaimed during the funerary rites (or: at the tombs) for his death, and let his memorial be crowned.

If they do not do everything that was commanded for them in the decree, let the one who goes against what is written pay one hundred drachmas to the association (or: to the common fund; *koinon*). If someone is considered unrighteous by the association, let him be liable to the established law. It is permitted for a member of the club to propose the penalty. Let the decree have authority for all time, and it is not permitted for leaders or for regular members to change or to write a motion, or for the ones leading to propose that there is a need to invalidate the honors granted to Dionysodoros. Let the one who writes or who proposes such things pay the written penalty of one hundred drachmas, and let his motion be invalid, and let him be liable to the unalterable law.

(E) After Dionysodoros was honored with a perpetual crown with a commendation and with both a gold crown and a crown of white poplar, he (a functionary) will proclaim the honors during the meetings (*synodoi*) and the libations at the burial places for all time.

256. Grave of Iacchos and Dionysodoros, Alexandrian Immigrants

Rhodes, town of Rhodes (Dodecanese). *IRhodM* 46 = Gabrielsen 1994 = PH191495.

Second century BCE

Rectangular altar, now in the Museum of Rhodes.

(A) Grave of Dionysodoros of Alexandria, benefactor and head of the club (*archeranistēs*).

(B) Grave of Iacchos and Dionysodoros, Alexandrians, benefactors. They have been honored by the association (*koinon*) for benefactions and with freedom from duties of all kinds for life, and they have been crowned, with a commendation, with a laurel crown. Dionysodoros has also been honored by the association of the Haliasts with freedom from duties of all kinds for life and with a proclamation of the honors at the burial places, and he was crowned with a commendation at the burial places for all time. He has also been honored by the association of Dionysiasts for benefaction and with freedom from duties of all kinds for life, and he was crowned with a gold crown with a commendation for virtue. This is the work (?) of Dionysios the Alexandrian and Ithakes the Solian.

257. Victories in Contests and an Association of Immigrants

Rhodes, town of Rhodes (Dodecanese). *IG* XII,1 127 = F. Bechtel and H. Collitz, eds., *Sammlung der griechischen Dialekt-Inschriften*, 4 vols. (Göttingen: Vandenhoeck & Ruprecht, 1884–1915), 3:4108 = PH138664.

Early second century BCE

Slab of marble found (in 1885) reused in a church. This inscription documents victories in contests organized by groups of immigrants or resident foreigners in Rhodes, mirroring the activities of the official tribes. Some members or leaders are identified as "Rhodians," however. It concludes with a list of donors who belonged to the association of immigrants. Those named throughout include immigrants from Ephesos, Ilion, Knidos, Chios, Kyzikos, Selge, Soloi in Asia

Minor, from Alexandria in Egypt (or in Asia Minor), from Antioch
in Syria (or in Asia Minor), and from Amphipolis in Thracia.

When Satyros the Ephesian was director of contests, to whom the right of
residence has been granted, the Nikasioneian tribe was victorious under
the direction of the tribal leader, Zenodotos son of Satyros the Ephesian,
and head of the gymnasium, Damatrios son of Damatrios the Rhodian.

When Metrodoros son of Tenios was director of contests, the Nikasioneian tribe was victorious under the direction of the tribal leader, Dorion
the Antiochian, and head of the gymnasium, Poseidonios son of Poseidonios the Rhodian.

When Apollonidas son of Lysimachos was director of contests, the
Nikasioneian tribe was victorious under the direction of the tribal leader,
Dion the Phrygian, and head of the gymnasium . . . *Name* the Antiochian.

When *Name* . . . was director of contests . . . (*remaining lines of this
victory missing*).

When Agathanor of Phaselis was director of contests, the Nikasioneian
tribe was victorious under the direction of the tribal leader, Apollonios the
Selgian, and head of the gymnasium, Apollonios the Amphipolitan.

When Philon the Alexandrian was director of contests, the Basileian
tribe was victorious under the direction of the tribal leader, Soterichos the
Antiochian, and head of the gymnasium, Keraias the Solian.

When Dromon the Antiochian was director of contests, the Olympian
tribe was victorious under the direction of the tribal leader, Gorgon the
Knidian, and head of the gymnasium, Apollonidas the Antiochian.

When Hermon the Antiochian was director of contests, the Basileian
tribe was victorious under the direction of the tribal leader, Philon (?) the
Ilian, and head of the gymnasium . . . *Name*. . . .

The male and female benefactors of the association (*koinon*): Nikasion
of Kyzikos to whom the right of residency was granted, founder of the
association; Olympias the Solian; Nikasion son of Nikasion, the Rhodian;
Basilis daughter of Demetrios; Demetrios son of Nikasion, the Rhodian;
Demetrios II the Rhodian; Hermokreon son of Thaliarchos, the Rhodian;
Theon the Antiochian to whom the right of residency was granted; Eirena
the Solian; Eukleitos, son of Damainetos, the Rhodian; Aristokrates son
of Aristophanes the Rhodian; Satyros the Ephesian to whom the right of
residency was granted; Zenodotos son of Satyros, the Ephesian; Nestor of
Hermione; Hermias of Symbra; Achias the Chian; Olympias son of Nikasion; Nikasion son of Archias and Kallistratos son of Archias; Diogenes
son of Archaias; Damatrios II the Rhodian; Agathokles the Solian; Bathip-
pos the Alexandrian; Menandros son of Kratinos, the Rhodian; Iphidias
son of Mikon, the Rhodian; . . . *Name* the Antiochian.

258. Honors by Devotees of the Samothracian Gods and Aphrodite for an Idumean

Syme (Dodecanese). *IG* XII,3 6 = PH75516.

Late first century BCE

> Found reused in the exterior wall of a church. Idumea (Edom) was
> a region south of Judea. The association that set up these honors is
> either an association of immigrants from the island of Samothrace
> or a group devoted to both Aphrodite and the Samothracian gods
> (but the meaning of *Borboritai* is uncertain). The association of
> Syrian immigrants that had previously honored the man was
> devoted to several deities (perhaps from the homeland), including
> those identified with Adonis, Aphrodite, and Asklepios.

The association (*koinon*) of the Samothracian Aphrodisian *Borboritai* set
this up on behalf of Euphrosynos the Idumean, resident foreigner and
benefactor of the association. The association praises and crowns him
with a gold crown on account of his virtue and goodwill which he continues to demonstrate to us all the time. Also, he has been crowned by us
with gold crowns for the third time, he has been crowned by the Adonian
Aphrodisian Asklepiasts of Syrians with a gold crown, by the . . . *Name*
district . . . with a gold crown, and by the Epibomous district with a gold
crown, all on account of his extreme goodness which he continues to demonstrate to the association.

This is dedicated to the gods.

Northern Islands
(off the coasts of Macedonia and Mysia)

259. Dedication of a Statue of Aphrodite by an Association of Leather Workers

Lesbos, city of Mytilene (Northern Aegean). *SEG* 26 (1976), no.
891 = *IG* XII,2 108 + 109 = PH322710.

Undated

> Two marble fragments.

To most sacred Artemis Thermia ("of the Hot Springs") Homonoia ("Concord"). Telesphoros son of Symphoros and Flavia Tycha have dedicated
the bronze image according to the divine command and decree, and the
workers in the leather craft consecrated the customary statue of Aphrodite
in the sacred area.

260. Dedication to Dionysos and the Initiates

Lesbos, city of Mytilene (Northern Aegean). *IG* XII,8 643 = Jaccottet 2003, vol. 2, no. 12 = PH79850.

Imperial period

> This inscription is not from Skopelos as originally thought (as in *IG*; see *SEG* 45 [1995], no. 1093).

Gaius Coelius Pankarpos set up the shrine and the place in front of it for the god Dionysos and for the initiates (*mystai*) in the place.

261. Dedication to Emperor Antoninus Pius, Dionysos, and the Initiates

Prokonnesos, north of Kyzikos (Northern Aegean). *IMT* 1306 = PH288610.

138–161 CE

Dedicated to emperor Caesar Aelius Hadrian Antoninus Augustus Pius, to the god Dionysos, and to the initiates (*mystai*). Tiberius Claudius Rufus set this up.

262. Regulations of a Society Dedicated to the God Herakles

Thasos (Northern Aegean). *SEG* 2 (1924), no. 505 = Picard 1923, 243 = PH322429.

Early fifth century BCE

> Marble block.

For the society (*thiasos*) of Herakles. Neither goat nor pig are to be sacrificed. Women are banned. A ninth portion must be left. The offering may not be divided. No one may look at the sacrifice.

263. Honorary Decree of an Association of Devotees of the God Sarapis

Thasos (Northern Aegean). *IG* XII,Suppl 365 = Robert K. Sherk, "The Eponymous Officials of Greek Cities V," *Zeitschrift für Papyrologie und Epigraphik* 96 (1993): 291–95 = PH79925.

Second century BCE

> Stone block.

For good fortune! The Sarapiasts resolved to honor the position of the eponymous official of the Sarapiasts. The person in the position of the eponymous official will receive the following benefits from the association (*koinon*): He will recline at the sacred banquet having a white priestly headband. He will be crowned in public at each meeting (*synodos*) by the host with the eponymous crown, having been announced by the sacred herald. He will receive from the association, eternally as long as he shall live, his surname on the administrative proceedings which the Sarapiasts administer. At the banquet he will be entitled to vote along with the priest and the secretary, according to what is set out in the law.

The purchaser of the position of the eponymous official will give the first installment in the month of Galaxion in the year of Leonidas (current eponymous official of the group or of Thasos), and the second in the year after Leonidas, and the third in the year after in this manner. From this balance, the eponymous official and the secretary are required to engrave the decrees in the sanctuary and engrave the names of the one holding the position of the eponymous official and the fellow Sarapiasts. These shall be engraved in the sanctuary in the most visible place, or wherever the eponymous official desires. Hypsikles son of Stasimenes bought the position for ninety-six drachmas.

Eponymous official: Hypsikles son of Stasimenes.

Sarapiasts: Diodoros son of Archedemos, Aristes son of Parmenos, Paiestratos son of Pythippos, Polykrates son of Philokrates, Philiskos son of Kleon . . . (*the other names are lost*).

264. Honors by a Dionysiac Association for a Prominent Official and Hierophant

Thasos (Northern Aegean). *IG* XII,Suppl 447 = Jaccottet 2003, vol. 2, no. 33 = PH80009.

150–200 CE

> Large monolithic statue base with a hole to support the statue. The description of this man's role as "ducenarian" indicates that he was paid two hundred thousand sesterces and was likely an imperial procurator.

For good fortune! The Baccheion (*bakcheion*) before the city (*pro poleōs*) honored Titus Aelius Magnus, the most outstanding ducenarian, foremost man of the city, high priest of the gladiators for two terms, and their own revealer of sacred things (*hierophantēs*), on account of his honor and benefaction. Prosper!

265. Honors by a Dionysiac Association for a Hierophant

Thasos (Northern Aegean). *IG* XII,8 387 = *IMakedD* 1412 = Jaccottet 2003, vol. 2, no. 34 = PH79580.

211–217 CE

> Inscription found on one of four high bases flanking each side of the middle part of a triumphal arch. A separate base has a relief of the honoree.

For good fortune! The most sacred, new Baccheion (*bakcheion*) honored the remarkable Junius Laberius Makedon, their own revealer of sacred things (*hierophantēs*), and no one has opposed. Prosper!

GREATER SYRIA AND THE EAST

266. Honors by a Sacred Association of Performers for a Performer

Apamea (Syria). *SEG* 48 (1998), no. 1844 = *AÉ* (1976), no. 686 = PH305967.

117–138 CE (time of Hadrian)

> Panel, the last four lines of which are somewhat damaged.

The sacred synod (*synodos*) of worldwide performers (*technitai*) gathered around Dionysos and emperor Caesar Trajan Hadrian Augustus son of Trajan, grandson of the god Nerva, the crowned sacred victors (*hieronikai*), and their fellow competitors (*synagōnistai*) honored Julius Paris, citizen of Claudia, also known as Apamea, and citizen of Antioch, who has also been honored in the (Roman) colony of Berytos, tragic pantomimic actor, high priest for life at the place, and crown bearer of Apollo Archegetes ("the Founder"). This was done on account of his honor and benefaction.

267. Grave of a Shipper Erected by an Association of Transporters

Ascalon (Palaestina). *SEG* 51 (2001), no. 2016.

100–250 CE

> Rectangular white-yellow marble plaque with a Latin inscription repeated in Greek. It seems the word "house" is used here in the sense of "guild" (as suggested by *SEG*). The association may have transported wine, an important export from Askalon.

In memory of Gaius Comisius Memor, a shipper from the "house" (*oeco/ oikos*) of transporters.

268. Guild of Builders

Gadara (Palaestina). *SEG* 44 (1994), no. 1354.

First century CE (or later)

> Hexoganal dark gray basalt base. The inscription appears on the side of the upper decorative moulding.

The guild (*syntechnia*) of builders (*oikodomoi*).

269. Honors by Linen Workers for a Patron of the City

Gerasa (Arabia). *SEG* 7 (1934), no. 827 = A. H. M. Jones, "Inscriptions from Jerash," *Journal of Roman Studies* 18 (1928): 171 (no. 39) = PH305125.

ca. 250 CE

> Cylindrical column (*cippus*).

The eternal sacred guild (*technē*) of linen weavers honored Aurelius Julianus on account of services rendered as patron of the city and holy president (*proedros*).

270. Dedication of a Synagogue by Theodotos

Jerusalem (Judea). *CIJ* 1404 = John S. Kloppenborg, "Dating Theodotus (CIJ II 1404)," *Journal of Jewish Studies* 51 (2000): 243–80.

Before 70 CE

> Block of limestone designed for mounting on a wall.

Theodotos son of Vettenus, priest and head of the synagogue (*archisynagōgos*), son of a head of the synagogue, and grandson of a head of the synagogue, built the synagogue (*synagōgē*) for the reading of the law and for the teaching of the commandments, as well as the guest room, the chambers, and the water fittings as an inn for those in need from abroad, the synagogue which his fathers founded with the elders and Simonides.

271. Painted Grave for Soldiers from Kaunos

Sidon (Syria/Phoenicia). Th. Macridy, "A travers les necropoles sidoniennes," *Revue biblique* 13 (1904): 549–50 (A) = OGIS 592.

Early second century BCE (Seleucid era)

Slab used as a grave, found in a house at Sidon in 1897. The painting depicts two soldiers with helmets and armor. The association here is a group of immigrant soldiers from Kaunos, a town on the border of Caria and Lycia on the southern coast of Asia Minor.

The corporate body (*politeuma*) of Kaunians set this up for Hippolytos (?) and Apollonides, sons of Hermagoras, Zenon son of Zenon, . . . *Name* son of Zenon, Isidoros son of Athenodoros (?), Hermonax son of Artemidoros, their fellow citizens.

272. Painted Grave of a Soldier from Thyatira

Sidon (Syria/Phoenicia). Th. Macridy, "A travers les necropoles sidoniennes," *Revue biblique* 13 (1904): 549–50 (B) = Gustave Mendel, *Catalogue des sculptures grecques, romaines et byzantines* (Constantinople: En vent au, 1912–1914), 263–64 (no. 104).

Early second century BCE (Seleucid era)

Slab of limestone. The painting depicts a standing soldier with helmet, shield, and lance.

The companions (*hetairoi*) set this up for Hekataios son of Menogenes, the Thyatiran. Farewell courageous Hekataios!

273. Painted Grave of a Soldier from Pisidia

Sidon (Syria/Phoenicia). Th. Macridy, "A travers les necropoles sidoniennes," *Revue biblique* 13 (1904): 551 (no. 2) = Gustave Mendel, *Catalogue des sculptures grecques, romaines et byzantines* (Constantinople: En vent au, 1912–1914), 262–63 (no. 103)

Early second century BCE (Seleucid era)

Slab of limestone with a niche, at the Imperial Museum at Constantinople in 1904. The painting depicts a soldier with helmet, shield, and weapon.

Saettas son of Trokondos, Pisidian of the Termessians near Oenoanda, fellow soldier. The corporate body (*politeuma*) of the Pisidians of the Termessians near Oenoanda set this up for their own citizen. Farewell courageous one!

274. Painted Grave of a Soldier from Lycia

Sidon (Syria/Phoenicia). Th. Macridy, "A travers les necropoles sidoniennes," *Revue biblique* 13 (1904): 551–52 (no. 3) = Gustave Mendel, *Catalogue des sculptures grecques, romaines et byzantines* (Constantinople: En vent au, 1912–1914), 266–67 (no. 106)

Early second century BCE (Seleucid era)

> Slab of limestone with a niche. The painting depicts a standing soldier with helmet and shield. The city of Pinara is located in western Lycia, north of Xanthos.

The corporate body (*politeuma*) of Pinarians set this up for Kartadis son of Hermaktibilos, Lycian. Farewell courageous and painless one!

275. Dedication by the Association of Cutlery Makers

> Sidon (Syria/Phoenicia). *SEG* 55 (1995), no. 1660 = Waltzing 1895–1900, vol. 3, no. 94.

48/47 BCE

> Marble slab. Theos Hagios ("Holy God") may here refer to a deity identified as Asklepios, as in another dedication to "Theos Hagios Asklepios" by a priest of Mithras at Sidon (ca. 140 CE).

Year 64. Heliodoros son of Apollonios dedicated this to Theos Hagios ("Holy God") when Apollophanes was head of the cutlery makers (*machairopoioi*) on behalf of the association (*koinon*).

276. Dedication by an Association of Couch Makers

> Sidon (Syria/Phoenicia). *SEG* 55 (1995), no. 1654 = *AÉ* (2005), no. 1569.

98 CE

> Slab of Marble.

For good fortune! Year 208 (Sidon era), first day of the month of Dystros. Using their own resources, the fifth guild (*technē*) of couch makers dedicated the building to emperor Caesar Augustus, god . . . (*four erased lines*).

277. Construction of a Building by an Association of Barbers

> Sidon (Syria/Phoenicia). *SEG* 54 (1994), no. 1628.

104 CE

> Slab of white marble.

Year 214, twentieth day of the month of Panemos. Dorotheos son of Demostratos, Alexandros son of Nikaios, Secundus, Heliodoros, Apollodoros, and Felix, the members of the guild (*technē*) of barbers constructed this from their own resources, along with their wives and children.

278. Honors by an Association of Barbers for a Leader

Sidon (Syria). *SEG* 55 (1995), no. 1655.

132 CE

> Slab of marble, broken into five pieces.

For good fortune! Year 242, twentieth day of the month of Dystros. For the salvation of lord Hadrian Gaius Cassius, son of Gaius, son of Maikia Alexandros II, head craftsman of the barbers (*koureus*). . . . The association set this up from its own resources.

EGYPT

Delta Region

279. Dedication by a President of a Synod

Alexandria (Nile Delta, Lower Egypt). *IAlexandriaK* 96 (with plate XLVII) = PH227188.

30 BCE–14 CE

> Statue base of black granite, now at Alexandria, Magasin des fouilles polonaises à Kôm el-Dik (inv. no. R/1598/70).

Ammonios, perfumer (*myropoles*), former president, dedicated this to the synod (*synodos*). The . . . *x*th year of Caesar.

280. Decree of a Synod Devoted to the Emperor

Alexandria (Nile Delta, Lower Egypt). *SB* XXII 15460 = Brashear 1993, 14–15.

5 BCE (August 21)

> Papyrus (38 × 15 cm) now in the Staatliche Museen in Berlin (P. Berol. inv. no. 25159). This is the same association as that in the next inscription (**281**).

In the twenty-fifth year of Caesar, on the twenty-eighth day of the month of Mesore, at the assembly (*synagōgē*) which met in the house of the synod (*synodos*) of the principal followers (*archakolothoi*) of emperor Augustus Caesar, the son of god Zeus Eleutherios ("Deliverer"), whose synagogue leader (*synagōgos*) is Primos and whose president is Ioukoundos . . . and during his tenure he showed himself not to have neglected anything in relation to the synod. Likewise also for the current year . . . and at all times during the tenure of his office he conducted himself with enthusiasm and . . .

For good fortune! By common consent it was agreed to honor him with the lifetime title "beloved by all" (*pamphilos*) and at the banquet that occurs in . . . to honor him with a distinguished crown so that the new . . . might know . . . and to know what kind. . . . It is not permitted for anyone to imagine the reversal of the matters that have been decided but, if this should happen, the one who proposes that this arrangement is not acceptable shall be fined five hundred silver drachmas. This memo, written in duplicate, is valid.

281. Loan Payment by a Synod of Caesar

Alexandria (Nile Delta, Lower Egypt). *BGU* IV 1137.

6 CE (November 19)

> Papyrus (19 × 14 cm), now in the Ägyptisches Museum in Berlin (inv. no. P. 13137 Ro). This is the same association as in the papyrus immediately above (**280**).

In the twenty-fifth year of Caesar, on the twenty-second of the month of Hathyr, at the assembly that occurred in Paratomos of the synod (*synodos*) of the god emperor Caesar Augustus, whose synagogue leader (*synagōgos*) and president (*prostatēs*) is Primos, a slave of Caesar, and whose priest is Ioukoundos, a slave of Caesar, and whose head of the gymnasium is Alexandros, with most of the members assembled. Whereas we have ordered the aforementioned priest Ioukoundos to take funds which he has the authority to draw from the synod and to pay the one hundred twenty Ptolemaic silver drachmas that Syntrophos owes to . . . *Name*, the slave (?) of Caesar, on behalf of Syntrophos, a slave of Caesar and member of the synod, before the thirty-first day of the present year (i.e., within one month).

By common consent it was agreed, first, that Ioukoundos should pay in full, before the thirtieth of Hathyr, the one hundred twenty silver drachmas on behalf of Syntrophos, without charging any interest, and second, that the funds that he has received from the synod be credited to Ioukoundos against what he owes to the synod and that Ioukoundos should not be accountable in regard to these matters. No one is permitted to take an action against this payment or to . . . such things, for the signed document written in duplicate is valid . . . the one . . . the other.

282. Dedication of a Statue by an Association of Women

Alexandria (Nile Delta, Lower Egypt). *IAlexandriaK* 70 = PH227160.

Early first century CE

> Statue base of black granite, now in the Alexandria Greco-Roman Museum, Bahnassa (inv. no. 211, catalogue 170).

The high priestess and president (*prostatis*) Tetiris dedicated this to the Apollonian (?) women's synod (*synodos*) in the . . . *x*th year of Caesar, on the first of the month Pachon.

283. Dedication of a Statue to a Synagogue by a President

> Alexandria (Nile Delta, Lower Egypt). *IEgJud* 20 = *IAlexandriaK* 92 = *CIJ* 1447 = PH227184.

Imperial period

> Statue base of black granite, now at Saint Petersburg, Hermitage.

Artemon son of Nikon, having been president (*prostatēs*) in the eleventh year, dedicated this to the synagogue (*synagōgē*). . . .

284. Dedication by an Association to a Chief Physician

> Alexandria (Nile Delta, Lower Egypt). *IAlexandriaK* 97 = PH227189.

7 CE

> Statue base of marble, still in location in the Zenat al-Sittât quarter of Alexandria.

The association (*plēthos*) of physicians (*iatroi*) . . . in Alexandria set up this statue of Gaius Procleius Themison, chief physician (*archiatros*), on account of his good will . . . in the thirty-seventh year of Caesar in the month of Phaophi.

285. Dedication by a Founder and President of an Association

> Kanopus (Nile Delta, Lower Egypt). *IGRR* I 1095 = *IDelta* I 11 = PH228250.

29/28 BCE

> Statue base.

Synistor, having assembled (*synagōgeō*) (the association) and having been president in the second year of Caesar, dedicated this.

286. Dedication by a Synagogue Leader of a Sambathic Association

Naukratis (Nile Delta, Lower Egypt). *IGRR* I 1106 = *IDelta* II 28 = *IEgJud* 26.

30 BCE–14 CE

Statue base of limestone.

. . . *Name* son of Ammonios, synagogue leader (*synagōgos*), dedicated this to the Sambathic synod (*synodos*). Year . . . *x* of Caesar, Phamenoth 7.

287. Decree Honoring a Donor to a Synod of Farmers

Psenamosis (Nile Delta, Berenike nome, Lower Egypt). *IDelta* I 446 = PH228299.

67, 64 BCE

Two inscribed decrees from 67 and 64 BCE, now in the Greco-Roman Museum, Alexandria (inv. no. 22175).

For good fortune!

Year 15, the twenty-first of Thoth. At the assembly (*synagōgē*) of fellow farmers (*syngeorgoi*) who hold the property around Psenamosis in the district (nome) of Berenike, after discussions concerning other things resolved: Since Paris, a kinsman who conducted himself in a generous way toward the synod (*synodos*) and favorably received everyone both collectively and individually, had some empty land suitable for the construction of a gymnasium and a shrine (*oikos*); and since, when we wished to buy it so that we could build a gymnasium and a shrine and conduct sacrifices on behalf of the kings, he did not insist on receiving payment, but donated it and registered it as a free gift to the synod; therefore, it was decided to approve this and to honor him with two statues which are to be set up in the gymnasium and in the shrine respectively, and to crown these statues on the eponymous days on which we come together to sacrifice on behalf of the kings. Likewise, it was decided that he shall have a seat on the first couch at the banquet for life; that a day will be observed in his honor each year at those places; and that a plaque will be inscribed saying "Paris, the kinsman, dedicated this place to the synod of landowners (*geouchoi*)" andthe plaque will be set up on the gateway.

For it is just for those honorable persons who join the association to charge an entrance fee (*timē*) from them, but if out of his ambition he should leave something else to the association (*koinon*), it is resolved that another day in his honor will be observed in the city (i.e., Alexandria).

When they hold their banquet, a statue of him will be crowned during the toasts, and three men, who he shall propose to be honored, will be received into the synod without an entrance fee, whose names he shall supply.

For good fortune! Below are written the twenty-nine members.

In the eighteenth year, in the month of Phaophi: Since Paris the kinsman has continued to act in a kindly and generous manner toward us. Formerly, when there was the land that belonged to him in Psenamosis that happened to be opportune for us to build a shrine and a gymnasium, we offered to pay its price, yet he did not insist on receiving payment but gave it to us freely. For this reason he has received from us the honor of two statues that have been confirmed by the preceding decree, which are to be set up in the gymnasium and in the shrine, and which are to be crowned on the eponymous days on which we gather to sacrifice on behalf of the kings. Likewise, he shall have a seat on the first couch at the banquet for life, and we will observe a day in his honor yearly at those places, and a plaque will be inscribed on the gateway saying: "Paris the kinsman dedicated this place to the synod of landowners." For while it is just for those honorable persons who join the association to charge an entrance fee (*timē*) from them, it is resolved to accept into the synod without any entrance fee three men that he will propose to be so honored, whose names he will give us.

And now in the twentieth year, since he had been eager to expand our synod, since he had made gifts for holding two additional days in his honor yearly, with the result that there are now three days this year namely: one day in Alexandria in the month of Thoth, when we set up his engraved image and crown it when we are feasting; one day in Psenamosis in the month of Pharmouthi, after the first day of Apollos, just as was resolved beforehand; and, yet another day in the month of Mesore at the time of vintage, for which days he has given one thousand silver drachmas, so that from the interest of two hundred silver drachmas that is collected each year, the expenses of the other two days may be met. It is further resolved that he be named priest for life, and that he be free from further dues, free from contributions for the banquets, free from monthly dues, free from the services (*leitourgia*), and exempt from levies. Furthermore, he will receive a double portion of food and, if he is not present at the banquet, it will be sent to him, and his statue will be crowned by the association at the toasts with a special wreath. And when he dies in old age, the synod will yearly observe for him the customary rites of the dead at the tomb and will crown him from common funds with a special crown at the toasts. The synod will inscribe a decree on a plaque regarding all the aforementioned things, and erect it at the gate of the sanctuary, concerning the three days that are held yearly in his honor and the three statues, in accordance with these decrees. For good fortune!

All those members who are present whose names are written below approved, and did everything as indicated above. At the bottom are written their names, all approving.

288. Dedication of a Gateway for a Prayer House

Xenephyris (Nile Delta, Lower Egypt). *IEgJud* 24 = *CIJ* 1441 = PH229360.

140–116 BCE

> Slab of limestone with letters inscribed and painted black, now in the Alexandria Museum (inv. no. 19398).

On behalf of King Ptolemaios, Queen Kleopatra the sister, and Queen Kleopatra the wife, the Judeans of Xenephyris dedicated the gateway of the prayer house (*proseuchē*), when Theodoros and Achillion were presidents (*prostatēs*).

Fayûm Region

289. Letter of Resignation by a Patron

Karanis (Arsinoites, division of Herakleides, Fayûm, Egypt). *PMich* IX 575.

184 CE (July 25)

> Papyrus (9.5 × 7.5 cm), now at the University of Michigan (inv. no. 5374 28–B163A-A). This is a poorly written document with a variety of grammatical errors. The letter is written on the reverse side (verso): on the front side (recto) is a receipt for 18 1/16(?) *artabai* of wheat.

To Thrax, the supervisor (*epimelētēs*) and to the members of the synod (*synoditai*), from Epiodoros. Since I am impoverished and unable to make contributions to the association (or: common fund; *koinon* [?]), I ask that you accept my resignation. Farewell.

Year 24. Farewell. First of the month of Mesore.

To the fellow members of the synod.

290. Letter Concerning Transportation of a Corpse

Kerkesoucha Orous (Arsinoites, division of Herakleides, Fayûm, Egypt). *PPetaus* 28.

Second century CE

> Papyrus (11 × 16.2 cm), now in Cologne (Papyrussammlung inv.
> no. 318). The sender and the addressee appear to be members of a
> transportation guild. Asklas is addressed as both "brother" (open-
> ing) and "friend" (end), which suggests the fictive use of sibling lan-
> guage here among fellow members of an occupation or guild. See
> Daniel (1979).

Papsaus to Asklas his brother (*adelphos*), many greetings. I greet you and
your entire household. I am already writing to you a second letter regarding the body of the soldier from Ouisemtos, a legionary, whose remains
the transporters from Tmounache and Phebechis, Kuiteilis and his partner brought, whom they gave to your son. The evidence: they have attached
a staff to his back and, casting him on donkey belonging to you and your
son, together with your son brought him to you.

Now I am writing to you about him, so that you will bring him to his
village. Since I have experienced a great insult and they almost brought me
before the governor. Wasn't this because of what you have done to me? I
offer another piece of evidence about him: your wife, when she came out,
bought spices for four obols for the sailor from Tmunache named Kuit-
eileis. You have not treated me honestly, not bringing him to his proper
place. I greet you and your son and your entire house. I pray that you are
well. Nineteenth of the month of Pharmouthi.

(*reverse side [verso]*)

Deliver this to Ke . . . to Askas, from Papaus, his friend (*philos*).

291. Dedication of a Statue by a Synod

> Krokodilopolites (Arsinoites, Fayûm, Egypt). *IFayum* III 204 = *SB*
> I 4211 = PH216120.

68 BCE

> Slab, poorly preserved, now in the Ny Carlsberg Glyptothek in
> Copenhagen (AEIN 826).

On behalf of king Ptolemaios, Philopater ("Father-loving") and Philadelphos ("Brother-loving") god. This statue was dedicated to Isis Esenchebis,
the great goddess, by the synod (*synodos*) of Esenchebis, whose synagogue
leader (*synagōgos*) is Helenos. They have dedicated the land to the north
and south, from the enclosure that Helenos constructed to the walkway,
and the land from the west to the east, from the assembly place to the
temple.

292. Letter of Complaint from Therous and Teos Against a Society Regarding Funeral Fees

Magdôla (Arsinoites, division of Polemon, Fayûm, Egypt). *PEnteuxeis* 21.

218 BCE

Four fragments.

To king Ptolemaios, greetings from Therous and Teos. We have been wronged by Temsois and Senemenopis and Teteim . . . and Herieus and by the other women who are fellow members of the society (*synthiasitidai*) who are from Kerkethoeris in the division of Polemon. Soeris my sister and wife of the aforementioned Teos, a fellow member of the society (*thiasos*) along with the aforementioned women, who held the priesthood of the society for four years, happened to die. . . . Since she had no relatives except us, when the aforementioned women were asked, they did not reimburse the funeral fee (*taphikon*). We beg you therefore, O king, to order Diophanes the commander (*stratēgos*) to write to Ptolemaios the superintendent (*epistatēs*), so that if they now will submit to pay us the funeral fee the matter will rest. But if not, we ask that you send them to Diophanes so that he may compel them to reimburse us, so that through you, O king, I may have justice. Farewell.

(second hand)

To Ptolemaios. Do your best to resolve the dispute of the parties. If that is not possible, send them to me—after the tenth of the month of Choiak—so that the case may be heard at the proper court. Year 4, twenty-seventh of the month of Daisios, which is the twenty-ninth of the month of Hathyr.

(reverse side)

Year 4, twenty-seventh day of Daisios which is the twenty-ninth of Hathyr. Therous and Teos versus Temsois and her fellow association members, in regard to a funeral fee.

293. Letter of Complaint from Krateia Against a Society Regarding Funeral Fees

Magdôla (Arsinoites, division of Polemon, Fayûm, Egypt). *PEnteuxeis* 20.

215 BCE

Six fragments of a papyrus.

To King Ptolemaios greetings, from Krateia who is from the people of Alexandrou Nesos. I have been wronged by Philippos and Dionysios. My brother Apollodotos was a fellow member of the society with them . . . for Maron, the one (Philippos) being the priest and the other (Dionysios) being the head of the society (*archithiasitēs*). When my brother died, they did not provide a funeral for him or accompany him to the burial, in violation of the society's regulations, and they did not reimburse the funeral fee (*taphikon*) that had accrued to him. I beg you, therefore, O king, if it please you to order Diophanes the commander (*strategos*) to compel them to reimburse me the funeral fee. For if this has been done, I shall have been furnished with justice by you, O king. Farewell.

(*second hand*) After examining the association's laws, compel the parties to come to a fair resolution. And if they contest this, send them to me.

(*reverse side*)

Year 1, twenty-eighth day of the month of Gorpiaios, which is the twelfth of Tybi.

Year 1, twenty-eighth of Gorpiaios, which is the twelfth of Tybi.

Krateia versus Philippos and Dionysios, regarding a funeral fee.

294. Dedications to the Gods Anubis and Apollo by Two Synods

Narmouthis (Arsinoites, division of Polemon, Fayûm, Egypt). *IFayum* III 171–72 = PH216087–PH216088.

First to second century CE

> Both inscriptions, which are no longer visible, were found in situ along the processional way leading to the south temple of Medinet Madi.

no. 171:

To Anubis the greatest god. The synod (*synodos*) dedicated this in accordance with a vow in the eighth year in the month of Mechir.

no. 172:

The synod dedicated this to Apollo the greatest god.

295. Regulations of an Association of Zeus Hypsistos

Philadelphia (Arsinoites, Fayûm, Egypt). *PLond* VII 2193 = Roberts, Skeat, and Nock 1936, 39–88 = *NewDocs* I 5.

69–58 BCE

> Papyrus (25.3 × 18 cm), cut from a roll, with a join running down the center, now in the British Museum (inv. no. 2710). This is

thought to be a copy or the first draft of a document, final copies
of which would be placed in the association's archive in the temple
and perhaps inscribed on a monument.

(*front side [recto]*)

Horion son of Haryotes . . . thirty-two. Total: 32.

For good fortune!

The law which those belonging to the synod (*synodos*) of Zeus Hypsistos ("Highest") devised jointly to be binding. Acting in the prescribed
manner, they first chose for themselves Petesouchos the son of Teephben-
nis as their leader (*hēgoumenos*), a learned man, worthy of the place and of
the banqueting hall (*andrōn*), for a year from the month and day written
above. You shall arrange one banquet a month in the sanctuary of Zeus for
all the contributors, at which they should in a common banqueting hall
pour libations, pray, and perform the other customary rites on behalf of
the god and lord, the king.

Further everyone must obey the leader and his assistant in matters
concerning the association (*koinon*) and they shall be present for all occasions that have been prescribed for them, at meetings (*synlogous*), gatherings (*synagōga*), and outings (*apodēmia*). It is not lawful for any one of
them to . . . (*unknown verb*), or to establish factions, or to depart from the
brotherhood (*phratra*) of the leader to join another brotherhood, or for
men to argue about one another's genealogies at the banquet (*symposion*)
or to abuse one another verbally at the banquet, or to chatter or to indict or
accuse another, or to resign for the course of the year, or to be absent from
the banquet, or . . . , or to steal the wife of another member, or to obstruct
the leader (?) . . . public . . . at the marriages and . . . each shall contribute
their dues (?) . . . and if any of them becomes a father (?), he shall receive
(?) . . .

(*reverse side [verso]*)

Pnepheros 2 for ?: 1,200; 3 Apollonios: 800; Sokrates 3 for the current
year (?): 1,200; 4 Petosiris: 1,200; Petesouchos, 2 for ?: 1,200; 3 . . . Kaleibis:
1,100.

296. Letter of Complaint by a Guild of Wool Weavers

Philadelphia (Arsinoites, Fayûm, Egypt). *BGU* VII 1572.

139 CE (December 17)

Now in the Ägyptisches Museum in Berlin (P. 11713).

To Dion, commander (*stratēgos*) of the division of Herakleides of
the Arsinoite district (nome), from the wool weavers of the village of

Philadelphia. Since we have recently received . . . *x* drachmas from the public treasury that we might prepare military clothing . . . some men from our guild (*ergasia*) . . . to complete what was ordered . . . four of them have been given . . . for public service, they have been taken from us and they went to Alexandria and what is more, we are. . . .

And so we are forced to come to you and request, if it please you, to grant those of us who are left to remain exempt from all public services, so that we may complete the clothing that has been ordered and deliver it, especially because we have received another order for military clothing which we must complete next, so that we may obtain redress. Initially, we were twelve men, of whom four have been taken away, so that now we are only eight men.

In the third year of emperor Caesar Titus Aelius Hadrian Antoninus Augustus Pius, on the twentieth of the month of Hadrianos.

297. Honorary Decree of a Synod of Dionysiac Performers

Ptolemais Hermou (Arsinoites, division of Herakleides, Fayûm, Egypt). *OGIS* 50 = *RIG* 1018 = PH218975.

ca. 269–246 BCE

> Limestone slab with a triangular top (pediment), discovered in 1884, now in the Museum in Giza.

The guild of performers (*technitai*) devoted to Dionysos and to the Brother Gods, and those who share membership in the synod (*synodos*) resolved that Dionysios son of Musaeos, president (*prytanis*) for life, be crowned with a wreath of ivy, in accordance with ancestral custom, on account of the good will that he has shown to the city of Ptolemais and to the performers associated with the great Dionysos and the brother gods. Further, it was resolved to announce the crowning to the Dionysiac performers and to inscribe this decree on a monument and to set it up in front of the temple of Dionysos. The treasurer (*oikonomos*) Sosibios will pay for the cost of the monument.

298. Honorary Decree and Membership List of a Synod of Dionysiac Performers

Ptolemais Hermou (Arsinoites, division of Herakleides, Fayûm, Egypt). *OGIS* 51 = *RIG* 1017 = PH218976.

269–246 BCE

> White limestone slab with a triangular top (pediment), discovered in a house in Menshieh (Ptolemais), now in the Museum in Giza.

The performers associated with Dionysos and the Brother Gods resolved: Since Lysimachos son of Ptolemaios of the Sostratic deme, the cavalry commander and president (*prytanis*) for life has first of all displayed good will—and even now in many ways continues to do so—to the king and to the king's parent, and conducts himself in a pious and holy manner toward Dionysos and the other gods. Since he had also dealt with the performers in a generous fashion (*philanthrōpōs*) and assisted each member individually and everyone collectively with zeal, giving himself intensely to the growth of the theatrical profession; and since it is good to honor such distinguished men as these with the appropriate honors, the association (*koinon*) of the performers devoted to Dionysos, whose names are subscribed, resolved to crown Lysimachos with an ivy wreath in accordance with ancestral custom on the eleventh of the month of Peritios at the Dionysia festival, on account of the excellence and piety that he has shown to King Ptolemaios and to Dionysos and the good will he has toward the king and his parents and to the association of the performers. For good fortune! They shall also set up a carved image of him in the vestibule of the civic president's building (*prytaneion*). And the secretary of the association, Demarchos, shall inscribe this decree on a plaque and set it up in front of the temple of Dionysos. Sosibios the treasurer (*oikonomos*) shall pay the expenses for these things.

(*column 1*)

Zopyros, who is in charge of the sacred rites for the triennial and annual festivals and his brothers, Dionysios and Taurinos. Tragic poets: Phainippos and Diognetos; comic poets: Stratagos and Mousaios; epic poets: Demarchos, Theogenes, Artemidoros; singers with a lyre: Menippos; lyre player: Herakleitos; dancer: Ptolemaios; . . .

(*column 2*)

tragic actor: Metrodoros; comics actors: Telemachos, Agathodoros, Apollonios, Asklepodoros son of Apollonios, Apollonios, Diodoros; tragic fellow competitors: Apollonides, Archonos, Kleitos, Ptolemaios, Zopyros; chorus director: *Name(s)*; . . .

(*column 3*)

tragic flute player: Thraikides; trumpet player: Thrasymachos; makers of masks and stage-props: Baton; guests: Demetrios, Phaidimos, Artemidoros, Spoudias, Dionysios; friends of the performers (i.e., honorary members; *philotechnitai*): Demetrios, Stephanos, Leon, Artemidoros, Demetrios, Aristonous.

299. Regulations of a Demotic Cult Association

Tebtynis (Arsinoites, division of Polemon, Fayûm, Egypt). *PCair-Dem* 30606 = de Cenival 1972, 45–58.

158/157 BCE

> Papyrus (70 × 32 cm). The English text below is a translation of de Cenival's translation of the demotic original with the list of names added from Wilhelm Spiegelberg, *Die demotischen Denkmäler 30601–31270, 50001–50022 II: Die demotischen Papyrus* (Catalogue général des antiquités égyptiennes du Musée du Caire 39; Strasbourg: W. Drugulin, 1908), 26–29 (no. 30606). The sums in column 2 appear to represent the full yearly dues and the monthly equivalent.

(*column 1*)

In year 24, Mesore . . . of king Ptolemaios and Kleopatra, children of Ptolemaios and Kleopatra, the Epiphanes ("Manifest") gods, when Ptolemaios the son of King Ptolemaios and Kleopatra, the Philometor ("Mother-loving") gods, was priest of Alexander, the savior gods, the brother gods, the benefactor gods, the Philopater ("Father-loving") gods, the Epiphanes gods, and the Philometor gods; when the lady Nike daughter of Hieronymos was the prize bearer (*athlophoros*) of Berenike, the benefactor god; when lady Arsinoe daughter of Charimortos (?) was the basket bearer (*kanēphoros*) of Arsinoe Philadelphos ("Brother loving"); when the lady Timarion daughter of Metrophanes was the priestess of Arsinoe Philopater:

The regulations which have been adopted by the members of the association and the priest of the devotees of the crocodile god, who gather before Souchos and the gods associated with Souchos, in the cemetery of the crocodile of the village of Sobek Tebtynis (Soknebtynis) in the division of Polemon, Arsinoite district (nome).

They say: We shall apply the regulations from year 24, month of Mesore until year 25, month of Mesore, which makes one year, or twelve and one-sixth months, or a year, saying together: We shall hold an assembly before Souchos and the gods associated with Souchos for the festivals and processions of Souchos and the gods associated with Souchos and on the days which those of the House have adopted as assembly dates during the aforesaid period. We shall contribute our dues every month, besides the contributions for functions for which we must make payment. We shall hand them over to the representative of the House when they become due each month.

If one of our members does not pay his dues each month and does not hand them over to the representative of the House as stipulated above, the representative of the House shall go to his house and shall seize a surety for the aforementioned money. If he attacks him or one of his agents, the fine shall be twenty-five debens (= 500 copper drachmas) . . . and he will continue until he pays the debt. Whoever takes up the collection shall establish the due date for the people of the House, each two shares per person valued at five debens per share. And each shall make a pledge of resin, ointment, wreaths, greenery, ricinus, and wood for the funds of the House. If one of our members is told to bring money on the fixed day and he does not do so, his fine will be twenty-five debens.

We shall perform the sacrifices and the libations for the king Ptolemaios and Queen Kleopatra, children of Ptolemaios and Kleopatra, and the sacrifices and offerings of Souchos and the gods associated with Souchos, on the aforesaid festivals and processions and on the days which those of the House will have adopted as meeting days, during the aforesaid period.

. . . If one of our members will not go out with us to pull the statue of the god and will not escort him to his tomb during the aforesaid period, his fine is . . . x debens and the curses of the god Souchos shall follow him, except in the case that he is ill or in prison or is in court with the royal treasury.

If one of our members dies in the House, we shall mourn for him and then escort him to the necropolis all together. We shall contribute for him the money for dues which those of the House will have agreed to give for his burial and embalming, and we shall let them levy eight shares for him. If one of our members will not mourn him, the fine will be five debens, except in the cases enumerated above. Moreover, if one of our members dies away from the village, we shall designate ten (?) men from the House and send them after him, that they might do for him in accordance with what is written above. If one of the members who is told "go after him," does not go, his fine is ten debens, except in the cases enumerated above. If one of our members whose father, mother, brother, sister, son, daughter, or wife dies, we shall mourn that one and escort him to the necropolis and we shall levy for him twenty shares. If one of our members will not mourn with him, the fine is five debens, except in the cases enumerated above. If one of our members has a son who dies at a tender age, we shall drink beer with him and comfort his heart.

If one of our members calumniates one of the members before a military or civil official or a police officer (?) without first bringing a complaint before those of the House, his fine will be fifty (?) debens. If one of the members says to one of us, "you are a leper," though he is not a leper, his fine is one hundred debens and they shall expel him from the House. If one of our members brings a complaint against one of us to a military official, civil official, or police officer (?), without first bringing the complaint before those of the House, his fine is twenty-five debens. If he brings a complaint against him (?) after he has received justice from them, when he brings a complaint against him (?) in that affair, his fine is thirty debens.

If one of our members insults one of us, his fine is twenty-five debens. The insult of the president: . . . x debens; if he commits it again: . . . x debens . . . the insult of the vice president: . . . x debens; if he commits it again, thirty-five debens; the insult of a nonmember: forty debens; if he commits it again: sixty debens; if one of our members strikes another member, his fine is sixty debens. The striking of the president: . . . debens; if he commits it again: eighty debens; the striking of the vice president (?): . . . debens; if he commits it again: . . . five debens; the striking of an ordinary member: eighty debens; if he commits it again, ninety debens.

If one of our members finds another member on the riverband (?) road or similar and he says, "can you give me some money . . ." and he does not give it, his fine is . . . x debens, except if he swears an oath before the god, saying, "I cannot give him anything." If one of our members is summoned for a ruling of the association or . . . and does not appear, his fine is . . . x debens if he has not made an appeal about it before. If one of our members goes to supplicate the god or is imprisoned, or takes asylum in the god's temple, the representative of the House shall assist him and give him five shares. If one of our members is involved in an unjust trial, we shall give the dues that those of the House decided to provide for his trial.

If a member whom those of the House decided shall be the representative of the House refuses to be representative, his fine is twenty-five debens. If one of our members refuses to meet with us during the aforesaid period, or after he has drunk beer . . . with us, his fine is twenty-five debens. If one of our members insults the representative of the House, and bribes him in any matter, his fine is twenty-five debens. The representative of the house is the one who has authority in anything he will discuss with us, by virtue of everything aforesaid, and we shall do them at his command without delay.

(*column 2*)

Their names: Pates (?) son of Pachois (?) the priest: 372 debens (per year) = 31 debens (per month); Onnophris son of Tše, the vice president: 300 debens = 25 debens; Marres *p3-sif* (?) . . . son of Sokonopis (?), the priest of the gods: 260 debens = 21 5/10 debens; Horos (?) son of Petos, the servant of the God Soknebtynis: 270 (?) debens = 22(?) 7½/10 debens; Patos (?) son of Horos the servant of *Name* . . . , the great god: 112 debens = 9 2½/10 debens; Phaneis, son of Peteharpsenesis, the priest of Horos: 108 debens = 9 debens; . . . *Name* son of . . . *Name*, the priest of Isis: 90 debens = 7½ debens . . . Pmenches son of Sokonopis (?): 6 debens; Haryothes son of Pachois: 6 debens. . . .

300. Regulations of a Guild of Sheep and Cattle Owners (?)

Tebtynis (Arsinoites, division of Polemon, Fayûm, Egypt). *PMich* V 243.

14–37 CE (time of Tiberius)

> Papyrus (37 × 23 cm), now in Ann Arbor, Michigan (P. Mich. inv. no. 720). The papyrus is from the archive of Kronion, the writer of laws (nomographer) of Tebtynis.

. . . in the *x*th year of Tiberius Caesar Augustus, Heron son of Orseus, with whom they must have a monthly banquet on the twelfth of the month, each member contributing monthly dues of twelve silver drachmas which have been determined for each on an equal basis. The president (*prostatēs*) is permitted to exact a pledge from anyone who fails to pay his dues in these or any other matters. If a member behaves badly owing to drunkenness, he shall be fined whatever the association (*koinon*) decides. If a member is sent an announcement of the meeting (*syllogos*) and does not attend, he shall be fined one drachma if the meeting is in the village and four drachmas if it is in the city.

A member shall contribute two drachmas if he marries, two drachmas for the birth of a male child, one drachma for the birth of a female child, four drachmas if land is purchased, four drachmas for a flock of sheep, and one drachma for cattle. If a member ignores someone (i.e., another member) who is in distress and does not assist in helping him out of his trouble, he shall pay eight drachmas.

Anyone who shoves in front of another at the banquets and takes his seat shall pay an extra three obols to sit in his own place. If a member prosecutes or calumniates another member, he shall be fined eight drachmas. If a member commits intrigue against, or corrupts the home of another member, he shall pay sixty drachmas. If a member has been arrested for a private debt, they shall stand surety for him for up to one hundred silver drachmas for thirty days, during which time he shall release the men from their pledge.

May health prevail! If one of the members (*synoditai*) should die, all of the members shall be shaved and shall hold a banquet for one day, each member contributing one drachma and two loaves immediately. In the case of other deaths (i.e., the death of family members), they shall hold a banquet for one day. Whoever does not shave his head shall be fined four drachmas. Whoever does not defile himself (i.e., attend the funeral and encounter corpse impurity) or has not put a wreath at the tomb shall be fined four drachmas. Other matters shall be as the association decides.

This law shall be valid when signed by the majority of members. When validated, it shall be returned to the president.

Herakleios son of Aphrodisios, about forty-two years old, with a scar between his eyebrows; Orses son of Kronides, about forty-five years old, with a scar on an eyebrow; Mieus son of Harmiusis, about forty-six years old, with a scar on the left side of his face; Harmiusis son of Phasos, about fifty-five years old, with a scar . . . right.

(*second hand*) I, Heron son of Orseus, president approve this as it has been set forth.

(*third hand*) I, Soterichos son of Soterichos, approve.

(*fourth hand*) I, Patron son of Patunis, approve.

(*fifth hand*) I, Herodes son of Soterichos, approve.

(*sixth hand*) I, Psenobastis son of Herodes approve.

(*seventh hand*) I, Herodes son of Herodes, also called Isidorus, approve.

(*eighth hand*) I, Orsenouphis son of Harmiusis, approve.

(*ninth hand*) I, Apollonios son of Aphrodisios, approve.

(*tenth hand*) We, Herakles son of Aphrodisios, Harmiusis son of Phasos, Orses son of Kronides, and Mieus son of Harmiusis give our approval as indicated above. Nikanor son of Heliodoros wrote for them because they are illiterate.

(*eleventh hand*) I, Orsenouphis son of Horos, approve.

I, Orsenouphis son of Aphrodisios, approve.

I, Herakles son of Ptolemaios, approve.

Orsenouphis son of Horos, also called . . . wrote for them because they are illiterate.

301. Regulations of an Association of Apolysimoi

Tebtynis (Arsinoites, division of Polemon, Fayûm, Egypt). *PMich* V 244.

43 CE

Papyrus (32 × 28.5 cm) from the archives in Tebtynis, now in Ann Arbor, Michigan (inv. no. 1277). The precise meaning of *apoly-simoi* here is unclear, but it suggests that these people have been "released," "discharged," or "exempted" from particular duties or services. They may be a group of exempted tenant farmers who work on the estate. Cf. *SB* VI 9224, likely involving an "exempted tenant farmer" (*apolysimos g[eōrgos]*).

In the third year of emperor Tiberius Claudius Caesar Augustus Germanicus, in the month of Kaisareios, on the third supplementary day, at Tebtynis in the division of Polemon of the Arsinoite district (nome). Having assembled, the undersigned men of Tebtynis, who are exempted ones (*apolysimoi*) from an estate of emperor Tiberius Claudius Caesar Augustus Germanicus, decided by common consent to elect one of their number, a most excellent man, Kronion son of Herodes, to be supervisor (*epimelētēs*) for one year from the month of Sebastos of the coming fourth year of emperor Tiberius Claudius Caesar Augustus Germanicus. The same Kronion will collect the public charges of the head tax (*laographia*) of the same exempted ones (*apolysimoi*) and all the expenses of the association (*plēthos*).

If the leader (*hēgoumenos*) gives a command to attend a meeting in the village and someone is not present at the meeting, he shall be fined two silver drachmas payable to the association, except in the case that . . . one drachma. If the meeting is not at the usual place, he shall be fined four drachmas; and if it is in the metropolis, eight drachmas.

If any of the undersigned men is arrested for a debt up to the amount of one hundred silver drachmas, the association will stand surety for him for a period of sixty days. But if someone fails to pay his dues and does not pay some of the head tax or some of the expenses, Kronion shall have authority to exact a pledge from him, whether in the town square or in his house, and to hand over either him or his slaves.

Agreed that the undersigned men shall pay out of the common fund (*koinon*) to the above-mentioned estate on behalf of the above-mentioned Kronion the head tax for the coming fourth year of emperor Tiberius Claudius Caesar Augustus Germanicus. Agreed that they shall drink (i.e., hold a banquet) monthly on the days of the god Augustus, with the above mentioned Kronion supplying drink for the toasts, and everyone shall obey the leader (*hēgoumenos*).

If one of the leaders should die, or his father or mother or wife or child or brother or sister and any of the undersigned men does not defile himself (i.e., attend the funeral and encounter corpse impurity), he shall be fined four drachmas payable to the association. The one who is bereaved shall be feasted by the association (*koinon*) for one day. If anyone fails to pay his dues and likewise does not pay some of his contributions and expenses, the aforementioned leader is authorized to exact a pledge from him and hand him over as mentioned above.

(*column 1*)

Kronion son of Herodes, leader, about thirty-five years old, with a scar on his left shin; Onnophris son of Nepheros, about forty years old, with a scar on the left eyebrow; Psenkebkis son of Marres, about thirty-eight years old, with a scar on his forehead to the left above the eyebrow; Panesneus son of Harmiusis, about thirty years old, with a scar on his right eyebrow; Sigeris son of Pakebkis, about twenty-nine years old, with a scar on his forehead to the left by the temple; Pakebkis son of Sigeris, about thirty-five years old, with a scar on his left thumb; Sekonopis son of Papontos, who is also called Diodoros, about thirty-two years old, with a scar in the middle of his forehead; Anchious son of Anchious . . . , about thirty years old, with a scar on his right shin; Orseus the younger, son of Petermouthis, who is also called Kuberomnis, about thirty-three years old, with a scar on his left thumb; Papnebtunis son of Papnebtunis, about thirty-three years old, with a scar above his right cheek; Kronion son of Labesis, about thirty (?) years old, with a scar on his nose under the eyebrows; Eutychos son of Eutychos, son of *Name* . . . , about thirty years old, with a scar on his right thumb; Orseus son of Petesouchos, also called Ph . . . , about fifty years old, with a scar on his right forearm; Petesouchos son of Protos, also called Hermais, about thirty-five years old, with a scar on his right forearm;

(*column 2*)

Sisoeis son of Eutychos, the carpenter, about thirty-eight years old, with a scar in the middle of his forehead; Labesis son of Labesis, about thirty-five years old, with scars on his forehead; Harmaeis son of Harmaeis, about thirty-three years old, with a scar on his left thumb; Komon son of Anchious, about thirty-seven years old, with a scar on his forehead to the right; Orseus son of Papnebtunis, about thirty years old, with a scar on the little finger of his left hand; Hermas son of Anchious, about thirty-three years old, with a scar on his left knee; Orseus son of Haruotes, son of Nanas, about thirty-four years old, with a scar on the first finger of his left hand; Amaeis son of Marres, about thirty-five years old, with a scar on his left eyebrow; Horos son of Harmiusis, about thirty-two years old, with a scar on the first finger of his right hand; Papontos son of Papnebtunis, about thirty-two years old, with a scar on his left foot.

(*secondhand*) I, Kronion son of Herodes, president, have cast my vote in favor, as has been indicated above.

(*thirdhand*) I, Eutychos son of Eutychos, also called . . . have cast my vote.

(*reverse side [verso]*)

Hand-written copy (chirograph) of Kronion, son of Herodion.

302. Regulations of the Salt Merchants

Tebtynis (Arsinoites, division of Polemon, Fayûm, Egypt). *PMich* V 245.

47 CE (August 18)

> Papyrus (12.9 × 28.7 cm), now in Ann Arbor, Michigan (inv. no. 657).

In the seventh year of emperor Tiberius Claudius Caesar Augustus Germanicus, on the twenty-fifth of the month Kaisareios. Coming together, the undersigned men, salt merchants (*halopōlai*) of Tebtynis, have decided by common consent to elect one of their number, a good man, Apynchis son of Orseus, both supervisor (*epimelētēs*) and collector of the public taxes for the coming eighth year of emperor Tiberius Claudius Caesar Augustus Germanicus. The aforementioned Apynchis is to collect all the public taxes for the same trade (*ergasia*) for the coming year. All, acting together, shall sell salt in the aforementioned village of Tebtynis. Orseus alone has obtained the sole right by lot to sell gypsum in the aforementioned village of Tebtynis and in the nearby villages, for which he shall pay, apart from the portion of the public charges that falls to him, another sixty-six silver drachmas. Likewise, it is agreed that the same Orseus has obtained the sole right in Kerkesis to sell salt, for which he shall likewise pay another eight silver drachmas. And it is agreed that Harmiysis, also called Belles son of Harmiysis, has obtained the sole right to sell salt and gypsum in the village of Tristomos, also called Boukolos, for which he shall pay, apart from the portion of the public charges that falls to him, another five silver drachmas. This is upon the condition that they shall sell high quality salt at the rate of two and one-half obols, the light salt at the rate of two obols, and the lighter salt at one and one-half obol, by our measure or that of the warehouse. If someone sells salt at a lower price than these, he shall be fined eight silver drachmas, payable to the common fund and the same to the public treasury. And if any of them is found to have sold more than one coin's (stater's) worth of salt to a store, he shall be fined eight silver drachmas, payable to the common fund and the same amount to the public treasury.

If the merchant intends to buy more than four drachmas of salt, it is necessary that all sell to him jointly. If someone imports gypsum and wants to sell it outside the area, it must be left in the storerooms of Orseus son of Harmiysis, until he takes it outside the area and sells it.

It is agreed that they shall drink always on the twenty-fifth of each month with each member having a liquid measure (*chous*; i.e., about 3.25 liters) of beer. If someone fails to attend a meeting in the village he shall be fined one drachma; if the meeting is outside the village, the fine is four drachmas, and if it is in the metropolis, eight drachmas. If someone fails to pay his dues and does not pay any of the public charges or fines (?) laid against him, Apynchis has the authority to arrest him, whether in the town square or in his house or in the field, and to hand him over as was indicated above.

Apynchis son of Orseus (?), leader (*hēgoumenos*), about thirty-two years old, with a scar on the right side. . . ; *Name* . . . about thirty-one years old, with a scar on his left hand; . . . *Name* about fifty-five years old, with a scar on his . . . foot; . . . *Name* about . . . years old with a scar . . . ; . . . *Name* about . . . years old with a scar. . . .

Upper Egypt

303. Imperial Letters to an Athletic Synod and the "Diploma of the Boxer"

Hermopolis Magna (Hermopolite nome, Upper Egypt). *PLond* III 1178, lines 1–37 = *GCRE* 27, 28, and 37.

194 CE (collecting letters by Claudius from 46 CE and from 47 CE, and by Vespasian from ca. 69–79 CE)

> A papyrus roll with 102 lines (only lines 1–37 are translated here), now in the British Museum. The first letter (lines 1–7) is from one branch of the synod to another, confirming that Hermeinos the boxer had paid his entrance fee. (This letter is repeated again in lines 37–44.) This is followed by two earlier letters of emperor Claudius (lines 8–31) and the letter from emperor Vespasian (lines 32–36), all from the first century. Then comes the diploma of Hermeios itself (ca. 194 CE), which is divided into a formal notification of his admission as a member (lines 37–44) and a list of the club's officials (lines 50–56), including three chief priests (lines 50–57), a president of the games (lines 58–59), a treasurer, and a secretary (lines 60–65). This is followed by the signatures of those named (lines 66–83). Finally there is another certificate indicating Hermeinos' payment of an additional fifty denarii at the great games of Asia in Sardis (lines 84–102).

(*lines 1–7*)

Hermeinos, also called Moros, from Hermopolis, a boxer. The sacred, traveling athletic synod (*synodos*) of athletes who honor Augustus Hadrian Antoninus Septimius, to those belonging to the same synod, greetings.

Know that Hermeinos, also called Moros, a boxer from Hermopolis about . . . *x* years old is a member of our synod (*synoditēs*), and has fully paid the entrance fee of one hundred denarii in accordance with the regulation.

We have written to you, therefore, so that you might know. Farewell.

First Letter from Claudius (lines 8–15)

Tiberius Claudius Caesar Augustus Germanicus Sarmaticus, greatest high priest (*pontifex maximus*), with tribunician power for the sixth time, consul designate for the fourth time, proclaimed emperor (*imperator*) twelve times, father of the fatherland, to the athletic synod of traveling athletes, greetings.

The golden crown that was sent by you for the victory over Britain I have gladly accepted as a symbol embracing the piety that you have for me. Your envoys were Tiberius Claudius Hermas, Tiberius Claudius Kyros, Dion son of Mikkalos of Antioch. Farewell.

Second Letter from Claudius (lines 16–31)

Tiberius Claudius Caesar Augustus Germanicus Sarmaticus, greatest high priest, with tribunician power for the seventh time, consul for the sixth time, proclaimed emperor (*imperator*) for the eighteenth time, father of the fatherland, to the athletic synod of traveling athletes of Herakles, greetings.

In the two decrees that were shown to me at the same time . . . you commended to me Gaius Julius Antiochus, the king of Commagene, and Julius Polemo, the king of Pontus, honorable men and my friends. They have acted toward you energetically and generously at the time that they held the games which were established by them in my name. I have acknowledged your gratitude toward them, and I recognized, rather than being surprised at, the goodwill that they show toward me and the generosity shown to you. Those who are mentioned in the decree are Diogenes son of Mikkalos of Antioch, who is to be the next high priest of the synod, whom I have considered to be worthy of Roman citizenship along with his two daughters, Sandogene and . . . of Mikkalos of Antioch. Farewell.

Letter from emperor Vespasian (lines 32–36)

Emperor Caesar Vespasianus Augustus, to the sacred athletic synod of traveling athletes of Herakles, greetings.

Recognizing your athletic accomplishment and honor, I, the god Claudius concede to you all the privileges for which you asked, and I myself propose to maintain them. Farewell.

304. Loan of Money from the Treasurer of an Association

Oxyrhynchos (Oxyrynchites, Upper Egypt). *PRyl* IV 586.

99 BCE (October 17–November 15)

> Papyrus (10 × 24.5 cm), now at Graz, Universität Ms. I 1933 and
> Manchester, John Rylands Library Gr. 586. The term "Persian of
> descent" seems to be used in this period to refer to a Hellenizing
> Egyptian that had risen above the status of a "mere" Egyptian.
> While the term perhaps originally referred to members of the Per-
> sian military settlement or their descendants, all such "Persians"
> in the early Ptolemaic period bear Greek names and lack any clear
> indication of military status.

. . . Persian of the descent of the village of Aphrodite Bernike Polis . . . from
their common money, the sum of fifty-three talents, . . . thousand drachmas in copper, with an interest rate of two drachmas per month for each
mina (i.e., 24 percent per year). Let Demetrios repay the fifty-three talents
and . . . thousand drachmas with interest in the . . . month of the sixteenth
year, to the lenders or to the treasurer of the association (*koinon*) who will
be appointed for that year. If he does not repay the loan in accordance with
what is written here, Demetrios must repay to the lenders or to the treasurer of the association who will be immediately appointed both the loan
and the interest when the time that has been indicated has elapsed. The
surety for all the provisions in this agreement guaranteeing full payment
is Demetrios' wife Asklepias daughter of Sosibios, a Persian of the descent,
acting with the same guardian. The right of execution shall be with the
lender or with the treasurer of the association who will be appointed, on
both of them or against whichever they should choose, and against all of
their possessions, as if by a legal decision. The contract is valid.

(*secondhand*) Simaristos, aged about sixty, bald with a long face and
a scar on the right forehead; Didymos, aged about fifty-three years, with
his forehead bald and a long and smooth face, with a scar under this
right . . .; Demetrios, aged about thirty-three, smaller than . . . on the
ankle, and a scar on the right temple and another just below it.

Cyrenaica

305. Honors by a Corporate Body of Judeans for a Benefactor

Berenike (Cyrenaica). *IBerenike* 18 = *SEG* 16 (1976), no. 931 =
CJZC 70.

Late first century BCE (March 30)

> Slab of marble with moulded gable and moulded base, heavily worn
> on the top left section (hence the fragmentary beginning). The
> term *politeuma* (translated "corporate body" in this volume), which

can also be used in reference to a body of citizens (as at Chios), is attested for associations of various types, including those formed by military settlers (see the inscriptions from Sidon, under Syria). It does not necessarily connote a body formally recognized by political institutions as previously believed (see Lüderitz 1994). This group uses the same self-designation in another inscription, and it seems that the same group also referred to itself as a "synagogue" in later decades (see **306–7**).

In third year on the fifth of Phamenoth, during the leadership (archonship) of . . . (*missing names*) . . . Dorion son of Ptolemaios, Zela . . . son of Gnaius, Ariston son of Arasas (?), . . . son of Andromachos, Nikias son of . . . , *Name* son of Simon.

Whereas Decimus Valerius Dionysios son of Gaius . . . is an honorable and good man and continues . . . and does good whenever he is able, both for the community and for each of the citizens individually, and . . . he had the amphitheater floors plastered and the walls painted.

The leaders and the corporate body (*politeuma*) of the Judeans in Berenike resolved to engrave his name in the . . . and to be free from services (*leitourgia*) of every kind. Likewise they resolved to also crown him with an olive crown and wool ribbon at each meeting (*synodos*) and new moon. Now after they have engraved the decree on a monument of white Parian stone, let the leaders (*archontes*) place it in a conspicuous place in the amphitheater.

All pebbles white (i.e., unanimous positive results of the vote).

Decimus Valerius Dionysios son of Gaius plastered the floors and painted the amphitheater at his own expense, a contribution to the corporate body.

306. Honors by a Corporate Body of Judeans for a Roman Provincial Official

Berenike (Cyrenaica). *IBerenike* 17 = *CJZC* 71 = *IGRR* I 1024.

24 CE (if the fifty-fifth year refers to the Actian era) or, less likely, 41 BCE (if it refers to the Cyrenaican era)

> Slab of marble, in the Musée St. Raymond at Toulouse in 1977. The presence of a Roman citizen within the Judean group at the time of this inscription suggests that the date of 24 CE is more likely.

In the fifty-fifth year, on the twenty-fifth of Phaoph, at the assembly of the feast of Tabernacles, during the leaderships (archonships) of Kleandros son of Stratonikos, Euphranor son of Ariston, Sosigenes son of Sosippos, Andromachos son of Andromachos, Marcus Laeilius Onasion son of

Apollonios, Philonides son of Hagemon, Autokles son of Zenon, Sonikos son of Theodotos, and Josepos son of Straton:

Whereas Marcus Tittius son of Sextus, member of the Aemilia tribe, an excellent man has, since he arrived in the province over public affairs, performed his governorship over these affairs in a good and humane manner and has always displayed a calm disposition in his behavior. He has shown himself to be nonburdensome not only in these affairs but also with the citizens who meet with him individually. Furthermore, in performing his governorship in a useful way for the Judeans of our corporate body (*politeuma*), both individually and as a group, he never fails to live up to his own noble rank.

For these reasons, the leaders and the corporate body of Judeans in Berenike decided to praise him, to crown him by name at each gathering and new moon with a crown of olive branches and ribbon, and to have the leaders engrave the decree on a monument of Parian stone which is to be set up in the most prominent place in the amphitheater. All pebbles white (i.e., unanimous positive results of the vote).

307. List of Donors to the Renovation of a Synagogue Building

Berenike (Cyrenaica). *IBerenike* 16 = *CJZC* 72 = *SEG* 17 (1977), no. 823.

55 CE (December 3)

> Marble panel with a moulding on the left and right, found reused in ancient walls but likely destroyed in World War II. Most of the donors are designated by their role as leader (archon), with one designated as a priest. Two of the donors of five drachmas are women.

(*column 1*)

In the second year of emperor Nero Claudius Caesar Drusus Germanicus, on the sixth of the month of Choiach. It seemed good to the synagogue of the Judeans in Berenike that they should inscribe on a monument of Parian stone the names of those who contributed toward the restoration of the synagogue (*synagōgē*):

Zenion son of Zoilos, leader (*archōn*): ten drachmas; Eisidoros son of Doseitheos, leader: ten drachmas; Doseitheos son of Ammonion, leader: ten drachmas; Pratis son of Ionathas, leader: ten drachmas; Karnedas son of Cornelius, leader: ten drachmas; Herakleides son of Herakleides, leader: ten drachmas; Thaliarchos son of Dositheos, leader: ten drachmas; Sosibios son of Iason, leader: ten drachmas; Pratomedes son of Sokrates, leader: ten drachmas; Antigonos son of Straton, leader: ten drachmas; Kartisthenes son of Archias, priest (*hiereus*): ten drachmas; Lysanias son of Lysanias: twenty-five drachmas; Zenodoros son of Theuphilos: twenty-eight drachmas; Marion son of . . . *Name*: twenty-five drachmas . . .

(*column 2*)

Alexandros son of Euphranor: five drachmas; Eisidora daughter of Serapion: five drachmas; Zosime daughter of Terpolios: five drachmas; Polon son of Dositheos: five drachmas.

ITALY AND THE WESTERN PROVINCES

Italy

308. Donation to the Association of Silvanus

Caposele (Lucania, Italy). *CIL* X 444 = *ILS* 3546 = Waltzing 1895–1900, vol. 3, no. 1636.

81–96 CE (time of emperor Domitian)

Latin inscription.

Dedicated to Silvanus, in fulfillment of a vow for the welfare of our emperor Domitian Augustus.

Lucius Domitius Phaon, in order to ensure for all time the cult, the maintenance, and the sacrifices for the members who are now in the association (*collegium*) of Silvanus and who will be in the future, has allotted his own estates (*fundus*)—called "Iunianus," "Lollianus," "Percennianus," and "Statuleianus"—along with their villas and enclosed territories. He has also stipulated that the income that comes from the aforementioned estates shall be used on the following days: on the Kalends of January (January 1); on the third of the Ides of February (February 13), which is the birthday of our Empress Domitiana; on the fifth of the Kalends of July (June 27), which is the dedication of the association to Silvanus; on the twelfth of the Kalends of July (July 20) at the Rose festival (*rosalia*); and, on the ninth of the Kalends of November (October 23), which is the birthday of our Domitian Augustus. They shall perform the sacred ceremonies in his presence, and those in the association (*collegium*) shall gather for a banquet under the supervision of the magistrates (*magistri*) for that year.

(*line 20*)

They shall do everything mentioned above without deceit, and so that all know that it is for the welfare of our most excellent leader (*princeps*) and lord (*dominus*) that the estates listed below [*sic*] have been dedicated and the days of sacrifice fixed. Further, the area—the field and the forest situated in the reserve and which is delimited by the borders around the statue of Silvanus—is dedicated to Silvanus and the road which leads to the statue of Silvanus through the estate of "Quaesicianus" shall be accessible to everyone. The wood also, and the water used for the purpose of the sacrifices shall be gathered from the estate of Gallicianus and from the adjacent reserve.

L. Domitius Phaon, owner of all the lands, thus ordered that these donations be made, accomplishing all of these presentations without deceit.

309. Bequest to an Association of Rag Dealers by a Woman

Cemelenum (Gallia Cisalpina, Italy). *CIL* V 7906 = *ILS* 8374 = Waltzing 1895–1900, vol. 3, no. 608.

Uncertain date

Latin inscription.

To Publius Etereius Quadratus son of Publius, of the Quirina tribe: his mother Etereia Aristolais set up a statue. For its dedication she provided the customary banquet to the association (*collegium*) of rag dealers and gave . . . *x* denarii. Annually and in perpetuity on the birthday of Quadratus, April 9th, at the place where he is buried they shall use the interest on this sum to offer a sacrifice (*unknown words*); they shall hold the customary banquet in the temple; and, they shall bring an offering of roses in season and cover and crown the statue. They have agreed that they (i.e., the members) will do this.

310. Regulations of the Worshippers of Diana and Antinoüs

Lanuvium (Campania, Italy). *CIL* XIV 2112 = *ILS* 7212 = Bendlin 2011.

136 CE (June 9)

Marble plaque with a Latin inscription, broken into sixty-five pieces and found in 1816, now in the Museo nationale romano alle Terme di Diocleziano (inv. no. 1031). The inscription may have been attached to the wall of a public bath or located near a cemetery.

In the year that Lucius Commodus and Sextus Vettulenus Civica Pompeianus were consuls, five days before the Ides of June (June 9), (*column 1*) at Lanuvium in the temple of Antinoüs, in which Lucius Caesennius Rufus, patron of the municipality had directed that a meeting be called through Lucius Pompeius . . . *Name*, president (*quinquennalis*) of the worshipers of Diana and Antinoüs, he promised that he would give them, out of his generosity, the interest on fifteen thousand sesterces, namely, four hundred sesterces on the birthday of Diana on the Ides of August (August 13), and four hundred sesterces on the birthday of Antinoüs, five days before the Kalends of December (November 27). He also instructed that the bylaws established by them should be inscribed on the inner side at the bottom of the four-columned porch (tetrastyle) of the temple of Antinoüs as recorded below.

In the year that Marcus Antonius Hiberus and Publius Mummius Sisenna were consuls, on the Kalends of January (January 1), the benevolent association (*collegium salutare*) of Diana . . . and Antinoüs was founded, Lucius Caesennius Rufus son of Lucius, of the Quirinia tribe, being for the third time sole magistrate (*dictator*) and also patron.

(*line 10*)

Clause from the decree of the Senate of the Roman People: *These are permitted to assemble, convene, and have an association* (collegium): *those who desire to make monthly contributions . . . may assemble in such an association, but . . . not . . . in the name of such an association except once a month for the sake of . . . , to provide burial for them when they die.*

May this be favorable, propitious, and happy to the emperor Caesar Trajan Hadrian Augustus and to the entire imperial house, to us, to our families, and to our association, and may we have made proper and careful arrangements for providing decent arrangements at the departure of the dead! Therefore we must all agree to contribute faithfully, so that our association may be able to continue in existence a long time.

(*line 20*)

You who desire to enter this association as a new member must first read the bylaws carefully before entering, so as not to find cause for complaint later or bequeath a lawsuit to your heir.

Bylaws of the Collegium

[1] It was voted unanimously that whoever wishes to enter this association shall pay an initiation fee of one hundred sesterces and an amphora of good wine, and shall pay monthly dues of five *asses* (= 1.25 sesterces).

[2] It was voted further that if anyone has not paid his dues for six consecutive months and the common lot of humankind befalls him, his claim to burial shall not be considered, even if he has provided for it in his will.

[3] It was further voted that upon the death of a paid-up member of our body there will be due him from the treasury three hundred sesterces, from which sum will be deducted a funeral

fee of fifty sesterces, which will be distributed at the funeral pyre (among those attending); the obsequies, furthermore, will be performed on foot.

[4] It was further voted that if a member dies farther than twenty miles from town and the association is notified, three men chosen from our body will be required to go there to arrange for his funeral; they will be required to render an accounting in good faith to the membership (*populus*), and if they are found guilty of any fraud they shall pay a quadruple fine. They will be given money for the funeral expenses (*funeraticium*), and in addition a round trip travel allowance of twenty sesterces each.

(*line 30*)

But if a member dies farther than twenty miles from town and notification is impossible, then he who has carried out the funeral shall claim his funeral expenses (*funeraticium*) from the association. The seals of seven Roman citizens must be attached to the documents and the matter has been approved. And security must be given that no one else is going to claim a further sum, and that the stipends and the money spent on the obsequies in accordance with the bylaws of the association have been deducted. Let no bad faith attend!

Also let no patron or patroness, master (*column 2*) or mistress, or creditor have any right of claim against the association, unless he has been named heir in a will. If a member dies without a will, the details of his burial (*funus*) will be decided by the president (*quinquennalis*) and the membership (*populus*).

[5] It was voted further that if a slave member of this association dies and his master or mistress unreasonably refuses to relinquish the body for burial, and he has not left written instruction, a funeral with an image of him will be held.

[6] It was further voted that if any member takes his own life for any reason whatever, his claim to burial shall not be considered.

(*line 40*)

[7] It was voted further that if any slave becomes free, he must give an amphora of good vine.

[8] It was voted further that if any master (*magister*), in the year when it is his turn in the membership list to provide dinner,

fails to comply and provide a dinner, he shall pay thirty sesterces into the treasury. The man next in line shall be required
to give the dinner, and the delinquent shall be required to
reciprocate when it is the latter's turn.

[9] Roster (*ordo*) of dinners: eight days before the Ides of March
(March 8), on the birthday of Caesennius . . . the father; five
days before the Kalends of December (November 27), on
birthday of Antinoüs; on the Ides of August (August 13), the
birthday of Diana and of the association (*collegium*); thirteen
days before the Kalends of September (August 20), on the
birthday of Caesennius Silvanus, his brother; the day before
the Nones of (?) (September 12 [?]), the birthday of Cornelia Procula, his mother; nineteen days before the Kalends of
January (December 14), the birthday of Caesennius Rufus,
patron of the municipality.

[10] Masters (*magistri*) of the dinners in the order of the membership list (*album*), appointed four at a time in turn, shall be
required to provide an amphora of good wine each, and for
as many members as the association has, bread costing two
asses, four sardines, the setting, and warm water with service.

(*line 50*)

[11] It was voted further that any member who becomes president
(*quinquennalis*) in this association shall be exempt from contributions for the term when he is president, and that he shall
receive a double share in all distributions.

[12] It was further voted that the secretary (*scriba*) and the messenger (*viator*) shall be exempt from such obligations and
shall receive a share and a half in every distribution.

[13] It was voted further that any member who has administered
the office of president honestly shall receive a share and a half
of everything as a mark of this honor, so that other presidents will also hope for the same by discharging their duties
properly.

[14] It was voted further that if any member wishes to lodge any
complaint or discuss business, he is to bring it up at a business
meeting, so that we may have the banquet in peace and good
cheer on festive days.

[15] It was further voted that any member who moves from one
seat to another so as to cause a disturbance shall be fined four
sesterces.

(line 60)

> Any member, moreover, who speaks abusively of another or causes an uproar shall be fined twelve sesterces. Any member who uses any abusive or insolent language to a president at a banquet shall be fined twenty sesterces.

[16] It was further voted that on the solemn days of his term each president is to conduct worship with incense (?) and wine and is to perform his other functions clothed in white, and that on the birthdays of Diana and Antinoüs he is to provide oil for the association in the public bath before the banquet.

311. Bequest to an Association of Rag Dealers by a Freedman

Mevania (Umbria, Italy). *CIL* XI 5047 = Waltzing 1895–1900, vol. 3, no. 1890.

Uncertain date

> Marble slab with a Latin inscription between reliefs of two Corinthian columns. The decorative triptych top depicts a woman in the center panel with a swan in the panel on either side. The base has a roughly cut tenon that could be inserted into a socket.

Gaius Atticus Januarius, a freedman of Gaius Atticus, one of the Six *Sacris faciundis* (i.e., a priestly college) and one of the Eight Men of Valetudo, bequeathed to the association (*collegium*) of rag dealers one thousand sesterces. No fewer than twelve men shall use the annual income to hold a banquet at his tomb on the festival of the Parentalia. This is in the care of the association of rag dealers.

312. Honors by a Synod of Alexandrian Athletes for a Priest with a List of Victories

Neapolis (Campania, Italy). *INapoli* I 51 = *IGRR* I 446 = PH177663.

ca. 100 CE

> The Greek term *pankration*, literally meaning "all powers" but translated "kickboxing" here, refers to a combat sport that combined boxing and wrestling with the use of punching, kicking, choking, and pressure holds (cf. Philostratos, *On Gymnastics*). (For a mosaic from Ostia depicting a wrestling match, see figure 17.)

For good fortune! The emperor-loving, Roman-loving, traveling, pious synod of Alexandrians honored T. Flavius Archibios of the Quirinia tribe, Alexandrian, high priest for life of the whole athletic meeting, and marvelous victor. At the 220th and 221st Olympic games, he won the men's kickboxing (*pankration*) competition. At the Capitolinian games in Rome, he won the crown for the youths' (lit.: beardless) kickboxing at the third quinquinenial (i.e., every four years) gathering; he won the men's kickboxing at the fourth; he won the crown for men's kickboxing at the fifth; and, he likewise won the crown for men's kickboxing at the sixth, placing first. At the games at Herakleia in honor of emperor Nero Trajan Caesar Augustus Germanicus Dacicus, he was crowned for victory for the men's kickboxing. At the Pythian games, he won the youths' kickboxing and both the men's wrestling and kickboxing in successive Pythiads, as well as placing first in the men's kickboxing. At the Nemean games, he won the boys' kickboxing and placed first among men three times in succession . . . men's kickboxing. At the Actian games, he won the youths' wrestling and kickboxing, as well as placing first among men in kickboxing. At the games at Neapolis, he won the youths' kickboxing and the men's kickboxing twice in succession . . . the youth's wrestling and kickboxing, as well as winning the men's wrestling and kickboxing twice in succession and placing first in the men's kickboxing in succession. At the Ephesian Balbilleian games, he placed first in the men's wrestling, boxing, and kickboxing. In the sacred, quinquennial games at Antioch in celebration of the battle of Actium, he won the boys' kickboxing, the youths' wrestling and kickboxing in quinquennial succession and the men's kickboxing in succession, as well as placing first in the men's kickboxing in succession. At the games of the provincial assembly of Asia at Smyrna, he won the youth's wrestling and kickboxing. At the sacred, quinquennial games in Alexandria in celebration of the battle of Actium, he won the boys' kickboxing and, after one quinquennial, he won the men's kickboxing, as well as winning the men's kickboxing in succession and placing first in the men's wrestling and kickboxing in succession. And he has also won the boys', youths', and men's wrestling and kickboxing at the shield-of-Argos festival and numerous other quinquennial games.

313. List of Society Members and Donors to a Temple

Ostia, port city of Rome (Latium, Italy). *CIL* XIV 246 (addenda) = Waltzing 1895–1900, vol. 3, no. 2227.

140–172 CE

Table of marble with a Latin inscription, now lost. The first lines form a title running across the entire inscription; below this are seven columns of names.

In the year that emperor Caesar Titus Aelius Hadrian Antoninus Augustus Pius, father of the fatherland (*pater patriae*) for the third time, and

Figure 17
Mosaic depicting two wrestlers from Ostia (photo by Ascough).

Marcus Aelius Aurelius Caesar were consuls, the following was the roster (*ordo*) of society members (*corporati*) who contributed money for the
enlarging of the temple:

Patrons: Titus Prifernius Paetus Rosianus Geminus son of Sextus
(Prifernius), Marcus Stlaccius Albinus, Trebellius Sallustius Rufus, Mar-
cus Sedatius Severianus son of Gaius (Sedatius), Titus Prifernius Paetus
Rosianus Geminus son of Titus (Prifernius), Marcus Sedatius Severus
Julius Reginus son of Marcus (Sedatius), Gaius Allius Fuscianus son of
Gaius (Allius), Titus Statilius Taurus son of Titus (Statilius), Tiberius
Aterius Saturninus, Gaius Pantuleius Graptiacus, Gaius Allius Fuscus son
of Gaius Allius.

(*column 2*)

President (*quinquennalis*) for life: Gaius Sossius Benedictus; president: Aulus Egrilius, an Augustalis; presidents: Publius Sulpicius Hera, Lucius Naevius Saecularis.

In the year that the two Quintilii were consuls: president: Aulus Egrilius Faustus.

In the year that Silvanus and Augurinus were consuls: presidents: Titus Fisevius Nicephorus, Lucius Naevius Proculus.

In the year that Laelianus and Pastor were consuls: president: Titus Fisevius Priscianus.

In the year that Clarus and Cethegus were consuls: president: Marcus Magius Marsus.

In the year that Maximus and Orfitus were consuls: president: Lucius Helvius Restitutus

Aulus Egrilius Faustus, by his will bequeathed four thousand sesterces on the following condition: that from the interest on above-mentioned sum they shall hold a banquet on the fifth of the Kalends of December (November 27) each year.

(*A list of 181 names follows in seven columns. Column 3: 31 names; column 4: 31 names; column 5: 33 names; column 6: 40 names; column 7: 46 names; for a total of 181 names in columns 3–7*).

314. Two Lists of Leaders and Members of an Association of Sailors and Accountants

Ostia, port city of Rome (Latium, Italy). *CIL* XIV 250, 251 = *ILS* 6174–75; Waltzing 1895–1900, vol. 3, nos. 2231–32.

152, 193 CE

> Two tables of marble, each with Latin inscriptions. The second is much larger than the first.

CIL XIV 250

In the year that Manius Acilius Glabrion and Marcus Valeius Homulum were consuls, the following was the roster (*ordo*) of the sailors, accountants, and assistants of Ostia.

Patrons: Marcus Sedatius Severianus, son of Gaius (Sedatius), Titus Prefernius Paetus Rosianus Geminus, son of Sextus (Prefernius), Marcus Sedatius Severus Julius Reginus, son of Marcus Sedatius, Gaius Aleius Fuscianus, son of Gaius Aleius, Lucius Volusius Maecianus, Lucius Julius Memor, Marcus Cipius Proclianus, Titus Aurelius Strenion, a freedman of Augustus, Lucius Marius Germanus.

President (*quinquennalis*) for life: Marcus Cornelius Epagathus.

Presidents: Marcus Antistius Helius and Marcus Cornelius Secundus son of Marcus Cornelius.

Members (*plebs*) (*125 names in four columns*).

CIL XIV 251

In the year that emperor (*imperator*) Caesar Augustus Publius Helvius Pertinax was consul for the second time: The roster (*ordo*) of the sailors, accountants, and assistants of Ostia.

(*column 1*)

Senatorial patrons: (*name erased*), Lucius Fabius Cilo Septiminus, and Marcus Umbilius Maximinus.

Equestrians: Lucius Furius Publicius Marcellus, father; Marcus Cornelius Valerianus; Sextus Sextilius Julianus, the son; Lucius Valerius Daphnus; Sextus Sextilius Julianus, the father.

President (*quinquennalis*) for life: Marcus Publicius Ostiensis, senior; president for the second time: Marcus Cornelius Valerianus; president for life: Lucius Valerius Daphnus; president for life: Marcus Cipius Victor; president for life: Sextus Sextilius Julianus, the father; presidents: Marcus Curtius Victorinus, Aulus Herenuleins Vettianus.

(*column 2*)

Members (*plebs*): Publius Cornelius Phoebus . . . (*258 names in seven columns*).

315. Dedication by an Association to the Unconquered God

Paestum (Bruttium and Lucania, Italy). *AÉ* (1975), no. 236.

Uncertain date

> Table of bronze with Latin inscription found in the temple. The "unconquered god" invoked here refers to Mithras.

The association (*collegium*) erected this monument to the unconquered god (*deus invictus*) for Aurelius, a freedman, from their own resources.

316. Dedication to Phrygian Zeus by a Corporate Body of Phrygians from Alexandria

Pompeii (Campania, Italy), originally from Alexandria, Egypt. *IAlexandriaK* 74 = *IG* XIV 701 = *IGRR* I 458 = PH227164.

3 BCE

> Base of black basalt. Found in the forum of Pompeii in 1818, originally from Alexandria in Egypt (as indicated by the form of dating).

It was brought to Pompeii before the volcanic eruption of 79 CE, perhaps by Hephaistion himself or other members of this Phrygian association.

Gaius Julius Hephaistion, son of Hephaistion, having served as priest of the corporate body (*politeuma*) of Phrygians, dedicated this to Phrygian Zeus. The twenty-seventh year of Caesar (Augustus), month of Pharmouthi, Augustan day.

317. Letter of the Tyrian Settlers at Puteoli to the City of Tyre

Puteoli (Campania, Italy). *IG* XIV 830 = *OGIS* 595 = Sosin 1999, 276–78 = PH141062.

174 CE

> Slab of marble, now in the Capitoline Museum in Rome. This monument presents two documents. The first is a letter from Tyrian merchants settled in Puteoli to their home city of Tyre in Phoenicia, requesting help in making payment for the continuation of their "station," the building used by this group of immigrants. The second, partially preserved, document is a portion of the minutes of the civic Council meeting at Tyre, responding to the request. Unfortunately, the inscription breaks off in the middle of the discussion. Sosin (1999) suggests the possibility that the debate was between Philokles, who was actually trying to do away with the station at Puteoli, and Laches, who was defending the independent existence of the Puteoli group. Regardless of the nature of the debate, which is difficult to determine, what is clear is that the group at Puteoli was successful in gaining the help of their home city of Tyre, for the Tyrians at Puteoli subsequently paid to have these documents engraved on this monument. Another fragmentary inscription, which involves the god Helios Sareptenos (= Baal of Sarapta), attests to the presence of Tyrians at Puteoli as early as 79 CE (*OGIS* 594). That god may be among the Phoenician, "ancestral gods" mentioned in our inscription here.

This is a letter which was written to the city of Tyre, the sacred, inviolable, and autonomous metropolis of Phoenicia and of other cities, and mistress of a fleet.

To the civic leaders (*archontes*), Council and People of their sovereign homeland, from those settled in Puteoli (*hoi en Potiolois katoikountes*), greetings.

Because of the gods and the fortune of our lord, the emperor, if there are any other stations in Puteoli, our station (*station*) is better than the others both in adornment and in size, as most of you know. In the past, this was cared for by the Tyrians settled in Puteoli, who were numerous and wealthy. But now our number has dwindled to a few and, since we pay the expenses for the sacrifices and services to our ancestral gods established here in temples, we do not have the means to pay the station's annual payment of two hundred fifty denarii, especially as the expenses for the bull sacrifice at the games in Puteoli have been imposed on us. We therefore beg you to provide for the station's continued existence. Now it will continue if you make provision for annual payment of two hundred fifty denarii. For we took care of the other expenses and those incurred in the restoration of the station for the sacred day of our lord, the emperor, so as not to burden the city (i.e., Tyre). We also remind you that no income accrues either from shippers (*nauklēroi*) or from merchants (*emporoi*) to our station, as is the case with the station in royal Rome. We therefore beg you to make provision in this circumstance.

Written in Puteoli, July 23, during the consulship of Gallus and Flaccus Cornelianus.

From the records of the Council conducted on the eleventh of the month of Dios in the year 300 (= December 8, 174 CE), when C. Valerius Kallikrates son of Pausanias was presiding for the day as president. The letter of the Tyrian station was read, having been brought by Laches, one of them. In the letter, they asked to make provision of the two hundred fifty denarii for them for the sacrifices and services of our ancestral gods which are established in temples there, since they do not have the means to supply the payment for the station, two hundred fifty denarii each year, and the expenses for the bull sacrifice at the games in Puteoli have been imposed on them. For they took care of the other expenses and those incurred in the restoration the station for the sacred day of our lord, the emperor, so as not to burden the city (i.e., Tyre). They also remind us that no income accrues either from shippers or from merchants, as is the case in the station in royal Rome.

After which, Philokles son of Diodoros said: "The members of the station (*statiōnarioi*) in Rome have always had the custom of furnishing the two hundred fifty denarii for those in Puteoli from what they (i.e., those in Rome) themselves receive. Now the members of the station in Puteoli also request to maintain these same arrangements for them; or, if those in Rome are not willing to furnish it for them, they undertake combining the two stations under the same leadership." They exclaimed: "Philokles speaks well! Rightly do those in Puteoli make the request. It has always been done this way, so let it continue now. This is advantageous for the city. Preserve the custom."

A written message was submitted by Laches son of Premogeneia and by Agathopous, his son, a Tyrian member *stationarius* of the Tyrian station, which is in the colony of Augusta Puteoli. In the message, they demonstrated that our homeland furnished both stations, the one in royal Rome. . . .

318. Election of a Patron by an Association of Laborers and Rag Dealers

Regium Lepidum (Aemilia, Italy). *CIL* XI 970 = Waltzing 1895–1900, vol. 3, no. 1819.

190 CE

> Table of bronze with a Latin inscription.

In the year that the emperor Caesar Marcus Aurelius Commodus Antoninus Augustus Pius Felix, for the sixth time, and Marcus Petronius Septimianus, were consuls, on March 23 in the temple of the association (*collegium*) of laborers and rag dealers of Regium. Whereas on the proposal of the treasurers, Publius Saenius Marcellinus and Gaius Aufidius Dialogus, it was stated that Tutilius Julianus, a generous man distinguished for his manner of life, his unassuming nature, and his innate modesty, ought to be adopted by our association as its patron, so that the evidence of our decision might serve as an example to other prospective benefactors. Concerning what we were pleased to see done concerning this matter, it was resolved as follows: We feel, one and all, that this most honorable proposal has been made by the treasurer and masters (*magistri*) of our society with good counsel; that therefore apologies should certainly be made to the honorable gentleman Julianus for the unavoidableness of this belated consideration of ours; that he should be asked to undertake, if he please, the function of patron of our association; and, that a bronze tablet inscribed with this resolution should be placed in his house. Adopted.

319. Honors by Paean Singers for a Prophet and "Father"

Rome (Latium, Italy). *IGUR* 77 = R. E. A. Palmer, "Paean and Paeanist of Serapis and the Flavian Emperors," in *Nomodeiktes: Greek Studies in Honor of Martin Ostwald*, ed. Ralph M. Rosen and Joseph Farrell (Ann Arbor: University of Michigan Press, 1993), 355–66 = *IG* XIV 1084 = PH187710.

146 CE (May 6)

> Slab found at the church of Santa Maria on Via Lata, near the ancient location of the sanctuaries of Isis and of Sarapis. This group,

who sang paeans (songs of victory or chants), probably included members from Alexandria in Egypt, as indicated by the method of dating. The same group is attested in the fragmentary *IGUR* 35, which preserves part of an imperial reply (in Latin) to the Paeanists' petition (in Greek).

The sacred order (*taxis*) of the Paeanists of Zeus Helios, the great Sarapis, in Rome and of the Augusti (*Sebastoi*) gods (i.e., members of the imperial family) honored Embes, prophet and father (*patēr*) of the order mentioned above, with a marble bust which was set up in the house (*oikos*) of the Paeanists on the day before the Nones of May, which is the eleventh of the month of Pachon according to the Alexandrians. This was done when Meteilius Ampliatus the elder was curator, during the consulship of Sextus Erucius Clarus—consul for the second time—and Gnaeus Claudius Severus.

320. Dedication and Imperial Letter from Emperor Hadrian Involving an Athletic Synod

Rome (Latium, Italy). *IGUR* 235 = *GCRE* 86 = PH187869.

143 CE, copying an earlier imperial letter from 134 CE

> Large base of white marble, in the Archaeological Museum at Naples in 1971. This dedication to the emperor Antoninus Pius along with an earlier imperial letter from emperor Hadrian is one of several inscriptions involving M. Ulpius Domesticus or the synod of athletes (see *IGUR* 235–50). It is not clear what documents or contracts the synod planned to modify, but the emperor was unconcerned.

(*front*)

For good fortune! M. Ulpius Domesticus, the high priest of the whole athletic meeting and officer in charge of the Augustan baths dedicated this to Marcus Aelius Aurelius Caesar, son of Titus Aelius Hadrian Antoninus Augustus Pius.

(*side*)

For good fortune! Emperor Caesar Trajan Hadrian Augustus, son of god Trajan Parthicus, grandson of god Nerva, greatest high priest (i.e., *pontifex maximus*), with tribunician power for the eighteenth time, consul for the third time, father of the fatherland, to the athletic synod of victorious and crowned athletes gathered around Herakles, greetings.

I will order that a place be given to you there as you wish, as well as a building to store your common documents. If you also consider the modification of the contracts necessary, that is up to you. Ulpius Domesticus was ambassador. Farewell.

May 5, from Rome.

321. Dedication and Imperial Letter from Antoninus Pius Involving an Athletic Synod

Rome (Latium, Italy). *IGUR* 236 = *GCRE* 128 = PH187870.

143 CE

> Base of white marble, in the Archaeological Museum at Naples in 1971.

(*front*)

M. Ulpius Domesticus, the high priest of the whole athletic meeting and officer in charge of the Augustan baths dedicated this to emperor Caesar Titus Aelius Hadrian Antoninus Augustus Pius.

(*side*)

For good fortune! Emperor Caesar T. Aelius Hadrian Antoninus Augustus, son of god Hadrian, grandson of god Trajan Parthicus, great-grandson of god Nerva, greatest high priest (i.e., *pontifex maximus*), with tribunician power for the sixth time, proclaimed emperor (*imperator*) for the second time, father of the fatherland, to the athletic synod of victorious and crowned athletes gathered around Herakles, greetings.

I ordered that you receive a space in which to place the sacred objects and the documents, near the hot baths themselves, those which were built by my grandfather, where you often come together for the Capitoline games. Farewell. Ulpius Domesticus was the ambassador, officer in charge of my baths.

This was written May 16 from Rome in the consulship of Torquatus and Herodes.

322. Regulations of the Association of Aesculapius (Asklepios) and Hygiae

Rome, Campus Martius district (Latium, Italy). *CIL* VI 10234 = *ILS* 7213 = Waltzing 1895–1900, vol. 3, nos. 268–71.

153 CE

> Marble plaque with a Latin inscription, now in the Vatican (Sala dell'Apoxyomenos, inv. no. 1172). "Aesculapius" is the Latin version

of Asklepios, god of healing. The goddess Hygiae (Latin equivalent of Hygieia) was often portrayed as the daughter of Asklepios.

Bylaws of the association (*collegium*) of Aesculapius and Hygiae ("Health"):

Salvia Marcellina daughter of Gaius (Salvius), in memory of Flavius Apollonius, procurator of the Augusti, who was in charge of the picture gallery in the palace, and in memory of Capito, imperial freedman, his assistant and her most excellent and pious husband, donated as a gift to the association (*collegium*) of Aesculapius and Hygiae the land for a chapel with a shop and a marble statue of Aesculapius and an attached covered solarium in which the membership (*populi*) of the above-named association can hold a banquet. This is located on the Via Appia near the temple of Mars, between the first and second milestones, on the left if one is leaving the city, between the property of Vibius Calocaerus and the public land. Likewise the same Marcellina donated to the sixty members of the above-named association fifty thousand sesterces, on the following conditions:

- that no more members be elected than the above-mentioned number;
- that the place of deceased members shall be sold, and free persons shall be elected to membership or, if anyone wishes to bequeath his place to a son or a brother or a freedman, he may do so provided that he contribute to our treasury (*arca*) one-half of the funeral dues;
- that they use the above-mentioned funds for no other purpose than holding meetings on the days listed below;
- that, if they realize any income from the interest from this sum, they shall give presents (*sportulae*) to the sixty members—a provision that was approved unanimously at a plenary meeting convened in the temple of the deified Caesars, in the shrine of the deified Titus, on March 11, in the year that Bruttius Praesens and Junius Rufinus were consuls; and,
- that they shall distribute the presents on the 19th of September, which is the birthday of our emperor Antoninus Pius, father of the country.

This was approved in the temple of the deified Caesars, in the shrine of the deified Titus. Gaius Ofilius Hermes, president (*quinquennalis*) for life, or whoever it might be at that time, shall receive three denarii; Aelius Zenon, father of the association (*pater collegi*), shall receive three denarii; Salvia Marcellina, mother of the association (*mater collegi*), shall receive three denarii; dues-exempt members (*immunes*) shall receive two denarii each; the supervisors (*curatores*) shall receive two denarii each; and, members (*populus*) shall receive one denarius each.

It was also agreed that on the 9th of November, the anniversary of the association, they shall distribute the following from the above-mentioned interest in our meeting place (*schola*) near the temple of Mars: to the president (*quinquennalis*), six denarii; to the father of the association (*pater collegi*), six denarii; to the mother of the association (*mater collegi*), six denarii; to dues-exempt members, four denarii each; to the supervisors (*curatores*), four denarii and bread worth three asses each. Measures of wine: to the president (*quinquennalis*), nine measures (*sextarii*; about 5 liters, since a *sextarius* was about 0.546 liters); to the father of the association (*pater collegi*), nine measures; to dues-exempt members, six measures each; to the supervisors (curatores), six measures each; and, to individual members, three measures each.

It was also agreed that on the 4th of January they shall distribute the New Year's presents in the same way prescribed above on September 19th.

Also, on the 22nd of February, on the day of our beloved agreement, in the same place near the temple of Mars, they shall distribute the presents (*sportulae*) of bread and wine as prescribed above for the 9th of November.

It was also decided that on the day before the Ides of March there shall be a banquet in the same place, which Oflius Hermes, the president (*quinquennalis*), has promised to provide each year for all who are present, and to give out the presents as it is customary.

It was also decided that in the same place on the 22nd of March, on the day of violets, the presents of wine and bread should be distributed as stipulated above.

It was also decided that on the 11th of May, on the day of roses in the same place, the presents of wine and bread shall be distributed to those present, as stipulated above. This is done on the condition that the full assembly agrees that on the above-mentioned days the presents, both bread and wine, of those who did not attend the banquet should be sold and the proceeds distributed to those who are present, except for the presents of those who were overseas or prohibited by some serious condition.

Likewise, Publius Aelius Zenon, imperial freedman, donated to the same above-mentioned association ten thousand sesterces—in the memory of Marcus Ulpius Capito, an imperial freedman and his most pious brother—so that from the income from this sum presents might be distributed.

If any of this above-mentioned money, which Salvia Marcellina daughter of Gaius Salvius and Publius Aelius Zenon, imperial freedman, gave and donated to the above-mentioned association is used for another purpose than what is authorized above and agreed to by the membership of our association, and if they do something else or fail to do what is

outlined regarding all the days that are mentioned above on which something is to occur, then those who happen at that time to be the president or
supervisors of the above-mentioned association will pay as a penalty into
our treasury (*arca*) the sum of twenty thousand sesterces.

This decree was approved by the roster of members in a full meeting
held in the temple of the deified Caesars in the shrine of the deified Titus
on the 11th of March in the year that Gaius Bruttius Praesens and Junius
Rufinus were consuls, when the president was Gaius Ofilius Hermes, and
the supervisors were P. Aelius Onesimus, freedman of Augustus, and
G. Salvius Seleucus.

323. Graves of a Family Association

Rome (Latium, Italy). *CIL* VI 10260–10264; *CIL* IX 9148, 9149.

Second century CE

Small slabs of marble with Latin inscriptions.

(A) The association (*collegium*) of the family of Sergia Paullina,
    daughter of Lucius (Sergius Paullinus) dedicated this to Cer-
    don, fellow slave. In memory (*CIL* VI 10260).

(B) To the divine spirits. Dedicated to Pardo who is also called
    Hiarine. The association (*collegium*) which is in the household
    of Sergia Paullina, daughter of Lucius (Sergius Paullinus) and
    Pyrrhus made this monument for his spouse. Well deserving
    (*CIL* VI 10261).

(C) Dedicated to Sergius Pius, well deserving. His wife Sergia
    Hesperis, who is from the association (*collegium*) that is in the
    household of Sergia Paullina, made this monument. He lived
    seventy years (*CIL* VI 10262).

(D) To the divine spirits. Dedicated to Lucius Sergio Trophimus,
    beloved father. Sergia Eutychia his daughter, who belongs to
    the association (*collegium*) of the family of Sergia Paullina,
    made this monument (*CIL* VI 10263).

(E) To the divine spirits. The tomb of Eutychia. The association of
    the great and small (*collegium maiorum et minorum*) which is
    in the household of Sergia Paullina daughter of Lucius Sergius
    made this monument (*CIL* VI 10264).

(F) To the divine spirits. To Hermerotus the treasurer who lived
    thirty-four years. The association (*collegium*) that is in the
    household of Sergia Paullina, Agathermer and Chreste
    Arescon made this monument for their blessed brother (*CIL*
    IX 9148).

(G) To the divine spirits. Dedicated to Hilarus the goldsmith. The association (*collegium*) that is in the household of Sergia Paullina, daughter of Lucius (Sergius Paullinus). His fellow slaves from the same household. . . . He lived thirty years . . . (*CIL* IX 9149).

324. Dedication to the Goddess Kore for a Group of Immigrants from Sardis

Rome (Latium, Italy). *IGUR* 86 = *IG* XIV 1008 = PH187719.

Late second to third century CE

> Base (?) found in a house in the area of Alteriorum near the church of Saint Marcus. There is another similar dedication involving Kore and the Sardians (*IGUR* 87).

Goddess Kore. Lucius Aurelius Satyros, freedperson of Augustus, has set this up for the Sardians.

325. Honors by a Sacred Synod of Athletes for M. Ulpius Domesticus

Rome (Latium, Italy). *IGUR* 237 = *IGRR* I 150 = PH187871.

Mid-second century CE

> Monument of marble. M. Ulpius Domesticus is described primarily as a citizen of Ephesos in *IGUR* 238, which involves honors for his son, M. Ulpius Firmus Domesticus, who was likewise high priest of the athletes.

The sacred athletic synod of settlers gathered around Herakles and lodging in royal Rome honored M. Ulpius Domesticus, head of the athletes for life and high priest of the whole athletic meeting, incredible victor in all the important games, officer in charge of the Augustan baths, their own patron and ambassador who requested the sanctuary for the whole athletic meeting.

Mettius Amerimnus set up the honor when L. Vennius Agrippianus and M. Mettius Amerimnos were leaders (*archontes*).

326. Dedication to the Gods and a Sacred Company by Priests of Dionysos

Rome (Latium, Italy). *IGUR* 156 = *IG* XIV 977 = Jaccottet 2003, vol. 2, no. 182 = PH187790.

Second to third century CE

> Base. The use of the term *speira* (here translated "company") for a Dionysiac association is common in Asia Minor. Other Greek inscriptions from Rome and vicinity refer to the role of the hierophant (the revealer of sacred things) in mysteries for Dionysos (*IGUR* 157, 159, and 160).

Priests of the god Dionysos have set this up for the gods which are placed here and for the sacred company (*speira*). T. Aelius Eros, Ouphenia Pauleina, Gamourena Kosmias, and T. Julius Masklion.

327. Grave of a Boy and Initiate in the Mysteries

Rome, Albani village (Italy). *IGUR* 1169 = *CIG* 6206 = Jaccottet 2003, vol. 2, no. 195 = PH188808.

Third to fourth century CE (?)

> Slab of Tiburtine stone.

Here I lie, Aurelius Antonios, who was priest of all the gods, first of Bona Dea ("Good Goddess"), then of the Mother of the gods and Dionysos Kathegemon ("Dionysos the Leader"). I always performed the mysteries (*mystēria*) for these deities in a reverent manner. Now I left behind the revered, sweet, holy light of the sun. From now on, initiates (*mystai*) and friends (*philoi*) of every way of life, seize (or, possibly: question) the revered mysteries of life immediately. For no one is able to unwind the thread of the Fates. For I, Antonius this revered one, lived seven years and twelve days.

328. Grave of a Boy Who Performed the Rites of Dionysos

Rome (Latium, Italy). *IGUR* 1228 = PH188867.

Undated

> Slab of marble decorated with Dionysiac symbols. The frescoes at the Villa of the Mysteries in Pompeii similarly depict a child playing a role in rites of Dionysos (figure 18).

To the gods of the underworld (chthonic deities). Not yet having tasted youth, I slipped into the realm of Hades, leaving behind tears and groans to my parents for my short time. Nor was I meant to reach the life span of mortals. I lived only seven years and two months, of which three years I accomplished and spoke the rites (*orgia*) for Dionysos. Now my father and revered mother called me Herophilos. Oh passerby, you now know who I was. I was not even brought into being.

Figure 18
*Fresco depicting a child reading during preparations for initiation into the mysteries of
Dionysos, from the Villa of the Mysteries at Pompeii (photo by Harland).*

329. Grave Inscriptions from Various Neighborhoods Mentioning Synagogues

Rome (Latium, Italy). *JIWE* II 165, 170, 189, 288.

Third to fourth century CE (?).

> Plaques of marble from places of burial (catacombs) in various
> districts or neighborhoods of Rome, as indicated below. As the

following inscriptions suggest, several of the synagogues at Rome were named after the neighborhood where they met (the Calcaresians in the lime burner's district, the Campesians in the Campus Martius, and the Siburesians in the Subura district); others point to the geographical origins of the Judeans who founded the group (e.g., Judeans from the city of Tripolis or from the city of Elaia); and, still others named themselves in honor of a prominent figure (e.g., the Augustesians after Augustus or some other emperor, the Agrippesians likely after Marcus Agrippa, and the Volumnesians after a figure named Volumnius).

Monteverde district catacombs:

(A) Here lies Poly . . . nis, head of the synagogue (*archisynagōgos*) of the synagogue of the Vernaclesians, fifty-three years old. His sleep is in peace. (*JIWE* II 117)

(B) Here lies Pomponis who was twice leader (*archōn*) of the synagogue of the Calcaresians. He lived sixty years. His sleep is in peace. (*JIWE* II 165)

(C) Here lies Proclus, leader of the synagogue of the Tripolitans. May he sleep in peace. (*JIWE* II 166)

(D) Here lies Hilaros, leader of the synagogue of the Volumnesians, having lived thirty-five years. His sleep is in peace. His memorial. (*JIWE* II 167)

(E) Here lies Kailis, patron of the Agrippesians. May he sleep in peace. (*JIWE* II 170)

(F) Here lies Quintianus, chief elder (*gerousiarchēs*) of the Augustesians, who lived fifty-four years. His sleep is in peace. (*JIWE* I 189)

Trastevere district catacombs:

(G) Here lies . . . *Name* Marcella, mother (?) of the synagogue of the Augustesians. May she be remembered (?). . . . Her sleep is in peace. (*JIWE* II 542)

Vigna Randanini district catacombs:

(H) Here lies Annianus, leader, child son of Julianus, the father of the synagogue of the Campesians, eight years and two months old. His sleep is in peace. (*JIWE* II 288)

Unknown provenance:

(I) Here lies Neikodemos, the leader of the Siburesians and loved by all of them, thirty years and forty-two days old. Have courage, Ablabius the younger, no one is immortal. (*JIWE* II 557)

(J) Here lies Pancharios, father (*patēr*) of the synagogue of Elaia, 110 years old, who loved his people and loved the commandments, living a good life. His sleep is in peace. (*JIWE* II 576)

(K) Here lies Solo daughter of Galias who was father of the synagogue of the Hebrews. She lived forty-one years. Her sleep is in peace. (*JIWE* II 578)

330. Statue for Pompeia Agrippinilla Dedicated by Initiates of the God Dionysos

Torre Nova (Sicily, Italy). *IGUR* 160 = Achille Vogliano, "La grande iscrizione bacchica del Metropolitan Museum," *American Journal of Archaeology* 37 (1933): 215–31 = Scheid 1986 = McLean 1993 = Jaccottet 2003, vol. 2, no. 188.

160–170 CE

> Statue base of marble with the inscription on three sides, found near Torre Nova, where a villa of Gallicanus was located. The priestess of this association, Pompeiia Agrippinilla, was the wife of Gavius Squilla Gallicanus, consul at Rome in 150 CE and proconsul of Asia in 165 CE. This family's ancestors included Theophilos of Mytilene (friend and historian of Pompey in the mid-first century BCE) on the island of Lesbos. Many of the members of the household that participated in this association (both men and women, slaves and freedpersons) have Greek names indicating origins in Asia Minor.

The initiates (*mystai*) written below set this up for the priestess Agrippinilla (*List of members follows*).

Description of membership list

There are about 402 members organized by roles (many other names are now missing or illegible). Here is an overview of the functionaries and roles:

- Roles mentioned in column 1: one male "hero"; one female torch bearer (*dadouchos*) named Kethegilla (the daughter of Agrippinilla); seven male priests (including Gallicanus himself); two female priestesses; one male revealer of the sacred objects (*hierophantēs*); two male god bearers (*theophoroi*); one male assistant (*hypourgos*) who is also described as the one who keeps order among the Silenoi (*seilēnokosmos*); three female basket bearers (*kistaphoroi*); three male head cowherds (*archiboukoloi*); and eight male sacred cowherds (*boukoloi*), with the last one starting at the top of the list on column 2.

- Roles mentioned in column 2: two male heads of the male bacchic devotees (*archibassaroi*); two male "flourishing children" (*amphithaleis*); three female winnowing basket bearers (*liknaphoroi*); one female phallus bearer (*phallophoros*); two male fire bearers (*pyrphoroi*); one male sacred official (*hieromnēmōn*); one male head of the youths (*archineaniskoi*); four female heads of the female bacchic devotees (*archibassarai*); eleven male cowherds (*boukoloi*).
- Roles listed in columns 3, 4, 5, and 6: approximately 128 members (91 men and 37 women) described simply as those wearing the special garment or "the bacchic devotees wearing the special garment" (*bacchoi apo katazōseōs*).
- Roles listed in columns 6 and 7: forty-six male sacred bacchants (*hieroi bacchoi*).
- Roles listed in columns 8 and 9: seventy legible male names, many others lost or illegible.
- Roles listed in column 10: twenty-seven female names, likely under the role of "cave guards" (*antrophylakes*) mentioned at the end of column 9.

331. Grave of a Patron of the Worshippers of the Goddess Diana

Tusculum (Latium, Italy). *CIL* XIV 2633 = *ILS* 7317a = Waltzing 1895–1900, vol. 3, no. 2326.

Date uncertain

> Slab with Latin inscription, originally housed in the Capitoline Museum but currently lost.

To the divine spirits. Antestius Victorinus and Agathemer and Asclepiodotus made this for Julius Severinus, patron of the worshippers (*cultores*) of Diana, well deserving!

332. Election of a Patroness by an Association of Builders

Volsinii (Etruria, Italy). *CIL* XI 2702 = *ILS* 7217 = Waltzing 1895–1900, vol. 3, no. 1846.

224 CE

> Table of bronze with Latin inscription, discovered in the ruins of a Roman house that probably belonged to Laberius Gallus.

In the year that Appius Claudius Julianus, for the second time, and Lucius

Bruttius Crispino were consuls, on 10th of the Kalends of February (February 20):

In the meeting place (*schola*) of the association (*collegium*) of builders (*collegium fabri*) of the city of Volsinii, which Titus Sossius Hilarus and Caetennius Onesimus, presidents (*quinquennales*) convened, the same presidents made the following motion:

Laberius Gallus, a centurion of the first military unit in the legion (*primipilaris*) and a distinguished man made it his practice to act toward our association with much love and affection. This is confirmed by his benefactions that he has showered on us for a long time. For these reasons, let us choose his wife, Ancharia Luperca—the daughter of the late Ancharius Celer of sacred memory—as patronness of our association, whose progeny and family served in all magistrate offices of our city with sincerity and in a faithful manner. Let us choose her in their honor and because of the chastity of her way of life and the purity of her sacred habits. We shall also erect a bronze statue for her in the meeting place (*schola*) of our association beside that of her husband, Laberius Gallus.

When this matter was put to the vote, all unanimously decided that our presidents had rightly and justly proposed that we should choose Ancharia Luperca, an honorable matron of a pure character and way of life, as a most worthy patroness, endowed with reverence, in honor of her husband Laberius Gallus—a centurion of the first military unit in the legion, a distinguished man and a patron of our association—and in memory of her father, the late Ancharius Celer. We also decided that we should erect a bronze statue of her in the meeting place (*schola*) of our association beside that of her husband, Laberius Gallus, so that her goodwill, her devotion toward us, and our goodwill toward her will be visible for all in the public view, and also that a patron's plaque (*tabula patronatus*) be attached to a wall in her house.

Western Provinces

333. Grave of a Goldsmith Who Was a Member of an Association of Carpenters

Amsoldingen (Germania Superior). *CIL* XIII 5154 = *ILS* 7687 = *AÉ* (1974), no. 434 = Waltzing 1895–1900, vol. 3, no. 2175.

First to second century CE

Slab with a Latin inscription, broken in two pieces.

To the divine spirits. This is the tomb of Camillus Polynices, by origin a Lydian, by occupation a goldsmith (*aurifex*), a member of the body (*corpus*) of carpenters (*fabri tignuarii*), who discharged all of their offices (*honores*) . . . and lived sixty years, and of Camillius Paulus, his son, of the same occupation and the same association, who lived thirty-three years.

334. Grave of a Carpenter

> Colonia Claudia Ara Agrippinensium (Germania Inferior). *CIL* XIII 8344 = *AÉ* (1899), no. 10 = *IKöln* 442.
>
> Second century CE

> > Gravestone of marble with a Latin inscription and a relief of the deceased above (now missing), now in the Römisch Germanisches Museum in Cologne (figure 19). The inscription demonstrates that sometimes associations were organized into "companies" (*centuriae*), possibly to help organize social events and firefighting duties (see also **L40**).

For Quintus Vetinius Verus. His mother Quintinia Materna made this monument for her dearest son, a member of the association (*collegium*) of carpenters (*fabri*), third company (*centuria*), who died at thirty-one years, seven months, twenty-six days.

335. Dedication by a Member of the Millers

> Colonia Claudia Ara Agrippinensium (Germania Inferior). *CIL* XIII 8255 = *IKöln* 215.
>
> Second to third century CE

> > Decorative plaque of marble with a Latin inscription, now in the Römisch Germanisches Museum Köln (inv. no. 711).

In honor of the divine imperial household, . . . ius Servandus, a member of the association (*collegium*) of millers (*pistores*) established in Colonia Claudia Ara Agrippinensium, donated and consecrated this monument.

336. Dedication by Soldiers Who Are Members of an Association

> Corstopitum, now Corbridge, Northumberland (Britannia). *AÉ* (1995), no. 1012 = *RIB* 1136.
>
> Second to third century CE

> > Altar with a Latin inscription built into Orchard Farm, Corbridge, still in situ.

Figure 19
*Monument of the Carpenters from Germania, now in the Römisch Germanisches Museum in Cologne (**334**; photo by Ascough).*

Dedicated to the holy god Silvanus by the soldiers from a detachment (*vexillatio*) of the Second Augustan Legion and the association (*collegium*) of the Silvanists (*Silvaniani*), who willingly and freely erected this altar from their own resources.

337. Dedication of a Temple to Neptune and Minerva

Noviomagus, now Chichester, West Sussex (Britannia). J. E. Bogaers, "King Cogidubnus in Chichester: Another Reading of *RIB* 91," *Britannia* 10 (1979): 243–54 (ph.) = *RIB* 91 = *CIL* VII 11, addit p. 305 = Waltzing 1895–1900, vol. 3, no. 1379.

First century CE

> Tablet with handles made from Purbeck (gray Sussex) marble with a Latin inscription, still located in the west face of Council Chamber at Chichester.

The association (*collegium*) of builders (*fabri*) and those belonging to it donated this temple dedicated to Neptune and Minerva from their own resources, for the welfare of the Divine Family, by the authority of Tiberius Claudius Cogidubnus, king of Magna Britannia. Pudens son of Pudentinus donated the piece of ground.

BUILDINGS AND MEETING PLACES

SOUTHERN AND CENTRAL GREECE

B1. Temple (*hieron*) of the Worshippers of Dionysos (*Dionysiastai*)

Piraeus (Attica)

Second century BCE

> *IG* II² 1326 (**21**); *IG* II² 1008, 1011, 1028, 1029, 1039. Robert Garland, *The Piraeus: From the Fifth to the First Century B.C.*, 2nd ed. (London: Bristol Classics Press, 2001), 146; Jon D. Mikalson, *Religion in Hellenistic Athens* (Hellenistic Culture and Society 29; Berkeley: University of California Press, 1998), 205 n102.

Located due west of modern Plateia Korais, this courtyard is surrounded by a colonnaded hall (21m wide) with eight columns on one side and an unknown number on the other. On the eastern side is a large rectangular building (40m × 23m) divided into many small rooms. It also included a window with a rectangular frame intersected by Ionic columns that Garland calls "the most remarkable" found from the Greek world. This feature indicates the wealth and importance of the building. Excavations at the site suggest that a large house may have been converted for use as the temple.

B2. Hall of the Iobacchoi

Athens (Attica)

Second century CE

> *IG* II² 1368 (**7**). Wilhelm Dörpfeld, "Die Ausgrabungen am Westabhange der Akropolis. II. Das Lenaion oder Dionysion in den

Limnai," *MDAI(A)* 20 (1895): 161–206 (with plan of the Baccheion in Taf. 4); Walther Judeich, *Topographie von Athen* (Handbuch der Altertumswissenschaft; Munich: C.H. Beck'sche Verlagsbuch-handlung, 1931), 291 (with plan of the Baccheion); Schäfer 2002 (with plan of the area around the building on p. 209).

The building, or Baccheion, is located between the Pnyx and the Areopa-gos near the western slope of the Acropolis. The rectangular hall measures 11m × 18m and has two rows of four columns with a quadrangular apse on the eastern end, which is where the column with the regulations of the Bacchic devotees inscribed on it was found (see 7). The altar in the apse is decorated with Dionysiac scenes, including a sacrificial goat, a satyr (male attendant of Dionysos), and a maenad (female attendant). A fragment of a statuette of Dionysos was also found in the building. Objects involving other gods that were discovered within the building include a statuette of Pan, a statuette of Aphrodite, a statuette of Artemis, an altar for Artemis, votives for Cybele, a statuette of Athena Parthenos, a relief of Athena, and an altar for Hadrian (see Schäfer 2002, 189–202).

MACEDONIA

B3. Sanctuary of the Worshippers of Silvanus

Philippi (Macedonia)

Second to third century CE

> *CIL* III 633 (**41**). Peter Pilhofer, *Philippi*, Band 1, *Die erste christli-che Gemeinde Europas* (WUNT 87; Tübingen: Mohr Siebeck, 1995), 108–13.

The rock face of the acropolis was quarried to serve as the rear wall of a sanctuary dedicated to Silvanus. Four Latin inscriptions that list various members of the association were engraved on this rear wall. One of the inscriptions documents some members' donations to the building of the temple, including four hundred roofing tiles and entrance steps cut into the extant rock. The interior included two bronze statues of Silvanus, a painting of Olympus, and marble statues of Herakles, Mercury, and Liber.

ASIA MINOR

B4. Meeting House of a Dionysiac Association

Ephesos (Ionia)

Late second century CE

> Peter Scherrer, *Ephesus* (Istanbul: Österreichisches Archäologisches

Figure 20
*Overview of the meeting room and courtyard of a house in which a Dionysos association
met in Ephesos (**B4***; photo by Ascough).*

Institut, 2000), 105–12 (plan); Hilke Thür, ed., *Hanghaus 2 in Ephesos. Die Wohneinheit 4: Baubefund, Ausstattung, Funde. Textband*
(Forschungen in Ephesos VIII/6; Vienna: Österreichischen Akademie der Wissenschaften, 2005), esp. 424–26 and 430–34 (English
summary); Ascough 2007b, 89 (photo); Schäfer 2007 (plan).

In the housing complex designated "Terrace House 2" (figure 20) is a large
private house measuring 950m² that includes a two-story colonnaded
court, marble-paneled room (H2/31), and a barrel-vaulted meeting room
(*basilica privata*, H2/8). An inscription and artistic themes suggest that
this room was used by an association dedicated to Dionysos.

B5. Banqueting House of an Association

Ephesos (Ionia)

Second century CE

Peter Scherrer, *Ephesus* (Istanbul: Österreichisches Archäologisches
Institut, 2000), 100–104 (plan); Ascough 2007b, 89.

In the housing complex designated "Terrace House 1" is a large house with
a colonnaded court with 6 × 10 columns dating from the first century
BCE. This house was adapted in the early second century CE to serve as a
banqueting facility for an association. The adaptation took over about half

the complex (*insula*). Further modifications were made in the late second century.

B6. Hall of Benches (*Podiensaal*) of the Dionysiac Cowherds (*boukoloi*)

Pergamon (Mysia)

Second to fourth century CE

> *IPergamon* II 485 (**115–16**). Wolfgang Radt, *Pergamon: Geschichte und Bauten einer antiken Metropole* (Darmstadt: Primus Verlag, 1999), 196–99 (photos); Schwarzer 2002 (plans; reconstruction; photos); Pilhofer 2002 (plans; photo); Ascough 2007b, 85–86 (photo).

This is a rectangular building measuring 24m × 10m (figure 21). The building is oriented with the long side running east-west along the main street, although it is set back behind a row of shops and workshops. A small alley led through to the paved yard in front of the building. Across from the doorway is a cult niche and together these divide the interior into two banqueting rooms with three benches each (*triclinia*). Each of the rooms consisted of a raised podium, or bench, 1m high and 2m wide, with a marble shelf set slightly lower in order to accommodate food and drink. The entire building could accommodate about seventy diners.

GREEK ISLANDS OF THE AEGEAN

B7. Temple of Sarapis ("Sarapieion A")

Delos (Cyclades)

220 BCE

> IG XI/4 1299. L. Michael White, *The Social Origins of Christian Architecture*, vol. 1, *Building God's House in the Roman World: Architectural Adaptation Among Pagans, Jews and Christians* (HTS 42; Valley Forge, Pa.: Trinity Press International, 1990), 33–40 (plan); McLean 1996, 205–11 (plan).

A small temple sits above a courtyard, from which there are other rooms at various levels, including a banqueting facility (room E). The temple was built by extending the existing domestic complex (*insula*). A household association of Sarapis worshippers expanded after two generations and undertook the building known to archaeologists as Sarapieion A. Eventually, this site was further developed and is designated the "Terrace of the Foreign Gods."

Figure 21
*Banqueting hall of the Dionysiac cowherds at Pergamon showing the two facing triclinia. The doorway is in the middle of the southeast wall (right side of photo) with a cult niche on the opposite wall, which housed the altar now lying in the middle (**B6**; photo by Ascough).*

B8. Meeting Place of the Berytian Merchants Devoted to Poseidon (*Poseidonistai*)

Delos (Cyclades)

153 BCE or earlier

> *IDelos* 1520 (**224**), 1778 (**226**), 1779 (**227**), 1782 (**228**), 1783 (**225**); *IDelos* 1773–96; Picard 1920; Meyer 1988 (plan); McLean 1996, 196–205; Monika Trümper, "Das Sanktuarium des 'Ésablissement

des Poseidoniastes de Bérytos' in Delos: Zur Baugeschichte eines griechischen Vereinsheiligtums." *Bulletin de correspondence hellénique* 126 (2002): 265–330.

This is a large structure containing a courtyard surrounded by columns to the northeast (where there was also a cistern), a large courtyard to the northwest, and a smaller courtyard to the southwest. There is also a series of small to medium-sized rooms along the south side (probably residential accommodation and warehouses). Along the southwest side are four small shrines devoted to the deities of the homeland (likely Poseidon, Astarte, and Melqart) and to the goddess Roma. Sacrifices to these gods most likely took place in the smaller courtyard. The complex underwent at least one major renovation before the first half of the first century BCE, after which the building was destroyed.

ITALY

B9. Meeting Place of the Augustales at Herculaneum

Herculaneum, regio I vi 21 (Italy)

Early first century CE

CIL X 1412. Bollmann 1998, 348–54 (A47; figs. 35–37).

Located in the center of the city near the southeast corner of the forum, this rectangular building (ca. 15m × 12.5m) has its main room divided into three naves by four Tuscan columns. At the back of the building (across from the entrance and raised slightly above the rest of the building) is a shrine that can be accessed by two steps. The entire room is decorated with frescos depicting the story of the god Hercules, particularly his final heroic deeds, painted in the IV style (figures 22 and 23). An inscription on the wall clearly identifies the location as the meeting place of the Augustales.

B10. Meeting Place of the Augustales at Misenum

Misenum, regio I (Italy)

First to second century CE

A. De Franciscis, *Il sacello degli Augustali a Miseno* (Naples: Arte tipografica, 1991), esp. 45; Bollmann 1998, 356–63 (A50; fig. 29; photos 8,1, 8,2); Paola Miniero, ed., *The Sacellum of the Augustales at Miseno* (Naples: Soprintendenza Archeologica di Napoli e Caserta, 2000), esp. 9–20 (figs. 1–10); D'Arms 2000.

Figure 22
Wall mural in the shrine inside the meeting place of the Augustales at Herculaneum
*(***B9***; photo by Ascough).*

Figure 23
Detail of a wall mural depicting mythology associated with Hercules from the meeting
*place of the Augustales at Herculaneum (***B9***; photo by Harland).*

These are three adjacent rectangular rooms that contained statues of various emperors. The central room is temple-like in its structure, with a columned porch. A mosaic at the entrance of the eastern room identifies it as a banqueting hall (*triclinium constantiae*). Many inscriptions found here attest to active patronage and honors for association members and donors.

B11. Meeting Place of the Ferrymen (*lenuncularii*)

Ostia, regio I ii 3 (Italy)

Early second century CE

> Hermansen 1981, 65, 115–19 (fig. 46); Bollmann 1998, 275–78 (A27; fig. 48; photos 11,1 11,2).

The main hall of the building measures 16m × 8m, including the vestibule (figure 24). The hall could be entered through two doorways, one from the Decumanus and the other from the Square of the Lares. The building includes an apse that may have functioned as a sanctuary. There is a long hall along the east side, as well as a smaller room and a latrine on the

Figure 24
Meeting place of the ferrymen in Ostia, viewed from vestibule on the south side
(**B11**; *photo by Ascough*).

north. An inscription from the time of Gordion III (238–244 CE) connects the building with the ferrymen. Hermansen notes that membership in the association must have been small.

B12. Hall of the Augustales at Ostia

Ostia, regio I ix 4 (Italy)

Late first to early second century CE

> Meiggs 1973, 219–20; Hermansen 1981, 79–81 (fig. 27); Laird 2000, 72–80 (plan; photos).

Measuring about 137m², this complex (*insula*) on the north side of the main street (the Decumanus) is constructed similar to a temple, being raised above street level by six steps with a six column façade (hexastyle). The rectangular portico leads to a central sanctuary (*cella*; 11.7m²) with a narrow hall on each side and a platform on the rear wall. The original excavator suggested that this might be the meeting place of the Augustales but later rejected the idea in favor of it being identified as the meeting hall

Figure 25
*A funerary statue of a woman standing in the accentuated room before the apse in the meeting place of the Augustales at Ostia (**B12**; photo by Ascough).*

Figure 26
*Remains of the meeting place of the caulk workers at Ostia (**B13**; photo by Ascough).*

of the city council (the *curia*), an identification supported by Hermansen. Meiggs argues in favor of the connection with the Augustales, as does Laird in much more detail. For a photo of a statue in this building, see figure 25.

B13. Meeting Place of the Makers of Caulking (*stuppatores*)

Ostia, regio I x 3–4 (Italy)

Early third century CE

> Hermansen 1981, 61–62, 119–20 (fig. 47); Hermansen 1982 (plan; photos); Bollmann 1998, 278–82 (A28; fig. 23); Egelhaaf-Gaiser 2002, 154–55 (fig. 12).

A doorway on the west side opens to a courtyard (figure 26). Opposite the courtyard is a sanctuary with a temple platform, although the temple itself was never completed and later the area was used as a Mithraeum, a meeting place for devotees of the god Mithras. A portico lines the other three sides, and off the northern portico is a long (14.3m), undivided room used for meetings and banquets.

B14. Meeting Place of the Carpenters (*fabri tignuari*)

Ostia, regio I xii 1 (Italy)

Second to fourth century CE

> Meiggs 1973, 140, 244, 324n4 (fig. 8); Hermansen 1981, 62–63 (fig. 12); Bollmann 1998, 284–88 (A30; fig. 1; photos 1,2, 1,2, 2,1); Egelhaaf-Gaiser 2002, 136–38 (figs. 2, 3).

An entrance from the main street (the Decumanus) leads into a courtyard in which there is a tablinum-type sanctuary. In the southwest corner there is a kitchen and the east wing contains four dining rooms with three benches (*triclinia*), after which the building is named as *Casa dei Triclini* (House of the *Triclinia*). For a photo of one dining room (*triclinium*), see figure 27.

Figure 27
One of the three-bench dining rooms (triclinia) *in the builders' meeting place*
(**B14**; *photo by Harland*).

B15. Meeting Place of the Grain Measurers (*mensores*)

Ostia, regio I xix 1–3 (Italy)

Early second to third century CE

> Meiggs 1973, 324–25; Hermansen 1981, 65–66 (fig. 14); Bollmann
> 1998, 291–95 (A32; fig. 30); Egelhaaf-Gaiser 2002, 138–40 (fig. 4).

An entrance from Via della Foce leads to a temple of Ceres Augusta.
Immediately behind the temple is a garden with a well, and to the west is
a large meeting hall. A latrine and smaller rooms line the east wall. First
built in the early second century, it was refurbished in the third century,
including the addition of a mosaic floor depicting a man carrying grain
alongside helpers and a controller (figure 28). Meiggs thinks the building
is too small to be the main headquarters of the association.

Figure 28
Mosaic floor depicting a man carrying grain from the meeting place of the grain measurers
(**B15**; *photo by Harland*).

B16. Forum of the Corporations

Ostia, region II vii 3 (Italy)

First century BCE to second century CE

> Meiggs 1973, 283–86; Hermansen 1981, 84–85; Bollmann 1998, 298–300 (A34; figs. 56, 57; photo 13,1).

This large rectangular area is the location of the offices of some of the most important merchants and shippers of Ostia, which line the two long sides on the east and west and the shorter north side (figure 29). At the south side is a theater while to the north just beyond the forum is the Tiber River, which was lined with warehouses. The complex took shape toward the end of the first century BCE under Augustus and was developed under subsequent emperors. Under Claudius (41–54 CE) an arcade was built around three of the four sides, and this was restored at the end the second century CE. At this time, the entire square was raised 40cm and black and white mosaics were laid in the floor of the arcade and the buildings. These

Figure 29
*View of the east porticus (looking north) of the forum of the corporations at Ostia (**B16**).
Black and white mosaics demarcate the nature of the shop (photo by Ascough).*

mosaics often name the association housed in that particular building and sometimes include a pictorial depiction (e.g., a scene depicting the loading of amphora from one ship to another). A temple to Ceres lies in the center of the forum.

B17. Temple Building of the Ship Builders (*fabri navali*)

Ostia, regio III ii 1–2 (Italy)

Late second century CE

> Meiggs 1973, 327–28; Hermansen 1981, 63–64 (fig. 13); Bollmann 1998, 304–7 (A36; fig. 21; photo 7,1; reconstruction 7,2); Egelhaaf-Gaiser 2002, 145–46 (fig. 8).

The long rectangular building is entered from the main street (the Decumanus) through a corridor, which leads into a courtyard with a portico. At the far side of the courtyard is a raised temple accessed by marble steps (figure 30). A smaller portico courtyard lies behind the temple, and likely

Figure 30

*The courtyard of the temple building of shipbuilders at Ostia seen from the main entrance, looking southeast (**B17**). At the rear are the marble steps leading up the platform upon which the temple was built (photo by Ascough).*

accommodated association meetings and banquets. There is a mosaic of a ship in the front entrance hall. A statue base with a dedication to the patron of the ship builders and a membership list (*album*) were found in the temple.

B18. Meeting Place and Temple of the Worshippers of Bellona (*hastiferi*)

Ostia, regio IV i 4 (Italy)

140–160/170 CE

> Meiggs 1973, 359–60; Hermansen 1981, 69–70 (figs. 16, 17, 20; photos 18, 19, 21, 22); Bollmann 1998, 320–23 (A40; figs. 38, 39; photo 15,2); Egelhaaf-Gaiser 2002, 146 (fig. 9).

This is a small square building measuring about 5.5m × 5.5m, which served as the hall for banqueting and meetings of the worshippers of Bellona, goddess of war. Five marble steps lead up to the entrance, which is flanked by a column on each side. The lance bearers (*hastiferi*) also had a small, separate temple (7m × 5.75m) of red and yellow brick on the inside, including a porch (*pronaos*) and inner chamber (*cella*). Both buildings are enclosed by walls.

B19. Meeting Place of the Ship Owners (*navicularii*)

Ostia, regio IV v 15 (Italy)

End of the second century CE

> Hermansen 1981, 71–74 (fig. 23); Bollmann 1998, 323–27 (A41; fig. 13; photos 5,1, 5,2, 15,1); Egelhaaf-Gaiser 2002, 140–43 (fig. 6).

A four-columned entryway along the main street (the Decumanus) leads to an elaborate vestibule, with a number of anterooms along each side. The vestibule opens up into a large courtyard that housed a sanctuary with an apse. The sanctuary resembles the living room of a house, and the mosaic floor indicates that this was a room with three benches used for banquets (a *triclinium*). There is a long, narrow water basin (*nymphaeum*) running through the courtyard, just off center. The complex is named the *Schola del Traiano*, although inscriptions found there clearly indicate that it was the meeting house of the association of ship owners. The structure is located across the main road from the meeting place of the ship builders (*fabri navali*, **B17**). Hermansen calls the ship owners' building "the largest and most impressive of all possible guild seats" at Ostia.

B20. Meeting Place of the Augustales at Ostia

Ostia, regio V vii 2 (Italy)

ca. 150 CE, restored in the third to fourth century CE

> . Hermansen 1981, 62, 111–12 (fig. 43); Bollmann 1998, 335–40 (A44;
> fig. 2; photo 2,2); Laird 2000, 41–72 (plan; photos); Egelhaaf-Gaiser
> 2002, 147 (fig. 11).

A long, narrow antechamber leads from the main street (the Decumanus)
to a courtyard on the right. There is a sanctuary at the far end of the courtyard. This building was enlarged in the third century by the addition of an
apse that extends into a private house, probably already in the possession
of the Augustales. A series of rooms surround the courtyard's north, east,
and south sides. Hermansen (1981, 62) confidently identifies this building
as the meeting location of the Augustales, but this has been called into
question by Laird (2000).

B21. The House of Themistocles

Ostia, regio V xi 1–3 (Italy)

ca. 194 CE

> Meiggs 1973, 329; Hermansen 1981, 64, 96–111 (figs. 33, 40, 41; pho-
> tos 34–39, 42); Bollmann 1998, 340–45 (A45; figs. 20, 94; recon-
> struction 6,1).

This is a large complex of buildings that includes an apartment block
(*insula*) and a house (originally owned by a single person). The complex
underwent numerous changes, including the addition of a temple in the
west wing around 194 CE. An entrance off the main street (the Decumanus) leads into the temple courtyard with a portico and a centrally placed
altar. An association likely used the entire complex, not just the temple.
The stores (*tabernae*) along the main street may have been used by individual guild members (who tended to cluster by occupation in various
cities). The stores were all interconnected, suggesting cooperation among
different merchants or workers. The apartment rooms likely housed the
workers and their families, while other rooms were used for storage. Overall, the complex is not luxurious and suggests persons of humble status.
Hermansen suggests that the carpenters (*fabri tignuari*), who clearly used
a building across the street (**B14**), may have also used this complex.

B22. Meeting Place of the Wool Workers (*fullones*)

Pompeii, regio VII xi 1 (Italy)

First century CE

> Moeller 1972; Bollmann 1998, 451–55 (B14; fig. 83); Paul Zanker,
> *Pompeii: Public and Private Life* (Cambridge, Mass.: Harvard University Press, 1998), 93–101 (fig. 45; photos 46–50).

This is a large rectangular building with an open courtyard surrounded by a colonnade (*porticus*), behind which is a three-sided covered gallery (*cryptoporticus*). The building is entered through a spacious portico with four recesses for statues. Opposite the entrance is an apse in which was found a statue of Concordia Augusta. At each end of the wall with the apse are exedrae, probably for statues of members of the imperial family. Originally identified as the wool market, the building was reassessed by Moeller as the headquarters of the association of wool workers (*fullones*, clothing fullers and dyers). Only part of the building was used as a wool exchange (*chalcidicum*).

Bollmann challenges this interpretation and excludes the building from her list. During the reign of Tiberius, a civic priestess named Eumachia dedicated the building to the cult of Concordia Augusta and Pietas. Her statue was found in the cryptoporticus. The accompanying inscription indicates that the wool workers had dedicated the statue.

B23. House of the *Triclinia*

Pompeii, regio I (Italy)

First century CE

> L. Richardson, *Pompeii: An Architectural History* (Baltimore: Johns Hopkins University Press, 1988), 307–8; Bollmann 1998, 368–71 (A52; fig. 12)

This is a rectangular building, only partially excavated at the north (short) end. There is a central garden courtyard surrounded by columns with three rooms measuring 4.6m × 4.8m occupying the north side, each of which is laid out as a dining room (*triclinium*). Excavations along the east side have revealed two similar dining rooms (4.3m × 4.4m), but there are no such rooms along the western side in the area so far excavated. The rooms are decorated in marble and wall paintings, with a black and white mosaic in the pavement in front. Each room has three masonry benches; the benches have a shallow channel along the front into which water was jettisoned. Richardson identifies the building as the clubhouse of an unidentified association, but suggests that the design lends itself more to drinking than to eating.

B24. Meeting Places in the Amphitheater

Puteoli, regio I (Italy)

Mid-first century CE

> Bollmann 1998, 374–78 (A56; figs. 58–60).

The amphitheater has three concentric circles of passageways on the ground floor, between which are radial rooms underneath the stairway ramps. In the southern half, seven of these rooms have been identified as having been used for cultic purposes by occupational associations (*collegia*): rooms 1, 6, 10, 59, 60, 64, and 69. Only one of the associations has been identified by name—the castanet players (*scabillarii*) of room 10. Inscriptions from the amphitheater attest to the presence of the meeting places of a group involved in sacred rites (*schola org[iophantarum]*) and the association of ship owners (*navicularii*), but the locations where these inscriptions were found are not known.

B25. Meeting Place of the Woodcutters (*dendrophori*)

Rome, regio II, Caelius (Italy)

ca. 150 CE

> L. Richardson, Jr., *A New Topographical Dictionary of Ancient Rome* (Baltimore: Johns Hopkins University Press, 1992), 52 (s.v. "Basilica Hillariana"); Bollmann 1998, 239–44 (A4; figs. 4, 5); Amanda Claridge, *Rome: An Oxford Archaeological Guide* (Oxford: Oxford University Press, 1998), 53.

This is a large basilica with a nave and double-side aisles located in the grounds of the military hospital and only partially excavated. The building was set into the ground and one descended twelve marble steps in order to enter the vestibule covered by a black and white mosaic within which an inscription welcomes those who enter (*CIL* VI 30973b). An inscription on a statue base in the vestibule honors Manius Poplicius, a dealer in pearls, who likely built the building (*CIL* VI 30973a). The building underwent expansions and renovations in the early third century and then again in the fifth and sixth centuries.

B26. Shrine of the Merchants (*negotiantes*) in the Warehouse of Agrippiana

Rome, regio VIII, Forum Romanum (Italy)

Late first century BCE to early second century CE

L. Richardson, Jr., *A New Topographical Dictionary of Ancient Rome* (Baltimore: Johns Hopkins University Press, 1992), 192 (s.v. "Horrea Agrippiana"); Bollmann 1998, 252–54 (A11; fig. 34).

This is a large trapezoidal warehouse complex, probably multistoried. It was built by Agrippa in the late first century BCE under the northwest slope of the Palatine. A series of chambers lie around the periphery and open toward the central courtyard, which contains a small shrine (*sacellum*) at its center with a mosaic floor that dates from the early second century CE. An inscribed marble statue base found at the back of the shrine identifies the dedicators as a society of merchants (*negotiantes*).

B27. Association of the Public Heralds (*praecones*)

Rome, regio X, Palatine (Italy)

Early third century CE

> L. Richardson, Jr., *A New Topographical Dictionary of Ancient Rome* (Baltimore: Johns Hopkins University Press, 1992), 346 (s.v. "Schola Praeconum"; fig. 63); Bollmann 1998, 261–65 (A18; fig. 7); Katherine M. D. Dunbabin, *The Roman Banquet: Images of Conviviality* (Cambridge: Cambridge University Press, 2003), 100–101 (photos 52, 53).

This partially excavated building is located on the southwest slope of the Palatine between the back of Domitian's palace and the Circus Maximus. The central colonnaded courtyard has three vaulted chambers on the northeast side; the middle vaulted chamber is slightly larger than the others and has a niche in the end wall. The building has been tentatively identified with the heralds of the *Domus Augustiana* ("Emperor's Palace") from the wall paintings in the eastern side room. Seven life-sized figures are depicted as servants greeting guests arriving at a banquet. A black and white mosaic floor depicts two processions, with four men carrying the emblems of the heralds in each procession.

B28. Warehouse of the Association of Wine Dealers

Rome, regio XIV, Trastevere (Italy)

Early second century CE

> *CIL* VI 8826; *CIL* VI 10251. L. Richardson, Jr., *A New Topographical Dictionary of Ancient Rome* (Baltimore: Johns Hopkins University Press, 1992), 80 (s.v. "Cellae Vinariae Nova et Arruntiana"); Bollmann 1998, 271–72 (A23; fig. 14); http://staging.digitalaugustanrome.org/, map 10.

A trapezoid-shaped building lies south of the Villa Farnesina on the west bank of the Tiber. The main building was a warehouse with a lower story of vaulted cellars and an upper story of rooms of equal size built around colonnaded courts. The inner brick columned portico changes direction multiple times. A second part of the building has a double colonnade on the east side and a gutter on the west, with a row of large storage jars (*dolia*) just outside the gutter. An inscription found in the main building identifies it as belonging to the *collegium* of wine dealers (*CIL* VI 8826). The building's unusual plan, however, suggests to Bollmann that it may not have functioned as the primary meeting place of the association. A second inscription found on an altar in the warehouses attests to the presence of another association (*collegium*) connected with the goddess Fortuna Reducis ("Fortune Returning"; *CIL* VI 10251), which Bollmann suggests may have been formed by an administrator of the warehouses.

LITERARY REFERENCES

GENERAL REFERENCES
(chronological by author)

L1. Aristotle, *Eudemian Ethics* (*Ethica eudemia*) 7.1241b.24–26 (7.9)

> Written ca. 360–322 BCE in the context of discussing the ethics of friendship and partnership (Greek).

The other partnerships (*koinoniai*) are a component part of the partnerships of the city (*polis*), such as the members of a brotherhood (*phrateres*), sacrificing associates (*orgeōnes*), or business partnerships.

L2. Isaeus of Athens, *Orations* 9.30.3–4 (*De Astyphilo.*)

> Speech delivered in Athens ca. 400–350 BCE to refute a forged will in which a more distant relative falsely claimed the right to the estate of Astyphilos, Isaeus' half brother (Greek).

My father took Astyphilos as a child with him to sacred rites everywhere, as he did with me [Isaeus]. And he introduced him into the membership of the Heraklean society (*thiasōtai*) so that he might participate in the fellowship (*koinōnias*). The society members themselves will testify to this for you.

L3. Demosthenes of Athens, *On the Crowns* (*De corona*) 18.258–60

> Speech delivered at Athens ca. 330 BCE in response to Aeschines' objection to Demosthenes receiving an honorary crown (Greek).

As if the jury did not know all about you [Aeschines, the opponent of Demosthenes]: from the beginning you read the books while your mother performed the rites, spending your time as a child in societies (*thiasoi*) with drunken men. . . . During the day you led your honorable societies (*thiasoi*) through the streets, their heads crowned with fennel and white poplar, as you tightly held the reddish-brown snakes or hung them above your head, shouted "euoi saboi!," and danced to the tune of "Hyes Attes! Attes Hyes!" You were greeted by all the old women with such proud titles as leader, instructor, basket bearer (*kistophoros*), and winnowing basket bearer (*liknaphoros*), receiving your reward of crumbled cakes, twisted pastries, and fresh buns. With such rewards who would not consider himself truly happy and favored by fortune?

L4. Polybius of Megalopolis (Arcadia, Greece), *Histories* (*Historiae*) 20.6.1, 5–6

Written ca. 180–120 BCE, concerning the supposed decline of Boeotia in the late third and early second centuries BCE (Greek).

Social life in Boeotia had fallen into such a bad state of being that for nearly twenty-five years neither civil nor criminal justice had been administered by them. . . . In similar fashion to these things was another unsavory zeal: when men died without children they did not leave their property to their nearest relatives, as was their former habit (*ethos*), but arranged for feasting and drinking and made it the common property of their friends. Even many who had families distributed the greater part of their property among the clubs (*syssitioi*), so that there were many Boeotians who were attending more monthly dinners than there were days appointed for the month!

L5. Varro, *On Agriculture* (*De re rustica*) 3.2.16

Written ca. 36 BCE relating a supposed discussion among Varro's consular friends regarding raising the funds to purchase and maintain a nice villa near Rome with an indoor bird sanctuary (Latin).

"Sixty thousand," I said. "Well, but in order attain such a fortune, you will need a banquet (*epulum*) or someone's triumph, like that of [Quintus Caecilius] Mettelus [Pius] Scipio [consul in 52 BCE and father-in-law of Pompey] at that time, or the dinners of associations (*collegia*), which are now so innumerable that they inflate the price of food in the markets." I [Varro] said: "Although in all other years you cannot expect such a fortune, I hope your aviary will not go bankrupt on you. Unless these habits decline, it will only rarely be that your goal eludes you. For how rare is it these days that you don't see a banquet (*epulum*) or a triumph or the associations (*collegia*) not feasting."

L6. Diodorus of Sicily, *Historical Library* (*Bibliotheca historica*) 4.24.6

Written ca. 59–30 BCE, discussing the ninth labor of Herakles (Greek).

Now the whole population [of Agyrium in Sicily], both freepersons and slaves, was in agreement in arranging for the household slaves to gather together in their own societies (*thiasoi*) to honor the god [Herakles], coming together to engage in festivities and to perform sacrifices to the god.

L7. Strabo of Amaseia (Pontus), *Geography* (*Geographica*) 17.1.8

Written ca. 7–18 CE, describing the city of Alexandria in Egypt (Greek).

The Museum is part of the royal buildings. It has a public walk, an alcove with seating, and a large building in which the educated men who share the Museum have a common hall (*syssition*). This synod (*synodos*) holds common properties and has a priest in charge of the Museum, who was formerly appointed by the kings but now is appointed by Caesar.

L8. Philo of Alexandria (Egypt), *On Drunkenness* (*De ebrietate*) 20–21 and 23

Written in the first century CE, providing an allegorical interpretation of the vice of drunkenness (Greek).

(20) Now to bring contributions and club fees (*eranoi*) with a view to participating in the best possession, practical wisdom, is praiseworthy and advantageous. But to do so with a view to the worst of all objects, foolishness, is disadvantageous and blameworthy. (21) Therefore, contributions for the most excellent object are the desire for virtue, the imitation of good people, continued care, laborious practice, incessant and unwearied labors. The contributions for the opposite object are relaxation, indifference, luxury, weakness, and a complete desertion of what is right. . . . (23) [All] those who bring festal-club fees for the destruction of learning injure the most important thing in them, namely, their mind. They cut off

everything that might save it, including prudence, temperance, courage, and justice. . . . [T]hose who bring forward attempts at virtue as their contributions and club fees wound, lacerate, and cut to pieces souls that are obedient and love learning to the point of complete destruction.

L9. Philo of Alexandria (Egypt), *On the Contemplative Life* (*De vita contemplativa*) 40, 64, and 83–89

Written in the first century CE, asserting the superiority of the activities of a Judean group (the *therapeutai*; i.e., servants of God) in Egypt in comparison with Greek and Roman gatherings (Greek).

(40) I also want to speak about the common assemblies (*synodoi*) [of the Judean therapeutists in Egypt], and their very cheerful meetings at banquets (*symposia*), contrasting them to the banquets (*symposia*) of other people. When others drink strong wine, it is as if they had been drinking not wine but some agitating and maddening drink, or even the most dangerous drink that can be imagined for driving a man out of his mind. They shriek, rage, and tear things to pieces like ferocious dogs. And they rise up and attack one another, biting and gnawing each other's noses, ears, fingers, and other parts of their body. . . . (64) I will contrast the banquets of those [Judean therapeutists] who have dedicated their own lives and themselves to knowledge and contemplation of the characteristics of nature according to the most sacred instructions of the prophet Moses. . . . [T]hey pray to God that their feasting (*euōchia*) may be acceptable and take place in accordance with his will. . . . (83) After the dinner (*deipnon*) they celebrate the sacred festival through the whole night. . . . (84) [T]hey sing hymns which have been composed in honor of God in many meters and tunes, sometimes singing together and at other times moving their hands and dancing in corresponding harmony. . . . (85) Then, when each chorus of the men and each chorus of the women has feasted separately by itself, like persons in the Bacchic festivities, drinking the pure wine of the love of God, they join together and the two become one chorus in imitation of that chorus that was established in ancient times by the Red Sea, on account of the wondrous works which were displayed there. . . .

L10. Philo of Alexandria (Egypt), *Against Flaccus* (*In Flaccum*) 135–37

Written after a Judean embassy to emperor Gaius in 39 or 40 CE, regarding the use of associations by Isidoros, a Greek opponent of Philo and the Judeans in Alexandria (Greek).

Such, then, was the character of Lampo, who was now one of the accusers of Flaccus [governor of Egypt]. And Isidoros was in no way inferior to him in wickedness. He was a man of the mobs, a demagogue, one who had continually studied to cause disorder and confusion, an enemy to all peace and stability, and very clever at exciting new seditions and disturbances while also fostering and worsening those that were already there. He was always careful to keep around him a disorderly and promiscuous mob of the worst of the people, which he had divided into sections (*symmoria*). There are societies (*thiasoi*) in the city with a large membership whose fellowship (*koinōnia*) is founded on no good principle. Instead, they are united by strong wine, drunkenness, drinking, and the outcome of those indulgencies: wanton violence. Their meetings are called "synods" (*synodoi*) and "dining couches" (*klinai*) by the locals. In all these societies, or the majority of them, Isidorus held the highest place and was called leader of the banquet (*symposiarchos*), chief of the dining couch (*klinarchēs*), and disturber of the city. Then, whenever he wanted to cause some damage, at his signal they all came together in a body, and they did and said whatever they were told.

L11. Dio Chrysostom of Prusa (Bithynia), *Orations* 34.21–23

Deliberative speech delivered to the People of Tarsus, ca. 80–110 CE, dealing with the exclusion of linen workers (*linourgoi*) from the political body (Greek).

Moving on from the discord involving the Council and People and involving the Youth and the Elders, there is a significantly sized group which is, as it were, left outside the body of citizens. Some call them "linen workers" (*linourgoi*). Now sometimes the citizens are irritated by them and assert that they are a useless rabble and responsible for tumult and disorder in Tarsus. Yet at other times they regard them as a part of the city and hold the opposite opinion of them. Well, if you regard them as instigators of insurrection and confusion, you should expel them completely and not admit them to the civic assemblies. But if, on the other hand, you regard them as being in some sense citizens, not only because they are resident in Tarsus but also because in most instances they were born here and know no other city, then it is not appropriate to dishonor them or exclude them. Yet, as it is, they are forced to remain separated in their disposition from what is advantageous to the community, being reviled and viewed as outsiders. But there is nothing more harmful to a city than such conditions, nothing more conducive to strife and disagreement. . . . I call on you to enroll them all as citizens . . . and not to reproach them or cast them off, but rather to regard them as members of your body politic, as in fact they are. . . . If a man works with linen, it cannot be that he is inferior to his neighbor and deserves to have his occupation reproached and reviled while, if he is a dyer (*bapheus*) or a leather cutter (*skytotomos*) or a carpenter (*tektōn*), it is not appropriate to reproach these occupations.

L12. Dio Chrysostom of Prusa (Bithynia), *Orations* 45.8

> Speech delivered to the People of Prusa, perhaps ca. 101–102 CE, concerning his positive relations with his hometown (Greek).

I held that, if possible, no other man should introduce such a practice or govern by means of associations (*hetaireia*) or split the city into factions. But, if they did, that I at least should avoid such faults, even if it meant that I should have much less influence than any of those others and be considered of no importance at all.

L13. Aelius Aristides of Smyrna (Ionia), *Orations* 45.27–28

> Written ca. 140–180 CE in praise of the Greco-Egyptian deity Sarapis (Greek).

People make this god [Sarapis] alone a full partner in sacrifices, inviting him to the meal (*hestia*) and making him both chief guest and host. So while different gods contribute to different club feasts (*eranoi*), he is the one who completes all feasts and has the rank of leader of the banquet (*symposiarchēs*) for those who assemble at times. . . . He is a participant in the libations and the one who receives the libations. He comes to the celebration and invites those celebrating, who perform a dance under his direction.

L14. Artemidoros of Daldis (Ionia), *Dream Interpretations* (*Oneirocritica*) 4.44 and 5.82

> Written in the second century CE, providing a guidebook on the interpretation of dreams of various sorts (Greek).

(4.44) Someone who belonged to an association (*symbiōsis*) and brotherhood (*phratria*) dreamt he lifted up his clothes in front of his association members (*symbiōtais*) and urinated upon each of them. He was expelled from the brotherhood as dishonorable. For it is understandable that those who engage in such drunken behavior would be hated and expelled.

(5.82) A man dreamt that his association members (*symbiōtai*) and brothers (*phratores*) suddenly appeared and said to him, "Receive us as guests and provide us dinner." He replied, "I do not have the money nor the means to receive you." Then he sent them away. On the next day, he was in a shipwreck, facing extreme danger and barely escaping with his life. . . . For it is customary for members of an association (*symbiōtai*) to go to the house of the deceased and to dine there, and it is said that the reception is given by the deceased in return for honors paid to him by the members of the association. . . . It was a shipwreck because he sent them away due to a lack of funds.

L15. Lollianus, *Phoenician Tales* (*Phoenikika*) B.1 recto, lines 10–16

Fragment of a Greek novel involving a criminal association of initiates, written in the second century CE (Greek).

Another naked man, who was wearing a red loincloth, passed by. Throwing the body of the child (or slave [*pais*]) on its back, he cut it up. And he tore out its heart and placed it on the fire. Then, he took it up and sliced it up to the middle. And on the surface (of the heart) . . . he sprinkled . . . and wet it with oil. When he had sufficiently prepared them . . . (he gave them?) to the initiates (*myoumenoi*), and those who held (the pieces of the heart began?) . . . to swear on the blood of the heart that they would neither give up nor betray. . . .

L16. Lucian of Samosata (Syria), *The Dance* (*De saltatione*) 15 and 79

Written ca. 150–180 CE, involving a dialogue in which Lycinus convinces the Cynic Crato of the value of panomimic dancing (Greek).

(15) I doubt I [Lycinus] need to explain that ancient rites of initiation (*teletē*) do not take place without dancing. Orpheus and Musaeus, the best dancers of their time, established these. The laws they passed on this show the value they attached to rhythm and dance as a means to be initiated. Thus, with regard to keeping the rites secret from the uninitiated, everyone knows that they say that those who reveal the mysteries are "dancing them out.". . .

(79) Despite being limited to satyric subjects, Bacchic dancing is particularly popular in Ionia and Pontus. It has taken such possession of people there, that, when the season comes around in each city, they leave everything else and sit for days watching Titans and Corybantes, satyrs and

cowherds (*boukoloi*). Those of noble birth and the highest positions are not ashamed to take part in these performances. Indeed, they pride themselves more in these activities than in nobility, civic services, and reputable ancestries.

L17. Lucian of Samosata (Syria), *The Passing of Peregrinus* (*De morte Peregrini*) 11

Written ca. 150–180 CE, involving a satirical biography of the philosopher Peregrinus (Greek).

It was then that [Peregrinus] learned the marvelous wisdom of the Christians by associating with their priests and scribes in Palestine. And—what else would you expect?—in a moment he made them all look like children, for he was prophet, leader of the society (*thiasiarchēs*), head of the synagogue (*xynagōgeus*), and everything else, all by himself. He interpreted and explained some of their books and even wrote many others. They stood in awe of him as though he was a god, proclaimed him a lawgiver, and titled him a protector, next after that other, to be sure, whom they still worship, the man who was crucified in Palestine because he introduced this new initiation (*teletē*) into the world.

L18. Tertullian of Carthage (North Africa), *Apology* (*Apologeticus*) 38–39

Written ca. 197 CE in defense of the legitimacy of Christian associations (Latin). Tertullian asserts the harmless and indeed beneficial character of Christian groups.

(38) Next, is not a more lenient treatment appropriate, that is, shouldn't this [Christian] sect (*secta*) be enrolled among the legitimate associations (*factiones*), when it commits none of the things that are often feared from illegal associations (*factiones*)? Unless I am wrong, the reason for prohibiting associations (*factiones*) has to do with the concern for public order, so that the city not be torn into factions (*partes*), which would likely disturb the elections, assemblies, senates, public meetings, even shows, by the contentions of partisans, especially since people had already begun to think of violence as a revenue source, and to think of it as their own livelihood. But as far as we are concerned, we who are indifferent to all the glory and dignity (of public matters), meeting together (*coetus*) is not a necessity; there is nothing more foreign to us than the state. One state we recognize: the universe.

We also renounce your public games, just as much as their origins, which we know are conceived from superstition; we leave to one side the events that have occasioned them. For us, there is nothing to say, to see, or to hear in relation to the craziness of the circus, with the impudence of the theater, the atrocities of the arena, and the vanity of the gymnasium. Why do we offend you, if we prefer different pleasures? If we don't want to be amused by the latest things, it is our loss, indeed, not yours. But we reject the things that please you; nor do our pleasures please you. But it was permitted for the Epicureans to maintain their idea of pleasure, namely calm of mind; and for the Christians there is enough to occupy us.

(39) Now I will show what is beneficial about the occupations of the Christian association (*factio*), as I have already shown that they are not evil. We are a partnership (*corpus*) with a common knowledge of reverence (*religio*), a discipline (*disciplina*), and a union of hope. We gather together for meeting (*coetus*) and assembly (*congregatio*) to approach God like a band (of soldiers), encompassing him with prayers. This kind of "violence" pleases God. We pray also for the emperors, for their ministers and those in authority, for the stability of the world, for general peace and quiet, and for the postponement of the end. We come together to read the divine writings, if the current state of affairs requires us either to be warned or makes us realize something. In any case we feed our loyalty with these holy words, we nurture our hope, we strengthen our faithfulness, and we reinforce the teaching by strengthening our precepts. There are also exhortations, corrections, and divine judgments. . . . Approved elders (*seniores*) preside, not those who have purchased this office for a price, but those who have obtained it on the basis of reputation (*testimonium*). For nothing concerning God can be obtained through money.

Even if we have a kind of treasury (*arca*), it is not for dispensing honoraria (or: it is not comprised of entrance fees), as if it were collected as a matter of a contract. Each person brings a small donation (*stips*) once a month, or when he wishes, and only if he is able. For no one is compelled, but each does so voluntarily. These are the deposits of piety. Now, these sums are not spent on banquets, drinking, or ungracious eating houses. Instead, that sum is spent on feeding and burying the poor, and on boys and girls who do not have parents, on aged domestic slaves, shipwrecked persons, and any who are in the mines, on islands, or in prisons, provided that they are in such places for the sake of God's sect (*secta*), who thus become pensioners of their confession.

The practice of this kind of love marks us in the eyes of some. They say, "See how they love one another"—they themselves hate each another. They say, "They are prepared to die for each another"—they will be more prepared to kill each another. But they think us insane for the fact that we call each other "brothers." I think, this is because among themselves every term relating to blood relationship is assumed to be phony. . . .

For you attack our little dinners (*coenulae*) as extravagant quite apart from any crimes committed there. Of course it was about us that Diogenes uttered his saying: "The Megarians buy food as if they were to die tomorrow, but they build as if they will never die!" But one sees a speck more easily in another's eye than a log in one's own. With so many tribes and senates and decurions belching, the air becomes sour. When the Salii (i.e., priests of Mars) dine, a money lender is needed; public accountants will have to total the expenditure of Heracles' tithes and banquets. At the Apaturia festival, Dionysia, and the Attic mysteries, they have a conscription: of cooks! And at the smoke of Sarapis' banquet the firefighters will have to get up. Yet, it is only the three-bench dining room (*triclinium*) of the Christians that is criticized.

The name of our dinner (*coena*) reveals its significance: it is called by the name which among the Greeks means affection (*delictio*). Whatever the cost, it is a gain to spend in the name of piety, for with this refreshment we assist those who are poor, not as it is with you, parasites who strive for the glory of selling their freedom, authorized by their belly to fatten themselves amid insults; rather, because for God there is greater consideration for the poor. If the reason for our banquet is an honest one, judge the rest of our discipline from this motive. As it is concerned with our pious duty, it allows nothing vile, nothing immodest. We do not recline before we have first tasted prayer to God; we only eat enough to satisfy hunger; and we only drink as much as is appropriate for the modest. . . . Likewise prayer closes the feast. The meeting then breaks up, not into violent groups or bands running about, nor for outbursts of lust, but to pursue the same care for modesty and chastity, as persons who have dined not so much on a dinner as on discipline.

If any one complains about Christians with the same complaint that is made about associations (*factiones*), this meeting (*coetus*) of Christians might be called illicit, I admit; that is, if it were the same as the illicit meetings, which certainly should be condemned. But for whose injury have we ever met? We are just the same when we assemble as we are when we are dispersed: what we are together we are also individually, injuring no one, grieving no one. When decent, good people come together, when the pious and pure gather, it is to be called not an association (*factio*), but a council chamber (*curia*).

L19. Origen of Alexandria (Egypt), *Against Celsus (Contra Celsum)* 1.1; 3.23; and 8.17

Written ca. 244–249 CE in response to portions of a work by Celsus which criticized Christianity (Greek). Quotation marks indicate likely citations from Celsus' work, which was perhaps composed around 177–180 CE.

(1.1) The first point which Celsus makes in his desire to discredit Christianity is that the Christians secretly form associations (*synthēkai*) with each other in violation of the law, because "among associations, those that are open are considered in keeping with the laws but those that are concealed violate the laws." He wants to slander the so-called "love (*agapē*) that Christians have toward one another," "because it exists for the common danger and is more powerful than an oath." Since he goes on and on about "the common law," saying that "the associations of the Christians violate this," I must reply. Take, for instance, a person living among Scythians—whose laws were, in fact, unlawful—and had no opportunity to leave and was compelled to live among them. This person would, with good reason, for the sake of the true law, which the Scythians would regard as violating their law, form associations (*synthēkai*) with like-minded people in violation of those laws. So, if truth is the measure, the laws of the nations concerning images and godless (atheistic) polytheism are, so to speak, Scythian laws or even more impious than those, if that is even possible. Therefore, it is not unreasonable to form associations against the laws for the sake of truth. For just as it would be right for people to form a concealed association to kill a tyrant who had seized control of their city, so also Christians, who are being tyrannized by the devil, as they call him, and by falsehood, form associations in violation of the laws of the devil. That is, they form associations against the devil and on behalf of the safety of others whom they may persuade to revolt against the law of the Scythians, as it were, and of a tyrant.

(3.23) When our Jesus, "appeared to the members of his own society (*thiasōtai*)," to use Celsus' own words, he really did appear, and Celsus makes a false accusation in saying that he appeared as a shadow [i.e., a ghost].

(8.17) After these things [viz., accusing Christians of failing to honor the true God as they claim] Celsus then says that we "avoid raising altars, images, and temples," since, he thinks, this is "a true sign of a concealed and secret association (*koinōnia*)." He does not realize that our altars are the soul of each righteous man, from which rises a sweet-smelling incense which is true and intelligible, namely prayers ascending from a pure conscience.

L20. Cyprian of Carthage (North Africa), *Epistles* (*Epistulae*) 67.6.2

Letter written ca. 257 CE to churches in Spain concerning the heretics Basilides and Martial (Latin).

Basilides and Martial have been contaminated by the abominable certificate of idolatry. . . . Martial also, in addition to the long-term frequenting of the disgraceful and filthy banquets (*convivia*) of the Gentiles in their association (*collegium*) and placing his sons in the same association, after the manner of foreign nations, among profane graves, and burying them together with strangers, has also affirmed, by acts which are publicly taken before a ducenarian procurator, that he had given himself to idolatry and had denied Christ.

L21. Eusebius of Caesarea, *Ecclesiastical History* (*Historia ecclesiastica*) 10.1.7–8

Written ca. 323–324 CE, covering the time of Constantine (Latin).

Finally a bright and shining day, overshadowed by no cloud, illuminated with beams of heavenly light the assemblies of Christ throughout the entire world. And not even those outside of our society (*thiasos*) were prevented from sharing in the same things, or at least from coming under their influence and participating in what was being obtained from God.

DEALINGS WITH CIVIC OR IMPERIAL AUTHORITIES
(arranged chronologically by incidents described)

L22. Plutarch of Chaeronea (Boeotia, Greece), *Lives* 17.1–3

Written ca. 70–120 CE, referring to the time of Numa Pompilius, king of Rome ca. 715–673 BCE (Greek).

Now of all [king Numa Pompilius'] administrative actions, the one greatly admired was the distribution of the multitude into groups according to trades (*technai*). For the city consisted of two tribes (*genē*), as has been said, seeming to stand together but divided into parts, and in no way desiring to become one or cover over differences and distinctions, but unceasingly making comparisons and loving strife (*philoneikia*) among the parts. Therefore, aware that hard substances which do not readily mix may be crushed and ground up and thus more easily mix on account of their smallness relative to one another, [Numa] decided to divide further all the multitude, and out of this place them into other distinctions, to eradicate the first and great distinction, which would be lost among the lesser distinctions. Thus, he distributed them by trades (*technai*), into musicians (*aulētai*), goldsmiths (*chrysochooi*), carpenters (*tektones*), dyers (*bapheis*), leather cutters (*skytotomoi*), leather dressers (*skytodepsai*), coppersmiths (*chalkeoi*), and potters (*kerameis*). The remaining trades he grouped together, and made one body (*systēma*) out of all who belonged to them. He also established social gatherings (*koinōnia*) and assemblies (*synodoi*) and honors for the gods as appropriate for each tribe (*genos*). In this way, he first removed from the city the practice of some who spoke and thought as Sabines and others as Romans, or of some as being of Tatius and others of Romulus, so that his division was harmonious and intermingled everyone together.

L23. Livy of Patavium (Italy), *History of Rome* (*Historia Romana*) 39.8–18 (selections)

Written during the time of emperor Augustus, concerning associations in Rome devoted to the god Dionysos, or Bacchus, ca. 186 BCE (Latin).

(39.8) The following year [186 BCE] diverted the attention of the consuls, Spurius Postumius Albinus and Quintus Marcius Philippus, from the army and the administration of wars and the provinces to the suppression of a conspiracy at home. . . . Both the consuls were given the responsibility of investigating clandestine conspiracies. First, a low-born Greek came to Etruria, but with none of the many skills that they [Greeks] have brought to us for the cultivation of mind and body, but a dabbler in sacrifices and a fortune-teller. Nor was he one who, by openly professing his business and his teaching, filled people's minds with error, but instead a priest of secret nocturnal rites. At first there were only a few who received these rites, but then they began to spread among both men and women. Added to the pleasure of piety, there was drinking and feasting, by which more souls were added. When wine inflamed them, and the nightly mingling of men with women and the young with the old had destroyed all sense of modesty, all varieties of corruption began to be practiced, since everyone had pleasures at hand to satisfy the craving to which his nature was most inclined. Neither was there just one form of vice, that is, the promiscuous intercourse of men and women. There were also false witnesses, forged documents and wills, and false information all coming from the same workshop, as well as poisonings and secret murders so that the bodies could not even be found for burial. Many crimes were committed by deceit, but most by violence. The violence was concealed because amid the noise of drums and cymbals, the cries of those who were being violated or murdered could not be heard.

(39.9) The destructive evil penetrated from Etruria to Rome like a plague. At first, the size and extent of the city, with its room and tolerance for such evils, concealed it. Eventually, information reached the consul Postumius in the following way: Publius Aebutius, whose father had served in the cavalry, had been left to guardians at his death. On the guardians' deaths, he had been brought up under the care of his mother Duronia and his stepfather Titus Sempronius Rutilus. The mother was devoted to her husband and his stepfather, who administered his guardianship in such a way that he could not render an account. He wished that his ward would either die, or be made dependent on them through some tie. One method of corrupting him was through the Bacchanalia (i.e., rites in honor of the god Bacchus = Dionysos). The mother told the youth that while he was sick she had taken a vow on his behalf that as soon as he recovered, she would initiate him into the Bacchic mysteries; now she was bound to fulfill the vow, because of the kindness of the gods. He had to continue in continence for ten days; then, after a banquet on the tenth day and purification, he had to go to the shrine. . . .

(39.10) In a jesting manner, [Aebutius] told [his lover, Hispala Fecenia, a freedwoman and courtesan] not to be surprised if he were away for some nights. It was a pious duty to discharge a vow made while he was ill, and he intended therefore to be initiated into the Bacchic mysteries. When she heard this she was very upset and exclaimed, "The gods forbid." It is better, she said, for both to die than that he should do this. Then she called down curses on the heads of those persons who had given him this advice. Astonished at her language and perturbance, the youth asked her to stop cursing: it was his mother who had commanded this, with the consent of his stepfather. "Perhaps it is not right to accuse your mother," she replied. "Your stepfather, then, is hurrying to destroy your virtue, your reputation, your hope, and your life." Even more astonished, he asked her what she meant. With a prayer to the gods and goddesses to forgive her if, constrained by her affection, she disclosed what ought to be concealed. She explained that when she was a slave she had attended the shrine with her mistress, but that as a freed woman she had never visited it. She knew it to be an office of every sort of corruption, and it was known that no one had been initiated for the last two years above the age of twenty. As each person was brought in, he was handed over to the priests like a victim and taken into a place which resounded with yells and songs, and with the jangling of cymbals and drums, so that no cry from those who were suffering violation could be heard. She then begged and implored him to end the matter in whatever way he could, and not to plunge into a place where he would first have to endure, and then to commit, every disgraceful practice. She would not let him go until he had given his word to keep clear of these rites. . . .

[Summary of following sections: After refusing to participate in the mysteries and being rejected by his mother and stepfather, Aebutius consulted with his aunt, Aebutia, and reported the whole situation to the consul, Postumius (39.12). The consul concluded that Aebutius' report was trustworthy and dismissed Aebutia, and asked his mother-in-law to send for Hispala, the freedwoman. She was brought into an inner apartment where the consul and his mother-in-law were present, and the consul told her that there was nothing to be afraid of if she could make up her mind to speak the truth. She might trust the pledged word of such a woman as Sulpicia and his own promise of safety, but she must give him a description of what usually went on at the Bacchic rites in the grove of Simila. Hispala was initially afraid to speak, but when she recovered, she reported that as a girl she had been initiated, together with her mistress. But since she had been manumitted, now some years ago, she knew nothing of what went on there. The consul commended her for having confessed that she had been initiated and begged her to be equally truthful in the rest of her story. She avowed that she knew nothing further, at which point the consul warned her that she would not receive the same consideration and indulgence as she would if she made a voluntary confession. He added that the person who had heard these things from her had disclosed everything to him. Hispala, convinced that Aebutius was the informer, flung herself at Sulpicia's feet and implored her not to let a conversation between a freedwoman and her lover be treated so seriously as to amount to treason (39.13). What she had told him was for the purpose of frightening, not because she really knew anything. The consul, Postumius, was angry,

*and told her that she must be imagining that she was joking
with her lover, and not speaking in the house of an important and revered lady and in the presence of the consul. At
that point, Hispala gave an account of the origin of the rites
as follows.]*

[Hispala reported that] at first it was a ritual for women and no man was
admitted. There had been three established days in the year on which persons were initiated during the daytime, and matrons were chosen to act as
priestesses. When she was priestess, Paculla Annia of Campania, changed
all of this, as though by divine command. For she was the first to initiate men and she initiated her own sons, Minius Cerinnius and Herennius
Cerinnius. At the same time, she made the rite a nighttime one instead of
a daytime one, and instead of three days in the year, she established five
times a month. From the time that the mysteries were performed in common, with men and women mingling and with the freedom of darkness
added, no crime, no wrongful deed, was left undone. There were more
shameful acts practiced between men than between men and women. If
someone would not submit to defilement or was reluctant to violate others,
he was sacrificed as a victim. To regard nothing as wrong was the very sum
of their piety. The men, as if insane and with frenzied distortions of their
bodies, shrieked out prophecies. Matrons, dressed as bacchants [i.e., devotees of Bacchus] with their hair disheveled, ran down to the Tiber with
burning torches, plunged them into the water, and drew them out again,
the flame undiminished, because they were made of sulphur mixed with
lime. Men were fastened to a machine and hurried off to hidden caves, and
they were said to have been carried away by the gods. These were the men
who refused to join their conspiracy or take a part in their crimes or submit to pollution. They [members of the group] formed a large multitude,
almost equal to the population of Rome. Among them were members of
noble families, both men and women. In the last two years, it had been
made a rule that no one more than twenty years old should be initiated. . . .

(39.14) [*The above information was then shared with the senators*]. The
Fathers were greatly alarmed for the public safety, lest these conspiracies and nocturnal gatherings were a danger to the state. They were
also alarmed for themselves, lest their own relations and friends might
be involved. They passed a vote of thanks to the consul for having conducted his investigations so carefully and without creating any public
disturbance. Then, arming the consuls with extraordinary powers, they
placed in their hands the inquiry into the proceedings at the Bacchanalia
and the nocturnal rites. They were to take care that Aebutius and Fecenia

suffered no injury for the information they had given, and they were to offer rewards to induce other informers to come forward. Those who pre-sided over these mysteries were to be sought out not only in Rome, but everywhere where people were in the habit of assembling, so that they might be delivered up to the consuls. Edicts were published in Rome and throughout Italy forbidding any who had been initiated from meeting together to celebrate their mysteries or performing any rites of a similar character. Above all, strict inquiry was to be made in the case of those who attended gatherings in which crime and debauchery had occurred. These were the measures which the Senate decreed. The consuls sent orders to the curule aediles [civic officials at Rome] to search out all the priests of those rites and, when they were arrested, to keep them in such custody as they thought best until their trial. The plebeian aediles were to see that no rites were performed openly during the day. The police commissioners were instructed to post watches throughout the city and take care that no nocturnal gatherings took place. . . .

(39.18) So great, however, was the number of those who fled from the city that law-suits and rights of property were in numerous cases lost by default. . . . Those who had simply been initiated, who, that is, had repeated after the priest the prescribed form of imprecation which pledged them to every form of evil and impurity, but had not been either active or passive participants in any of the proceedings to which their oath bound them, were detained in prison. Those who had polluted themselves by outrage and murder, those who had stained themselves by giving false evidence, forging docu-ments and wills and by other fraudulent practices were sentenced to death. The number of those executed exceeded the number of those sentenced to imprisonment. There was an enormous number of men as well as women in both groups. The women who had been found guilty were handed over to their relatives or guardians to be dealt with privately; if there was no one capable of inflicting punishment, they were executed publicly.

The next task awaiting the consuls was the destruction of all the Bac-chic shrines, beginning with Rome, and then throughout the length and breadth of Italy, except where there was an ancient altar or a sacred image. The Senate decreed that for the future there should be no Bacchanalian rites in Rome or in Italy. If any one considered that this form of worship was a necessary obligation and that he could not dispense with it without incurring guilt, he was to make a declaration before the city praetor and the praetor was to consult the Senate. If the Senate gave permission, not fewer than one hundred senators being present, he might observe those rites on condition that not more than five persons took part in the service, that they had no common fund, and that there was no priest or conductor of the ceremonies.

L24. Cicero (Quintus Tullius), *Handbook of Electioneering* (*Commentariolum petitionis,* or *De petitione consulatus*) 8.29–30

Written ca. 65–64 BCE by the younger brother of M. Tullius Cicero as a handbook on running for the consulship (Latin).

Therefore, take care to secure all the centuries [divisions of the population of Rome] through many friends of different sorts. First and most obviously draw to yourself senators, Roman knights, active and influential men of other ranks. . . . Then, take into account the whole city: all the associations (*collegia*), the wards, the hills. If you establish a friendship with the leading men from among their number, you will easily secure, through them, the remaining masses.

L25. Cicero (M. Tullius), *For Sestius* (*Pro Sestio*) 13 §§31–32, 34, and 25 §55

Written ca. 56 BCE in defense of Publius Sestius, concerning the actions of the two consuls of 58 BCE and their ally, Publius Clodius Pulcher (Latin).

(13 §31) Although you are listening to me most attentively, gentlemen, . . . still I fear that some of you may perhaps wonder what is my object in tracing things back so far, or what connection the offences of those men who trouble the Republic before Publius Sestius was tribune have with his cause now. But my intention is to show that the entire policy and object of his tribuneship was to heal the misfortunes of the afflicted and ruined Republic as far as was in his power. . . . And pardon me, if in exposing those wounds, I appear to say rather too much about myself. For you and all loyal citizens decided that that disaster which befell me was the heaviest possible blow to the Republic. Publius Sestius is a defendant, not on his own account, but on mine. For since he devoted all the strength of his tribuneship to promoting my welfare, it is inevitable that I should look upon my own cause in past time as united with the defense which I am now making for him. (13 §32) The Senate then was in grief, and all citizens wore the drab garments of mourning, by a public resolution. There was no town in all Italy, no colony, no prefecture, no company of men or tax farmers, no association (*collegium*) or council, no public body, in short, of any kind whatever, which had not passed most honorable resolutions

concerning my safety, when suddenly the two consuls issue an edict that the senators are to return to their former dress. . . .

(13 §34) With the same consuls [Lucius Calpurnius Piso Caesoninus and Aulus Gabinius] looking on, a levy of slaves was held before the tribunal of Aurelius, on the pretext of forming associations (*collegia*): men were enlisted according to their districts (*vici*), divided into divisions of ten (*decuries*), and stirred up to violence, arms, murder, and plunder. It was while these same men were consuls, that arms were openly carried into the temple of Castor, and the steps of the temple were pulled up. Armed men occupied the forum and the assemblies of the people. Slaughter and stonings took place. There was no Senate, and no magistrates were left. One man [Clodius] by arms and the violent tactics of a pirate seized all the power of all the magistrates not by any power of his own. Rather, having bribed the two consuls to desert the republic by the treaty respecting the provinces, he insulted every one, domineered over every one, made promises to some, held down many by terror and fear, and gained over more by hope and promises. . . .

(25 §55) For laws were passed while those consuls, shall I say, were silent— yes, rather while they actually approved of them. These were laws to the effect that the notice of the censors and the most important decisions of the most holy magistrates should be abolished; that not only those ancient associations (*collegia*) which had existed before should be restored in defiance of the resolution of the Senate (*senatus consultum*), but that innumerable new associations should be established by one gladiator.

L26. Cicero (M. Tullius), *Against Piso* (*In Pisonem*) 4.9

Written by Cicero ca. 55 BCE as a speech against Lucius Calpurnius Piso Caesoninus, the father-in-law of Julius Caesar, concerning incidents during Piso's consulship in 58 BCE (Latin).

Therefore, after you [Piso] had laid these foundations for your consulship [58 BCE], three days after, while you were looking on in silence, the Aelian and Fufian law, that fortress and wall of tranquillity and peace, was overturned by that fatal prodigy and monster of the republic [Publius Clodius]. Not only the associations (*collegia*) which the Senate had abolished were restored, but countless new ones were established made up of all the scum of the city and even slaves. The same man [Clodius], immersed in unheard of and nefarious debaucheries, abolished the old precepts of decency and modesty, the severity of the censor, while you [Piso] in the meantime, you sepulcher of the Republic, you who say that you were at that time consul at Rome, never by one single word intimated any opinion of your own amid such a terrible shipwreck of the state.

L27. Cicero (M. Tullius), *On His House* (*De domo sua*) 27 §§73–75

Written as a speech ca. 57 BCE to the college of priests upon Cicero's return from exile, an exile which had resulted from a law introduced by Clodius ca. 58 BCE (Latin).

(73) For what public deliberative body is there in the whole world, whether important or unimportant, which has not expressed that opinion of my deeds that is most desirable and most honorable for me? The greatest council of the Roman people—and of all peoples, nations, and kings—is the Senate; this decreed that all who desired the safety of the Republic should come forward to defend me alone, and showed its opinion that the Republic could not have been saved if I had not existed, and could not last if I did not return. (74) The next in rank to this dignified body is the equestrian order. All the companies for the collection of public revenues passed most favorable and honorable decrees respecting my consulship and my actions. The public scribes, who are much connected with us in matters relating to public registers and monuments, took good care that their sentiments and resolutions respecting my services to the Republic should not be left in doubt. There is no association (*collegium*) in all this city, no body of men either from the villages or the highlands—for our ancestors thought fit that the common people of the city should also have places of meeting and some sort of deliberative assemblies—which has not passed most honorable resolutions, not merely respecting my safety, but relating also to my dignity. (75) For why need I mention those divine and immortal decrees of the municipal towns, and of the colonies, and of all Italy, by which, as by a flight of steps, I seem not only to have returned to my country, but to have mounted up to heaven?

L28. Cicero (M. Tullius), *In the Senate after His Return* (*Post reditum in senatu*) 13 §33

Written as a speech ca. 57 BCE delivered to the Senate after Cicero's return from exile, referring to the period leading up to his exile (Latin).

Two parties were supposed to exist in the republic, the one was thought out of its hostility to me [Cicero], to demand my surrender [viz., those

associated with Clodius and the consuls Lucius Calpurnius Piso Caesoninus and Aulus Gabinius]; the other was timid in my defense, because
of the fear of the bloodshed that they thought clung to me. . . . Conse-
quently, when I realized that the Senate was deprived of leaders, and that
the magistrates had either attacked me, or betrayed me, or deserted me,
and that slaves had been enrolled by name under some pretext of forming an association (*collegium*), that all the forces of Catiline were recalled
to their original hopes of massacre and incendiarism under almost the
same leaders as before [referring back to Catiline's use of associations in
64 BCE], and when I saw that the Roman knights were under the same fear
of proscription as before, and when I saw that the municipal towns were in
fear of being pillaged, and every one in fear of his life—I might—I might,
I say, O conscript fathers, still have been able to defend myself by force,
and many wise and brave men advised me to do so. I was not lacking in
the same courage that I had shown before, and which was not unknown to
you. But I saw that if I was victorious, I still had too many others behind
who must also be defeated. And if I were defeated, many virtuous men
would fall for my sake, fall with me and even after me. And I saw that the
avengers of the blood of the tribunes were present, but that all satisfaction
for my death must be exacted by the slow progress of the law, and reserved
for posterity.

L29. Asconius (Quintus Asconius Pedianus), *Commentary on* [Cicero's] *Against Piso* (*In Pisonem*) 320.8–90

Written ca. 54–57 CE, concerning incidents in 64 BCE and 58
BCE (Latin).

In the consulship of L. Julius and C. Marcius [64 BCE], whom Cicero mentions earlier, a decree of the Senate abolished the associations (*collegia*) as
being contrary to the interest of the people. The magistrates of these associations were in the habit of wearing the toga of office when holding the
Compitalician games, just like the leaders of the districts (*vici*). The games
came to an end with the abolition of the associations. Six years after the
abolition [58 BCE], P. Clodius, the tribune of the common people, restored
them by legislation. So Cicero puts the blame for this restoration on
Piso. . . .

L30. Asconius (Quintus Asconius Pedianus), *Commentary on* [Cicero's] *For Cornelius* (*Pro Cornelio*) 75C

Written ca. 54–57 CE, concerning incidents in 64 BCE (Latin).

Meetings frequently took place at the time, attended by seditious men without the authority of the people with damaging consequences. As a result, the associations (*collegia*) were abolished by senatorial decrees and a number of laws later on, except for a few specified ones with a clear benefit for the people, such as those of carpenters and potters (*fabrorum fictorumque*).

L31. Dio Cassius of Nikaia (Bithynia), *Roman History* (*Historiae Romanae*) 38.13

Written ca. 229 CE, concerning incidents in the time of Clodius, ca. 62–58 BCE (Greek).

[Cicero was] disliked and hated even by those very persons whom he otherwise pleased. Because of this situation, Clodius therefore hoped to prepare the Senate, the knights, and the populace to defeat [Cicero] quickly. So [Clodius] went to distributing free wheat. (For when Gabinius and Piso had now become consuls, he [Clodius] had introduced his motion that it should be doled out to the needy.) He also revived the associations (*hetairika*), called "collegia" (*kollēgia*) in the native language, which had existed since ancient times but had been dissolved for some time.

L32. Suetonius, *Lives of the Caesars*, "Julius" (*Divus Julius*) 42

Written ca. 90–130 CE, concerning actions of Julius Caesar ca. 47–46 BCE (Latin).

[In connection with various other actions, Julius Caesar] dissolved all associations (*collegia*) except those of ancient foundation (*antiquitus constituta*).

L33. Josephus, *Jewish Antiquities* (*Antiquitates judaicae*) 14.213–16

Document attributed to Julius Caesar ca. 47–46 BCE, collected and edited by Josephus ca. 80–100 CE along with other ostensibly official documents from the mid-late first century BCE (Greek).

"Julius Gaius, praetor and consul of the Romans [ca. 47–46 BCE], to the leaders, Council, and People of the Parians, greetings. The Judeans on Delos and some of the neighboring Judeans, in the presence of your ambassadors, explained to us that, by decree, you forbid them to engage in their ancestral customs and sacred rites. Now it does not please me that such decrees should be made against our friends and allies in such a way that they are forbidden to live according to their own customs or to collect funds for common meals and sacred activities, while they are not forbidden to do so even at Rome itself. For even Gaius Caesar, our praetor and consul, passed a decree preventing societies (*thiasoi*) from gathering together in the city [of Rome], yet he did not prevent these [Judeans] alone from collecting funds or having common meals. Likewise, when I prevent other societies (*thiasoi*), I permit these [Judeans] alone to gather together according to their ancestral customs and laws, and to feast. Therefore, it would be good for you to, if you have passed any decree against our friends and allies, to cancel the decree because of their virtue and goodwill toward us."

L34. Suetonius, *Lives of the Caesars,* "Augustus" (*Divus Augustus*) 32.1

Written ca. 90–130 CE, concerning actions of Augustus (Latin).

Many of the most evil practices which threaten the destruction of the public order had survived as a result of the lawless habits of the civil wars, or had even arisen in time of peace. For many brigands went about openly with swords by their sides, supposedly to protect themselves, and travelers in the country, freemen and slaves alike, were seized indiscriminately and confined in the workhouses of the landowners. Many groups (*factiones*) formed societies (*societates*) bearing the title of a new association (*collegium*) to commit nothing that was not outrageous. Therefore [Augustus] restrained the brigandage by stationing guards wherever it seemed opportune, he inspected the workhouses, and dissolved the associations (*collegia*), except those that were long-standing and formed for legitimate purposes (*antiqua et legitima*).

L35. Appian of Alexandria (Egypt), *Civil Wars* (*Bella civilia*) 5.132

Written before ca. 165 CE, concerning the time of Octavius, later Augustus (Greek).

Octavius was now twenty-eight years old [ca. 35 BCE]. . . . At this time Italy and Rome itself were openly infested with bands (*systaseis*) of brigands, whose activities were more like blatant plunder than secret theft. Octavius chose Sabinus to correct this disorder. Sabinus executed many of the captured brigands, and within one year brought about a condition of complete security. They say that the customary arrangement of having cohorts of night watchmen, which is still in force, began at that time. Octavius caused amazement by having put an end to this problem with exceptional speed.

L36. Philo of Alexandria (Egypt), *Against Flaccus* (*In Flaccum*) 4–5

Written after a Judean embassy to emperor Gaius in 39 or 40 CE, concerning Aulus Avilius Flaccus, the governor in Egypt from 32–38 CE (Greek).

[During his time as prefect, Flaccus] prohibited the gathering of riotous and promiscuous mobs of men. Also, he dissolved the associations (*hetaireia*) and synods (*synodoi*), which were always feasting together under pretence of sacrifices and causing problems with their drunken behavior. He dealt harshly and forcibly with the ones that rebelled.

L37. Philo of Alexandria (Egypt), *On the Embassy to Gaius* (*Legatio ad Gaium*) 311–13

Written for a Judean embassy to emperor Gaius in 39 or 40 CE, referring to earlier actions of Augustus (Greek).

Though I would be able to demonstrate to you the wishes of Augustus, your great grandfather, with an abundance of evidence, I will be content with two. For, in the first place, he sent a letter to all the governors of the provinces in Asia, because he heard that the sacred first fruits were being treated with disrespect. He ordered them to permit only the Judeans to come together in gatherings (*synagōgia*). For these synods (*synodoi*) were not based on drunkenness and drunken behavior to cause disturbance. Instead, they were schools of temperance and justice, where people practiced virtue and contributed the annual first fruits every year, sending sacred ambassadors to take them to the temple in Jerusalem. Then he commanded that no one should hinder the Judeans from gathering, collecting funds, or sending ambassadors to Jerusalem according to ancestral custom.

L38. Dio Cassius of Nikaia (Bithynia), *Roman History* (*Historiae Romanae*) 60.6.6–7

Written ca. 229 CE, concerning the time of emperor Gaius (31–41 CE) and emperor Claudius (41–54 CE) (Greek).

The Judeans had increased so greatly that, due to the size of the population, it would be difficult to shut them out of the city without causing a disturbance. So [the emperor Claudius] did not drive them out. Instead he ordered them not to hold meetings while continuing their traditional mode of life. He also disbanded the associations (*hetaireia*), which had been reintroduced by Gaius. Moreover, seeing that there was no use in forbidding the populace from doing certain things without changing their daily life, he abolished the taverns where they gathered and drank and he commanded that no boiled meat or hot water should be sold. He also punished some who disobeyed in this matter.

L39. Tacitus, *Annals* (*Annales*) 14.17

Written ca. 100–110 CE, concerning an incident in 59 CE in and around the amphitheater at Pompeii (Latin). See figure 31 for a photo of a fresco from Pompeii that seems to depict this same event.

About the same time, a trivial incident led to terrible slaughter between the inhabitants of the colonies of Nuceria and Pompeii, at gladiatorial games presented by Livineius Regulus, who, as I have related, had been removed from the Senate. During an exchange quite typical of impudent small towns, they began with abusive language against each other, then

Figure 31
Wall painting from a house at Pompeii depicting a riot in and around the amphitheater, now in the archaeological museum at Naples (L39; photo by Harland).

stones, and then steel weapons. The people of Pompeii, where the show was taking place, gained superiority. Therefore, a number of Nucerians were carried to the city [Rome] with their bodies mutilated by wounds, while many lamented the deaths of children or parents. The emperor entrusted the judgment of the case to the Senate, and the Senate assigned it to the consuls. When the case was again referred back to the Fathers [i.e., senators], the people of Pompeii were forbidden from having such public gatherings for ten years, and all associations (*collegia*) formed in defiance of the laws were dissolved. Livineius and the others who had fomented the disturbance were punished with exile.

L40. Pliny the Younger, *Epistles* (*Epistulae*) 10.33–34, 10.92–93, and 10.96–97

Initially written ca. 109–110 CE, while Pliny was legate of the province of Bithynia-Pontus in northern Asia Minor (Latin).

(10.33) Pliny to the emperor Trajan.

While I was traveling about in a different part of the province, an enormous fire broke out at Nikomedia, which not only consumed many private houses, but also two public buildings—the elders' meeting place (*gerousia*) and the temple of Isis—although the road runs between them. It was spread partly because of a strong wind and partly through the inactivity of the people, who it is agreed, stood by idly and immobile watching the disaster without doing anything to stop it. Actually, there is not a single fire engine in the town, nor buckets, nor any apparatus for fighting fires. However, I have now given directions to have these supplied.

Will you, Sir, consider whether you think an association of builders (*collegium fabrorum*) be formed, limited to one hundred fifty members. I will see that no one is admitted who is not a builder, and that the privileges granted them shall not be used for another purpose. It will not be difficult to monitor such small numbers.

(10.34) Trajan to Pliny.

You have had the idea that it would be proper to form an association of builders (*collegium fabrorum*) in Nikomedia, following the model of those existing elsewhere. But we must remember that societies (*civatates*) of this sort have been responsible for the disturbances in your province, especially in the towns. Under whatever name they assemble and for whatever reason we give, they soon turn into a political club (*hetaeria*). It is a better policy, then, to provide the equipment necessary for dealing with fires, and to instruct the owners of estates to suppress fires, and, if necessary, to call on the help of the people.

(10.92) To the emperor Trajan.

By your indulgence, the free and confederate city of the Amisus has the privilege of administering its own laws. I have subjoined to this letter a petition handed to me there concerning clubs (*erànoi* [the Greek term is used]) so that you may decide, Sir, whether and to what extent this should be permitted or prohibited.

(10.93) Trajan to Pliny.

If the Amisenians, whose petition you have sent to me, are allowed by their own laws, granted them by formal treaty, to form a club (*eranus*), we should not oppose it, especially if the contributions are used not for the purpose of disturbances and illicit assembly (*coetus*), but for the support of the indigent (*tenuiores*). However, in other cities which are subject to our laws, these are to be prohibited.

(10.96) Pliny to Trajan.

It is my custom, Sir, to refer to you in all cases where I am in doubt, for who can better clear up difficulties and inform me? I have never been present at any examination (*cognitio*) of the Christians. Therefore, I do not know what are the usual punishments given out to them, or the extent of those punishments, or how far an examination should go. Nor am I sure whether any distinction should be made in regard to the age of the accused, or if youths and adults should be treated the same way, or whether a pardon should be granted to someone who retracts his belief, or if he had once professed to be a Christian he should gain nothing by renouncing it. And whether the name of Christian itself should be punished, even though otherwise innocent of crime, or only the crimes that associated with the name?

In the meantime, this is the plan which I have adopted in the case of those Christians who have been brought before me. I ask them whether they are Christians. If they admit it, then I repeat the question a second and a third time, warning them of the punishments involved. And if they persist, I ordered them to be led away (for execution) (*perseverantes duci iussi*). For, whatever the nature of their confession, I have no doubt that their stubbornness (*pertinacia*) and unyielding obstinacy (*obstinatio*) surely ought to be punished. Others who showed similar madness, who were Roman citizens, I reserved to be sent to Rome.

Now, as is commonly the case, the fact of my entertaining the question led to a multiplying of accusations and a variety of cases were brought before me. An anonymous pamphlet was issued, containing many names. Those who denied that they were or had been Christians, I acquitted, when they called upon the gods with the usual formula, reciting the words after me, and those who offered incense and wine before your image (which I had ordered to be brought forward for this purpose, along with the regular statues of the gods), and, furthermore, they had cursed the name of Christ, which it is said genuine Christians cannot be induced to do.

Other names were supplied by an informer. These first said they had been Christians, but then denied it, insisting they had been but were so no longer. Some of them had recanted many years ago, and more than one twenty years ago. These all reverenced your image and the god's statues and cursed the name of Christ. But they said that the sum total of their guilt or error was this: on a fixed day they used to meet before dawn and recite a hymn (*carmen*) among themselves to Christ, as though he were a god. So far from binding themselves by oath (*sacramentum*) to commit any crime, they swore to keep from theft, robbery, adultery, breach of faith, and not to deny any trust money deposited with them when called upon to deliver it. After this ceremony, they used to depart and meet again to take food, but of an ordinary and entirely harmless type. They also had ceased from this practice after the edict I issued, by which, in keeping with your orders, I banned all associations (*hetaeria*).

I then thought it the more needful to get to the facts behind their statements. Therefore I placed two women, whom they call "servants" (*ministrae*), under torture, but I found only a depraved and immoderate superstition (*superstitio*).

I have postponed my examination, and immediately consulted you. This seems a matter worthy of your prompt consideration, especially as so many people are endangered. Many of all ages and both sexes are put in peril of their lives by their accusers, and this will continue, for the contagion of this superstition has spread not merely through the free towns, but into the villages and farms. Still I think it can be halted and things set right. Beyond any doubt, the temples, which were nearly deserted, are beginning again to be crowded with worshippers. The sacred rites, which long have lapsed, are now being renewed, and the food for the sacrificial victims is again finding a sale, though until recently it had almost no market. So one can safely infer how vast numbers could be reclaimed, if only there were given an opportunity for repentance.

(10.97) Trajan to Pliny

You have adopted the right procedure in examining the cases of those cited before you as Christians, my dear Pliny. It is impossible to have a general rule covering such a wide question. The Christians are not to be hunted out. If they are brought before you, and the offense is proved, they are to be punished; but if any one denies he is a Christian and makes it clear he is not by offering prayer to our gods, then he is to be pardoned on his recantation, no matter how suspicious his past. As for anonymous pamphlets, they are to be discarded completely, whatever crime they may charge, for they are not only a precedent of a very bad type, but they are not in keeping with the spirit of our age.

L41. Athenaeus of Naukratis (Egypt), *The Banquet of the Learned (Deiphnosophistae)* 5.185b

Written in the late second century CE (Greek).

The lawgivers, providing for present-day dinners (*deipna*), prescribed both tribe dinners (*phyletika*) and subdivision dinners (*dēmotika*), and beyond these the dinners of the societies (*thiasoi*), the brotherhood (*phratrika*) dinners, and again those that are called "orgeonic" [i.e., run by sacrificing associates].

L42. Augustan History, "Alexander Severus" (*Scriptores historiae Augustae*, "Alexander Severus") 33

Written in the late third or fourth century, concerning the time of emperor Alexander Severus, ca. 222–235 CE (Latin).

He appointed fourteen supervisors (*curatores*) of the city of Rome, chosen from among those who had been consuls, and commanded them to hear city cases in conjunction with the prefect of the city, giving orders that all of them, or at least a majority, should be present whenever the records were made. He also formed partnerships (*corpora*) of all the wine dealers, the green grocers, the shoemakers, and, in short, of all the skilled trades, and he granted them advocates chosen from their own numbers and designated the judge to whose jurisdiction each should belong.

LEGAL DOCUMENTS IN THE *DIGEST* OF JUSTINIAN (CA. 527–565 CE)

(arranged chronologically by jurist)

Order of passages in the *Digest* of Justinian

1.12.1.14	= **L47**. Ulpian, *On the Duties of the Urban Prefect*
2.4.10.4	= **L49**. Ulpian, *On the Edict* 5
3.4.1	= **L43**. Gaius, *On the Provincial Edict* 3
3.4.2	= **L50**. Ulpian, *On the Edict* 8

4.2.9.1	= **L51**. Ulpian, *On the Edict* 11
10.4.7.3	= **L52**. Ulpian, *On the Edict* 24
27.1.17.2–3	= **L45**. Callistratus, *On Judicial Inquiries* 4
47.22.1	= **L53**. Marcianus, *Institutes* 3
47.22.2	= **L48**. Ulpian, *On the Duties of Proconsul* 7
47.22.3	= **L54**. Marcianus, *Public Prosecutions* 2
47.22.4	= **L44**. Gaius, *On the Law of the Twelve Tables* 4
50.6.5.3, 5, 6–7, 9, 12–13	= **L46**. Callistratus, *On Judicial Inquiries* 1

Gaius (ca. 130–180 CE)

L43. Gaius, *On the Provincial Edict (Institutiones)* 3 = *Digest* 3.4.1

Gaius was a Roman jurist, born in the time of emperor Hadrian and active under the emperors Antoninus Pius and Marcus Aurelius, but we know almost nothing about him (not even his full name) beyond citations of works attributed to him (Latin).

Permission has not been granted to any persons to form either a society (*societas*), an association (*collegium*), or a similar partnership (*corpus*), for this is regulated by laws, decrees of the Senate, and edicts of the emperors. In a few instances, partnerships (*corpora*) of this kind are authorized: as, for example, the right to form partnerships is permitted to those engaged as partners in the collection of taxes, or associations of workers in the gold-mines, silver-mines, and salt-mines. Certain associations at Rome have been confirmed by decrees of the Senate, and edicts of the emperors, as, for example, those of bakers (*pistores*) and of some other trades, as well as those of ship owners (*navicularii*), which also exist in the provinces.

(1) When persons are allowed to form a partnership (*corpus*) under the title of an association (*collegium*), society (*societas*), or some other name, they are, like a municipality (*res publica*), entitled to hold property in common, have a common treasury (*arca*), and have an agent or advocate (*syndicus*). And just as in the case of a municipality, whatever he contracts or does is considered to be contracted and done by all in common.

(2) Where no one defends them in a suit, the proconsul will order their common property to be seized and if, having been warned, they do not take measures to defend themselves, he will order the property to be sold. We understand that an association has no agent or advocate when he is absent, or prevented by a serious condition (i.e., illness), or is otherwise incapable of transacting business.

(3) Where a stranger appears to defend a company (*universitas*), the proconsul permits him to do so, as it happens in the case of the defense of private individuals; because in this way the condition of the company is improved.

L44. Gaius, *On the Law of the Twelve Tables (Institutiones)* 4 = *Digest* 47.22.4

This passage attributed to Gaius includes citation of a law (in Greek) attributed to Solon, the Athenian lawmaker (ca. 638 BCE–558 BCE) (Latin and Greek).

Members (*sodales*) are those who belong to the same association (*collegium*), which the Greeks call *hetaireia*. The law allows them to enter into whatever contracts they may wish with one another, provided they do nothing to corrupt the public interest. This law appears to have been taken over from a law of Solon, which is as follows [in Greek]: "If the people (*dēmos*), or brothers (*fratres*), or those engaging in sacred rites (*orgia*), or sailors (*nautai*), or feasting mates (*syssitoi*), or those who are buried in the same tomb (*homotaphoi*), or members of a society (*thiasōtai*) who generally live together, enter into any contract with one another, whatever they agree upon is binding, unless the public laws forbid it."

Callistratus (ca. 198–211 CE)

L45. Callistratus, *On Judicial Inquiries* 4 = *Digest* 27.1.17.2–3

The Roman jurist Callistratus was active under the emperors Septimius Severus and Caracalla, but little is known about him beyond citations of his works (Latin).

[Quoting the Imperial Constitutions]: (2) Those who belong to certain partnerships (*corpora*), for example, builders (*fabri*), who we declare to have an exemption (*immunitas*) in respect to the guardianship of persons not belonging to their partnership will be excused, even if their property has been subsequently increased, in order to compel them to undertake other public employments. This is provided for by the Imperial Constitutions.

(3) Not all partnerships (*corpora*) or associations (*collegia*), nevertheless, enjoy a release from the duties of guardianship, although they may not be obliged to assume municipal offices, unless this privilege has been expressly granted them.

L46. Callistratus, *On Judicial Inquiries* 1 = *Digest* 50.6.5.3, 5, 6–7, 9, 12–13

These passages attributed to Callistratus are focused on imperial grants of freedom from public service, which were granted to certain associations for their supply of services important to imperial rule: the supply of grain to Rome (traders and ship owners) and firefighting or other services (builders/carpenters) (Latin).

(3) Traders (*negotiatores*) who help in the grain supply of the city as well as ship owners (*navicularii*) who also provide for the grain supply obtain exemption (*immunitas*) from public office (*munera*), as long they are involved in this occupation.
. . .

(5) The divine Hadrian [ca. 117–138 CE] confirmed in a rescript that ship owners who provide the grain supply have an exemption from public office.

(6) If it is permitted for someone to belong to a partnership of ship owners who neither owns a ship or a vessel nor anything else that is provided for by the Imperial Constitutions, he cannot use the privilege conceded to ship owners. . . .

(7) This must be said in respect to exemptions: that if someone who has been summoned to municipal service (*munera*) before he began to act as a trader, or before he was admitted to an association (*collegium*) which had obtained immunity, or before he became seventy years old, and before he publicly stated these facts, or before he had the requisite number of children, he should be compelled to assume the office (*honor*) to which he was appointed. . . .

(9) The divine (Antoninus) Pius [ca. 138–161 CE] confirmed in a rescript that whenever a question was raised as to whether anyone was a ship owner, it should be ascertained whether he had assumed the identity of a ship owner in order to escape public service. . . .

(12) To certain associations (*collegia*) or partnerships (*corpora*) which are given the right to assemble by law, exemption from public service is granted. This applies to associations or partnerships to which a person is admitted by virtue of his occupation, such as the partnership (*corpus*) of builders (*fabri*), provided they have the same origin, that is, if they have been founded to perform some work necessary for the public interest.

Exemption is not indiscriminately granted to all who are admitted to these associations, but only to artisans (*artificii*). Nor may they choose persons of all ages, as the divine (Antoninus) Pius decreed, who disapproved of the admission of those of an advanced or weak age. And in order that individuals who had become wealthy might not avoid the responsibility attaching to public service (*munera*), it was decided in many places that persons could avail themselves of the privileges which had been granted by such associations to anyone in reduced circumstances (*tenuiores*).

(13) If those who have been elected to a partnership that offer exemption, such as the ship owners, obtain the decurionate, they are to be compelled to accept public service.

This seems to have been confirmed by a rescript of the divine Pertinax [193 CE].

Ulpian (ca. 170–223 CE)

L47. Ulpian, *On the Duties of the Urban Prefect* = *Digest* 1.12.1.14

Domitius Ulpianus was a Roman jurist and legal compiler who was born in Tyre (Phoenicia) and served in significant imperial positions before being assassinated while prefect of the praetorians in about 223 CE (cf. Cassius Dio, *Roman History* 80.1.1; 80.2.2–3) (Latin).

The divine Severus [193–211 CE] issued a rescript saying that those who are said to have held an unlawful association (*collegium*) are to be prosecuted before the city prefect.

L48. Ulpian, *On the Duties of Proconsul* 7 = *Digest* 47.22.2

(Latin).

Whoever becomes a member of an unlawful association (*collegium*) is liable to the same penalty as persons who have been convicted of occupying public places or temples by means of armed men.

L49. Ulpian, *On the Edict* 5 = *Digest* 2.4.10.4

(Latin).

Whoever is manumitted by a partnership (*corpus*), an association (*collegium*), or by a city, can summon any member of the same to court, for he is not the freedman of any of them (individually). He is required, however, to show respect to all collectively. And if he wishes to bring an action against a municipality (*res publica*) or a partnership, he must ask permission to do so under the edict, although he may intend to summon one who has been appointed the agent of the others.

L50. Ulpian, *On the Edict* 8 = *Digest* 3.4.2

(Latin).

Where the citizens of a municipality (*municipes*) or members of any company (*universitas*) appoint an agent to take care of their legal interests, it is not said that he has thus been given this charge only by several individuals, for he acts in a legal capacity on behalf of the municipality or the whole company, and not for the members individually.

L51. Ulpian, *On the Edict* 11 = *Digest* 4.2.9.1

(Latin).

[The praetor in this section speaks generally, not in relation to specific cases]. Therefore, whether it is individual persons who intimidate, or a mob, or a municipality, or an association (*collegium*), or a partnership (*corpus*), the edict will apply.

L52. Ulpian, *On the Edict* 24 = *Digest* 10.4.7.3

(Latin).

It is possible to sue a municipality (*municipes*) to force it to disclose something, because it has the power of delivery; for it can assume possession by adverse possession (*usucapio*). The same rule also applies to associations (*collegia*) and other partnerships (*corpora*) like them.

Marcianus (ca. 222–235 CE)

L53. Marcianus, *Institutes* (*Institutiones regulae*) 3 = *Digest* 47.22.1

Aelius Marcianus was a Roman jurist and legal compiler who worked during the time of emperors Septimius Severus and Caracalla (Latin).

By the decrees of the emperors, the governors of the provinces have orders not to allow associations (*collegia sodalicia*), not even soldiers' associations.

But the poor (*tenuiorum*; i.e., the poor among the soldiers) are permitted to contribute a monthly donation to a common fund, and are allowed to assemble only once a month, but not as a pretext to convene an unlawful association (*illicitum collegium*), which the divine Severus [193–211 CE] said in a rescript should not be tolerated, not only at Rome, but also in Italy and the provinces.

(1) But it is not forbidden to assemble for religious purposes (*religionis causa*) if one does not act against the decree of the Senate which forbade unlawful associations.

(2) It is not permitted to join more than one lawful association (*collegium licitum*), as has been decided by the divine Brothers [joint emperors Caracalla and Geta; ca. 209–211 CE]. And if anyone becomes a member of two associations, the rescript requires that he must choose the one that he likes better, and he shall obtain from the association from which he withdraws the property to which he may be entitled from the common property.

L54. Marcianus, *Public Prosecutions* 2 = *Digest* 47.22.3

(Latin).

If associations (*collegia*) are unlawful (*illicita*), they will be dissolved in accordance with the imperial mandates and constitutions and the decrees of the Senate. When they are dissolved, the members are allowed to divide among themselves the money held in common, if there is any money in common.

(1) In sum, unless an association or any partnership (*corpus*) of this description convenes with the authority of the decree of the Senate, or of the emperor, this assembly is contrary to the provisions of the decrees of the Senate and the imperial mandates and constitutions.

(2) It is also permitted for slaves to join an association of the poor (*collegium tenuiorum*), if they have the permission of their owners. And the supervisors of these kinds of associations should know that they cannot accept a slave into an association of the poor without the approval and knowledge of the owner; if they do they will be liable to a penalty of a hundred gold pieces (*aurei*) for every slave admitted.

ANNOTATED BIBLIOGRAPHY

Abbott, Frank Frost. 1911. "Some Reflections on Corporations and Trade-Guilds." In *The Common People of Ancient Rome: Studies of Roman Life and Literature*, ed. Frank Frost Abbott, 205–34. New York: Scribner.

> A. briefly traces the history of Roman labor associations from their mythical establishment by King Numa to the empire. Associations were formed for companionship and mutual help and met at fixed times, as well as on special occasions, usually in a temple. Initiation fees, monthly dues, donations, and fines funded them. Membership was limited to the lower strata of society, who banded together for social importance, reproducing the Roman leadership structure in miniature.

Alföldy, Géza. 1958. "Collegium-Organisationen in Intercisa." *Acta Antiqua Academiae Scientiarum Hungaricae* 6:177–98.

> Although the city of Intercisa never attained the status of a *municipium*, which was necessary for the establishment of *collegia* (associations), three verifiable *collegia* did exist there during the second quarter of the third century CE. The authorization for their establishment in settlements without municipal law was exceptional, and in the case of Intercisa is linked to Severus Alexander's policy of supporting *collegia* among the poor (who in turn supported him).

Alföldy, Géza. 1966. "Zur Inschrift des Collegium Centonariorum von Solva." *Historia* 15:433–44.

> A. provides the missing information in the prescript of an inscription of the *collegium centonariorum* (textile workers) that includes a letter of Septimius Severus and Caracalla concerning the

centonarii of Solva. The members named are likely the recipients of the privileges outlined in the decree. Also addressed is a dispute over required monetary contributions by wealthy members and the right of poor members to hold municipal office.

Alikin, Valeriy A. 2010. *The Earliest History of the Christian Gathering: Origin, Development and Content of the Christian Gathering in the First to Third Centuries.* VC Supplements 102. Leiden: E.J. Brill.

Builds on recent work demonstrating early Christian communities were similar in function and practices to associations to provide a reconstruction of how the Christians' weekly gatherings originated and developed in form and content, giving attention to the timing of the feast day (each Sunday) and the preaching, praying, singing, and reading at these gatherings.

Aneziri, Sophia. 2003. *Die Vereine der dionysischen Techniten im Kontext der hellenistischen Gesellschaft: Untersuchungen zur Geschichte, Organisation und Wirkung der hellenistischen Technitenvereine.* Historia Einzelschriften 163, 542. Stuttgart: Franz Steiner Verlag.

A. analyzes the name, formation, structure, and informal cooperation of Dionysiac associations of performers (or artists) and their relationship to the *polis* (city) in Athens, Isthmia, Asia Minor, and Egypt. Membership issues examined are functionaries, discipline, honorary membership, gender composition, familial relationships, geographic origins, and legal and social position. Included are issues of property and finances and the roles played by the performers in the Hellenistic festivals. An appendix collects eighty-seven relevant inscriptions.

Arnaoutoglou, Ilias N. 1994a. "ΑΡΧΕΡΑΝΙΣΤΗΣ and Its Meaning in Inscriptions." *Zeitschrift für Papyrologie und Epigraphik* 104:107–10.

It is not possible to maintain that the office of *archeranistēs* (head of the club) denotes superiority or prominence since associations varied from city to city and adapted their structure and nomenclature to fit their individuality. For example, in Rhodes the *archeranistēs* was prominent and authoritative and always appeared among fellow *eranistai* (club members), whereas in Athens the *archeranistēs* was not necessarily prominent and appeared in groups not called *eranistai.*

Arnaoutoglou, Ilias N. 1994b. "Associations and Patronage in Ancient Athens." *Ancient Society* 25:5–17.

Ancient Greek associations (*orgeōnes* and *thiasōtai*) were not the actual vehicle for clientelism since the associations did not garner much participation from the elite. However, clientelism was not compatible with the ideal of citizenship in Athens, and the power of wealthy patricians was limited by the emphasis on political equality and by the municipal responsibility for liturgy and financial remuneration of the judiciary and civic participants. Friendship (*philia*), an essential part of the Athenian civic community, was based upon proportionate returns and therefore impermanent.

Arnaoutoglou, Ilias N. 1998. "Between *Koinon* and *Idion*: Legal and Social Dimensions of Religious Associations in Ancient Athens." In *Kosmos: Essays in Order, Conflict, and Community in Classical Athens*, ed. Paul Cartledge, Paul Millett, and Sitta von Reden, 68–83. Cambridge: Cambridge University Press.

Association inscriptions are unhelpful for information on the founding and dissolution of associations, or legal rights and duties, because they had no juristic personality. Socio-culturally, however, associations were important participants in the honorific system, and their "rituals of conviviality" not only strengthened internal associative links but also served to assimilate novices and foreigners into the fabric of the Athenian city. Associations reflected the dominant social order and helped replicate the conditions necessary to preserve this social order.

Arnaoutoglou, Ilias N. 2002. "Roman Law and *Collegia* in Asia Minor." *Revue internationale des droits de l'antiquité* 49 (3rd ser.): 27–44.

Associative life in Asia Minor was not restricted to specific areas, nor did it disappear after the Roman domination of the area. Any interventions or restrictions by Roman authorities were temporary. Restrictions were placed not on associations as such but on occupational groups that were less organized and thus had potential to promulgate anti-Roman attitudes and initiatives.

Arnaoutoglou, Ilias N. 2003. *Thysias Heneka kai Synousias: Private Religious Associations in Hellenistic Athens*. Academy of Athens. Yearbook of the Research Centre for the History of Greek Law, Supplement 37/4. Athens: Academy of Athens.

A. examines several topics regarding associations, including association terminology (chap. 1; *orgeōnes* was characteristic of the fourth to third centuries BCE, *thiasōtai* developed out of the phratries, and *eranistai* appeared in the first century BCE), organizational structure (chap. 2), legal standing (chap. 3), and integration within the *polis* (city; chap. 4).

Arnaoutoglou, Ilias N. 2005. "*Collegia* in the Province of Egypt in the First Century AD." *Ancient Society* 35:197–216.

> The discrepancy among restrictive Roman legislation on *collegia* (associations), the *lex Iulia de collegiis* (the Julian law on associations), and the evidence from Philo on the continued activity of *collegia* in first-century CE Egypt (**L10**) can be reconciled by attributing the collegial ban to Alexandria's prefect, Flaccus (32–38 CE). Nonetheless, there are at least nine inscriptions and papyri from Egypt bearing witness to the continued activity of associations during the first-century CE ban.

Arnaoutoglou, Ilias N. 2007. "Group and Individuals in *IRhamnous* 59 (*SEG* 49.161)." In *Individus, groupes et politique à Athènes de Solon à Mithridate*, ed. Jean-Christophe Couvenhes, 315–37. Perspectives historiques 15. Tours: Presses Universitaires François Rabelais.

> A. addresses the problem of the interaction among individuals, groups, and politics using *IRhamnous* 59 (224 BCE), which demonstrates that there was a single group that bore two different names (rather than two different groups): the *politai* (for their right to acquire land) and *Sarapiastai* (committed to Sarapis).

Arnaoutoglou, Ilias N. 2011. "Status and Identity in Private Religious Associations in Hellenistic Athens." In *Political Culture in the Greek City after the Classical Age*, ed. O. M. van Nijf and R. Alston, 27–48. Groningen-Royal Holloway Studies on the Greek City after the Classical Age 2. Leuven: Peeters.

> The wide array of association names can be linked to each group's sense of its own collective identity, which was developed through activities such as rituals, festivals, sacrifices, feasts, celebrations, and reunions. Such activities helped assimilate them into the wider civic context. Thus, it is not correct to imagine in Hellenistic Athens that civic and private associations were two separate and parallel groups, for the private were assimilating into the civic.

Ascough, Richard S. 1997. "Translocal Relationships among Voluntary Associations and Early Christianity." *Journal of Early Christian Studies* 5:223–41.

> Some associations had translocal links, while early Christian groups were primarily focused on their own locale. Thus, there is

more coherence among associations and Christian groups than scholars often allow.

Ascough, Richard S. 1998. *What Are They Saying about the Formation of Pauline Churches?* New York: Paulist Press.

A. outlines strengths and weaknesses of four scholarly models useful for understanding Pauline Christian groups: synagogues, philosophical schools, the mysteries, and associations.

Ascough, Richard S. 2000a. "Benefaction Gone Wrong: The 'Sin' of Ananias and Sapphira in Context." In *Text and Artifact in the Religions of Mediterranean Antiquity: Essays in Honour of Peter Richardson*, ed. Stephen G. Wilson and Michel Desjardins, 91–110. ESCJ 9. Waterloo: Wilfrid Laurier University Press.

Inscriptions regarding the "purchase" of honor in ancient associations are used to illuminate the "sin" of Ananias and Sapphira in the book of Acts. The author portrays their primary sin as lying, motivated by desire for worldly honor, which is contrasted to the value of divine concerns.

Ascough, Richard. S. 2000b. "The Thessalonian Christian Community as a Professional Voluntary Association." *Journal of Biblical Literature* 119:311–28.

The Thessalonian community would appear to outsiders and function internally as an association. Paul's letters discursively reflect his awareness of associations.

Ascough, Richard S. 2001. "Matthew and Community Formation." In *The Gospel of Matthew in Current Study: Studies in Memory of William G. Thompson, S.J.*, ed. David E. Aune, 96–126. Grand Rapids: Eerdmans.

Conflict resolutions found in Matthew 5:1–7:29 and 18:15-22 are similar to those of many associations which proscribe internal conflict. However, associations' detailed punitive measures can be contrasted to Matthew's emphasis on forgiveness and the abrogation of honor codes.

Ascough, Richard S. 2002. "Greco-Roman Philosophic, Religious, and Voluntary Associations." In *Community Formation in the Early Church and the Church Today*, ed. Richard N. Longenecker, 3–19. Peabody, Mass.: Hendrickson.

Three types of associations are discussed in relation to organization, membership, functionaries, finances, meetings, meeting places, patronage, and behavioral regulations. These groups varied widely in organizational structures but were similar with respect to honorary activities, banquets, burials, and agonistic ranking.

Ascough, Richard S. 2003. *Paul's Macedonian Associations: The Social Context of Philippians and 1 Thessalonians*. WUNT 2/161. Tübingen: Mohr Siebeck.

Greco-Roman associations can be used as a comparative model for understanding early Christian community organization. Community language and practices of associations are reflected in 1 Thessalonians and Philippians, and these groups both appeared to outsiders as associations and functioned internally as associations.

Ascough, Richard S. 2004. "A Question of Death: Paul's Community Building Language in 1 Thessalonians 4:13-18." *Journal of Biblical Literature* 123:509–30.

Burial of members was not simply a benefit of association membership but also demonstrated postmortem community connection. In 1 Thessalonians 4:13-18 Paul reassures the Thessalonians that their dead members are still considered part of the living community and the living can still continue commemorative rituals typical of associations.

Ascough, Richard S. 2006. "Voluntary Associations and the Formation of Pauline Churches: Addressing the Objections." In *Vereine, Synagogen und Gemeinden im kaiserzeitlichen Kleinasien*, ed. Andreas Gutsfeld and Dietrich-Alex Koch, 149–83. STAC 25. Tübingen: Mohr Siebeck.

Common scholarly objections to using associations as a comparator for early Jesus groups cannot be sustained in the face of a broad database regarding association terminology, officials, egalitarianism, exclusivity, translocal links, morality, and cultic activities.

Ascough, Richard S. 2007a. "Defining Community-Ethos in Light of the 'Other': Recruitment Rhetoric among Greco-Roman Religious Groups." *Annali di storia dell'esegesi* 24:59–75.

Greco-Roman associations, including Jewish and Christian groups, established their community's ethos through contrast with other groups. Such "rhetoric of recruitment" can seem combative, yet exchanges with real or imagined "others" allowed associations to forge and proclaim identity while gaining and retaining members.

Ascough, Richard S. 2007b. "'A Place to Stand, a Place to Grow': Architectural and Epigraphic Evidence for Expansion in Greco-Roman Associations." In *Identity and Interaction in the Ancient Mediterranean: Jews,*

Christians and Others. Festschrift for Stephen G. Wilson, ed. Zeba A. Crook and Philip A. Harland, 76–98. Sheffield: Sheffield Phoenix Press.

> Although a (modern) Christian understanding of "mission" and "evangelism" is not applicable to recruitment practices among associations, evidence regarding association buildings (at Pergamon and Ephesos) and membership lists (*alba*) shows that such groups could be successful at expanding their membership base.

Ascough, Richard S. 2008. "Forms of Commensality in Greco-Roman Associations." *Classical World* 102:33–46.

> Association meals served as locations of social interaction and group self-definition while inscribing community boundaries. Associations undertook, at various times and places, segregative commensality, exceptional commensality, transgressive commensality, and, in some cases, "extra-domestic" commensality.

Ascough, Richard S. 2010. "Of Memories and Meals: Greco-Roman Associations and the Early Jesus-group at Thessalonikē." In *From Roman to Early Christian Thessalonikē: Studies in Religion and Archaeology*, ed. Laura Nasrallah, Charalambos Bakirtzis, and Steven Friesen, 49–72. Harvard Theological Studies 64. Cambridge, Mass.: Harvard University Press.

> Associations at Thessalonica held common meals, around which they inscribed regulatory behaviors. Similar regulatory concerns can be discerned in 2 Thessalonians 3:6-14, suggesting that the Thessalonians shared a ritualized meal.

Ascough, Richard S. 2011. "The Apostolic Decree of Acts and Greco-Roman Associations: Eating in the Shadow of the Roman Empire." In *Das Aposteldekret und das antike Vereinswesen*, ed. Markus Öhler and Hermut Löhr, 297–316. WUNT 280. Tübingen: Mohr Siebeck.

> The author of Luke–Acts presents Jesus followers as an association that poses no threat to the established Roman order (*ordo*). The so-called Apostolic Decree of Acts 15 is framed in such a way as to lay out for Luke's time the means whereby Gentiles and Judeans can join together for common meals in a manner that is indistinguishable from other legal associations in the post-70 CE Roman world.

Aubert, Jean-Jacques. 1999. "La gestion des *collegia*: Aspects juridiques, économiques et sociaux." In *Cahiers du centre Gustave-Glotz. Revue reconnue par le CNRS*, 49–69. Publications de la Sorbonne 10. Paris: E. de Boccard.

Unlike medieval guilds, occupational associations did not play a determining economic role in Roman antiquity; their primary purpose was promoting the economic interests of a particular activity. The juridical status of *collegia* (associations) changed between the republican period (when they were outlawed but tolerated) and the early imperial period (when *collegia* began to have juridical identity).

Ausbüttel, Frank M. 1982. *Untersuchungen zu den Vereinen im Westen des römischen Reiches.* FAS 11. Kallmünz: Michael Laßleben.

A. provides a comprehensive overview of the distribution of the associations in the western part of the Roman Empire and the terminology they used for themselves (chap. 1), their membership structure (chap. 2), and their activities (chap. 3). A final chapter traces the development of the *collegia* up to the fourth century CE. Although many associations were involved in burial, there was no such thing as a separate category of "funerary *collegia*."

Avram, Alexandru. 2002. "Der dionysische *thiasos* in Kallatis: Organisation, Repräsentation, Funktion." In *Religiöse Vereine in der römischen Antike: Untersuchungen zu Organisation, Ritual und Raumordnung,* ed. Ulrike Egelhaaf-Gaiser and Alfred Schäfer, 69–80. STAC 13. Tübingen: Mohr Siebeck.

A. examines the organization and functions of a Dionysiac society (*thiasos*) at Kallatis in Skythia Minor, emphasizing its "public character" (see **73–74**).

Baldwin, Barry. 1963–1964. "Strikes in the Roman Empire." *Classical Journal* 59:75–76.

B. supplements MacMullen (1962–1963) by citing additional examples of strike activity (citing "strikes" by Cynic philosophers as discussed by Lucian in *Runaways*, by agricultural laborers in Roman Egypt, by Christian Circumcellions in North Africa [IV–V CE], and by bakers at Hippo in 362).

Barclay, John M. G. 2006. "Money and Meetings: Group Formation among Diaspora Jews and Early Christians." In *Vereine, Synagogen und Gemeinden im kaiserzeitlichen Kleinasien,* ed. Andreas Gutsfeld and Dietrich-Alex Koch, 113–28. STAC 25. Tübingen: Mohr Siebeck.

B. compares Jewish and Christian groups with ancient associations with regard to meals, meetings, instruction, religious rites, patterns of benefaction, patterns of leadership, monetary collections, and resource commitments. Doing so reveals new perspectives on the forms of solidarity, loyalty, social integration, and social differentiation these activities established.

Barton, S. C., and G. H. R. Horsley. 1981. "A Hellenistic Cult Group and the New Testament Churches." *Jahrbuch für Antike und Christentum* 24:7–41.

B. and H. compare an association of Zeus in Philadelphia (*SIG*³ 985 [**121**], I BCE) to Paul's early Jesus communities. Although both cults were concerned with moral purity and group building, early Christian morality was more rigorous and was not connected to mysteries and ritual purifications.

Baslez, Marie-Francoise. 1998. "Les associations dans la cité grecque et l'apprentissage du collectif." *Ktèma* 23:431–40.

During the Hellenistic period, most associations met in public places rather than private houses to avoid being labeled as "secret societies" involved in subversive activities.

Batten, Alicia. 2007. "The Moral World of Greco-Roman Associations." *Studies in Religion* 36:135–51.

Key expressions in the evidence for associations reflect moral conduct and may illuminate early Christian texts inasmuch as they share vocabulary with texts such as the Pastoral Epistles and 2 Peter.

Beck, Roger. 1992. "The Mithras Cult as Association." *Studies in Religion* 21:3–13.

The Mithraists' meals can be understood within the framework of associations. These groups fit with the values and aspirations of petty bureaucrats and soldiers.

Belayche, Nicole. 2003. "En quête de marqueurs des communautés 'religieuses' gréco-romaines." In *Les communautés religieuses dans le monde gréco-romain: Essais de définition*, ed. Nicole Belayche and Simon C. Mimouni, 9–20. Bibliothèque de l'École des Hautes Études sciences religieuses 117. Turnhout: Brepols.

Religious associations have an admittance ritual that demarcates the boundary between members and outsiders, conceptual markers that reflect specific notions on the world and the gods, behavioral markers such as purity regulations, and hierarchical markers in the form of leaders (president, priest, patron).

Bendlin, Andreas. 2002. "Gemeinschaft, Öffentlichkeit und Identität: Forschungsgeschichtliche Anmerkungen zu den Mustern sozialer

Ordnung in Rom." In *Religiöse Vereine in der römischen Antike: Untersuchungen zu Organisation, Ritual und Raumordnung*, ed. Ulrike Egelhaaf-Gaiser and Alfred Schäfer, 9–40. STAC 13. Tübingen: Mohr Siebeck.

> Ancient Roman society should be viewed as a node of different public spaces that together compose a social network. Recognition of the role associations (*collegia, sodalitates*, etc.) played as alternative spaces of political, social, and religious networking avoids a narrow focus on the elite.

Bendlin, Andreas. 2005. "'Eine Zusammenkunft um der religio willen ist erlaubt . . .'? Zu den politischen und rechtlichen Konstruktionen von (religiöser) Vergemeinschaftung in der römischen Kaiserzeit." In *Die verrechtlichte Religion: Der Öffentlichkeitsstatus von Religionsgemeinschaften*, ed. Hans G. Kippenberg and Gunnar Folke Schuppert, 65–107. Tübingen: Mohr Siebeck.

> Although unauthorized associations were normal, at moments of political crisis nominal laws were invoked to suppress meetings. The *senatus consultum* (senatorial decree) was limited to a special form of gathering and did not apply generally to associations. Early Christian and Jewish groups were de facto local and regional associations, but would not qualify for individual ratification as associations by the authorities.

Bendlin, Andreas. 2011. "Associations, Sociality, and Roman Law: A New Interpretation of the *cultores Dianae et Antinoi* in Lanuvium." In *Das Aposteldekret und das antike Vereinswesen*, ed. Markus Öhler and Hermut Löhr, 207–96. WUNT 280. Tübingen: Mohr Siebeck.

> B. provides a critical reappraisal of *CIL* XIV 2112 (see **310**) from Lanuvium and dispels many of Mommsen's well-entrenched interpretations, including issues surrounding political control of associations and the notion that this group can be used as a template for the study of associations generally.

Bennett, Julian. 2006. "New Evidence from Ankara for the *collegia veteranorum* and the *albata decursio*." *Anatolian Studies* 56:95–101.

> A first-century CE inscription from Ankyra involving an association of veterans (*collegium veteranorum*) is only the fifth inscription to attest to a veterans' association, about which little is known.

Benzina Ben Abdallah, Zeineb, and Jean Peyras. 1997. "Le *mibil*, association religieuse ou sanctuaire? Recherches sur une énigme épigraphique." *Antiquités africaines* 33:129–41.

Three inscriptions from *Africa Proconsularis* use the term *mibil*, which is crucial for understanding the texts but cannot be explained by Latin, Greek, or Hebrew. It refers either to a sanctuary or to the "brotherhood" that tended the temple, but in context cannot refer to both at once.

Berger, Adolf. 1947. "C.C.C. A Contribution to the Latin Terminology Concerning Collegia." *Epigraphica* 9:44–55.

The Latin abbreviation CCC in the inscription *CIL* VI 4416 (= VI 2193) is likely *c(ollegium) c(oire) c(onvenire)*, alluding both to the founding of the association and its continuing activity.

Boak, A. E. R. 1937a. "An Ordinance of the Salt Merchants." *American Journal of Philology* 58:210–19.

Analysis of *PMich* V 245 (inv. no. 657, 47–48 CE; see **302**) reveals that the salt merchants' association ran the salt and gypsum concessions in Tebtunis and the surrounding area, assuming collective responsibility for rendering payment to the state for this privilege.

Boak, A. E. R. 1937b. "The Organization of Gilds in Greco-Roman Egypt." *Transactions of the American Philological Association* 68:212–20.

Regulations of three Greek associations from first-century Tebtunis are compared to the laws of the association of Zeus Hypsistos (late first century BCE), the guild of bankers (ca. fifth century CE), and Egyptian Demotic texts of the second and third centuries. The laws were private contracts whose validity depended upon the voluntary, expressed consent of the members, and they were enforceable under the principles of private law.

Bollmann, Beate. 1998. *Römische Vereinshäuser: Untersuchungen zu den Scholae der römischen Berufs-, Kult- und Augustalen-Kollegien in Italien.* Mainz: Philipp von Zabern.

B. examines several issues regarding associations and their buildings, including the history of associations (chap. 2), difficulties in identifying association meeting places (*scholae*; chap. 3), types of archaeological remains (chap. 4), furnishings and monuments within these buildings (chap. 5; cf. appendix 3), a chronology of meeting places (chap. 6), and buildings at Rome and Ostia specifically (chap. 7). Overall, associations were more concerned with social than religious functions. There are three appendices (property law and associations, list of inscriptions from Roman associations, list of divinities and dedications) and three catalogues (A: seventy-nine probable meeting places from archaeological and epigraphic evidence; B: twenty-one doubtful meeting places; and C: eighty inscriptions referring to buildings whose whereabouts are unknown).

Bömer, Franz. 1981 [1958–1963]. *Untersuchungen über die Religion der Sklaven in Griechenland und Rom.* 2nd ed. Abhandlungen der Geistes- und Sozialwissenschaftlichen Klasse 10.4. Wiesbaden: Verlag der Akademie der Wissenschaften und der Literatur.

"Concerning Brotherhood in Religious Associations" (172–79, cf. 1092–97) argues that the use of familial terms, especially "brotherhood," did not occur in the Greek east and was rare in western cultural areas. Concepts of "brotherhood" were widespread in Christianity and from the beginning included slaves, which were excluded from such identification in associations.

Borgen, Peder. 1995. "'Yes,' 'No,' 'How Far?': The Participation of Jews and Christians in Pagan Cults." In *Paul in His Hellenistic Context,* ed. Troels Engberg-Pedersen, 30–59. Minneapolis: Fortress.

Evidence from Josephus and from inscriptions indicates that some Judeans participated in Hellenistic associations, and literary evidence suggests Christians engaged in some polytheistic practices. Philo, Josephus, Paul, and the writer of Revelation disapprove of such participation, particularly polytheistic festivities, athletics, and theater attendance.

Brashear, William M. 1993. *Vereine im griechisch-römischen Ägypten.* Xenia 34. Konstanzer Althistorische Vorträge und Forschungen 7. Konstanz: Universitätsverlag Konstanz.

B. provides the text, translation, and technical notes for *PBerol* 25159 (5 BCE), the decision of an Alexandrian association to honor its leader. The formation of associations primarily for social purposes within the cults of Egypt suggests their secularization in Greco-Roman times.

Bresson, Alain. 1997. "De Marseille à Milet: Lettres lunaires et associations cultuelles." *Revue des études anciennes* 99:491–506.

Linguistic evidence reveals that an altar found in Marseilles was set up by members of a subgroup of an association describing themselves as "brothers." Similar evidence redates to the second century BCE a funerary inscription from an association of *Temenitai* at Miletos (cf. **177**).

Buckler, W. H. 1923. "Labour Disputes in the Province of Asia." In *Anatolian Studies, Presented to Sir William Mitchell Ramsay*, ed. William H. Buckler and W. M. Calder, 27–50. Manchester: Manchester University Press.

> Strikes occurred from time to time, although the causes and objectives are obscure. Three second-century CE inscriptions discuss labor unrest from the province of Asia: the Ephesian bakers' strike, an edict of the Pergamon laborers, and the settlement of a building dispute at Miletos. In 459 CE there was a strike by the builders' association at Sardis.

Calhoun, George Miller. 1964 [1913]. *Athenian Clubs in Politics and Litigation*. Bulletin of the University of Texas 262. Humanistic Series 14. Austin: University of Texas Press.

> C. collects all available information on the aristocratic Athenian clubs (*hetairoi*; *synōmosiai*) of the sixth and fifth centuries BCE. Such associations probably offered many forms of assistance to fellow members, including monetary contributions, friendly prosecutions, countersuits, persuasion and dissuasion of witnesses through bribery and violence, influencing of juries and officials, and evidence suppression or fabrication. Associations sought to control the Athenian political assemblies by presenting and securing the election of their team of candidates.

Carrié, Jean-Michel. 2002. "Les associations professionnelles à l'époque tardive: Entre *munus* et convivialité." In *Humana sapit: Mélanges en l'honneur de Lellia Cracco Ruggini*, ed. Jean-Michel Carrié and Rita Lizzi Testa, 309–32. Bibliothèque de l'Antiquité tardive 3. Turnhout: Brepols.

> From the fourth to the mid-sixth century CE, membership in occupational associations became compulsory and universal rather than voluntary. The associations were required to collect and pay taxes to the state and fulfill other public services.

Cazanove, Olivier de, et al. 1986. *L'Association dionysiaque dans les sociétés anciennes: Actes de la table ronde organisée par L'École française de Rome (Rome 24–25 Mai 1984)*. Collection de l'école française de Rome 89. Paris: E. de Boccard.

> This is a collection of conference papers (in French and Italian) that cover Dionysiac associations in specific locales (Delphi, Gaul, Egypt, North Africa, Italy), as well papers on vase images, literary

texts (e.g., Ovid), and regulatory inscriptions (*IG* II² 1368 [**7**] and *IGUR* I 160 [**330**]). Also see Scheid (1986).

de Cenival, Françoise. 1969. "Les associations dans les temples égyptiens d'après les données fournies par les papyrus démotique." In *Religions en Egypte hellénistique et romaine: Colloque de Strasbourg, 16–18 mai 1967.* Bibliothèque des Centres d'études supérieures spécialisés, 5–19. Paris: Presses universitaires de France.

> The emphasis in Demotic texts on behavioral, legal, and financial matters, coupled with a relative scarcity of references to religious issues, suggests that the associations were more concerned with material than theological issues.

de Cenival, Françoise. 1972. *Les associations religieuses en Egypte d'après les documents démotiques.* 2 vols. Publications de l'Institut français d'archéologie orientale du Caire. Bibliothèque d'étude, vol. 46. Caire: Institut français d'archéologie Orientale.

> The first part of volume 1 provides transcription, French translation, and philological commentary for Demotic papyri concerned with religious associations in Egypt. The second part examines the associations' regulations, membership, activities, and legal status. Volume 2 contains photographic plates of the texts.

Chester, Stephen J. 2003. *Conversion at Corinth: Perspectives on Conversion in Paul's Theology and the Corinthian Church.* SNTW. London: T&T Clark.

> "Corinthian Conversion and Voluntary Associations" (227–66) suggests that the Christian group at Corinth was not an association with respect to issues of conversion, but its actions, customs, and practical arrangements are patterned on association behavior.

Clarke, Andrew D. 2000. *Serve the Community of the Church: Christians as Leaders and Ministers.* Grand Rapids: Eerdmans.

> "Leadership in the Voluntary Associations" (59–78) argues that careful gradations of honor, so apparent in the civic world, were replicated in the associations. Similar political and religious elements resulted in similar leadership rules and impacted the attitudes and practices of governments and other levels of society.

Clauss, Manfred. 1998. "Zur Integrationsleistung der römischen Vereinigungen—ein Kommentar." In *Gesellschaften im Vergleich: Forschungen aus Sozial- und Geschichtswissenschaften*, ed. Hartmut Kaelble and Jürgen Schriewer, 35–38. Komparatistische Bibliothek 9. Frankfurt: Peter Lang.

Associations had a stabilizing effect by organizing public gatherings and ceremonies for the emperor, and could serve as a means of control. They also contributed toward municipal projects. Moreover, the number of associations "exploded" with the spread of imperial cult and greatly decreased with its cessation.

Conrat (Cohn), Max. 1873. *Zum römischen Vereinsrecht: Abhandlungen aus der Rechtsgeschichte*. Berlin: Weidmann. Repr., Aalen: Scientia, 1969.

C. explores prohibitions against associations during republican times, as well as tolerance for those termed "ancient" (therefore harmless). C. refutes Mommsen by suggesting the term *collegia tenuiorum* refers to *collegia militum* (military associations). The final chapter examines the legal status of the *societates* (society members) and *collegia publicani* (associations of those working in imperial revenue and taxation).

Cotter, Wendy. 1996. "The Collegia and Roman Law: State Restrictions on Voluntary Associations, 64 BCE–200 CE." In *Voluntary Associations in the Graeco-Roman World*, ed. John S. Kloppenborg and Stephen G. Wilson, 74–89. London: Routledge.

C. argues that from the time of the late republic to the end of the second century, prohibition and dissolution of associations was frequently employed by the Romans. Despite this policy, associations continued to multiply, and this provides the sociopolitical context in which early Christian communities lived.

Countryman, William L. 1977. "Patrons and Officers in Club and Church." In *Society of Biblical Literature 1977 Seminar Papers*, ed. Paul J. Achtemeier, 135–43. SBLSP 11. Missoula, Mont.: Scholars Press.

Christian churches were similar to associations in that their memberships were voluntary, they organized around the worship of a heroized man, they stressed meals, and their patrons were encouraged to support the church. There was a marked difference in that the churches possessed two foci of power: the powerful minister and the rich layman.

Couvenhes, Jean-Christophe. 2007. "Les décrets des *paroikoi* de Rhamnonte." In *Individus, groupes et politique à Athènes de Solon à Mithridate*, ed. Jean-Christophe Couvenhes, 293–313. Perspectives Historiques 15. Tours: Presses Universitaires François Rabelais.

The decree of the *paroikoi* (settled foreigners) in the deme of Rhamnous reveals that this group functioned more like a group of foreigners adopted into the institutional practices of the city than as an association.

Cumont, Franz. 1933. "La grande inscription bacchique du Metropolitan Museum II." *American Journal of Archaeology* 37:232–67.

A number of archaisms demonstrate that the household Bacchic association of Pompeia Agrippinilla (*IGUR* 160, Torre Nova, ca. 150 CE; see **330**) had its origins in a much earlier form of Dionysiac religion. The many titles listed in the inscription are likely in their order of precedence in the sacred procession.

Daniel, Robert W. 1979. "Notes on the Guilds and Army in Roman Egypt." *Bulletin of the American Society of Papyrologists* 16:37–46.

PRyl IV 604 (III CE) is a letter from an important official (*xystarch*) of one athletic association to an official in another. The association members call one another "brothers," but it is not a Christian or military association. *PPetaus* 28 (see **290**), which likely involves an undertakers guild, once again attests to the use of fictive brother language.

D'Arms, John H. 2000. "Memory, Money, and Status at Misenum: Three New Inscriptions from the Collegium of the Augustales." *Journal of Roman Studies* 90:126–44.

A statue base with three inscriptions was set up by a freedman's wife, who was adlected into the Augustales' ranks a year after her husband's death (the first known case of the adlection of a woman to the all-male Augustales).

Demoulin, Hubert. 1897. "Les collegia iuvenum dans l'empire romain." *Le Musée belge. Revue de philologie classique* 1:114–36, 200–217.

A list of youth associations (*collegia iuvenum*) is followed by an analysis of their internal organization and structure, finances, and legislation, as well as their place in the city, their funerary activities, their organization of spectacles, and their military characteristics.

Demoulin, Hubert. 1899. "Encore les collegia iuvenum." *Le Musée belge. Revue de philologie classique* 3:177–92.

Lead *tessera* (tokens) from spectacles confirms Demoulin's earlier conclusions concerning the participation of the *collegia iuvenum* (youth associations) in staging spectacles and their role as part of the urban militia (includes an appendix listing the *tessera*).

Dill, Samuel. 1904. *Roman Society from Nero to Marcus Aurelius*. London: Macmillan.

"The Colleges and Plebeian Life" (251–86) summarizes various facets of Roman associations from the first century BCE to the fourth and fifth centuries CE. The proletariat evinced great pride in their occupations and, in the Augustan age, increasingly organized into *collegia*. Imperial suppression of *collegia* occurred from 64 BCE until the reign of Alexander Severus, after which *collegia* were more numerous.

Dissen, Margret. 2009. *Römische Kollegien und deutsche Geschichtswissenschaft im 19. und 20. Jahrhundert*. Historia Einzelschriften 209. Stuttgart: Franz Steiner.

An analysis of German scholarship on *collegia* (associations) reveals three clearly identifiable trends: (1) a focus on legal questions and state relations (beginning with Mommsen in 1843), (2) a turn to social and political issues (from the end of WWI to the 1970s), and (3) a sociological focus since the early 1980s, with scholars viewing associations in terms of their participation in and replication of the Roman social and political order.

Dittmann-Schöne, Imogen. 2001. *Der Berufsvereinen in den Städten des kaiserzeitlichen Kleinasiens*. Theorie und Forschung 690; Geschichte 10. Regensburg: S. Roderer.

This is a survey of occupational associations in Asia Minor during the Roman imperial period with attention to the diversity of nomenclature, inner structure, interactions with the state, civic disruptions, reserved seating in civic institutions, burial practices, and cultic activities. Part 2 presents 190 newly edited association inscriptions from Asia Minor (organized by province) with German translations.

Dittmann-Schöne, Imogen. 2002. "Götterverehrung bei den Berufsvereinen im kaiserzeitlichen Kleinasien." In *Religiöse Vereine in der römischen Antike: Untersuchungen zu Organisation, Ritual und Raumordnung*, ed. Ulrike Egelhaaf-Gaiser and Alfred Schäfer, 81–96. STAC 13. Tübingen: Mohr Siebeck.

Cultic activities were important within all types of associations, including occupational guilds in Asia Minor during the imperial period.

Dombrowski, Bruno W. 1966. "היחד in 1QS and τὸ κοινόν: An Instance of Early Greek and Jewish Synthesis." *Harvard Theological Review* 59:293–307.

The translation of *to koinon* as *hyḥd* in Hebrew, as seen in 1QS at Qumran, was a result of Hellenization of Jewish ideas and speech. Similarities between the Qumran group and associations can be seen in parallel language in the Manual of Discipline (150 BCE) and regulations of the guild of Zeus Hypsistos (*PLond* VII 2193, 69–58 BCE; see **295**), although there are also many differences. After 100 CE, *hyḥd* falls from use; a re-Judaizing orthodoxy deliberately avoided *hyḥd* and its Hebrew equivalent as a reaction to earlier Hellenization.

Donahue, John F. 2003. "Toward a Typology of Roman Public Feasting." *American Journal of Philology* 124:423–41. Reprinted in *Roman Dining: A Special Issue of American Journal of Philology*, ed. Barbara K. Gold and John F. Donahue, 95–113. Baltimore: Johns Hopkins University Press, 2005.

Drawing on categories associated with French commensality, D. outlines six possible taxa, suggesting that segregative commensality best applies to Roman associations (*collegia*). Their meals provided a means for the group to forge identity, monitor members, and solidify internal divisions or hierarchies.

Downs, David J. 2008. *The Offering of the Gentiles: Paul's Collection for Jerusalem in Its Chronological, Cultural, and Cultic Contexts.* WUNT 2/248. Tübingen: Mohr Siebeck.

D. examines the practice of benefaction in associations (73–118) as part of a broader study of the Apostle Paul's organization and collection of a relief fund for the Jerusalem church.

Drew-Bear, Thomas. 1980. "An Act of Foundation at Hypaipa." *Chiron* 10:534–36.

D.-B. publishes and discusses an inscription found at Hypaipa (*SEG* 30 [1980], nos. 1382(c) and 1383/4) and links this with others found there involving donations to six occupational associations (wool sellers, linen weavers, and others), including a vineyard.

Drexel, F. 1927. "Utriclarii." *Glotta* 15:156–58.

The *utriclarii* (shippers) were an auxiliary troop among the firefighters, rather than leaders of the *fabri* (builders) and the *centonarii* (textile workers).

Duff, P. W. 1938. *Personality in Roman Private Law.* Cambridge: Cambridge University Press.

"Collegia: The *Ius Coeundi*" (95–128) argues that after the Julian legislation (*lex Iulia*) around 30 BCE, all associations (*collegia*) needed authorization from the Senate or emperor. There were two types of illegal *collegia*: the seditious associations (*hetaeria*) and the innocently illegal, which were ignored by the state. A *collegium* applying for permission to exist had to prove only its harmlessness, not its usefulness (e.g., burial clubs for the poor). "Collegia and Corporate Capacity" (129–61) traces the history of the legal status of *collegia* from the early Republic through to the time of Marcus Aurelius.

Ebel, Eva. 2004. *Die Attraktivität früher christlicher Gemeinden: Die Gemeinde von Korinth im Spiegel griechisch-römischer Vereine.* WUNT 2/178. Tübingen: Mohr Siebeck.

Early Christian communities were perceived as associations and were in direct competition with other associations for new members. E. examines in detail the social organization of a number of specific associations, giving priority to the worshippers of Diana and Antinous at Lanuvium (*CIL* XIV 2112; see **310**) and the Iobacchoi at Athens (*IG* II² 1368; see **7**), with texts and a German translation of each. The final third of the book gives attention to the Christian associations at Corinth as a test case.

Edgar, C. C. 1925. "Records of a Village Club." In *Raccolta di scritti in onore di Giacomo Lumbroso (1844–1925)*, 369–76. Pubblicazioni di "Aegyptus." Serie Scientifica 3. Milan: Aegyptus.

Papyrus fragments from Philadelphia in the Fayûm testify to a servants' association that met frequently, probably monthly, for social purposes. Minutes were recorded, with information on the election and duties of officers, varying meeting places, and financial records of banquet disbursements for wine and flute players.

Egelhaaf-Gaiser, Ulrike. 2002. "Religionsästhetik und Raumordnung am Beispiel der Vereinsgebäude von Ostia." In *Religiöse Vereine in der römischen Antike: Untersuchungen zu Organisation, Ritual und Raumordnung*, ed. Ulrike Egelhaaf-Gaiser and Alfred Schäfer, 123–72. STAC 13. Tübingen: Mohr Siebeck.

After introducing ancient and modern conceptions of space, E.-G. compares the conceptual design and room organization of three association meeting places (*scholae*) in Ostia: carpenters (**B14**, **B21**), grain measurers (**B15**), and ship owners (**B19**). Compared to occupational associations, religious associations were more concerned with cult than with presenting themselves publicly and recruiting new members.

Egelhaaf-Gaiser, Ulrike, and Alfred Schäfer, eds. 2002. *Religiöse Vereine in der römischen Antike: Untersuchungen zu Organisation, Ritual und Raumordnung.* STAC 13. Tübingen: Mohr Siebeck.

> This edited collection contains papers presented during a 1999 conference in Potsdam. See the descriptions of Bendlin (2002), Rüpke (2002), Avram (2002), Dittmann-Schöne (2002), Egelhaaf-Gaiser (2002), Schäfer (2002), Schwarzer (2002).

d'Escurac, Henriette Pavis. 1990. "Dénominations des organisations artisanales dans l'occident romain." *Ktèma* 15:109–20.

> Roman association names were created by adding a generic noun to a specific noun (e.g., *corpus pistorum*). Starting in the second century CE, occupational associations used the terms *collegium* or *corpus*, which became synonyms in the late empire. Often the name of the city where the association was located was added to underline its local character (e.g., *fabri lignarii Lugudunenses*).

d'Escurac-Doisy, Henriette. 1967. "Notes sur le phénomène associatif dans le monde paysan à l'époque du Haut-Empire." *Antiquités africaines* 1:59–71.

> Two sets of African epigraphic documents show that Northern African veterans-turned-peasant landowners grouped together for mutual benefit in associations on the model of military associations familiar to them.

Fellmeth, Ulrich. 1990. "Politisches Bewußtsein in den Vereinen der städtischen Massen in Rom und Italien zur Zeit der Republik und der frühen Kaiserzeit." *Eirene* 27:49–71.

> Membership lists (*alba*) demonstrate that occupational associations and religious associations (*sodalitates*) differed in the social background and status of their members, with the highest social ranks found in the top administrative positions of occupational associations, and slaves, freedpersons, and poorer strata of society found in religious associations.

Ferguson, William Scott. 1910. "The Athenian Phratries." *Classical Philology* 5:257–84.

> Each of the twelve Attic phratries (*phratria*), which likely began in the sixth century BCE, must have contained about fifteen hundred

members. After 403 BCE, the phratries were broken up into their constituent *thiasoi* (societies), and these *thiasoi* were absorbed into the less artificial *genes* and *orgeōnes* ("sacrificing associates"), the latter initially consisting of those from the lower social strata.

Ferguson, William Scott. 1944. "The Attic *Orgeones* and the Cult of Heroes." *Harvard Theological Review* 37:61–140.

Athenian *orgeōnes* (sacrificing associates) from the pre-Solon era to the Roman era were both rural and urban, and their motivation was probably convivial. Membership in cults of heroes or heroines ("class A") was derived from hereditary citizenship, whereas cults of higher deities ("class B"), mostly of foreign origin, included foreigners and noncitizens.

Ferguson, William Scott. 1949. "Orgeonika." *Commemorative Studies in Honor of Theodore Leslie Shear.* Hesperia Supplement, vol. 8, 130–63. Athens: American School of Classical Studies at Athens.

F. continues his discussion in Ferguson (1944) with inscriptions relating to the cult of Bendis in classical Athens.

Fikhman, I. F. 1994. "Sur quelques aspects socio-économiques de l'activité des corporations professionnelles de l'Égypte byzantine." *Zeitschrift für Papyrologie und Epigraphik* 103:19–40.

Associations in Byzantine Egypt can be divided into two general classes: those "free" or independent from the state and those subject to the state. Free associations are further subdivided as (1) associations composed of "free," "independent" workers (the majority of associations) and (2) associations composed of workers who were dependent on large landowners for their livelihood (a small minority).

Fisher, Nicholas R. E. 1988a. "Greek Associations, Symposia, and Clubs." In *Civilization of the Ancient Mediterranean: Greece and Rome,* ed. Michael Grant and Rachel Kitzinger, 1167–97. New York: Charles Scribner's Sons.

F. surveys the early history of Greek *symposia* (banquets) and associations.

Fisher, Nicholas R. E. 1988b. "Roman Associations, Dinner Parties, and Clubs." In *Civilization of the Ancient Mediterranean: Greece and Rome,* ed. Michael Grant and Rachel Kitzinger, 1199–1225. New York: Charles Scribner's Sons.

F. surveys the history of associations and banquets in the Roman period, stressing the steady Hellenization of Roman social life and the growth of voluntary associations and their intermittent political significance. Three characteristics of the Roman practice differ from the Greek: greater emphasis on the meal, more participation of respectable women in both *symposia* and associations, and less religious support of same-sex encounters.

Flambard, Jean-Marc. 1977. "Clodius, les collèges, la plèbe les esclaves. Recherches sur la politique populaire au milieu de Ier siècle." *Ktèma* 89:115–56.

In the period 65–55 BCE, Clodius transformed traditional *collegia* (associations) into politically divisive groups called *operae* (hired aiders, parties; see **L25–L30**). These paramilitary groups were used as instruments of intimidation and as a method of controlling the lower classes and the streets. The *collegia* dissolved by an edict in 64 BCE were of many different types, but primarily occupational in nature.

Flambard, Jean-Marc. 1981. "Collegia compitalicia: Phénomène associatif, cadres territoriaux et cadres civiques dans le monde romain à l'époque républicaine." *Ktèma* 6:143–66.

There are traces of territorial associations—called *pagani* and *montani*—until the end of the republic. Whatever his tribal or social origins, a citizen could belong to such an association if he met all the criteria and the obligations. Neighborhood associations were mainly for the lower classes. Such associations were homogeneous in their membership and thus reproduced the social stratification and the ideological prejudices of Roman society.

Flambard, Jean-Marc. 1987. "Éléments pour une approche financière de la mort dans les classes populaires du Haut-Empire: Analyse du budget de quelques collèges funéraires de Rome et d'Italie." In *La mort, les morts et l'au delà dans le monde romain. Actes du colloque de Caen (20–22 novembre 1985)*, ed. F. Hinnard, 209–44. Caen: Université de Caen.

F. provides an overview of sources of funding and/or applications of collective wealth from association regulations. The groups in question had as their primary purpose the provision of "decent" funerals for group members funded through membership fees (*capitularium*), fines, and regular dues (*stips menstrua*).

Forbes, Clarence A. 1933. *Neoi: A Contribution to the Study of Greek Associations.* Philological Monographs of the American Philological Association 2. Middletown, Conn.: American Philological Association.

The *neoi* were public groups of state-sponsored young men older than nineteen or twenty (alumni of the younger *ephebes* [youths]). These institutions endured from the fourth century BCE to the third century CE and are found from Delphi in the west to Babylon in the east, from Kallatis (Thrace) in the north to Egypt in the south. The *neoi* pursued interests in athletics, rather than education, participated in processions and feasts, and honored their benefactors. Officials included a leader and patron (the *gymnasiarchēs*), and a treasurer to oversee finances.

Forbes, Clarence Allen. 1955. "Ancient Athletic Guilds." *Classical Philology* 50:238–52.

F. traces the rise and fall of athletic guilds in the Greco-Roman world, from the first century BCE to the late fourth century CE. In the first century BCE there appears to have been a victors' guild, composed of champion athletes, as well as a combined guild of the artists (or performers) of Dionysos and all professional athletes. Athletic guilds disappeared after the abolition of the Olympic games in 393 CE.

Foucart, Paul. 1873. *Des associations religieuses chez les Grecs: Thiases, èranes, orgéons, avec le texte des inscriptions relatives à ces associations.* Paris: Klincksieck.

F. surveys associations in the Greek period, with chapters on membership composition, laws and decrees, religious and civic functions, honorary decrees, finances, and legal standing. In general, the associations imitated the organizational form of the city and were tolerated by magistrates insofar as they maintained good order. However, the associations did not take on the role of benefit societies caring for the sick and needy. Many foreigners' associations focused on foreign deities, a situation encouraged by the state. In later periods the associations continued to flourish. F. includes sixty-eight Greek inscriptions.

Fraschetti, Augusto. 1989. "Collèges contre la cité collèges autour de la famille du prince." In *Aux sources de la puissance sociabilité et parenté. Actes du colloque de Roueu 12–13 novembre 1987,* ed. Françoise Thelamon, 57–62. CNRS URA 1274. Rouen: L'université de Rouen.

Festival and cult activities not only set the rhythm of life in and around Rome but also were important as forums for civil obedience or sedition. According to Cicero, the *pagani* and *montani*—inhabitants of the suburbs and inhabitants of the rural areas—were part of the urban *plebe*, but were very different from their urban counterparts, the *collegia* (associations). These differences became all the more pronounced as these groups were essentially "passed over" in the urban reorganization that took place in the first century BCE.

Gabba, Emilio. 1984. "The *Collegia* of Numa: Problems of Method and Political Ideas." *Journal of Roman Studies* 74:81–86.

> Plutarch's claim that Numa created Roman occupational associations in order to reconcile the Romans and the Sabines is a literary fiction aimed at drawing a parallel between Numa and the Athenian lawgiver, Solon (*Lives* 17.1–3; see **L22**). Cicero, Livy, and Dionysius of Halicarnassus make no mention of this.

Gabrielsen, Vincent. 1994. "The Rhodian Associations Honouring Dionysodoros from Alexandria." *Classica et mediaevalia* 45:137–60.

> G. examines the second century CE dossier of Dionysodoros, a foreigner from Alexandria who maintained memberships in several associations at Rhodes (see **255**). G. discusses the implications for multiple memberships. Associations had two internal sets of laws, the "unalterable law" containing the statutes of the association and the "open to revision laws" for administration, finances, and other structural issues. These features reflect the imitation of the *polis* (city) and its institutions.

Gabrielsen, Vincent. 2007. "Brotherhoods of Faith and Provident Planning: The Non-public Associations of the Greek World." *Mediterranean Historical Review* 22:183–210.

> Although private associations of the Hellenistic age often included noncitizens, in terms of structure and organization they replicated the *polis* (city). The dissemination of these groups following 300 BCE led to widespread opportunities for networking in the areas of religion, economics, and politics.

Geagan, Daniel J. 1972. "Hadrian and the Athenian Dionysiac *Technitai*." *Transactions of the American Philological Associations* 103:133–62.

> Eight pieces of a slab (stele) from Athens (ca. 128–129 CE) contain fragments of a series of letters from Hadrian to the synod of Dionysiac performers (*technitai*) at Athens (face A) and, likely, documents associated with the services of an Athenian priest and *archōn,* or civic leader (face B). Hadrian was the first emperor to be initiated into the secondary stage of initiation (*epopteia,* or "viewing") and may have been responsible for establishing the mystic synod of performers in Smyrna, Pergamon, or Ephesos.

Gillihan, Yonder Moynihan. 2012. *Civic Ideology, Organization, and Law in the Rule Scrolls: A Comparative Study of the Covenanters' Sect and Contemporary Voluntary Associations in Political Context.* Studies on the Texts of the Desert of Judah, vol. 97. Leiden and Boston: Brill

> Observing that associations tend to imitate civic structures, the author proposes a typology of associations, distinguishing between "assimilative associations," which function to incorporate small groups into civic structures, and "alternative civic associations," which claim superiority to the state. The Qumran *yahad* belongs to the latter type, reinforcing traditional Israelite distinctions between citizens and outsiders, full members and resident aliens, while claiming superiority and difference from the rest of the Judaean *politeia.*

Ginestet, P. 1991. *Les organisations de la jeunesse dans l'occident romain.* Collection Latomus 213. Brussels: Latomus.

> Institutionalized under Augustus, associations of young men (*collegia iuvenum*) consisted of youths from the equestrian and senatorial orders who learned skills such as riding, fencing, and self-defense.

Ginsburg, Michael S. 1940. "Roman Military Clubs and Their Social Functions." *Transactions of the American Philological Association* 71:149–55.

> Funerary associations incidentally helped their members by offering free banquets and distribution of food baskets and money allowances. Military clubs furthered this social insurance system. Veterans' associations instituted a system whereby half of the soldiers' cash bonus was held back until retirement, dismissal or death. A *collegium* of petty officers of Lambaesis (North Africa, 198 CE) is examined in detail.

Graeber, Andreas. 1983. *Untersuchungen zum spätrömischen Korporationswesen.* Europäische Hochschulschriften. Reihe III. Geschichte und ihre Hilfswissenschaften 196. Frankfurt: Lang.

> This is a study of primary and secondary literature on the occupational associations in the late Roman Empire that looks at the responsibilities and privileges of these associations, paying particular attention to the ship owners, bakers, and pig dealers. Associations were an essential component of the administration of the empire at this time.

Greenfield, J. C. 1974. "The *Marzeaḥ* as a Social Institution." *Acta Antiqua Academiae Hungaricae* 22:451–55.

> The *marzeaḥ*, known in Samaria, Judah, Palestine, Syria, Elephantine, Phoenicia, and Nabatea (fourth century BCE to third century CE), encompassed financial, social, and cultic aspects. Financially, *marzeaḥs* were known to possess fields, vineyards, permanent meeting places, and treasuries. Socially, they were wealthy dining institutions, with a leader (*symposiarch*), limited membership, benefaction system, banqueting facilities (*triclinia*), and burial rituals. They were devoted to a variety of gods.

Gros, Pierre. 1997. "Maisons ou sièges de corporations? Les traces archéologiques du phénomène associatif dans la Gaule romaine méridionale." *Comptes rendus de l'Académie des Inscriptions* 1997:213–41.

> Floor plans of buildings (*scholae*) that were built specifically for an association tended to reflect their specific functions. Converted residences tended to have fairly erratic floor plans, since additions had been added gradually. Artisans' buildings could be commercial sites for the sale of products (e.g., the Eumachia of Pompeii; see **B22**) and were often located in close proximity to their workshops (e.g., the *stuppatores* [caulk workers] of Ostia; see **B13**).

Gutsfeld, Andreas. 1998. "Das Vereinigungswesen und die Städte in der römischen Kaiserzeit." In *Gesellschaften im Vergleich: Forschungen aus Sozial- und Geschichtswissenschaften*, ed. Hartmut Kaelble and Jürgen Schriewer, 13–33. Komparatistische Bibliothek 9. Frankfurt: Peter Lang.

> Associations played an important integrative role in urban life and may even have been the most important social aspect of unity in two distinguishable forms: (1) normative—the promotion of values and objectives that are binding for the urban community—and (2) functional—the integration of the individual in certain positions and functions within the urban community.

Gutsfeld, Andreas, and Dietrich-Alex Koch, eds. 2006. *Vereine, Synagogen und Gemeinden im kaiserzeitlichen Kleinasien*. STAC 25. Tübingen: Mohr Siebeck.

> This is a collection of papers presented at a 2001 conference in Münster, Germany. See entries for Ascough (2006), Barclay (2006), Hirschmann (2006), Koch and Schinkel (2006), Schmeller (2006), Sirks (2006), and Sommer (2006).

Hanges, James C. 1998. "1 Corinthians 4:6 and the Possibility of Written Bylaws in the Corinthian Church." *Journal of Biblical Literature* 117:275–98.

> Paul's first letter to the Corinthians deals with issues similar to those found in the regulations of associations: cultic procedures, relations among members, sex, participation of women and slaves, orderly behavior, cultic attire, orderly worship, and the well-being of the state. Paul's reference to "that which is written" (*ha gegraptai*; 1 Cor 4:6) is an allusion to the bylaws of the Christian groups at Corinth.

Hardin, Justin K. 2006. "Decrees and Drachmas at Thessalonica: An Illegal Assembly in Jason's House (Acts 17.1-10a)." *New Testament Studies* 52:29–49.

> Jason's hosting of an assembly in his house, led by Paul and Silas, was understood as politically motivated, and thus Jason and the others with him were prosecuted and fined for forming an unauthorized association. As a result, Paul and Silas were banished by the group in order to protect themselves from further attention by the authorities.

Hardy, E. G. 1906. *Studies in Roman History* 1. London: Sonnenschein and Macmillan.

> In "Christianity and the Collegia" (129–50), H. demonstrates that during the reign of Augustus, the *lex Iulia* (Julian law) dissolved a large number of existing *collegia* (associations) and required the *collegia* to seek a senatorial license to exist. As a result, most associations, including Christian and Jewish groups, were illegal, but tolerated as insignificant. Under Marcus Aurelius partial recognition as a burial association (*collegia tenuiorum*) provided Christians with some protection and sanction, but still left them liable for persecution on more general grounds.

Harland, Philip A. 1996. "Honours and Worship: Emperors, Imperial Cults and Associations at Ephesus (First to Third Centuries C.E.)." *Studies in Religion* 25:319–34.

> Inscriptions from Ephesos demonstrate the significant part the emperors played within the life of associations, including festivals and internal rituals. Some groups, such as the hymn singers, participated directly in provincial imperial cult celebrations (see **160**).

Harland, Philip A. 2000. "Honouring the Emperor or Assailing the Beast: Participation in Civic Life among Associations (Jewish, Christian and Other) in Asia Minor and the Apocalypse of John." *Journal for the Study of the New Testament* 77:99–121.

> Associations in Roman Asia, including Jewish and Christian groups, were positively involved in imperial facets of civic life. Many associations could maintain positive relationships with imperial officials and could participate in honoring the emperor (as in 1 Pet 2:17). The author of Revelation disapproves of Christians who engaged in activities, such as honors for the emperor, that lessened tensions between group and society. This article was further developed in Harland (2003a).

Harland, Philip A. 2002. "Connections with Elites in the World of the Early Christians." In *Handbook of Early Christianity: Social Science Approaches*, ed. Anthony J. Blasi, Paul-André Turcotte, and Jean Duhaime, 385–408. Walnut Creek, Calif.: AltaMira.

> After outlining key social networks in the ancient context and their role in the formation of associations, H. explores the relation between associations of various kinds and the elite, including participation within networks of benefaction and the potential for social mobility among Christians and others.

Harland, Philip A. 2003a. *Associations, Synagogues and Congregations: Claiming a Place in Ancient Mediterranean Society*. Minneapolis: Fortress Press.

> Despite occasional tensions, there were ongoing positive interactions between unofficial associations, including synagogues and Christian assemblies, and society in the Roman province of Asia (first to third centuries CE). This study includes an examination of ancient associations generally (part 1), of associations' participation in imperial honors and connections (part 2), and of the involvements of Jewish and Christian groups in imperial related activities (with a focus on contextualizing John's Apocalypse; part 3). Tensions between Roman authorities and the associations tended to be sporadic and local.

Harland, Philip A. 2003b. "Christ-Bearers and Fellow-Initiates: Local Cultural Life and Christian Identity in Ignatius' Letters." *Journal of Early Christian Studies* 11:481–99.

> Bishop Ignatius of Antioch writes letters to Christian groups in various cities of Roman Asia drawing on images from the world

of religious processions, mysteries, and the cultural life of associations. This article is further developed in Harland (2009).

Harland, Philip A. 2003c. "Imperial Cults within Local Cultural Life: Associations in Roman Asia." *Ancient History Bulletin* 17:85–107.

Scholars have underestimated the social and religious significance of imperial cults in Asia Minor, and this is largely due to the imposition of modern distinctions between politics and religion and between private and public spheres. Associations engaged in various imperial related activities and honors. The performance of sacrifice, mysteries, or other rituals for emperors in the group setting was a symbolic expression of a worldview that encompassed interconnected social, religious, and political dimensions.

Harland, Philip A. 2005a. "Familial Dimensions of Group Identity: 'Brothers' (ἀδελφοί) in Associations of the Greek East." *Journal of Biblical Literature* 124:491–513.

Inscriptional and papyrological evidence from Asia Minor, Greece, Macedonia, the Danube, the Bosporus and Egypt indicates association use of fictive kinship language. This article is further developed in Harland (2009).

Harland, Philip A. 2005b. "Spheres of Contention, Claims of Preeminence: Rivalries among Associations in Sardis and Smyrna." In *Religious Rivalries and the Struggle for Success in Sardis and Smyrna*, edited by Richard S. Ascough, 53–63. ESCJ 14. Waterloo: Wilfrid Laurier University Press.

Associations contended with one another in giving and receiving benefaction through the process of monumentalization and the "rhetoric of rivalry." This article is further developed in Harland (2009).

Harland, Philip A. 2006a. "Acculturation and Identity in the Diaspora: A Jewish Family and 'Pagan' Guilds at Hierapolis." *Journal of Jewish Studies* 57:222–44.

Jewish funerary inscriptions at Hierapolis in Asia Minor illustrate that Judeans adopted and adapted to local cultural practices in interacting with their neighbors, and in some cases belonged to occupational associations. This article is further developed in Harland (2009).

Harland, Philip A. 2006b. "The Declining Polis? Religious Rivalries in Ancient Civic Context." In *Religious Rivalries in the Early Roman*

Empire and the Rise of Christianity, ed. Leif E. Vaage. ESCJ 18. Waterloo: Wilfrid Laurier University Press.

> Traditional cults and honors for the gods were not in decline in the Hellenistic era but rather thrived at least into the third century CE despite changes and innovations. Associations contributed to the vitality of the *polis* (city) both through mutual cooperation in benefaction and through identification with their *polis* in rivalry with other cities. Judeans and Christians also found it necessary to maintain their place in the *polis* through some form of participation in the social, economic, and cultural features of civic life.

Harland, Philip A. 2007a. "Familial Dimensions of Group Identity (II): 'Mothers' and 'Fathers' in Associations and Synagogues of the Greek World." *Journal for the Study of Judaism in the Persian, Hellenistic, and Roman Period* 38:57–79.

> The widespread use of parental and familial metaphors in cities and associations of the Greek East, and their westward to influence on Rome illuminates the Judean designations "father of the synagogue" and "mother of the synagogue." This article is further developed in Harland (2009).

Harland, Philip A. 2007b. "'These People Are . . . Men Eaters': Banquets of the Anti-Associations and Perceptions of Minority Cultural Groups." In *Identity and Interaction in the Ancient Mediterranean: Jews, Christians and Others. Festschrift for Stephen G. Wilson*, ed. Zeba A. Crook and Philip A. Harland, 56–75. Sheffield: Sheffield Phoenix Press.

> Charges against associations of wild transgressions such as human sacrifice, cannibalism, and sexual perversion in fictional and ostensibly historical writings are part of the methods and rhetoric of ancient ethnography in which the "other" is described and distanced from one's own cultural group. This article is further developed in Harland (2009).

Harland, Philip A. 2009. *Dynamics of Identity in the World of the Early Christians: Associations, Judeans, and Cultural Minorities*. New York: Continuum/T&T Clark.

> H. draws on insights from social identity theory and migration theory in order to explore dynamics of identity among associations, immigrants, and cultural minorities (including Judeans and Christians). There are chapters on Judean and Christian groups' shared terminology with associations (chap. 1), Ignatius of Antioch's characterization of Christian groups as "fellow initiates" (*symmystai*;

chap. 2), the use of brother language in associations (chap. 3), the use of parental language in associations and synagogues (chap. 4), acculturation among associations of Syrian and Judean immigrants (chaps. 5–6), and the nature of ethnic and other rivalries, including accusations of human sacrifice and cannibalism (chaps. 7–8).

Harland, Philip A. and David Instone-Brewer. 2008. "Jewish Associations in Roman Palestine: Evidence from the Mishnah." *Journal of Greco-Roman Christianity and Judaism* 5:200–221.

Passages in the Mishnah give some important glimpses into Jewish banqueting associations, including some that met in the first century CE, particularly around Passover meals.

Harrison, Jim. 1999. "Paul's House Churches and the Cultic Associations." *Reformed Theological Review* 58:31–47.

H. compares the charismatic nature of Paul's Corinthian house churches with five associations and speculates that Paul borrowed the concept of charisma from contemporary colloquial language and developed it into a technical term for the manifestation and operation of divine grace within Israel and/or the body of Christ. A key difference for Paul, however, is the belief that the Spirit helps Christians use their gifts for mutual and community up-building.

Hasegawa, Kinuko. 2005. *The Familia Urbana during the Early Empire: A Study of Columbaria Inscriptions*. BAR International Series 1440. Oxford: Archaeopress.

"The Burial Clubs for Slaves and Freedmen" (81–88) examines the organization of associations that managed the *columbaria* (burial vaults with recessed niches for human remains) for the burial of the non-elite staff of elite households.

Hatch, Edwin. 1881. *The Organization of Early Christian Churches: Eight Lectures*. Bampton Lectures. London: Rivingtons. Repr., Eugene, Ore.: Wipf & Stock, 1999.

"Bishops and Deacons" (26–54) argues that Christian churches were similar to Greco-Roman associations in several respects, including leadership structures (*episkopoi* and *epimelētai*) and terminology used for meetings (*synodoi* and *ekklēsia*). In both types of groups, members contributed to a common fund and a shared meal, and membership was open to women and strangers, freedmen, and slaves. There were a few differences, however, such as the Christian emphasis on charity and the office of bishop as the single religious head of the association, rather than the financial and administrative officer.

Hatzfeld, Jean. 1919. *Les trafiquants italiens dans l'orient hellénique*. Bibliothèque des écoles françaises d'Athènes et de Rome, 115. Paris: E. de Boccard.

> H. explores evidence for Roman and Italian traders and merchants (*Italikoi, Romaioi, negotiatores*) throughout the Hellenistic world, including their formation of immigrant associations or settlements (*conventi, kaitoikountes*) in the Greek cities. Part 1 provides a historical and geographical survey from the second century BCE through the Roman imperial period. Part 2 explores the activities, organization, and role of merchants and their associations.

Heinrici, Georg. 1876. "Die Christengemeinden Korinths und die religiösen Genossenschaften der Griechen." *Zeitschrift für wissenschaftliche Theologie* 19:465–526.

> At their foundational stage, the Christian groups in Corinth were Greek religious associations that do not significantly evidence Jewish traditions. Drawing on the pattern of existing organization helped Christian groups avoid the mistrust of the authorities.

Heinrici, Georg. 1877. "Zur Geschichte der Anfänge paulinischer Gemeinden." *Zeitschrift für wissenschaftliche Theologie* 20:89–130.

> Focusing on Corinth, H. suggests that Paul founded these Christian groups as quasi-religious domestic communities (families) and associations of tradesmen. These groups were first tolerated under a general concession allowing new groups, before their belief in another god was thought to be incompatible with the law and order of the Roman Empire. Independently from the first part of the article, H. argues that rites and customs of non-Christian religions and cultures had a degenerative influence on the Christian groups in the empire (119–30).

Heinrici, Georg. 1881. "Zum genossenschaftlichen Charakter der paulinischen Christengemeinden." *Theologische Studien und Kritiken* 54:505–24.

> H. provides further evidence from associations and the New Testament to support his argument that the early Christian groups were founded by Paul on the model of the associations.

Hemelrijk, Emily. 2008. "Patronesses and 'Mothers' of Roman *Collegia*." *Classical Antiquity* 27:115–62.

Women played a role in association life in two ways: (1) all-male occupational associations co-opted female patrons from among local elite families and (2) "mothers" were either members or relatives of members and were of the same social class as those in the association. The appendices contain data on the distribution and social status of the two categories.

Hermansen, Gustav. 1981. *Ostia: Aspects of Roman City Life*. Edmonton: University of Alberta Press.

H. surveys archaeological evidence for buildings at Ostia used by occupational associations (chap. 2). An appendix lists the occupational associations according to (1) grain shipping and related services, (2) commerce, (3) transport, (4) trades, (5) civil service, and (6) cults.

Hermansen, Gustav. 1982. "The *Stuppatores* and Their Guild in Ostia." *American Journal of Archaeology* 86:121–26.

H. discusses the building of the guild of *stuppatores* (caulk workers) in Ostia, which was not completed until 235 CE (see **B13**).

Herrmann, Peter. 1996. "Mystenvereine in Sardeis." *Chiron* 26:315–341.

H. documents and discusses inscriptions pertaining to *mystai* (initiates in the mysteries) at Sardis in Asia Minor.

Hirschmann, Vera. 2006. "Macht durch Integration? Aspekte einer gesellschaftlichen Wechselwirkung zwischen Verein und Stadt am Beispiel der Mysten und Techniten des Dionysos von Smyrna." In *Vereine, Synagogen und Gemeinden im kaiserzeitlichen Kleinasien*, ed. Andreas Gutsfeld and Dietrich-Alex Koch, 41–59. STAC 25. Tübingen: Mohr Siebeck.

H. presents epigraphic evidence for associations of Dionysos devotees at Smyrna and their integration into social and political networks there. This is contrasted with Christian groups in the same city, which did not become integrated, as can be seen in the narrative of the martyrdom of Polycarp from the second century CE.

Hogarth, D. G. 1891. "The *Gerousia* of Hierapolis." *Journal of Philology* 19:69–101.

The *gerousia* (elders' council), which possessed large sums of money in its treasury, was an important association in Hierapolis. In contrast, the *ephebes* (youths) and the *neoi* (young men), both large associations, were honored neither by responsibility for festivals nor with great sums of money.

Horsley, Richard. 2005. "Paul's Assembly in Corinth: An Alternative Society." In *Urban Religion in Roman Corinth: Interdisciplinary Approaches*, ed. Daniel Schowalter and Stephen J. Friesen, 371–95. Harvard Theological Studies 53. Cambridge, Mass.: Harvard University Press.

> "Social world" theories that draw on data from associations lack authority because the central features of the associations such as common terminology, regulations, patronage, and exclusively local linkages lack comparison in Paul's communities. Rather, Paul was spearheading "an international anti-imperial movement" (394).

Ismard, Paulin. 2007. "Les associations en attique de Solon à Clisthène." In *Individus, groupes et politique à Athènes de Solon à Mithridate*, ed. Jean-Christophe Couvenhes, 17–34. Perspectives Historiques 15. Tours: Presses Universitaires François Rabelais.

> I. examines the law of Solon (*Digest* 47.22.4; see **L44**) concerning associations and Cleisthenes' reforms in which the demes of Athens were created, arguing that Cleisthenes' reforms simply integrated the associations and reflect more of an evolutionary process than a radical shift in political organization.

Jaccottet, Anne-Françoise. 2003. *Choisir Dionysos. Les associations dionysiaques ou la face cachée du dionysisme*; vol. 1, *Texte*; vol. 2, *Documents*. Zurich: Akanthus.

> Volume 1 contains analysis of the evidence for Dionysiac associations (excluding the Dionysiac *technitai*). There are chapters on the history of the study of Dionysiac associations, gender, iconography, and rituals. J. argues that the notion of a large Bacchic movement was not part of the consciousness of the members of localized associations. Volume 2 contains two hundred Greek and Latin inscriptions, with French translation and commentary.

Jaccottet, Anne-Françoise. 2006. "Une dieu, plusieurs mystères? Les différents visages des mystères dionysiaques. In *Religions orientales—culti misterici: Neue Perspektiven—nouvelles perspectives—prospettive nuove*, ed. Corinne Bonnet, Jörg Rüpke, and Paolo Scarpi, 219–30. PAwB 16. Stuttgart: Franz Steiner.

> There were diverse manifestations of Dionysiac cult in antiquity, and not all of them can be classified as "mystery religions," unless there is evidence of *teletai* (initiations) or *orgia* (rites).

Jaczynowska, Maria. 1978. *Les associations de la jeunesse romaine sous le haut-Empire*. Archiwum Filologiczne 136. Wroclaw: Zaklad Narodowy imienia Ossolinskisch.

J. studies several aspects of Roman youth associations (*collegia iuvenum*), including their historical development, geographic distribution, social composition, organization, and social-religious activities. An appendix includes the texts of 223 inscriptions arranged geographically, while a second appendix lists the names and titles of the functionaries found in the inscriptions.

Jones, Nicholas F. 1995. "The Athenian *Phylai* as Associations: Disposition, Function, and Purpose." *Hesperia* 64:503–42.

Fourth-century BCE Athenian inscriptions pertaining to *phylai* ("tribes") bestowing honors on important officials of the city provide evidence for representative government in ancient Greece. The main purpose of the *phylai* was to maximize their members' influence within the central government.

Jones, Nicholas F. 1999. *The Associations of Classical Athens: The Response to Democracy*. New York: Oxford University Press.

The disenfranchisement of the majority of the Attic population by the democratic government of Cleisthenes in 508/507 BCE was ameliorated by Solon's early law on associations (595 BCE; see **L44**). This law engendered political stability for two centuries, for it encouraged state-association relations such as mediation between government and the individual, opportunities for upward mobility in the political or social hierarchy, and the development of important integrative roles. Deme associations, based upon residence in precise territorial boundaries, existed in conjunction with the constitutional deme, which was based upon legitimate descent. These local associations, with an outlying rural base, offered the advantages of familiarity, convenience of assemblance, and historical linkage with the past, none of which were offered by the urban governmental deme. New associations arose in response to areas of need such as burial of abandoned corpses and distribution of alms.

Jory, E. J. 1970. "Associations of Actors in Rome." *Hermes* 98:224–53.

Early associations of stage artists were modeled on those of Dionysiac performers and included both actors and poets, but evidence for the stage artists' associations disappears after the middle of the third century CE. An appendix includes twelve Latin inscriptions with commentary.

Judge, E. A. 1960. *The Social Pattern of Christian Groups in the First Century: Some Prolegomena to the Study of New Testament Ideas of Social Obligation*. London: Tyndale.

J. suggests that groups of Judeans and Jesus followers were viewed as "unincorporated" (rather than "illegal") associations during the first century. Differences between the associations and the Christian groups include the existence of international ("translocal") links among the latter and the broad constituency from which they drew, from the wealthy sub-elites down to slaves. Nevertheless, Christians and outsiders would have perceived Christian groups as associations.

Judge, E. A. 2003. "Did the Churches Compete with Cult Groups?" In *Early Christianity and Classical Culture: Comparative Studies in Honor of Abraham J. Malherbe*, ed. John T. Fitzgerald, Thomas H. Olbricht, and L. Michael White, 501–24. NovTSup 110. Leiden: E.J. Brill.

J. argues that there was no connection between the cult groups and the Christian *ekklēsia* ("churches") because "the first churches are all community and no cult, while so-called 'cult-groups' create far more cult than community" (502).

Kaizer, Ted. 2002. *The Religious Life of Palmyra: A Study of the Social Patterns of Worship in the Roman Period*. Stuttgart: Franz Steiner.

"Groups of Worshippers, Priests and Benefactors" (213–64) surveys evidence for occupational and banqueting associations at Palmyra in Syria within the context of associations and other groupings in the ancient Near East.

Kippenberg, Hans G. 2005. "'Nach dem Vorbild eines öffentlichen Gemeinwesens.' Diskurse römischer Juristen über private religiöse Vereinigungen." In *Die verrechtlichte Religion: Der Öffentlichkeitsstatus von Religionsgemeinschaften*, ed. Hans G. Kippenberg and Gunnar Folke Schuppert, 37–64. Tübingen: Mohr Siebeck.

K. examines Roman legal codes from the Twelve Tables to the codification of Roman law under the emperors Theodosius and Justinian. The laws allowed for the existence of private *collegia*, but they were restricted to three types of associations: occupational, funerary, and religious (*religio*). Other associations (e.g., political groups) were not allowed. Christian groups eventually presented themselves as a *religio* rather than a *superstitio* and thus were treated as licit associations.

Klauck, Hans-Josef. 1982. *Herrenmahl und hellenistischer Kult: Eine religionsgeschichtliche Untersuchung zum ersten Korintherbrief.* NTAbh 15. Münster: Aschendorff.

Literary testimony for association meals demonstrates that some of the ancient Greek association structures and nomenclature can also be found in Jewish groups (68–76). From an outsider's point of view, a Jewish group (and, by extension, a Christian group) could be seen as a cult association with a Hellenistic structure.

Klauck, Hans-Josef. 2000. *The Religious Context of Early Christianity: A Guide to Graeco-Roman Religions*. Edinburgh: T&T Clark.

K. describes the outward manifestations and terminology of associations, gives four specific examples, and concludes with Philo's comments as an example of an outsider's view of associations (42–54). Jewish and Christian groups could be seen as "mystery associations of a newly-imported oriental deity" (54). Christians may have distinguished themselves by intensifying social integration and charitable activity, as well as choosing the term *ekklēsia*.

Klinghardt, Matthias. 1994. "The Manual of Discipline in the Light of Statutes of Hellenistic Associations." In *Methods of Investigation of the Dead Sea Scrolls and the Khirbet Qumran Site: Present Realities and Future Prospects*, ed. John J. Collins, Michael O. Wise, Norman Golb, and Dennis Pardee, 251–70. Annals of the New York Academy of Sciences 722. New York: New York Academy of Sciences.

The Qumran Manual of Discipline (1QS) closely parallels the genre and content of statutes from Hellenistic associations.

Klinghardt, Matthias. 1996. *Gemeinschaftsmahl und Mahlgemeinschaft. Soziologie und Liturgie frühchristlicher Mahlfeiern*. TANZ 13. Tübingen: Francke.

Part 1 (21–174) provides a comprehensive survey of evidence for association meal practices and suggests that the meal practices of Jewish and early Christian groups can be understood in light of those of Hellenistic associations.

Kloppenborg, John S. 1993. "Edwin Hatch, Churches and Collegia." In *Origins and Method: Towards a New Understanding of Judaism and Christianity. Essays in Honour of John C. Hurd*, ed. Bradley H. McLean, 212–38. JSNTSup 86. Sheffield: JSOT Press.

K. assesses the largely negative reaction to Hatch's (1881) proposal that Christian groups were viewed as associations in antiquity. Exploring analogical rather than genealogical relations between associations and Christian groups helps us understand how Pauline churches functioned in imperial society, the ways they offered benefits (which were more than religious), and their internal structures and church-*polis* (city) relationships.

Kloppenborg, John S. 1996a. "Collegia and *Thiasoi*: Issues in Function, Taxonomy and Membership." In *Voluntary Associations in the Graeco-Roman World*, ed. John S. Kloppenborg and Stephen G. Wilson, 16–30. London: Routledge.

> K. suggests there were two main types of associations: (1) the official Roman sacerdotal colleges and sacred sodalities, which were established by an act of the senate and were composed of the elite, and (2) private associations, which were illegal, tolerated rather than encouraged, and composed of the non-elite. "Funerary associations" is a misleading category and was a legal fiction established only after Hadrian's time.

Kloppenborg, John S. 1996b. "Egalitarianism in the Myth and Rhetoric of Pauline Churches." In *Reimagining Christian Origins: A Colloquium Honoring Burton L. Mack*, ed. Elizabeth A. Castelli and Hal Taussig, 247–63. Valley Forge, Pa.: Trinity Press International.

> Paul's attempts at conflict resolution in the Corinthian groups (1 Cor 6) can be understood better when compared with associations that dealt with similar issues. Like the associations, Paul attempts to avoid public shaming in the civic courts of one member by another, but, unlike the associations, he was also attempting to subvert the relentlessly vertical character of Greco-Roman social life.

Kloppenborg, John S. 2006. "Associations in the Ancient World." In *The Historical Jesus in Context*, ed. Amy Jill Levine, Dale C. Allison, and John Dominic Crossan, 323–38. Princeton: Princeton University Press.

> K. divides associations into three overlapping categories: *phratriai* or family-based groups; religious groups; and, ethnic, neighborhood, and trade groups. Biblical texts and early Christian groups can be read in light of the data from associations.

Kloppenborg Verbin, John S. 1999. "Patronage Avoidance in James." *Hervormde Theologiese Studies* 55:1–40.

> Using Pseudo-Cicero's rhetorical form of the "elaboration on a theme," the biblical book of James proposes an effective argument against patronage, comparing God's honor and friendship to the shame of "flattery" and its guise of friendship. James' group is comparable to a non-elite association that provided dignity, economic support, and honor to its members.

Kloppenborg, John S., and Stephen G. Wilson, eds. 1996. *Voluntary Associations in the Graeco-Roman World*. London: Routledge.

>This is a collection of papers arising from a five-year seminar in the Canadian Society of Biblical Studies. See entries for Cotter (1996), Kloppenborg (1996a), Mason (1996), McCready (1996), McLean (1996), Remus (1996), Richardson (1996), Richardson and Heuchan (1996), Seland (1996), and Wilson (1996).

Kneissl, Peter. 1981. "Die *utriclarii*. Ihre Rolle im gallo-römischen Transportwesen und Weinhandel." *Bonner Jahrbübucher* 181:79–99.

>The *utriclarii* (attested in about twenty-seven inscriptions) were not likely shippers but rather transporters of wine and oil overland by wagon in leather containers.

Kneissl, Peter. 1994. "Die *fabri, fabri tignuarii, fabri subaediani, centonarii* und *dolabrarii* als Feuerwehren in den Städten Italiens und der westlichen Provinzen." In *E fontibus haurire: Beiträge zur römischen Geschichte und zu ihren Hilfswissenschaften*, ed. Rosmarie Günther und Stefan Rebenich, 133–46. Studien zur Geschichte und Kulture des Altertums 8. Paderborn: Ferdinand Schöningh.

>Associations of manual workers (*fabri*) could include members from other occupations. The common and main feature of the members of these associations was their service as auxiliary firefighters.

Kneissl, Peter. 1998. "Die Berufsvereine im römischen Gallien. Eine Interpretation der Epigraphischen Zeugnisse." In *Imperium Romanum: Studien zu Geschichte und Rezeption. Festschrift für Karl Christ zum 75. Geburtstag*, ed. Peter Kneissl and Volker Losemann, 431–49. Stuttgart: Franz Steiner.

>K. and S. survey epigraphic evidence for occupational associations in the Roman province of Gaul, including a discussion of their legal standing and their involvement in fire fighting (first to third centuries CE).

Koch, Dietrich-Alex, and Dirk Schinkel. 2006. "Die Frage nach den Vereinen in der Geistes- und Theologiegeschichte des 19. und 20 Jahrhunderts unter besonderer Berücksichtigung des zeitgenossischen Vereins. Wesens und der Wende in der protestantischen Theologie nach 1918." In *Vereine, Synagogen und Gemeinden im kaiserzeitlichen Kleinasien*, ed. Andreas Gutsfeld and Dietrich-Alex Koch, 129–48. STAC 25. Tübingen: Mohr Siebeck.

K. surveys interest in the associations among theologians and biblical exegetes in the nineteenth and the early twentieth centuries.

Koester, Helmut. 1999. "Associations of the Egyptian Cult in Asia Minor." In *Steine und Wege: Festschrift für Dieter Knibbe zum 65. Geburtstag*, ed. Peter Scherrer, Hans Taeuber, and Hilke Thür, 315–18. Österreichisches Archäologisches Institut, Sonderschriften 32. Vienna: Austrian Archaeological Institute. Reprinted in *Paul and His World: Interpreting the New Testament in Its Context*, 160–67. Minneapolis: Fortress Press, 2007.

K. discusses associations connected to the Egyptian gods in Asia Minor with the aim of demonstrating that it is not possible to extrapolate a general depiction of such associations from the more extensive evidence for Egyptian associations on Delos.

Kolb, Anne. 1995. "Vereine 'Kleiner Leute' und kaiserliche Verwaltung." *Zeitschrift für Papyrologie und Epigraphik* 107:201–12.

For the lower classes, joining an occupational or religious association was an opportunity to participate in public life as well as benefit from the social prestige of the associations, including connections with the imperial administration (as illustrated by three inscriptions involving workers on imperial estates).

Konen, H. 2001. "Die Schiffsbauer und Werften in den antiken Häfen von Ostia und Portus." *Münstersche Beiträge zur antiken Handelsgeschichte* 20:1–36.

A number of inscriptions and membership lists (*alba*) attest to the association of shipwrights (*fabri navales*) of Portus and Ostia, whose members were quite wealthy. By the third century, shipwrights in Portus were under imperial control (unlike the Ostian shipwrights) in connection with the supply of grain to Rome.

Krause, Marie-France Meylan. 2002. "Die Handwerker und die Stadt." *Archäologie der Schweiz* 24:50–59.

K. describes occupational associations active in the city of Aventicum (in modern Switzerland), many of which had their own buildings.

Kurz, K. 1960. "Methodische Bemerkungen zum Studium der Kollegien im Donaugebiet." *Acta Antiqua Academiae Scientiarum Hungaricae* 8:133–44.

The development of the *collegia* (associations) within the provinces around the Danube needs to be connected to an analysis of the life of the municipal population in those same provinces. The association of builders and textile workers (*collegium fabrum et centonariorum*) in Aquincum participated in fighting fires.

Labarre, Guy, and M.-Th. Le Dinahet. 1996. "Le métiers du textile in Asie Mineure de l'époque hellénistique a l'époque impériale." In *Aspects de l'artisanat du textile dans le monde méditerranée (Égypte, Grèce, Monde romain)*, 49–115. Collection de l'Institut d'archéologie et d'histoire de l'antiquité 2. Paris: E. de Boccard.

> This collection of eighty-two inscriptions deals with textile associations in Asia Minor and adjacent Aegean islands, including French translations and a synthesis of the evidence of the guilds with regard to distribution, terminology, and relations within local societies.

Ladage, D. 1979. "*Collegia Iuvenum*—Ausbildung der municipalen Elite?" *Chiron* 9:319–46.

> L. analyzes literary and epigraphic evidence attesting the *collegia iuvenum* (youth associations), which were established for the municipal elite youth and had no direct national or municipal responsibilities.

Lafer, Renate. 2001. *Omnes Collegiati! Brandbekämpfung im Imperium Romanum*. Grazer Altertumskundliche Studien 7. Frankfurt: Peter Lang.

> L. discusses the auxiliary and occupational firefighting groups in the Roman Empire. While professional fire brigades operated in Rome, voluntary firefighting groups consisting of *fabri* (builders), *centonarii* (textile workers), and *dendrophori* (woodcutters)—the so-called *tria collegia principalia* or *omnia collegia*—played a key role in other cities of the provinces.

Laird, Margaret L. 2000. "Reconsidering the So-Called *Sede degli Augustali* at Ostia." *Memoirs of the American Academy in Rome* 45:41–84.

> L. argues against the prevailing view that the meeting place of the Augustales in Ostia was the building labeled the "seat of the Augustales" (see **B20**). A much more likely candidate for the meeting place of the Augustales is the so-called Curia building (see **B12**).

La Piana, Georg. 1927. "Foreign Groups in Rome during the First Century of the Empire." *Harvard Theological Review* 20:183–354.

> L. discusses evidence for the cults and associations of foreigners settled in Rome. These cults remained foreign, isolated, and

independent, and although they enjoyed official favor and adapted somewhat, they did not undergo substantial Romanization.

Laum, Bernhard. 1914. *Stiftungen in der griechischen und römischen Antike: Ein Beitrag zur antiken Kulturgeschichte.* Leipzig: Teubner. Repr., Aalen: Scientia, 1964.

> L. gathers, translates (into German), and examines inscriptions pertaining to financial endowments in antiquity, including those involving associations and civic groups (151–66).

Le Guen, Brigitte. 2001. *Les associations de technites dionysiaques à l'époque hellénistique.* Vol. 1, *Corpus documentaire*; vol. 2, *Synthèse.* Études d'archéologie classique XI–XII. Nancy and Paris: Association pour la diffusion de la recherche sur l'Antiquite, and E. de Boccard.

> Volume 1 contains nearly one hundred geographically arranged epigraphic texts from the Hellenistic era (with French translation) and twenty literary texts concerning the Dionysiac performers (*technitai*). Volume 2 examines the evidence with respect to group composition, cultic and theatrical activities, and the overall function and importance of these associations.

Le Guen, Brigitte. 2004. "Le statut professionnel des acteurs grecs à l'époque hellénistique." In *Le statut de l'acteur dans l'antiquité. Actes du colloque international (Tours, 3–4 mai 2002),* ed. Ch. Hugoniot, F. Hurlet, and S. Milanezi, 77–106. Tours: Presses Universitaires François Rabelais, Tours.

> There were no associations of performers or actors (*technitai*) between 323 and 280 BCE; after that time until the first century BCE, only about 16 percent of actors were clearly members of an association. The prevailing scholarly view that after the death of Alexander the Great independent actors were incorporated into newly formed associations of Dionysiac performers is incorrect.

Le Guen, Brigitte. 2007a. "L'association des technites d'Athènes ou les ressorts d'une cohabitation réussie." In *Individus, groupes et politique à Athènes de Solon à Mithridate,* ed. Jean-Christophe Couvenhes, 339–364. Perspectives Historiques 15. Tours: Presses Universitaires François Rabelais.

> Associations of Dionysiac performers (*technitai*) in Athens modeled themselves on the *polis* (city), using similar organizational structures and titles for officials and engaging in similar honorary activities. These contacts with Hellenistic authorities explain the

harmonious relations these associations enjoyed with the municipal authorities.

Le Guen, Brigitte. 2007b. "Kraton, son of Zotichos: Artists' Associations and Monarchic Power in the Hellenistic Period." In *The Greek Theatre and Festivals: Documentary Studies*, ed. Peter Wilson, 246–78. Oxford Studies in Ancient Documents. Oxford: Oxford University Press.

> L. discusses the famous second-century BCE musician named Kraton, who had connections with five different associations of Dionysiac artists (*technitai*) in various locales around Asia Minor.

Leiwo, Martti. 1997. "Religion, or Other Reasons? Private Associations in Athens." In *Early Hellenistic Athens: Symptoms of a Change*, ed. Jaakko Frösén, 103–17. Papers and Monographs of the Finnish Institute at Athens. Helsinki: Finnish Institute at Athens.

> The main purpose of the associations in fourth- and third-century BCE Athens was not religious but social (*synousia*) with a focus on common meals and social, judicial, and financial support. L. also discusses the earliest meanings of *eranos* ("loan," "contribution," and "meal") and *thiasos* (involving a banquet with food, drink, and dances connected with cultic activities).

Levinskaya, Irina. 1996. *The Book of Acts in Its Diaspora Setting*. The Book of Acts in Its First Century Setting 5. Grand Rapids: Eerdmans.

> "God-fearers and the Cult of the Most High God" (83–104) argues that Theos Hypsistos ("Highest God") consistently has a Judean connection involving Gentile god fearers who worshipped the Judean God. "God-fearers: The Bosporan Kingdom" (105–16) argues that societies (*thiasoi*) devoted to Theos Hypsistos at Tanais were, in fact, associations of Gentile god fearers worshipping the Judean god. (See Ustinova [1999], who refutes this argument in relation to earlier work by Levinskaya.) Appendix 3 collects together inscriptions pertaining to Judeans (primarily manumissions) and associations in the Bosporan Kingdom (227–46).

Liebenam, Wilhelm. 1890. *Zur Geschichte und Organisation des römischen Vereinswesens: Drei Untersuchungen*. Leipzig: Teubner. Repr., Aalen: Scientia Verlag, 1964.

> L. examines the development of *collegia opificum* (tradesmen) from King Numa to the end of the republic, arguing that the Roman state placed no restrictions on associations until Augustus' *lex Iulia* (Julian law) (chap. 1); demonstrates that *collegia opificum*

were spread unevenly across Italy and the provinces, and that only a small fraction of workmen were united in associations (chap. 2); and explains the organization of *collegia opificum* during the empire (chap. 3).

de Ligt, Luuk. 2000. "Governmental Attitudes towards Markets and Collegia." In *Mercati permanenti e mercati periodici nel mondo romano: Atti degli incontri capresi di storia dell'economia antica, Capri 13–15 ottobre 1997*, ed. Elio Lo Cascio, 237–52. Bari: Edipuglia.

> The *senatus consultum de collegiis tenuiorum* (senatorial decree on associations for the poor), which allowed associations for funerary purposes, was issued soon after Augustus' reaffirmation of the Caesarian *lex Iulia* (Julian law), which had abolished nearly all associations.

de Ligt, Luuk. 2001. "D.47,22,1,pr.-1 and the Formation of Semi-Public *Collegia*." *Latomus* 60:354–58.

> L. extends the argument of his earlier work (de Ligt 2000) by compiling considerable evidence for the existence of a number of semi-public *collegia* (associations) that were not under a general imperial ban and thus did not have to apply for permission to exist. Those that did register their existence with the senate did so for reasons other than the request for permission. Thus, the ban against "all *collegia*" is in fact a ban against associations that were not under the control of imperial or municipal authorities.

Linderski, Jerzy. 1968. "Der Senat und die Vereine." In *Gesellschaft und Recht im griechisch-römischen Altertum: Eine Aufsatzsammlung*, ed. Mikhail N. Andreev, Elemér Pólay, Johannes Irmscher, and Witold Warkallo, 94–132. Deutsche Akademie der Wissenschaften zu Berlin 52. Berlin: Akademi Verlag.

> L. surveys the legal standing of associations under Roman rule.

Liu, Jinyu. 2007. "The Economy of Endowments: The Case of the Roman Collegia." In Πίστοι δὶα τὴν τεχνήν. *Bankers, Loans and Archives in the Ancient World. Studies in Honour of Raymond Bogaert*, ed. K. Verboven, K. Vandorpe, and V. Chankowski, 231–56. Studia Hellenistica 44. Leuven: Peeters.

> In the western Roman Empire, endowments to *collegia* (associations), both cash and revenue generating property, had a profound effect on the internal organization of associations and their roles as consumers, managers, and investors. Most endowments were given

to fund commemorative rites during festivals (e.g., the *rosalia*) or to celebrate the birthday of a patron or a deity, while some funding was designated for the maintenance of statues.

Liu, Jinyu. 2008. "Pompeii and *collegia*: A New Appraisal of the Evidence." *Ancient History Bulletin* 22:53–69.

Occupational and religious groups at Pompeii should not be considered *collegia* since none used the term. Nor is there any indication of the three most frequently attested types of *collegia*: *fabri* (smiths, builders, carpenters), *centonariorii* (textile workers), and *dendrophori* (woodcutters). The *fabri, centonariorii,* and *dendrophori* were part of a later diffusion of *collegia* that were formally and informally promoted by Roman authorities, particularly after the first century CE.

Liu, Jinyu. 2009. Collegia Centonariorum: *The Guilds of Textile Dealers in the Roman West.* Columbia Studies in the Classical Tradition 34. Leiden: E.J. Brill.

L. investigates the origins, functions, organizations, and legal status of the *collegia centonariorum* (textile workers) in the western part of the Roman Empire, drawing on 234 Latin inscriptions, which are collected in an appendix (most without translation). These associations, which were officially recognized early on, played a role in firefighting, but this was not their principal role.

Lüderitz, Gert. 1994. "What Is a *Politeuma*?" In *Studies in Early Jewish Epigraphy,* ed. Jan Willem van Henten and Pieter Willem van der Horst, 183–225. AGAJU 21. Leiden: E.J. Brill.

L. surveys the types of groups that used the self-designation *politeuma* ("corporate body"), including its use by political groups, by unofficial associations, and by Jews in Alexandria and in Berenike (see **305–306**). L. refutes the common suggestion (first proposed by Perdrizet in reference to Jews at Berenike) that *politeuma* pertains to a formally recognized public institution of immigrants or Jews with special privileges and some form of citizenship.

MacMullen, Ramsay. 1962–1963. "Note on Roman Strikes." *The Classical Journal* 48:269–73.

M. counters the view that an increase in strike activity toward the end of the Roman Empire is evidence for the compulsory guilds weakening the general economy and contributing to the decline of the empire.

MacMullen, Ramsay. 1974. *Roman Social Relations 50 B.C. to A.D. 284*. New Haven: Yale University Press.

> This social-historical study of rural and urban dwellers in the Roman Empire makes frequent reference to associations of various types (e.g., farmers, herders, craftsmen, youths, women) and the important social roles they played in civic and social life (e.g., voting, festivals, burial).

Malay, Hasan. 2005. "*ΦΙΛΑΝΠΙΛΟΙ* in Phrygia and Lydia." *Epigraphica Anatolica* 38:42–44.

> An inscription from Kotiaion (*SEG* 31 [1981], no. 1130) refers to an association calling itself *philanpiloi* ("new lovers of the vine"), not *philangeloi* ("friends-of-angels"), as Sheppard (1980–1981) had thought.

Martinez, David, and Mary Williams. 1997a. "*P. Erasm.* I 10: An Order for Payment from a Cult Association." *Zeitschrift für Papyrologie und Epigraphik* 118:263–66.

> A second-century BCE document from the Arsinoite nome in Egypt is an example of the bookkeeping in the association of the crocodile. The obscurity of the text leaves open at least three options in the relationship between lender and borrower.

Martinez, David, and Mary Williams. 1997b. "Records of Loan Receipts from a Guild Association." *Zeitschrift für Papyrologie und Epigraphik* 118:259–63.

> Three papyri loan receipts from an anonymous association in 182 or 156 BCE record the bookkeeping of an association that acts as a lending institution.

Mason, Steve N. 1996. "*Philosophiai*: Greco-Roman, Jewish, and Christian." In *Voluntary Associations in the Graeco-Roman World*, ed. John S. Kloppenborg and Stephen G. Wilson, 31–58. London: Routledge.

> M. argues that philosophical schools were associations with a language of conversion. Philo, Josephus, and the rabbinic tradition present Judaism as a philosophy. Christianity in the first generation (Paul) was only partly presented as a philosophy, but the second generation (Luke) adopted this approach more fully.

Masson, Olivier. 1987. "Le mot ΔΟΥΜΟΣ 'confrérie' dans les textes et les inscriptions." *Cahiers Ferdinand de Saussure* 41:145–52.

The designation *doumos* for an association has roots in Phrygia in the sixth century BCE, although it continued to be used into the third and fourth centuries CE.

McCready, Wayne O. 1996. "*EKKLĒSIA* and Voluntary Associations." In *Voluntary Associations in the Graeco-Roman World*, ed. John S. Kloppenborg and Stephen G. Wilson, 59–73. London: Routledge.

Although there are some similarities between Christian *ekklēsia* (churches) and the associations, this is outweighed by differences pertaining to the exclusivity of Christianity and the associations' emphasis upon fellowship rather than salvation.

McLean, Bradley H. 1993. "The Agrippinilla Inscription: Religious Associations and Early Church Formation." In *Origins and Method: Towards a New Understanding of Judaism and Christianity. Essays in Honour of John C. Hurd*, ed. Bradley H. McLean, 239–70. JSNTSup 86. Sheffield: JSOT Press.

The Dionysiac association attested on the base of a statue for Pompeia Agrippinilla was a household group consisting of freeborn Romans and Greek slaves and freedmen (*IGUR* 160, ca. 150 CE; see **330**). M. supplies the text and a translation, comparing the group with Pauline groups with respect to family-based structures and social hierarchies.

McLean, B. Hudson. 1996. "The Place of Cult in Voluntary Associations and Christian Churches on Delos." In *Voluntary Associations in the Graeco-Roman World*, ed. John S. Kloppenborg and Stephen G. Wilson, 186–225. London: Routledge.

M. explores the use of cultic space within associations of various kinds on the island of Delos, including the Berytians, Samaritans, and Judeans (with descriptions of building remains and translations of relevant inscriptions). Christian churches on Delos used cultic space in a manner similar to associations.

McLean, B. Hudson. 1999. "Hierarchically Organized Associations on Delos." In *XI Congresso Internazionale di Epigrafia Greca e Latina, Roma, 18–24 settembre 1997*, 361–70. Rome: Quasar.

M. proposes that there was a three-tiered internal structure within the associations of Berytians, Tyrians, and others on Delos: (1) the *thiasos* was probably the largest, most inclusive level that probably involved men, women, slaves, and some foreigners or guests; (2) the *koinon* was probably a large deliberatory group within the *thiasos*, with all male members who shared a common ethnic origin; and (3) the *synodos* was probably a subcommittee of the *koinon*, functioning in an executive mode.

McRae, Rachel M. 2011. "Eating with Honor: The Corinthian Lord's Supper in Light of Voluntary Association Meal Practices." *Journal of Biblical Literature* 130:165–81.

> Paul deplores the typical banqueting distinctions of the associations, which are being replicated in the divisions at the Lord's Supper at Corinth. Paul counters with teachings about equality, humility, and mutuality in which God is recognized as the divine patron deserving of the believers' honor and devoted service.

Meeks, Wayne A. 2003 [1983]. *The First Urban Christians: The Social World of the Apostle Paul.* 2nd ed. (new introduction). New Haven: Yale University Press.

> In an often cited passage, M. presents four different models for understanding the formation of early Pauline groups: households, associations, synagogues, and philosophic or rhetorical schools (75–84). Although there are some similarities between Christian groups and associations in the provision for burial of members and dependence upon patronage, the differences (e.g., exclusivity and translocal character of Christian groups) are far more prevalent.

Meeks, Wayne A. 2009. "Taking Stock and Moving On." In *After the First Urban Christians: The Social-Scientific Study of Pauline Christianity Twenty-Five Years Later,* ed. Todd D. Still and David G. Horrell, 134–46. London: T&T Clark.

> M. acknowledges the progress made in research on associations, which has led to "a correction of something I said earlier" (i.e., in Meeks 2003) regarding the comparability of associations and Christian groups (141). He modifies his "earlier suggestion that Christians and Jews were unique among urban organizations in the Roman cities in translocal sensibilities and practices," although he resists going "as far as Ascough (1997)" (141).

Meiggs, Russell. 1973 [1960]. *Roman Ostia.* 2nd ed. Oxford: Clarendon.

> "The Guilds of Ostia" (311–36) included trade guilds, religious associations, burial associations, youth organizations (*iuvenes*), and the *Augustales,* as well as two guilds that cannot be classified. Ostian guilds were relatively wealthy during the intensive rebuilding of the town in the second century, but declined in the third century when trade shrank and shifted to Portus.

Mendelsohn, I. 1940a. "Guilds in Ancient Palestine." *Bulletin of the American Schools of Oriental Research* 80:17–21.

Archaeological and literary evidence attests to associations in ancient Palestine before contact with the Hellenistic world. Evidence from potter's marks indicates the presence of ancient, large, well-equipped, and collectively owned associations. Neighborhood guilds were trade monopolies and closed corporations with legal rights of exclusion and protection against loss of tools, with their own religious and social institutions.

Mendelsohn, I. 1940b. "Guilds in Babylonia and Assyria." *Journal of the American Oriental Society* 60:68–72.

Legal and business documents show that occupational associations existed in Old and Neo-Babylonia and in Assyria. They had privileges and responsibilities, particularly with regard to the collection of taxes.

Merkelbach, Reinhold. 1988. *Die Hirten des Dionysos: Die Dionysos-Mysterien der römischen Kaiserzeit und der bukolische Roman des Longus.* Stuttgart: Teubner, 1988.

Chapter 2 (15–30) looks at some Dionysiac associations during the Roman imperial period, including the association of Agrippinilla in Rome (see **330**), a grotto on Thasos, the mysteries in Ephesos, Philadelphia (Lydia), Smyrna, and Magnesia, the cult of Bacchus in Numidia, and the Iobacchoi in Athens (see **7**).

Meyer, Hugo. 1988. "Zur Chronologie des Poseidoniastenhauses in Delos." *Mitteilungen des deutschen archäologischen Instituts (Athenische Abteilung)* 103:203–20.

M. discusses the development of the buildings used by the association of Berytians devoted to the god Poseidon on Delos (**B8**).

Millar, Fergus. 1999. "The Greek East and Roman Law: The Dossier of M. Cn. Licinius Rufinus." *Journal of Roman Studies* 89:80–108.

M. gathers together inscriptions regarding the activities and career of the jurist Licinius Rufinus, including three honorary inscriptions from Thyatira set up by a high priest of an athletic association (no. 1; see **137**), by a group of tanners (*byrseis*; no. 3), and by a group of gardeners (*kēpouroi*; no. 6).

Minns, Ellis H. 1913. *Scythians and Greeks: A Survey of Ancient History and Archaeology on the North Coast of the Euxine from the Danube to the Caucasus.* Cambridge: Cambridge University Press.

"Bosporus Cults" (615–25) draws on epigraphic and numismatic evidence to argue that the Greco-Iranian population of the Bosporan Kingdom engaged in a syncretistic popular religion, with the chief deity being Aphrodite Ourania ("of the Heavens"). Semiprivate associations (*thiasoi*, *synodoi*) had three objectives: worship of particular deities, burial of members, and education of the young.

Miranda, E. 1999. "La comunità giudaica di Hierapolis di Frigia." *Epigraphica Anatolica* 31: 109–55.

M. collects together twenty-three Judean grave inscriptions from Hierapolis (thirteen newly published), discussing the situation of Judeans in Asia Minor and the names that appear in the inscriptions, as well as providing an analysis of the P. Aelius Glykon inscription and the guilds involved (see **149–152**).

Moeller, Walter O. 1972. "The Building of Eumachia: A Reconsideration." *American Journal of Archaeology* 76:323–27.

The Pompeian building dedicated by the city priestess, Eumachia, to the cult of Concordia Augusta and Pietas was probably the headquarters of the Pompeian association of wool traders (*fullones*), rather than a wool market (see **B22**).

Mohler, S. L. 1937. "The Iuvenes and Roman Education." *Transactions of the American Philological Association* 68:442–79.

Associations of aristocratic youths (*iuvenes*) in Rome were often assigned important roles in local worship, and special games were given in their honor in the post-Augustan era. M. argues that the inclusion of alumni among their ranks suggests that these were associations of schoolboys whose groups developed along the lines of "funerary *collegia*."

Mommsen, Theodor. 1843. *De collegiis et sodaliciis Romanorum, accedit inscription lanuvina*. Keil: Schwers'sche Buchhandlung.

This work set the stage for most of the earliest research on *collegia* and associations generally. Drawing primarily on the association devoted to Antinous and Diana at Lanuvium, Italy (*CIL* XIV 2112; see **310**), M. argues for the existence of a category of "funerary associations" (*collegia funeraticia*) whose primary purpose was the burial of members and celebration of funerary rituals. These *collegia* were recognized as legal by the Roman authorities as they claimed an exemption from the general *senatus consultum*. Christian groups claimed this same status as a way to protect themselves from the authorities.

Mommsen, Theodor. 1907. "Zur Lehre von den römischen Korporationen." In *Gesammelte Schriften 3. Juristische Schriften*, 53–68. Berlin: Weidmannsche Buchhandlung.

> In Roman law, a *collegium* (association) had administrative and property rights like that of the *municipium*. Public and private *collegia* could thus own property, including their own slaves. Nevertheless, the abuses by some of the private *collegia* led to many restrictions of the rights of associations during the late republic and the imperial period. Permission was required for the formation of a *collegium* as a result of a specific senatorial decree (*senatus consultum*), although there was general permission for funerary associations (*collegia funeraticia*) consisting of the poor.

Monson, A. 2006. "The Ethics and Economics of Ptolemaic Religious Associations." *Ancient Society* 36:221–38.

> M. examines the economic status of members in Ptolemaic religious associations, concluding that they were relatively prosperous in relation to the villages where they were active. The associations' institutionalization of norms of behavior is characteristic of "trust networks" (as distinct from other social networks).

Muhs, Brian. 2001. "Membership in Private Associations in Ptolemaic Tebtunis." *Journal of the Economic and Social History of the Orient* 44:1–21.

> Crocodile associations in Ptolemaic Tebtunis involved the adoration and procession of mummified crocodiles, which represented the god Souchos, worshipped in the temples. These non-elite groups were similar to Hellenistic associations, upon which they were based.

Muszynski, Michel. 1977. "Les 'associations religieuses' en Égypte d'après les sources hiéroglyphiques, démotiques et grecques." *Orientalia Lovaniensia Periodica* 8:147–74.

> Texts in hieroglyphics, demotic, and Greek demonstrate that Egyptian religious associations are not the basis upon which later Christian monasteries were modeled. Nonetheless, they may be treated as precursors of Christian "brotherhoods" that later evolved into the monasteries.

Nigdelis, Pantelis M. 2010. "Voluntary Associations in Roman Thessalonikē: In Search of Identity and Support in a Cosmopolitan Society." In *From Roman to Early Christian Thessalonikē: Studies in Religion and Archaeology*, ed. Laura Nasrallah, Charalambos Bakirtzis, and Steven Friesen,

13–47. Harvard Theological Studies 64. Cambridge, Mass.: Harvard University Press.

> Forty-four Greek association inscriptions from Thessalonica (collected in an appendix) are used to illustrate the social history of the city in the Roman imperial period. N. categorizes the inscriptions into four groups: religious, occupational, household, and those formed for the purpose of entertainment.

Nijf, Onno M. van. 1997. *The Civic World of Professional Associations in the Roman East*. Dutch Monographs on Ancient History and Archaeology 17. Amsterdam: J.C. Gieben.

> N. explores the place of guilds within society in the eastern part of the Roman Empire (especially Asia Minor), demonstrating how these groups were involved within social, religious, and economic aspects of civic life. This includes extensive discussions of associations' participation in funerary activities (chap. 1), honorific customs (chap. 2), civic festivals (chap. 3), public banqueting (chap. 4), processions (chap. 5), and activities at theaters and stadia (chap. 6).

Nijf, Onno M. van. 2000. "Inscriptions and Civic Memory in the Roman East." In *The Afterlife of Inscriptions*, ed. A. Cooley, 21–36. Bulletin of the Institute of Classical Studies Supplements 75. London: Institute of Classical Studies.

> Public monuments were a form of collective self-representation by the Roman elite and by other groups. Associations used monuments to record their gratitude to benefactors and to reflect their solidarity with civic values.

Nijf, Onno M. van. 2002. "*Collegia* and Civic Guards. Two Chapters in the History of Sociability." In *After the Past: Essays in Ancient History in Honour of H. W. Pleket*, ed. Willem Jongman and Marc Kleijwegt, 305–40. Mnemosyne Supplement 233. Leiden: E.J. Brill.

> N. compares two culturally and temporally disparate types of associations: the ancient *collegia* and the Dutch civic guards of the sixteenth and seventeenth centuries. While both groups contributed essential civic functions—the *collegia* as firefighters and the civic guards as maintainers of law and order—their contributions have been overestimated and their primary function should be understood as social.

Nijf, Onno M. van. 2003. "Les élites comme patrons des associations professionalees dans l'orient romain." In *Les élites et leurs facettes. Les élites locales dans le monde hellénistique et romain*, ed. M. Cébeillac-Gervasoni and L. Lamoine, 307–21. École française de Rome. Paris: Presses universitaires Blaise-Pascal.

> Epigraphic production transformed the urban landscape and allowed associations to present themselves as integrated within the local hierarchy, rather than being alternatives to civic structures.

Nock, A. D. 1924. "The Historical Importance of Cult-Associations." *Classical Review* 38:105–8.

> Cult associations facilitated the evolution of new religious ideas and, being modeled on the family, provided freedom that contrasted to the uncompromising imperial cult. The underground basilica found near the Porta Maggiore at Rome in 1917 was the building of a small Dionysiac association (first century BCE or earlier), rather than a domestic chapel.

Nock, A. D. 1972. "*Magistri* and *Collegia*." In *Essays on Religion and the Ancient World*, ed. Zeph Stewart, 409–13. Oxford: Clarendon. Originally published as "Review of Johnson, *Excavations at Minturnae* II I," *American Journal of Philology* 56 (1935): 86–91.

> Inscriptions from the foundations of a temple erected at Minturnae (first century CE) probably testify to a local cult group that delegated a variety of religious functions to four or more distinct boards. In spite of the high proportion of slave members (83 percent), the cults administered by *magistri* and *magistrae* at Minturnae have been naturalized and are ranked as Italian.

Oehler, Johann. 1893. "Genossenschaften in Kleinasien und Syrien: Ein Beitrag zur Geschichte des Gewerbfleisses in der römischen Kaiserzeit." *Eranos Vindobonensis* 2:276–82.

> O. lists and discusses various occupational associations, mostly in Asia Minor, with a few from Syria.

Oehler, Johann. 1905. "Zum griechischen Vereinswesen." In *Jahres-Bericht des k.k. Maximilians-Gynasiums in Wien*, 1–30. Vienna: Selbstverlag des Gymnasiums.

> O. lists Greek associations by geographic location, with notes highlighting the expansion of the associations over time, and provides a view of association life in individual cities.

Öhler, Markus. 2002. "Römisches Vereinsrecht und christliche Gemeinden." In *Zwischen den Reichen: Neues Testament und römische Herrschaft: Vorträge auf der ersten Konferenz der European Association for Biblical*

Studies, ed. M. Labahn and J. Zangenberg, 51–71. TANZ 36. Tübingen: Francke.

> Ö. surveys Roman laws concerning associations (second century BCE to second century CE) and argues that Christian groups were perceived as *collegia* by those around them. Being part of the Jewish movement, they initially had the same privileges as the Jewish communities, falling under the definition of *collegia antiqua* and thus permissible. This changed with increasing tensions between Jews and Christians, first under Nero and then again under Trajan.

Öhler, Markus. 2004. "Iobakchen und Christusverehrer: Das Christentum im Rahmen des antiken Vereinswesens." In *Inkulturation: Historische Beispiele und theologische Reflexionen zur Flexibilität und Widerständigkeit des Christlichen*, ed. Rupert Klieber and Martin Stowasser, 63–86. Theologie Forschung und Wissenschaft 10. Vienna: LIT.

> Despite key differences (e.g., monotheism), early Christian groups shared much in common with associations such as the Iobacchoi at Athens (*IG* II^2 1368; see 7) and the group at Philadelphia in Lydia (*SIG*^{3} 985; see 121). Christian groups were attractive because they offered unrestricted access, no membership fees, and more frequent meal celebrations.

Öhler, Markus. 2005a. "Antikes Vereinswesen." In *Neues Testament und antike Kultur, II: Familie, Gesellschaft, Wirtschaft*, ed. Kurt Scherberich, 79–86. Neukirchen-Vluyn: Neukirchener.

> Associations played a significant role in society during the Greco-Roman period in serving as social networks and ameliorating challenges of the members' lives, including negative effects of immigration, poverty, and slavery. Christian communities were also considered associations.

Öhler, Markus. 2005b. "Die Jerusalemer Urgemeinde im Spiegel des antiken Vereinswesens." *New Testament Studies* 51:393–415.

> The author of Acts presents the early Christian group in Jerusalem in terms of an association, including family-like relations (e.g., "brothers"), friendship, joint property from individual benefaction, meal celebrations, meetings in private accommodation, hierarchical structure, and egalitarian organization (at least in principle). The Christian group differs with respect to leadership by low rank individuals, a lack of importance for the external status of the group, and unrestricted membership access.

Olivecrona, Karl. 1954. "'Corpus' and 'collegium' in D. 3. 4. 1." *Rivista internazionale di diritto romano e antico* 5:181–90.

A discussion of *Digest* 3.4.1 (see **L43**) demonstrates that Gaius used only the word *collegium* in the passage and that the word *corpus* is an interpolation, as are many other words and expressions in the same text.

Oliver, James H. 1941. *The Sacred Gerusia.* Hesperia Supplement 6. Athens: American School of Classical Studies at Athens.

Originally the sacred *gerousia* (elders' council) was an association of respected Greek citizens in Ephesos, but in the early third century BCE (under Lysimachos) the *gerousia* was given control of the temple of Artemis and became entrenched in the administrative machinations of the *polis* (city). Later the city took control of the temple and returned the *gerousia* to its former private character. It was not until the time of Hadrian in the early second century that the Ephesian *gerousia* rose again to importance, and at the same time similar institutions were established across the empire (for which we have scattered evidence into the third century). Part 2 collects the epigraphic evidence.

Oliver, James H. 1958. "*Gerusiae* und *Augustales.*" *Historia* 7:472–96.

This continuation of Oliver (1941) argues that in Western towns the *Augustales* served the public cult while in Greek cities the elders' councils (*gerousiai*) took on these roles.

Parker, Robert. 1996. *Athenian Religion: A History.* Oxford: Clarendon.

Appendix 3 (328–42) provides a detailed analysis of known religious associations, while appendix 4 (333–37) surveys Attic private associations chronologically, beginning in the fifth century. In Attica, locals and foreigners alike formed associations, but groups with a mixture of citizens and noncitizens became more common as time progressed.

Patterson, John R. 1992. "Patronage, *Collegia* and Burial in Imperial Rome." In *Death in Towns: Urban Responses to the Dying and the Dead, 100–1600*, ed. Steven Bassett, 15–27. Leicester: Leicester University Press.

To avoid burial in unmarked graves, individuals who could not afford burial expenses either sought a patron or joined an association in imperial Rome.

Patterson, John R. 1994. "The *Collegia* and the Transformation of the Towns of Italy in the Second Century AD." In *L'Italie d'Auguste à Dioclétien,*

227–38. Collection de l'École française de Rome 198. Rome: École française de Rome.

> As benefaction by the elite in Italian towns declined in the second century CE, benefactions by the lower strata, including *collegia* (associations), increased. Associations adopted civic nomenclature for their officers and erected statues to emperors and benefactors on behalf of the populace, thus becoming part of the maintenance of civic identity.

Pearse, J. L. D. 1980. "Three *Alba* of the *Collegium Fabrum Tignariorum* of Rome." *Bullettino della Commissione Archeologica Comunale di Roma* 85:163–76.

> Two new epigraphic fragments are compared to *CIL* VI 33856 (154 CE), 33857, and 33858 (198–210 CE) and shown to be part of the missing lower half of 33857. This is a list of sixty *decuriones* and six scribes of a *collegium* (association). In subsequent lists from the same association, *decuriones* increased in seniority and graduated either toward promotion to *magistri quinquennales* (presidents) or death or retirement.

Perry, Jonathan Scott. 2001. "Ancient *Collegia*, Modern Blackshirts? The Study of Roman Corporations in Fascist Italy." *International Journal of the Classical Tradition* 8:205–16.

> P. analyzes the writings of de Robertis in the 1930s and 1940s, demonstrating that unlike most of his colleagues he was able to maintain a distance between his work on the *collegia* (associations) and the demands by the Fascist regime to find ancient support for their doctrines and practices.

Perry, Jonathan Scott. 2006. *The Roman* Collegia: *The Modern Evolution of an Ancient Concept.* Mnemosyne Supplements, History and Archaeology of Classical Antiquity 277. Leiden: E.J. Brill.

> P. undertakes a historiographical study of scholarship on the ancient Roman *collegia* (associations), including discussions of Mommsen's problematic category of "funerary associations" (*collegia funeraticia*; chap. 1), Waltzing's category of "professional associations" and its links to the Christian democratic movement (chap. 2), the connections between Fascism in Italy and the study of associations (chaps. 3–5), and the shift toward social history in post-WWII research (chap. 6).

Perry, Jonathan S. 2011. "Organized Societies: *Collegia*." In *The Oxford Handbook of Social Relations in the Roman World*, ed. Michael Peachin, 499–515. Oxford: Oxford University Press.

>   P. surveys trends in the study of Roman associations, identifying dominant themes and scholars of different periods: social aspects (Waltzing), pursuit of honor and status (MacMullen; Alföldy), internal relationships and connections with civic institutions (Royden; Liu), and social mobility through patrons (Patterson; van Nijf). P. proposes that the *collegia* were used as a tool of the elites to organize and control the urban population and were tolerated only insofar as they remained loyal to those with wealth and power.

Picard, Charles. 1920. "Fouilles de Délos (1910): Observations sur la société des Poseidoniastes de Bérytos et sur son histoire." *Bulletin de correspondance hellénique* 44:263–311.

>   P. outlines the function and organization of the association of Berytians devoted to Poseidon on the island of Delos (see **224–228**) with attention to its membership and leaders before turning to the nature of the cult itself. The group was probably active from around 110–109 to 69 BCE.

Picard, Charles. 1923. "Un rituel archaïque du culte de l'Héraklès thasien trouvé à Thasos." *Bulletin de correspondance hellénique* 47:241–74.

>   P. explores an early-fifth-century inscription attesting to a ritual carried out by an association devoted to the god Herakles on the island on Thasos (*SEG* 2 [1924], no. 505; see **261**).

Piccottini, Gernot. 1993. "Ein römisches Handwerkerkollegium aus Virunum." *Tyche* 8:111–23 and Tafel 10.

>   An inscription from Virunum (Austria) lists fifty-two members of a local *collegium subaedianorum* (association of builders). The first and third columns list names of male members, whereas the second and fourth show names of female members, probably the respective wives or sisters of the men. The erasure of five names suggests these members either left the association or were divorced from their partners.

Pickard-Cambridge, Arthur Wallace. 1968. *The Dramatic Festivals of Athens*. 2nd ed. edited by J. Gould and D. M. Lewis. Oxford: Clarendon.

>   "The Artists of Dionysus" (279–321) traces the history of the associations of dramatic and musical performers from the inception of various branches in the early third century BCE to their merging

with the athletic association in the third century CE. The associations played an important role in establishing and enlarging festivals, and their members were held in high regard as full citizens. An international organization of performers was established during the reign of Claudius (ca. 43 CE), with Athens as the center in the east and Rome in the west, although local guilds retained a subordinate existence.

Pilhofer, Peter. 2002. "Ein andres Volk ohne Tempel. Die θίασοι der Dionysos-Verehrer. In *Die frühen Christen und ihre Welt: Greifswalder Afusätze 1996–2001*, ed. Peter Pilhofer, 123–38. WUNT 145. Tübingen: Mohr Siebeck.

The association of "Asians" at Thessalonica (*IG* X 2/1 185) had a priest but no temple, in continuity with its forbearers in Italy. In Pergamon the meeting hall of a Dionysos association (**B6**) was not related to the Dionysos temple down the road. Much like Jewish and Christian groups, both these associations looked to a savior in the here and now (Dionysos) and had eschatological hopes for the future, symbolized in their sharing of wine and meat. Judeans and Christians stood in competition with Dionysiac associations without temples.

Pleket, H. W. 1969. "*Collegium Iuvenum Nemesiorum*: A Note on Ancient Youth Organisations," *Mnemosyne* 22 (4th ser.): 281–98.

Examination of a Latin inscription from Vintium suggests that the *collegium iuvenum* there was primarily a youth organization that worshipped Nemesis as the patroness of hunting.

Pleket, H. W. 1973. "Some Aspects of the History of the Athletic Guilds." *Zeitschrift für Papyrologie und Epigraphik* 10:197–227.

In the Roman imperial period there were three types of Hellenistic athletic associations: ecumenical athletes (athletes from around the world, based in Asia Minor), sacred victors (*hieronikai*), and retired athletes. These associations merged in the second century CE, and the international synod (*synodos*) moved its headquarters to Rome during Hadrian's reign.

Pleket, H. W. 2008. "Berufsvereine im kaiserzeitlichen Kleinasien: Geselligkeit oder Zünfte?" In *Antike Lebenswelten: Konstanz—Wandel—Wirkungsmacht. Festschrift für Ingomar Weiler zum 70. Geburtstag*, ed. Christoph Ulf, 533–44. Philippika. Marburger altertumskundliche Abhandlungen 25. Wiesbaden: Harrassowitz.

P. considers the status and function of occupational associations in western Asia Minor, particularly those affiliated with textile manufacturing and trade. These groups were a constitutive part of the political structure.

Poland, Franz. 1909. *Geschichte des griechischen Vereinswesens.* Leipzig: Teubner. Repr., Leipzig: Zentral-Antiquariat der Deutschen Demokratischen Republik, 1967.

This examination of Greek associations was the foundation for much subsequent scholarly work on the topic. Major sections cover topics including terminology, taxonomic distinctions, membership (including discussions of women, children, and slaves in associations), organization (e.g., officials, honors), and finances. The final chapter provides a historical overview of Greek associations from classical Athens until the Roman period. There is an extensive list of inscriptions and papyri referenced throughout.

Poland, Franz. 1926. "Griechische Sängervereinigungen im Altertum." In *700–Jahr-Feler der Kreuzschule zu Dresden: Festschrift zur Jubelfeier der Kreuzschule 1926*, 46–56. Dresden: Dr. Guntzsche Stiftung.

P. surveys the development of associations of hymn singers in Asia Minor using evidence not available for Poland (1909).

Préaux, Claire. 1948. "A propos des associations dans l'Egypte gréco-romaine." *Revue internationale des droits de l'antiquité* 1 (2nd series): 189–98.

Using three papyri texts from associations of salt merchants (43 CE; see **302**), P. argues that Greek associations, indigenous Egyptian associations, and Greek-speaking associations in Egypt likely influenced one another insofar as their regulations and contracts were concerned. None of the associations required regular dues or fees from their members, although members did financially contribute to ceremonies, funerals, and festivals.

Puig, Marie-Christine Villanueva. 1998. "Le cas du thiase dionysiaque." *Ktéma* 23:365–72.

P. discusses "public" and "private" societies (*thiasoi*) of Dionysos, including the role of cities in controlling some practices of associations and in bringing them into the public sphere, particularly through festivals.

Radin, Max. 1910. *Legislation of the Greeks and Romans on Corporations.* New York: Tuttle, Morehouse & Taylor.

R. studies the legal standing of associations from the earliest legislation through the Roman period. From the Twelve Tables through Augustus, only foreign cults and special *collegia* or groups fell under restrictive statutes. As associations began to flourish in the early imperial period, they were granted privileges in exchange for public service. Many fell under centralized control during the reign of Nerva (96–98 CE), until finally all the occupational associations became public bodies under Alexander Severus (222–235 CE).

Raubitschek, A. E. 1981. "A New Attic Club (*Eranos*)." *J. Paul Getty Museum Journal* 9:93–98.

R. translates and discusses an inscription involving the *eranos* (festal club) of the Herakliasts in the Marshes, from Liopesi in Attica (ca. 100 CE; *SEG* 31 [1981], no. 122; see **9** and cover photo). The inscription deals with proper behavior at meetings, punishment of infringements, protection of endowments through interest payments on loans, and membership dues, as well as the supply of food for banquets.

Rauh, Nicholas K. 1993. *The Sacred Bonds of Commerce: Religion, Economy, and Trade Society at Hellenistic Roman Delos.* Amsterdam: Gieben.

R. surveys the evidence for ethnic associations on the island of Delos, discussing Tyrians, Berytians, and Italians, including special attention to the Roman-Italian Hermaists, Apolloniasts, Poseidonists, and Compitaliasts (28–41; see also **223–39**). Even the Italian groups could have members who were Greeks. The associations at Delos, particularly the *eranos* associations, served a variety of functions for their members, including financial functions such as lending (251–70).

Rebillard, Éric. 1999. "Les formes de l'assistance funéraire dans l'Empire romain et leur évolution dans l'antiquité tardive." *Antiquité tardive* 7:269–82.

R. surveys developing options for the poor to obtain a decent burial in the Roman Empire. These options were provided by the city, patrons, and the *collegia* (associations). The practices of the latter were picked up by the church with the support of the emperor and individual donors.

Rebillard, Éric. 2009. *The Care of the Dead in Late Antiquity.* Trans. Elizabeth Trapnel Rawlings and Jeanine Toutier-Pucci. Cornell Studies in Classical Philology. Ithaca, N.Y.: Cornell University Press. Translation of *Religion et sépulture: L'Église, les vivants et les morts dans l'antiquité tardive*. Civilisations et sociétés 15. Paris: Éditions de l'École des hautes études en sciences sociales, 2003.

> "Voluntary Associations and Collective Burial: The Church, Christians, and the *Collegia*" (37–56) discounts the specific category "funerary association" (*collegia funeraticia*) but notes that funerary activities were an important function of associations and were a model for collective Christian burial practice. Christians did not, however, officially organize in order to acquire legal status in the empire for the purpose of administering their cemeteries. Some Christians also continued their membership in *collegia*.

Reicke, Bo. 1951. *Diakonie, Festfreude, und Zelos in Verbindung mit der Altchristlichen Agapenfeier*. Uppsala Universitets Årsskrift 1951, no. 5. Uppsala: Lundequist and Harrassowitz.

> An excursus (320–38) surveys disturbances in Hellenistic and Roman associations as a means to understand warnings in New Testament letters against violence and conflict within the communities.

Remus, Harold E. 1996. "Voluntary Association and Networks: Aelius Aristides at the Asclepieion in Pergamum." In *Voluntary Associations in the Graeco-Roman World*, ed. John S. Kloppenborg and Stephen G. Wilso, 146–75. London: Routledge.

> In the second century CE, social networks help to account for the persistence of the Aesclepius cult, and the relatively slow growth of Christianity in Pergamon as a result. Aelius Aristides (117–180 CE) is the "focal individual" or "point of anchorage" for seven types of groups: co-incubants, acquaintances, companions, friends, *therapeutai* (attendants), physicians, and priests.

Renan, Ernest. 1869. *The Apostles*. Origins of Christianity 2. New York: Clarendon and Trübner. Translation of *Les apôtres*. Histoire des origins du christianisme 2. Paris: Michel Levy, 1866.

> "Religious Legislation of the Period" (278–89) argues that associations (including Jewish and Christian groups) were non-elite societies for mutual assistance with membership and behavioral regulations, a treasury, and regular meetings in gardens or small buildings. The Roman enactment of legislation curtailing the activities of associations was grounded in distrust of the associations' emphasis on solidarity of the poor and on their religious observances.

Richardson, G. Peter. 1996. "Early Synagogues as *Collegia* in the Diaspora and Palestine." In *Voluntary Associations in the Graeco-Roman World*, ed. John S. Kloppenborg and Stephen G. Wilson, 90–109. London: Routledge. Reprinted with revisions and new material on Rome as "Pre-70 Synagogues as *Collegia* in Rome, the Diaspora, and Judea," in *Building Jewish in the Roman East*, ed. Peter Richardson, 111–33.Waco, Tex.: Baylor University Press, 2004.

> Early synagogues in Egypt and Greece were uncomplicated structures with an emphasis on a democratic communal experience, and they were considered buildings for ethnic associations. The development of synagogue buildings before 70 CE cohered with the existing social character and legal definition of *collegia* (their architectural model was the *collegium*).

Richardson, Peter. 2002. "Building a *Synodos* . . . and a Place of Their Own." In *Community Formation in the Early Church and in the Church Today*, ed. Richard N. Longenecker, 36–56. Peabody, Mass.: Hendrickson. Reprinted with slight revisions in *Building Jewish in the Roman East*, ed. Peter Richardson, 187–205. Waco, Tex.: Baylor University Press, 2004.

> R. surveys archaeological and inscriptional evidence for associations in Asia Minor, Delos, Italy, North Africa, and Syria-Palestine to argue that synagogues adopted patterns of behavior similar to associations and utilized similar architectural characteristics in their buildings, such as benches, banqueting facilities, worship areas, and courtyards.

Richardson, Peter. 2003. "An Architectural Case for Synagogues as Associations." In *The Ancient Synagogue from Its Origins until 200 C.E.: Papers Presented at an International Conference at Lund University October 14–17, 2001*, ed. Birger Olson and Magnus Zetterholm, 90–117. CBNT 39. Stockholm: Almqvist and Wiksell. Reprinted with slight revisions in *Building Jewish in the Roman East*, ed. Peter Richardson, 207–21. Waco, Tex.: Baylor University Press, 2004.

> A comparison of Diaspora synagogues and association buildings demonstrates that the former are modeled architecturally on the latter.

Richardson, G. Peter, and Valerie Heuchan. 1996. "Jewish Voluntary Associations in Egypt and the Roles of Women." In *Voluntary Associations in the Graeco-Roman World*, ed. John S. Kloppenborg and Stephen G. Wilson, 226–51. London: Routledge. Reprinted in *Building Jewish in the*

Roman East, ed. Peter Richardson, 165–85. Waco, Tex.: Baylor University Press, 2004.

> There is some evidence that Egyptian Jewish groups in Leontopolis and the therapeutists (*therapeutai*) of Alexandria were viewed by their neighbors and themselves as associations.

de Robertis, Francesco Maria. 1987. *Scritti varii di diritto romano (Articoli da riviste e miscellanee).* 3 vols. Bari: Cacucci.

> This is a collection of publications by de Robertis, dealing primarily with the legal standing and socioeconomic role of associations. The collection includes: *Il diritto associativo romano dai collegi della Repubblica alle corporazioni del Basso Impero* [The Roman Right to Associate by Societies in the Republic to Corporations in the Early Empire] (Bari: Laterza, 1938); *Il fenomeno associativo nel mondo romano, dai collegi della Repubblica alle corporazioni del Basso Impero* [The Associative Phenomenon in the Roman World: From the Societies of the Republic to the Corporations in the Early Empire] (Naples: Libreria scientifica editrice, 1955); and, *Storia delle corporazioni e del regime associativo nel mondo romano* [History of the Corporations and of the Associated Groups in the Roman World] (Bari: Adriatica, 1971).

Roberts, Colin, T. C. Skeat, and A. D. Nock. 1936. "The Guild of Zeus Hypsistos." *Harvard Theological Review* 29:39–88. English translation and commentary republished in *Essays on Religion in the Ancient World*, ed. Zeph Stewart, 414–43. Oxford: Clarendon, 1972.

> This article publishes and translates a partial regulation of an Egyptian association devoted to Zeus Hypsistos ("Highest") written between 69 and 58 BCE (*PLond* VII 2193 = inv. no. 2710; see **295**), suggesting a Macedonian origin for the god.

de Rossi, Giovanni Battista. 1864–1877. *La Roma sotteranea cristiana.* Rome: Cromo-litografia Pontificia.

> Based on archaeological work on the catacombs at Rome, de Rossi argues Christians modeled themselves on the associations with respect to burial customs. In so doing, they were tolerated by the government as "funerary associations," particularly since they were linked to elite households.

Roueché, Charlotte. 1993. *Performers and Partisans at Aphrodisias in the Roman and Late Roman Periods. A Study Based on Inscriptions from the Current Excavations at Aphrodisias in Caria.* Journal of Roman Studies Monographs 6. London: Society for the Promotion of Roman Studies.

"The Organization of Performers" (49–60) summarizes how and why performers (*technitai*) formed associations. The success of these associations led to imitation by others, such as athletes. From the time of Augustus the performers' guilds formed a "worldwide" network of locally based groups. Appendix III, "The Activities of the Synodos" (223–37), includes six Greek inscriptions with translation, notes, and commentary.

Roueché, Charlotte. 1995. "Aurarii in the Auditoria." *Zeitschrift für Papyrologie und Epigraphik* 105:37–50.

The Greek use of the Latin term *aurarius* found inscribed on seats in the theater and in the stadium in Aphrodisias and on seats in the theater in Miletos refers to associations of gold workers who have some official governmental role, likely linked to taxation on gold in the late empire (see **183**).

Royden, Halsey L. 1988. *The Magistrates of the Roman Professional Collegia in Italy from the First to the Third Century A.D.* Biblioteca di studi antichi 61. Pisa: Giardini.

R. compiles data concerning leadership positions in the occupational *collegia* (associations) in Italy, particularly Rome and Ostia (first to third centuries CE). This includes a discussion of social standing, occupations, and administrative connections of these magistrates, as well as the internal organization and operation of the guilds. Some *collegia* were organized as fire brigades (the largest number of *collegia*). The appendices contain 350 inscriptions with commentary.

Royden, Halsey. 1989. "The Tenure of Office of the Quinquennalis in the Roman Professional *Collegia*." *American Journal of Philology* 110:303–15.

The terms of reference for *quinquennalis* changed from "chief magistrate," who served for five years (7 BCE to 60 CE), to "president," who served for a shorter term (second century CE), likely three to four years. Two large membership lists (*alba*) of a *collegium* (association) at Ostia contain the names of the magistrates and verify that at this time it was more likely a three- or four-year term.

Runesson, Anders. 2001. *Origins of the Synagogue: A Socio-Historical Study.* Stockholm: Almquest & Wiksell.

Synagogues developed in two different ways, according to their location. In Palestine they developed in the form of Hellenistic associations, in which people gathered in any available building for reading, teaching, and discussion, much like public assemblies in villages, towns, and cities. As a result, synagogue locations are not distinguishable from other meeting places. In the Diaspora, synagogues were regarded by non-Judeans and some Judeans as associations and were generally subject to the same laws as other associations. The arrival of immigrants from Palestine in Diaspora synagogues introduced Torah reading into the liturgy.

Runesson, Anders. 2003. "The Origins of the Synagogue in Past and Present Research—Some Comments on Definitions, Theories, and Sources." *Studia Theologica—Nordic Journal of Theology* 58:60–76.

> R. surveys the history of scholarship on the origins of the synagogue and demonstrates that the older paradigm that placed the origins of the synagogue in the Babylonian exile is no longer the consensus view. Synagogues developed by following the model of the associations, first during a period of relative prosperity in Palestine, and subsequently in the Diaspora.

Rüpke, Jörg. 2002. "*Collegia Sacerdotum*: Religiöse Vereine in der Oberschicht." In *Religiöse Vereine in der römischen Antike: Untersuchungen zu Organisation, Ritual und Raumordnung*, ed. Ulrike Egelhaaf-Gaiser and Alfred Schäfer, 41–67. STAC 13. Tübingen: Mohr Siebeck.

> R. reconstructs the organizational structures, functions, and perceptions of the banquets of the public *collegia* of priests at Rome, giving particular attention to their timing and location. This elite group was united in their desire to demonstrate their position and authority to themselves and to outsiders.

Salamito, Jean-Marie. 1987. "Les dendrophores dans l'empire chrétien: À propos de *Code Théodosien*, XIV, 8, 1 et XVI, 10, 20, 2." *Mélanges de l'École Française de Rome. Antiquité* 99:991–1018.

> The *dendrophori* (wood bearers, or wood transporters) differed from their contemporaries in that they were simultaneously an occupational association and a religious brotherhood. Along with the *fabri* (builders) and *centonarii* (textile workers), the wood bearers probably also acted as municipal fire brigades.

Salamito, Jean-Marie. 1990. "Les collèges de *fabri, centonarii* et *dendrophori* dans les villes de la *Regio X* à l'époque impériale." In *La città nell'Italia settentrionale in età romana*, 163–77. Collection de l'École Française de Rome 130. Rome: Università di Trieste and École Française de Rome.

> The *collegium fabrum* united builders of all kinds. The *centonarii* (textile workers) manufactured *centones*, wool coverings that

were soaked in vinegar and draped over war machines to protect them from incendiary arrows. The *dendrophori* were wood bearers who were merchants of some sort. All three groups were enlisted as municipal firefighters and were involved in local festivals, banquets, and celebrations, ensuring their continued sanction by the community and government.

San Nicolò, Mariano. 1913–1915. *Ägyptisches Vereinswesen zur Zeit der Ptolemäer und Römer. I: Die Vereinsarten; II: Vereinswesen und Vereinsrecht.* Münchener Beiträge zur Papyrusforschung und antiken Rechtsgeschichte. Munich: C.H. Beck.

Although there were no nonpublic associations prior to the Hellenistic period, once they arrived they spread rapidly throughout Egyptian society. Part I provides a survey of various topics including the gods worshipped in associations (chap. 1), age-based groups (*ephēboi, neoi, gerousiai*) (chap. 2), associations of Dionysiac performers and athletes (chap. 3), and occupational associations (chap. 4). Part II examines the formation of associations, their legal standing, their membership base, their conditions of admission and dissolution (mostly imposed as sanctions by the government), and their internal organization and leadership structures.

San Nicolò, Mariano. 1927. "Zur Vereinsgerichtsbarkeit im hellenistischen Ägypten." In *ΕΠΙΤΥΜΒΙΟΝ Heinrich Swoboda dargstellt*, 255–99. Reichenberg: Stiepel.

Similar to Greek and Roman associations, groups in Egypt had penal and judicial power over their members, based on the statutes of each individual group. The statutes functioned like contracts between the association or executive and the members, and they were binding for all parties.

Schäfer, Alfred. 2002. "Raumnutzung und Raumwahrnehmung im Vereinslokal der Iobakchen von Athen." In *Religiöse Vereine in der römischen Antike: Untersuchungen zu Organisation, Ritual und Raumordnung*, ed. Ulrike Egelhaaf-Gaiser and Alfred Schäfer, 173–200. STAC 13. Tübingen: Mohr Siebeck.

The Baccheion at Athens (**B2**) is an example of the composition and usage of multifunctional space in an association building, as seen through an examination of *IG* II² 1368 (see **7**) and a comparison with a similar building complex in the city of Melos.

Schäfer, Alfred. 2007. "Dionysische Grupen als ein städtisches Phanomen der römischen Kaiserzeit." In *Gruppenreligionen im römischen Reich:*

Sozialformen, Grenzziehungen und Leistungen, ed. Jörg Rüpke, 161–80. STAC 43. Tübingen: Mohr Siebeck.

A brief examination of Dionysos associations in Asia Minor and the Danube region demonstrates the integration of religious associations into the city. Space for private gatherings can be seen in the building remains at Ephesos (**B5**) and Apulum.

Scheid, John. 1986. "Le thiase du Metropolitan Museum (IGUR I 160)." In *L'association dionysiaque dans les sociétés anciennes: Actes de la table ronde organisée par l'école française de Rome (Rome 24–25 mai 1984)*, ed. Olivier de Cazanove et al., 275–90. Collection de l'école française de Rome 89. Paris: E. de Boccard.

Onomastic examination of *IGUR* I 160 (see **330**) demonstrates that the more than four hundred members of the association come from a single senatorial family grouping.

Scheid, John. 1990. *Romulus et ses frères: Le collège des frères arvales: Modèle du culte public dans la Rome des empereurs*. BEFAR 275, 806. Paris: E. de Boccard.

Part 1 surveys the literary, epigraphic, and archaeological sources for studying the Arval brothers, an association of powerful aristocrats who were active from the time of Augustus to 304 CE. Part 2 gives attention to the structure of the public religion represented by the Arvals. Part 3 examines the rituals themselves, giving particular attention to the relationship between the rituals and the restoration of an earlier agrarian cult group by Augustus.

Scheid, John. 2003. "Communauté et communauté. Réflexions sur quelques ambiguïtés d'après l'exemple des thiases de l'Égypte romaine." In *Les communautés religieuses dans le monde Gréco-Romain: Essais de définition*, ed. Nicole Belayche and Simon C. Mimouni, 61–74. Bibliothèque de l'École des Hautes Études sciences religieuses 117. Turnhout: Brepols.

In antiquity, all associations were organized around cult, thus the term "religious association" is a tautology. Judeans and Christians took on the risky form of a *collegium* (association), potentially perceived by Roman authorities as disorderly and thus viewed with suspicion.

Scheid, John. 2011. "Graeco-Roman Cultic Societies." In *The Oxford Handbook of Social Relations in the Roman World*, ed. Michael Peachin, 535–66. Oxford: Oxford University Press.

S. demonstrates the difficulty of separating "religious activity" or "cult" from other aspects of Greco-Roman life. Religious activity was undertaken in a communal setting, and every social grouping, including all associations, invoked some aspect of cult, as demonstrated through examples.

Schinkel, Dirk. 2008. "Kanzler oder Schriftführer? Apg 19,23–40 und das Amt des γραμματεύς in griechisch-römischen Vereinigungen." In *Paulus und die antike Welt: Beiträge zur zeit- und religionsgeschichtlichen Erforschung des paulinischen Christentums*, ed. David C. Bienert, Joachim Jeska, and Thomas Witulski, 136–49. FRLANT 222. Göttingen: Vandenhoeck & Ruprecht.

Reference to a *grammateus* (secretary) in the account of the silversmiths riot in Acts 19:23-40 may refer to an office within an association of silversmiths (rather than a civic functionary).

Schmeller, Thomas. 1995. *Hierarchie und Egalität: Eine sozialgeschichtliche Untersuchung paulinischer Gemeinden und griechisch-römischer Vereine*. SBS 162. Stuttgart: Katholisches Bibelwerk.

S. engages in a study of associations and Pauline groups, surveying the history of research (chap. 1), arguing that the social structure of associations is characterized by a connection of hierarchic and egalitarian elements (chap. 2), and providing comparative analysis of associations and Pauline groups of Jesus followers (chap. 3). Notions of the equality of members were more prevalent within the Pauline groups.

Schmeller, Thomas. 2003. "Zum Vergleich zwischen paulinischen Gemeinden und nichtchristlichen Gruppen." *Biblical Zeitschrift* 47:167–85.

Early Christian groups were perceived by outsiders as associations and thought of themselves as associations, yet most scholars of early Christianity did not accept this connection when it was first proposed in the nineteenth century by scholars such as Hatch (1881) and Heinrici (1876; 1877; 1881).

Schmeller, Thomas. 2006. "Zum exegetischen Interesse an antiken Vereinen im 19. und 20. Jahrhundert." In *Vereine, Synagogen und Gemeinden im kaiserzeitlichen Kleinasien*, ed. Andreas Gutsfeld and Dietrich-Alex Koch, 1–19. STAC 25. Tübingen: Mohr Siebeck.

S. provides an overview of scholarly work on the relationship between early Christian groups and associations, beginning with the nineteenth century and focusing on exegetical, confessional, social, and cultural factors that affected how the question of the relationship was approached.

Schmitt-Pantel, Pauline. 1990. "Collective Activities and the Political in the Greek City." In *The Greek City from Homer to Alexander*, ed. Oswyn Murray and Simon Price, 119–213. Oxford: Clarendon.

> Four categories of groups participated in the expression of political, civil, and social community in archaic Greek cities: (1) civic groups, (2) cult associations, (3) age-based groups, and (4) companion groups.

Schulz-Falkenthal, Heinz. 1965. "Zur Frage der Entstehung der römischen Handwerkerkollegien." *Wissenschaftliche Zeitschrift der Martin-Luthers Universität. Gesellsachatliche und Sprachwissenschaftliche Reihe* 14:55–64.

> Associations of handworkers were founded in the middle of the third century BCE when slaves started doing the same work in lower quality mass production than (usually better) qualified tradesmen. Motivations for the development of *collegia opificum* (tradesmen) in and around Rome included occupational competition, collective public representation, and development of a shared sense of community.

Schulz-Falkenthal, Heinz. 1966. "Zur Lage der römischen Berufskollegien zu Beginn des 3.Jhs. u.Z. (die Privilegien der centonarii in Solva nach einem Reskript des Septimius Severus und Caracalla)." *Wissenschaftliche Zeitschrift der Martin-Luthers Universität. Gesellsachatliche und Sprachwissenschaftliche Reihe* 15:285–94.

> S.-F. undertake a Marxist analysis of the social and economic changes in the cities of the Roman Empire from the end of the second century CE, which were an important factor in the demise of the culture of slavery. The concession of rights to slaves in order to stem potential unrest, particularly access to *collegia* (associations) and obligatory exercise of civil services, strengthened their position. Serving as auxiliary fire brigades, the *collegia* of *fabri*, *centonarii*, and *dendrophori* (= *tria collegia principalia*) were among the first slave groups to enter into a sociopolitical relation with the state and the cities.

Schulz-Falkenthal, Heinz. 1970. "Zur Frage der organisatorischen Vorbilder für den korporativen Zusammenschluss in den *collegia opificium* u. ihre Verhältnis zu den mittelalterlichen Zünften." *Wissenschaftliche Zeitschrift der Martin-Luthers Universität. Gesellsachatliche und Sprachwissenschaftliche Reihe* 19:41–50.

Associations usually copied the structure of the community in which their members were living (*pagi, vici, municipia*). Although there is no continuous development from the Roman associations to the European guilds, both the *collegia opificum* (tradesmen) and the European guilds emerged in times of important social and economic debates and changes (slavery in ancient Rome, feudalism in medieval Europe). Both were organized democratically, reflecting the social process of the division of labor (and further specialization of individual work branches/trades).

Schulz-Falkenthal, Heinz. 1971. "Gegenseitigkeitshilfe und Unterstützungstätigkeit in den römischen Handwerkergenossenschaften." *Wissenschaftliche Zeitschrift der Martin-Luthers Universität. Gesellsachatliche und Sprachwissenschaftliche Reihe* 20:59–78.

> Members of *collegia opificum* (tradesmen) helped and supported one another even without official regulations, from general socializing to burial and from the exchange of work experience to granting loans to members in need.

Schulz-Falkenthal, Heinz. 1972. "Zur politischen Aktivität der römischen Handwerkerkollegien." *Wissenschaftliche Zeitschrift der Martin-Luthers Universität. Gesellsachatliche und Sprachwissenschaftliche Reihe* 21:79–99.

> The difficult living conditions of tradesmen served as a potential source of social unrest and political action. However, there is no evidence that associations were dissolved because of political activities. The government gained more control over the associations by granting them privileges in exchange for loyal service.

Schulz-Falkenthal, Heinz. 1973. "Römische Handwerkerkollegien im Dienst der städtischen Gemeinschaft und ihre Begünstigung durch staatliche Privilegien." *Wissenschaftliche Zeitschrift der Martin-Luthers Universität. Gesellsachatliche und Sprachwissenschaftliche Reihe* 22:21–35.

> Members of Roman *collegia opificum* (tradesmen) were granted privileges by Rome in exchange for their services to the community, such as their work as firefighters. In order to avoid the abuse of these rights by individual members and to prevent associations from becoming too powerful within the state, the concession of privileges was accompanied by increasing control of the associations by the state.

Schwarzer, Holger. 2002. "Vereinslokale im Hellenistischen und römischen Pergamon." In *Religiöse Vereine in der römischen Antike: Untersuchungen zu Organisation, Ritual und Raumordnung*, ed. Ulrike Egelhaaf-Gaiser and Alfred Schäfer, 221–60. STAC 13. Tübingen: Mohr Siebeck.

> S. describes association buildings at Pergamon that were unattached to a public sanctuary, including the niche building on Theater Street used by the Attalists (devotees of Attalid royalty), the "Hall of Benches" (Podiensaal; see **B6**) used by the Dionysiac cowherds, and the banqueting benches in the Asklepios sanctuary used by an association devoted to Asklepios. The so-called *Mithräum im Felsheiligtum von Kapikaya* was dedicated to Cybele and likewise had benches for banqueting.

Schwarzer, Holger. 2008. *Das Gebäude mit dem Podiensaal in der Stadtgrabung von Pergamon: Studien zu sakralen Bankettträumen mit Liegepodien in der Antike.* Altertümer von Pergamon XV 4. Berlin: Deutsches archäologisches Institut.

> This is a detailed archaeological analysis of the remains of the "Hall of Benches" (Podiensaal) at Pergamon (see **B6**), which at one point served as the meeting place of a group of Dionysiac cowherds (*boukoloi*). S. documents phases in the history of the building and its area from about 150 BCE to the middle of the fourth century CE, placing his findings within the context of the history of Pergamon and the cult of Dionysos.

Seesengood, Robert P. 2002. "Rules for an Ancient Philadelphian Religious Organization and Early Christian Ethical Teaching." *Stone Campbell Journal* 5:217–33.

> The standards of morality and ethical behavior found among New Testament documents are not unique, as can be seen by examining the statutes of an association in Philadelphia, Asia Minor (*SIG*[3] 985, I BCE; see **121**).

Segal, Alan F. 2002. "The Jewish Experience: Temple, Synagogue, Home, and Fraternal Groups." In *Community Formation in the Early Church and in the Church Today*, ed. Richard N. Longenecker, 20–35. Peabody, Mass.: Hendrickson.

> Although their origins are unclear, synagogues existed at least from the first century as places for assembly, study, and prayer. There were neighborhood, occupational, rabbinic (*hābûrōt*), and burial (*hevra kadisha*) associations.

Seland, Torrey. 1996. "Philo and the Clubs and Associations of Alexandria." In *Voluntary Associations in the Graeco-Roman World*, ed. John S. Kloppenborg and Stephen G. Wilson, 110–27. London: Routledge.

Philo of Alexandria demonstrates an awareness about Greco-Roman associations in contrasting the self-restraint of the Jewish *therapeutai* (therapeutists) to the supposed excesses of the Greco-Roman banquets and association gatherings (see **L8–L10**). Philo alludes to—and does not totally reject the practice of—payments to associations, so long as the pursuit of a virtuous life is entailed. This would entail Jewish participation in the associations of others.

Sheppard, A. R. R. 1980–1981. "Pagan Cults of Angels in Roman Asia Minor." *Talanta* 12–13:77–101.

S. publishes an inscription from near Kotiaion (*SEG* 31 [1981], no. 1130) involving a vow to holiness and justice by an "association of friends of the angels," which suggests a group of non-Christians or non-Judeans who devoted themselves in some way to angels. (Sheppard's reading, especially the reference to angels, has since been challenged; see Malay [2005].)

Sifakis, Gregory M. 1965. "Organization of Festivals and the Dionysiac Guilds." *Classical Quarterly* 15:206–14.

S. demonstrates that the three musical and dramatic festivals linked to Dionysos—the Athenian, the Isthmian and Nemean, and the Ionian and Hellespontian—were open to participation by performers from all associations and not limited to those from particular locales.

Sirks, A. J. Boudewijn. 2006. "Die vereine in der kaiserlichen Gesetzgebung." In *Vereine, Synagogen und Gemeinden im kaiserzeitlichen Kleinasien*, ed. Andreas Gutsfeld and Dietrich-Alex Koch, 21–40. STAC 25. Tübingen: Mohr Siebeck.

S. examines Roman legislation concerning associations from the late Republic through to the Codex of Justinian, including a discussion of the rationale for forming associations and the frequency with which meetings were tolerated under the law.

Slater, William J. 2000. "Handouts at Dinner." *Phoenix* 54:107–22.

In writing against lawyers (*Ep.* 2.14.4), Pliny the Younger refers to spaces where associations met for meals and members received distributions of *sportulae* ("handouts"). Although some associations had their own buildings, often their dining spaces were open to public viewing.

Smith, Dennis E. 2003. *From Symposium to Eucharist: The Banquet in the Early Christian World*. Minneapolis: Fortress.

"The Club Banquet" (87–131) surveys the meal practices of classical Greek associations, Roman associations, and Greek associations in the Roman period. Whatever the purported reason for the formation of an association, banqueting was often the central activity.

Sokolowski, Franciszek. 1954. "Fees and Taxes in the Greek Cults." *Harvard Theological Review* 47:151–64.

Although not substantial, fees and taxes played an important role in the continuation of association activities when funds from benefaction, endowments, or subsidies were lacking.

Sommer, Stefan. 2006a. "Religion und Vereinigungsunruhen in der Kaiserzeit." In *Vereine, Synagogen und Gemeinden im kaiserzeitlichen Kleinasien*, ed. Andreas Gutsfeld and Dietrich-Alex Koch, 77–93. STAC 25. Tübingen: Mohr Siebeck.

While religion did not play a role in associations' involvement in civic unrest, it did so in the case of Christian groups, where unrest was linked to an emphasis on exclusivity.

Sommer, Stefan. 2006b. *Rom und die Vereinigungen im südwestlichen Kleinasien (133 v. Chr.–284 n. Chr.)*. Pietas 1. Hennef: Buchverlag Marthe Clauss.

S. explores questions about the position of associations in southwestern Asia Minor and the relationship among Roman authorities, civic authorities, and these groups. Roman imperial interference in the lives of associations was limited, and associations of various kinds were integrated within society in Asia Minor. Associations engaged in both external (civic) and internal rituals for the gods.

Sommer, Stefan. 2008. "Vereinigungen in Tarsos." In *A Roman Miscellany: Essays in Honour of Anthony R. Birley on His Seventieth Birthday*, ed. Hans Michael Schellenberg, Vera Elisabeth Hirschmann and Andreas Krieckhaus, 131–48. Akanthina 3. Gdánsk: Foundation for the Development of Gdánsk University.

Associations played a role in political disturbances at Tarsus, as first witnessed in Dio Chrysostom's oration on the exclusion of linen workers (34.15–25, ca. 113 CE; see **L11**).

Sosin, Joshua D. 1999. "Tyrian *stationarii* at Puteoli." *Tyche* 14:275–84.

S. republishes an inscription involving the Tyrian merchants' request for Tyre's assistance in paying rent at Puteoli in Italy, providing an English translation and commentary (*IG* XIV 830; 174 CE; see **317**). S. interprets the fragmentary minutes of the Tyrian civic body (the latter part of the inscription) in terms of an attempted takeover of the Tyrian group at Puteoli by the Tyrians settled at Rome.

Steimle, Christopher. 2006. "Das Heiligtum der ägyptischen Götter in Thessaloniki und die Vereine in seinem Umfeld." In *Religions orientales—culti misterici: Neue Perspektiven—nouvelles perspectives—prospettive nuove*, ed. Corinne Bonnet, Jörg Rüpke, and Paolo Scarpi, 27–38. PAwB 16. Stuttgart: Franz Steiner.

Associations in the sanctuary of the Egyptian gods at Thessalonica (as attested in inscriptions from the third century BCE to the second century CE) were generally coherent social groupings, mostly from the upper social strata of Romans.

Steimle, Christopher. 2008. *Religion im römischen Thessaloniki: Sakraltopographie, Kult und Gesellschaft 168 v. Chr.—324 n. Chr.* STAC 47. Tübingen: Mohr Siebeck.

The latter part of chapter 3 (168–200) examines the activities of associations at Thessalonica, with particular attention to youth groups (*neoi*), Roman merchants, Dionysiac groups, groups devoted to Egyptian gods, and occupational associations.

Steuernagel, Dirk. 1999. "Corporate Identity: Über Vereins-, Stadt- und Staatskulte im kaiserzeitlichen Puteoli." *Mitteilungen des deutschen archäologischen Instituts (Römische Abteilung)* 106:149–87.

S. surveys the religious history of Puteoli (a port city of Rome) during the imperial period, with attention to the associations, eastern religions, and the patron deities of the city. In the first century, a small group of elites were involved in building cultic structures, while associations and eastern religions remained marginal. By the second century, however, the associations increased in number and became more influential in civic life, as evidenced in their building projects.

Stowers, Stanley K. 1998. "A Cult from Philadelphia: Oikos Religion or Cultic Association?" In *The Early Church in Its Context: Essays in Honor of Everett Ferguson*, ed. Abraham J. Malherbe, Frederick W. Norris, and James W. Thompson, 287–301. NovTSup 99. Leiden: E.J. Brill.

The group at Philadelphia in Lydia (*SIG*³ 985 see **131**) is a private household cult, rather than a public association. Dionysios is the *kyrios* (master) of his household, and the regulations safeguard the lineage of his children and the breeding of slaves. There is no model of salvation and no egalitarianism reflected in the text.

Tatum, W. Jeffery. 1990. "Cicero's Opposition to the *Lex Clodia de collegiis*." *Classical Quarterly* 40:187–94.

Cicero and Ninnius, motivated by self-protection, limited their opposition to Clodius' law concerning associations at Rome (*Lex de collegiis*; cf. **L26, L28, L29, L31**). Cicero likely failed to stop Clodius' law because of a compromise negotiated by Clodius through the *optimates* (the circle of Cato and Hortensius), whose esteem Cicero honored and whose company he craved.

Taubenschlag, Rafael. 1959. "The Laws of Association in Greco-Roman Egypt." In *Opera Minora*, vol. 2, 521–26. Warsaw: Panstwowe Wydawnictivo Naukowe.

The ordinances of Athenian, Ptolemaic, and Roman associations show that they held contracts entered into voluntarily by their members.

Taussig, Hal. 2009. *In the Beginning Was the Meal: Social Experimentation and Early Christian Identity*. Minneapolis: Fortress.

T. summarizes recent scholarship on associations and meals to demonstrate that Christian meals would be similar to association meals insofar as they included members from a wide socioeconomic range, including the poor (88–102). Roman authorities were rightly suspicious of associations and their meals as loci for resistance. In replicating many of the association meal practices, Christian groups expressed in their commensality a process of "socializing resistance" to imperial rule (118–43).

Teixidor, Javier. 1981. "Le thiase de Belastor et de Béelshamen d'après une inscription récemment découverte à Palmyre." *Comptes rendus de l'Académie des Inscriptions et Belles Lettres* 34:306–14.

A multilingual (Palmyran and Syriac) funerary inscription from Palmyra, by the priests of the god Belastor, records the regulations of a society (*thiasos*) and attests to a god named Beelshamen (Baal Shamin; first century CE). The inscription underlines the importance of the banquet room as the locale in which the society members (*thiasōtai*) worshipped, voted, and passed judgment.

Tod, Marcus N. 1906–1907. "A Statute of an Attic *Thiasos*." *Annual of the British School at Athens* 13:328–38.

This is the first publication of *IG* II² 1275 (325–275 BCE; see **13**) concerning the obligations of members of a society (*thiasos*). T. includes a lengthy line-by-line discussion of the text.

Tod, Marcus N. 1932. "Clubs and Societies in the Greek World." In *Side-lights on Greek History: Three Lectures on the Light Thrown by Greek Inscriptions on the Life and Thought of the Ancient World*, 71–96. Oxford: Blackwell.

> T. surveys associations from fourth century BCE to the Byzantine period. The Greeks turned to associations for religious fellowship as a result of the decline of the *polis* (city-state) in the wake of Alexander the Great. The associations developed from cult *orgeōnes* (sacrificing associates) in the fourth century BCE to the social *thiasoi* (societies), socioeconomic *eranistai* (festal clubs), and secular *synodai* (synods) of imperial times. The inscription of the Iobacchoi at Athens (see 7) is translated into English and discussed.

Tod, Marcus N. 1934. "Greek Inscriptions at Cairness House." *Journal of Hellenic Studies* 54:140–62.

> This is the first publication (including an English translation) of *IDelos* 1520 (153/52 BCE; see **224**) involving the Berytians' honors for a Roman banker.

Tran, N. 2001. "Le collège la communauté et le politique sous le Haut-Empire romain. Historiographie du droit à la fin du XIXe siècle, 'tradition sociologique' et quelques recherches contemporaines." *Cahiers du Centre Gustave Glotz* 12:181–98.

> T. examines the scholarly interest in Roman *collegia* (associations) of the late empire that developed in conjunction with the 1884 French law on trade unions.

Tran, N. 2006. *Les membres des associations romaines. Le rang social des collegiate en Italie et en Gaules, sous le Haut-Empire*. Rome: École française de Rome.

> Part 1 argues that the heterogeneity (slaves, freed, free, and a few elite) of the associations in Italy and the West allowed for social integration and acquisition of social prestige. Part 2 examines the complex and ambiguous legal standing of the associations, which led to equally complex engagement with authorities. Part 3 argues that the social networks of members cannot be isolated from numerous other networks, such as neighborhoods, ethnic groups, friends, and families.

Trebilco, Paul R. 1999. "Jews, Christians and the Associations in Ephesos: A Comparative Study of Group Structures." In *100 Jahre österreichische Forschungen in Ephesos. Akten des Symposions Wien 1995*, ed. Barbara Brandt and Karl R. Krierer, 325–34. Österreichischen Akademie der

Wissenschaften. Philosophisch-historische Klasse Denkschriften 260. Vienna: Österreichischen Akademie der Wissenschaften.

> The organizational structures of Christian churches in Ephesos are compared both to the Jewish group, which had a citywide structure, and the associations, which followed two models, one independent and the other citywide. T. rejects theories of a single, merged Christian community in Ephesos and suggests that four or five distinct Christian groups likely existed.

Ustinova, Julia. 1991. "The *Thiasoi* of Theos Hypsistos in Tanais." *History of Religions* 31:150–80.

> U. rejects two rival theories concerning associations (*thiasoi*) of Theos Hypsistos ("Highest God") in Tanais: that Theos Hypsistos of the Bosporan inscriptions is the Judean God and that the Thracians influenced the cult. Instead, the associations were engaged in a traditional Iranian cult centered on a solar god, Pharsiris.

Ustinova, Julia. 1999. *The Supreme Gods of the Bosporan Kingdom: Celestial Aphrodite and the Most High God.* RGRW 135. Leiden: E.J. Brill.

> U. further develops her argument in Ustinova (1991) regarding the Iranian or Sarmatian background of associations in the Bosporan Kingdom, particularly associations devoted to Aphrodite Ourania ("of the Heavens") and Theos Hypsistos ("Highest God"). She surveys the membership, organization, and activities of societies of Theos Hypsistos in the city of Tanais, and argues that there is no evidence for a Judean connection as proposed by some scholars, such as Levinskaya 1996 (177–284).

Venticinque, Philip F. 2010. "Family Affairs: Guild Regulations and Family Relationships in Roman Egypt." *Greek, Roman, and Byzantine Studies* 50:273–94.

> The claim that people joined associations to compensate for deficiencies in their economic, social, or family life cannot be sustained in the face of evidence, particularly from Egypt, that demonstrates that many association members had ties to social and political elites in their communities. Ethical regulations of associations created and maintained bonds among members, many of whom were related to one another.

Verboven, Koenraad. 2007. "The Associative Order: Status and Ethos among Roman Businessmen in Late Republic and Early Empire." *Athenaeum: Studi periodici di letteratura e storia dell'antichità* 97:1–33.

Status enhancement among the lower classes (*humiliores*) was institutionalized through the associations, allowing successful businessmen the means to transform their economic capital into social, symbolic capital. The associations themselves were hierarchically ranked. The most prestigious were the *collegia* of the *seviri Augustales*, followed by the provincial or interprovincial associations (merchants in wine, olive oil, corn; land-routes controllers). Next on the social scale were the local associations of the *tria collegia* (*fabri, centonarii*, and *dendrophori*), and finally the smaller local associations such as mule drivers, stonecutters, fishermen, goldsmiths, and other laborers.

Verboven, Koenraad. 2009. "Magistrates, Patrons and Benefactors of Collegia: Status Building and Romanisation in the Spanish, Gallic and German Provinces." In *Transforming Historical Landscapes in the Ancient Empires. Proceedings of the First Workshop Area of Research in Studies from Antiquity, Barcelona 2007*, ed. I. B. Antela Bernárdez and T. Ñaco del Hoyo, 159–67. British Archaeological Reports, International Series 1986. Oxford: John and Erica Hedges.

Associations in the Gallic and German provinces contributed toward the integration of local elites and businessmen into the "New Roman Order" and were therefore a part of the process of Romanization. This was not the case in Spain, where associations are less evident.

Vesley, M. 1998. "Gladiatorial Training for Girls in the *Collegia Iuvenum* of the Roman Empire." *Échos du monde classique/Classical Views* 42:85–93.

V. examines three post-Augustan Latin inscriptions that suggest the *collegia iuvenum* (youth associations) included young females alongside the elite young males who were undergoing athletic and combat training.

Voutiras, Emmanuel. 1992. "Berufs- und Kultverein: Ein ΔΟΥΜΟΣ in Thessalonike." *Zeitschrift für Papyrologie und Epigraphik* 90:87–96.

An epitaph from Thessalonica (see **49**) is our earliest evidence for the use of the term *doumos* (common in Asia Minor) for an association in Greece.

Waltzing, Jean Pierre. 1892. *L'épigraphie Latine et les corporations professionnelles de l'empire Romain*. Ghent: A. Siffer.

W. justifies his new project in Latin epigraphy at the Université de Liège, particularly in connection with its relevance to modern unionization as a means to addressing social problems.

Waltzing, Jean Pierre. 1895. "Les corporations de l'ancienne Rome et charité." In *Compte rendu de troisième congrès scientifique international des Catholiques*, 165–90. Brussels: Société Belge de Librairie. Translated into English as "The Roman Guilds and Charity." *Charities Review* 4 (1895): 345–62.

While Roman occupational associations assured members of a decent funeral (as "funerary associations"), they did not provide social aid to their members who suffered economic hardship in this life; that is, they were not charitable organizations like the Christian churches.

Waltzing, Jean Pierre. 1895–1900. *Étude historique sur les corporations professionnelles chez les romains depuis les origines jusqu'à la chute de l'empire d'occident*. Mémoire couronne par l'Academie Royale des Sciences, des Lettres et des Beaux-Arts de Belgique. Louvain: Uitgeverij Peeters. Repr., Hildesheim: Georg Olms, 1970.

This four-volume work provides the earliest comprehensive picture of the legal history, organization, duties, and influence of the occupational associations (*collegia*) in the Roman world. The first part focuses on the legal position of *collegia*, as well as their structures and influence. The second part places guilds within the context of W.'s threefold typology: (1) occupational associations, (2) funerary associations, and (3) cultic associations. All three of these based their organization on the model of the city in some way, as leaders were elected and decisions were made democratically. Part 3 collects almost 2,500 Greek and Latin inscriptions with brief commentary, arranged geographically. Part 4 is a comprehensive index.

Waltzing, Jean Pierre. 1898. "Les collèges funéraires chez les romains." *Le musée Belge revue de philologie classique* 2:281–94 and 3:130–57.

W. lists 332 inscriptions that attest to his category of "funerary associations," providing data as to their origin, nature, purpose, internal organization, and influence on the life of the lower classes.

Waltzing, Jean Pierre. 1901. "Recueil des inscriptions grecques et latines relatives aux corporations romains. Ier supplément." *Le Musée Belge revue de philologie classique* 5:62–64, 127–35.

W. collects additional inscriptions to supplement Waltzing (1895–1900, vol. 3).

Weber, Volker. 1993. "Zu den Verhältnissen in Handwerk und Handel. III.1. Zum Kollegienwesen: Die Berufsvereine in Handwerk und Handel." In *Gesellschaft und Wirtschaft des römischen Reiches im 3. Jahrhundert: Studien zu ausgewählten Problemen von Gerda von Bülow, Hagen Fischer, Klaus-Peter Johne, Detlef Rößler und Volker Weber,* ed. Klaus-Peter Johne, 101–34. Berlin: Akademie Verlag.

At a time of decentralization of administrative organization in the republican and imperial periods, occupational associations made it easier for authorities to be in contact with members and to collect taxes. In the second and third centuries CE, the state became increasingly controlling, culminating with some occupational associations assuming obligatory state functions in the fourth century.

Weinfeld, Moshe. 1986. *The Organizational Pattern and the Penal Code of the Qumran Sect: A Comparison with Guilds and Religious Associations of the Hellenistic Period.* NovT et orbis antiquus 2. Göttingen: Vandenhoeck & Ruprecht.

The organizational pattern and penal code of the Qumran sect are largely congruent with those of the Greco-Roman associations. Similarities include the existence of membership requirements, designated officials, regulations, mutual aid, and private court structure. The Qumran group differed in its sacrificial rituals, burial customs, membership dues, pecuniary fines, religious-moralistic rhetoric, and apocalyptic vision of the future. Despite the similarities, no genealogical relationship existed between the Qumran group and the associations.

Weinreich, Otto. 1919. *Stiftung und Kultsatzungen eines Privatheiligtums in Philadelphia in Lydien.* Sitzungsberichte der Heidelberger Akademie der Wissenschaften, Philosophisch-Historische Klasse, Jahrg. 1919, Bericht 16 . Heidelberg: C. Winter.

W. publishes and discusses the regulation of an association in Philadelphia, Asia Minor, based on a close reading of *SIG*³ 985 (I BCE; see **131**).

Westermann, W. L. 1932. "Entertainment in the Villages of Graeco-Roman Egypt." *Journal of Egyptian Archaeology* 18:16–27.

After assembling evidence of village clubs and social parties in Egypt from the third century BCE to the sixth century CE, W.

concludes that dancing and musical entertainment were common to religious festivals, village associations, and private parties. The Greeks influenced the organization of these Egyptian associations. During Roman times, associations required official endorsement, but officials probably "closed their eyes" to the many small illegal innocuous associations.

Wilken, Robert L. 1971. "Collegia, Philosophical Schools, and Theology." In *The Catacombs and the Colosseum: The Roman Empire as the Setting of Primitive Christianity*, ed. Stephen Benko and John J. O'Rourke, 268–91. Valley Forge, Pa.: Judson.

W. describes how outsiders would have perceived Christianity in the first three centuries, emphasizing the model of the philosophical school and touching on the associations.

Wilken, Robert L. 1984. *The Christians as the Romans Saw Them*. New Haven: Yale University Press.

"Christianity as a Burial Society" (31–47) argues that by the early second century the Christian church was described as an association by outsiders (such as Pliny and Celsus) and by insiders (such as Tertullian).

Williams, Margaret. 1998. "The Structure of the Jewish Community in Rome." In *Jews in a Graeco-Roman World*, ed. Martin Goodman, 215–28. Oxford: Oxford University Press.

The Jewish communities at Rome were not viewed as *collegia* (associations) since superficial similarities are outweighed by the differences. The overall thrust is to emphasize the Jewish rather than Roman character of the Judeans at Rome.

Wilson, Stephen G. 1996. "Voluntary Associations: An Overview." In *Voluntary Associations in the Graeco-Roman World*, ed. John S. Kloppenborg and Stephen G. Wilson, 1–15. London: Routledge.

W. introduces associations and touches on key scholarly issues regarding social location, hierarchy, egalitarianism, women's participation, and the benefits of membership.

Wilson, Thomas. 1927. *St. Paul and Paganism*. Edinburgh: T&T Clark.

"St. Paul and the Pagan Guilds" (120–35) argues that Paul's churches would structure themselves as associations since many of the adherents were Gentiles rather than Judeans.

Wittenburg, Andreas. 1998. "Grandes familles et associations cultuelles à l'époque hellénistique." *Ktèma* 33:451–55.

W. suggests that the third and second centuries BCE witnessed an increase in aristocratic families' endowments to associations for the maintenance of the elite's funerary cults in Greek city-states.

Wischniter, Mark. 1950. "Notes to a History of Jewish Guilds." *Hebrew Union College Annual* 33:245–63.

W. traces the history of Jewish occupational associations, including those from the time of the Babylonian empire through the Byzantine period. In Roman Egypt, Judeans sometimes joined non-Jewish associations, but more often they had their own occupational associations, which were patterned on non-Jewish associations.

Youtie, Herbert Chayyim. 1948. "The *Kline* of Sarapis." *Harvard Theological Review* 41:9–29.

The "dining association" (*klinē*, lit. "couch") of Sarapis offered opportunities for socializing, dancing, worship, and commemorations such as marriage or coming of age. A new third-century CE papyrus text reveals that grades of initiation were part of the Sarapis cult.

Ziebarth, Erich Gustav Ludwig. 1896. *Das griechisches Vereinswesen*. Stuttgart: S. Hirzel. Repr., Wiesbaden: Martin Sändig oHG, 1969.

Z. provides a comprehensive study of Greek associations, dealing with household-based associations, associations centered on economics (private associations, lending societies, trade guilds), and associations formed for a specific purpose. In this latter category he devotes a chapter each to associations formed around cults, academics, politics, occupations, physical education, social pursuits, Roman-influenced groups, and Judean and Christian groups. The third section examines the organization of the associations, including terminology, entrance requirements, membership, constitution, administration, officials, finances, activities, and formulaic language. A final section surveys the purposes and activities of the associations.

Ziebarth, Erich Gustav Ludwig. 1900. "Zu den griechischen Vereinsschriften." *Rheinisches Museum für Philologie* 55:501–19.

This addendum to Ziebarth (1896) is organized by geographic regions from Greece around to Egypt and includes a number of new inscriptions and additions and corrections to texts published in the earlier volume, including two texts from associations from artists.

Ziebarth, Erich Gustav Ludwig. 1923. "Fünfundzwanzig Jahre griechischer Inschriftenforschung (1894–1919)." *Jahresbericht über die Fortschritte der klassischen Altertumswissenschaft* 193:60–78.

> Z. lists and briefly describes publications from 1894 to 1919 that discuss inscriptions and other documents regarding associations on Delos.

Zimmermann, Carola. 2002. *Handwerkervereine im griechischen Osten des Imperium Romanum.* RGZM 57. Mainz: Rudolf Habelt.

> Z. surveys occupational associations of artisans in the Greek east during the Roman imperial period with chapters on formal characteristics (legal standing and terminology), internal organization, membership, buildings, and occupations (textiles, pottery, stonemasonry, milling, baking). The final chapter considers the legal standing of the associations and their interactions with Roman authorities. Although there was some interference by the state in the affairs of the occupational associations, for the most part they remained relatively free and independent.

CONCORDANCE AND INDICES

Inscriptions and Papyri Cited

496	203	49 1827	149
503	176	50 876	240
823	307	51 2016	267
18 280	68	53 726	78
518	187	54 1628	277
555	103	55 937bis	245
26 826	66	1654	276
891	259	1655	278
1272	168	1660	275
1299	198	*SIRIS*	
28 603	76	5	4
953	107	109	47
1585	98	295	205
29 1205	126	301	169
30 1339	177	305	185
31 122	9	318	109
807	241	*SIG²*	
32 488	31	773	34
809	222b	*SIG³*	
810	222a	866	220
1203	194	985	121
34 1191	192	1098	14
35 714	36	1103	2
1327	93	1115	115
36 228	3	1140	34
1051	181	1263	186
1114	102		
1207	208	*TAM*	
39 649	61	V.2 924	128
41 1201	147	932	143
1202	148	935	136
42 157	4	955	142
625	49	959	135
43 510	89	966	138
898	101	972	129
44 556	59	978	132
1354	268	984	137
46 800	45	989	133
1519	123	995	140
1524	124	1002	131
1528	125	1019	141
1656	152	1055	139
47 1089	67	1098	130
48 716ter	33	1142	134
751	35	1148	144
1844	266		

LITERARY TEXTS CITED

INDEX OF SUBJECTS AND LOCALES

(Nb: all numbers refer to entry numbers not page numbers.)

linen workers/linen weavers, 172e,
181, 207, 210
merchants/traders, 5, 10, 32, 108, 143,
223, 224, 226, 227, 228, 234, 236,
239, 302, 317; B8, B16, B21, B26;
L46, Boak 1937a, Hatzfeld 1919; *see
also* shippers; oil merchants; salt
merchants; wine merchants
millers, 335
nail workers, 158
oil merchants, 234; Kneissl 1981
performers/artists of Dionysos,
178, 180, 184, 193, 212, 251, 266,
297, 298; Geagan 1972, Jaccottet
2003, Jory 1970, Le Guen 2001,
Le Guen 2004, Le Guen 2007b,
Pickard-Cambridge 1968, Pleket
1973, Roueché 1993, San Nicolò
1913–1915, Sifakis 1965, Ziebarth
1900, Ziebarth 1923
physicians, 165, 174, 174, 242, 284;
Remus 1996
porters/sack bearers, 111, 173 (?),
197, 199, 211
potters, L22, L30
purple dyers, 44, 55, 152, 155, 157,
158, 209
rag dealers, 309, 311, 318
sack bearers: see porters
salt merchants, 302
ship builders, B17, B19
shippers/ship owners, 5, 49, 81, 84,
94, 223, 224, 226, 227, 228, 239,
267, 317; B16, B19; Drexel 1927,
Graeber 1983, Hermansen 1981,
Kneissl 1981, Konen 2001, Rauh
1993, Voutrias 1992; *see also*
merchants/traders
sack weavers, 101
silversmiths, 40, 161, 164, 186;
Schinkel 2008, Trebilco 1999
slave merchants/slave brokers, 143
soldiers, 246, 253, 271, 272, 273, 274,
290, 336; L18; Alföldy 1958, Beck
1992

textile workers, 70; Labarre and
Le Dinahet 1996, Lafer 2001,
Liu 2009, Pleket 2008, Salamito
1990; *see also* wool workers; linen
workers
transporters, 54, 267, 290; Kneissl
1981; Salamito 1987; *see also* ship-
pers/ship owners; merchants/
traders
undertakers, 290; Daniel 1979
warehouse workers, 224, 226, 227,
228, 230; B26, B28
wine merchants, 236
wood cutters: *see* builders/
carpenters
wool workers/wool weavers/wool
cleaners/wool carders/wool dealers, 141, 156, 171, 172c, 211, 296;
B22; Drew-Bear 1980, Moeller
1972, Salamito 1990; *see also* linen
workers; textile workers
Odessos (Moesia Inferior), 79
officials and leadership in associations, Abbott 1911, Ascough 2000b,
Ascough 2002, Clarke 2000,
Cumont 1933, Countryman 1977,
Dill 1904, Gabrielsen 2007, Harland 2007a, Harland 2009, Hatch
1881, Jones 1995, Liebenam 1890,
McLean 1999, Öhler 2005b, Pickard-
Cambridge 1968, Poland 1909,
Roueché 1993, Royden 1989, San
Nicolò 1913–1915, Schmeller 1995,
Waltzing 1895–1900, Ziebarth 1896
administrator (*dioikētēs*), 63, (of
sacred affairs; of the taxes), 84;
(*artutēr*), 190, 243
advocate (*syndikos*), 8
archivist (*grammatophylax*), 243
assistant (*hypourgos*), 294, 330
attendant (*diakonos*), 1, 4, 19, 29, 36,
38
auditor (*logistes*), 9, 45, 206
basket bearer (*kanēphoros,*) 299;
(*kistaphoros*) 330; (*kistaphoros*) L3

S

sacrifice, 1,2, 6, 9, 11, 14, 15, 20, 21, 22,
52, 58, 94, 108, 117, 121, 140, 160, 163,
165, 178, 195, 223, 224, 243, 262, 287,
299, 308, 309, 317; B8; L6, L13, L23,
L36; Avram 2002, Judge 2003, Klinghardt 1994, McLean 1996, Puig 1998
Sadducees, Mason 1996
Sagalassos (Pisidia/Lycia), 209
salvation, 7, 80, 121, 182, 278;
McCready 1996, Seesengood 2002,
Stowers 1998, Weinreich 1919
sanhedrin: *see* associations, nomencla-
ture of
Sarapis: *see* gods and goddesses
Sardian immigrants: *see* associations,
ethnic
Sardis (Lydia), 122–27, 303, 324; Buck-
ler 1923, Drew-Bear 1980, Harland
2005b, Herrmann 1996
scholarship, Arnaoutoglou 2003,
Ascough 1998, Ascough 2006,
Bendlin 2002; Bendlin 2011, Dis-
sen 2009, Koch and Schinkel 2006,
Perry 2001, Perry 2006, Perry 2011,
Runesson 2003, Schmeller 2003,
Tran 2001
seating, 7, 105, 183, 199, 287, 300, 310;
L17; Dittmann-Schöne 2001, Roueché 1995
Seleucia (Cilicia), 218–19
Senate, Roman, 67, 170, 178, 310; L18,
L23, L25, L26, L27, L28, L29, L31,
L39, L43, L53, L54; Duff 1938, Kloppenborg 1996a, de Ligt 2001
senatorial decree (*senatus consultum*),
194; L25, L30; Bendlin 2005, Bend-
lin 2011, de Ligt 2000, de Ligt 2001,
Mommsen 1843, Mommsen 1907
sexuality, 22, 121; L23; Fisher 1988b,
Stowers 1998
shippers: *see* occupations
shrine, 5, 18, 52, 60, 122, 126, 130, 165,
195, 260, 287, 322; B8, B9, B26; L23;
Ferguson 1944, Ferguson 1949

Sidon (Syria/Phoenicia), 271–78
silversmiths: *see* occupations
slaves, 3, 12, 22, 29, 41, 45, 83, 86, 121,
124, 140, 143, 196, 197, 281, 301, 210,
323, 330; L6, L15, L25, L26, L28,
L34, L54; Bömer 1981, Fellmeth
1990, Hanges 1998, Harrison 1999,
Hasegawa 2005, Hatch 1881, Jones
1999, Judge 1960, McLean 1993,
McLean 1999, Mommsen 1907,
Nock 1972, Öhler 2005a, Poland
1909, Salamito 1990, Schulz-Falkenthal 1965, Schulz-Falkenthal 1966,
Schulz-Falkenthal 1970, Stowers
1998, Tran 2006
Smyrna (Ionia), 185–201, 206, 312;
L13; Geagan 1972, Harland 2005b,
Hirschmann 2006, Merkelbach 1988
social status, Bendlin 2011, Ebel 2004,
Parker 1996, Verboven 2007
soldiers: *see* occupations
Solon, 21; L44; Gabba 1984, Ismard
2007, Jones 1999, Radin 1910
Sparta (Peloponnesos), 29
sportula, 322; Ladage 1979, McRae
2011, Patterson 1994, Slater 2000
status, Renan 1869, Verboven 2009
Stobi (Macedonia), 46
Stoics, Mason 1996
strike, Baldwin 1963–1964, Buckler
1923, Kloppenborg 1996a, MacMullen 1962–1963, Schulz-Falkenthal
1972, Schulz-Falkenthal 1973
Switzerland, Krause 2002
Syme Island (Dodecanese), 258
synagogue, Judean, 46, 59, 86, 89,
105, 127, 145, 149, 196, 270, 283 (?),
286 (?), 307, 329; Ascough 1998,
Ascough 2006, Barclay 2006, Harland 2003a, Harland 2007a, Harland 2009, Heinrici 1876, Heinrici
1877, Klinghardt 1994, Klinghardt
1996, Kloppenborg 1993, La Piana
1927, McLean 1996, Meeks 2003,
Meeks 2009, Mendelsohn 1940a,